Mr and Mrs Samuel Carter Hall undertook several tours throughout Ireland in the first half of the nineteenth century. Their tour of 1840 led to the writing of *Hall's Ireland*, which was first published in 1841–3 in three volumes. Their county by county account of this journey provides us with a valuable record of pre-famine Ireland and an idiosyncratic, highly personal account of the country in the last century, their aim being 'to direct public attention to Ireland, and to induce visitors to examine it for themselves'.

Also by Michael Scott in Sphere Books:

IRISH FOLK AND FAIRY TALES Volume 1
IRISH FOLK AND FAIRY TALES Volume 2
IRISH FOLK AND FAIRY TALES Volume 3

HALL'S IRELAND

MR & MRS HALL'S TOUR OF 1840

EDITED BY

Michael Scott

VOLUME 1

SPHERE BOOKS LIMITED
London and Sydney

First published in Great Britain by
Hall, Virtue, and Co., 1841 in three volumes
Condensed edition published by Sphere Books Ltd 1984
30–32 Gray's Inn Road, London WC1X 8JL

TRADE
MARK

Set in Bembo

Printed and bound in Great Britain by
Cox & Wyman Ltd, Reading

There is no country in the world so safe or so pleasant for strangers, so that for every new visitor it receives, it will obtain a new friend.

Mr and Mrs S C Hall 1840

CONTENTS

LIST OF ILLUSTRATIONS

IRELAND
0 10 20 30 40
(English miles)
NORTH CHANNEL
IRISH SEA
ATLANTIC OCEAN
ST GEORGE'S CHANNEL
DONEGAL
LONDONDERRY
ANTRIM
TYRONE
L. Neagh
Belfast
Donegal Bay
FERMANAGH
ARMAGH
DOWN
Sligo Bay
SLIGO
MONAGHAN
MAYO
LEITRIM
CAVAN
LOUTH
ROSCOMMON
LONGFORD
L. Mask
L. Carrib
MEATH
WESTMEATH
GALWAY
Tullamore
KINGS COUNTY
Dublin
Dublin Bay
DUBLIN
Galway Bay
KILDARE
Maryborough
QUEENS COUNTY
WICKLOW
CLARE
Carlow
CARLOW
TIPPERARY
KILKENNY
Kilkenny
Limerick
Askeaton
River Shannon
LIMERICK
Tipperary
Cashel
Cahir
Callan
Clonmel
WEXFORD
Listowel
Tralee
New Ross
Wexford Haven
Wexford
Waterford
Killarney
WATERFORD
Lismore
Dungarvan
Waterford Harbour
KERRY
CORK
Kenmare
Macroom
Cork
Youghal
Bantry Bay
Bantry
Kinsale
Cork Harbour
Skibbereen

Introduction

Of the many tours undertaken through Ireland in the middle and latter half of the nineteenth century, those of Mr and Mrs Samuel Carter Hall stand out as the most comprehensive. Their county by county tours provide us with a valuable record of pre-famine Ireland, an Ireland that was to disappear when the Great Famine of 1846-7 ravaged the country. An entire way of life vanished then; whole towns and communities were decimated, customs, folk-lore and myths were lost forever as the blight spread across the country striking at the staple diet of the Irish people of the time: the potato.

Both Mr and Mrs Hall were Irish born and spent their formative years in Ireland, and this probably accounts for their undoubted fascination with and love of the country.

Anna Maria Hall (née Fielding) was born on 6th January 1800, in Anne Street, in Dublin. She spent her early years in Wexford, on the south-east coast of Ireland, before moving to London with her mother in 1815. A young woman of startling beauty, she met and, on 20th September 1824, married Samuel Carter Hall who was at that time a student of law.

Samuel Carter Hall was born on 9th May 1800, in the Geneva Barracks near Waterford, on the south coast, the son of middle-class English parents. His father, Robert Hall who had fought at Gibraltar, and had subsequently raised the short-lived regiment of the Devon and Cornwall Fencibles, moved to Ireland in 1795. With a regiment composed largely of Cornish miners, it seemed natural that Captain Hall should take an interest in copper mining in the south of Ireland. He invested a large portion of his personal fortune into this venture – and was subsequently ruined. His wife, Ann Hall, was forced to open a small millinery business in Cork in order to support her twelve children.

Samuel Carter Hall, the fourth son, came to London in 1821, and followed a varied career, mainly in journalism, and founded a number of literary and art journals, including the *Amulet*. He also edited many of the journals in which his wife's first writings appeared, particularly *The Spirit and Manners of the Age* in which *Master Ben,* her first work, appeared in January 1829.

Both Halls were keenly interested in philanthropic work, and Anna Maria is credited with having founded the Hospital for Consumption, the Governesses Institute, the Nightingale Fund and the Home for Decayed Gentlewomen. A woman of extraordinary energy and boundless enthusiasm, she was also a staunch supporter of the temperance cause, and this comes through clearly in *Hall's Ireland*, where many of the ills of the country are ascribed to the demon drink. She was also an early champion of women's rights, and wrote many tracts for the cause. However, combined with her eminently practical nature was a strong and unswerving belief in spiritualism, and that too found its way into her many books and pamphlets. Indeed, the number of her books and other writings is estimated to be in excess of four hundred, and cover a wide and varied list of subjects.

Anna Maria Hall was awarded a civil list pension of £100 in 1868. She died on 30th January 1881, and her husband died some eight years later on 16th March 1889. They are both buried in Addlestone churchyard, Surrey.

The Halls toured Ireland more than once – no mean achievement at a time when transport was primitive and roads crude or non-existent. Their first tour would seem to have taken place between 10th June and 6th September 1840, and forms the basis around which they – almost annually – toured the country. A contemporary account of the first edition of the work describes it as 'a standard work of beauty and permanent value,' giving a 'better and more truthful picture of Ireland and the Irish than any other book in the language.'

Hall's Ireland was first published between 1841 and 1843 in three volumes, beautifully illustrated with fine steel-engravings by some of the leading artists of the time. It was reprinted several times, with Mr and Mrs Hall adding new material to the books as they appeared. This is especially evident in the chapter on Dublin, where – in the revised work – Queen Victoria's visit to the capital in August 1849 is covered in the form of an additional long paragraph added at the close of the chapter.

The present edited version follows the text of the first edition and incorporates the notes and addenda of the 'new edition' published some ten years later. The only major noticeable change between this edition and the original three-volume work occurs where the footnotes in the original have been incorporated into the text, and the folklore has been removed to the appendices. If the Halls thought a county to be 'uninteresting' or 'devoid of interest' they often disgressed and discussed some of the many topics they considered to be of 'grave importance'. Some of these topics are covered in the appendices to volume two. It is also quite common to find several pages of folklore and legends inserted into the text in the original. Some of these stories are presented uncut and unchanged in the appendices to volume one of the present work, and explore aspects of the life and culture of the country people. Much of the 'historical' background presented by the Halls has been removed, not only because of its lack of veracity and dubious authority, but because it was felt that it intruded into the text; most of the figures have been removed for the same reasons.

Hall's Ireland presents an idiosyncratic, highly personal account of Ireland in the last century. It is filled with the prejudices of a typically genteel couple of the time, and while it is both patronising and condescending, a deep sympathy and a genuine understanding of the plight of the Irish people run through it at all times.

It is still possible to retrace their route, to follow the by-ways and high-ways that Anna Maria and Samuel Carter followed, to view the sights they viewed and, even allowing for the passage of time, much remains the same. That is part of the beauty of *Hall's Ireland*.

Preface

The introduction of steam has made the islands of Ireland and England one island as it were, and the voyage now, either from Liverpool to Dublin, or from Bristol to Waterford or Cork is far more comfortable and less fatiguing than a journey to York. The steam boats that ply beween the two countries have, in fact, facilitated intercourse almost as much as a bridge across St George's Channel would have done. The elegance with which they are fitted up, the moderate fares and the attention to comfort has made the journey from England to Ireland an excursion of pleasure instead of a weary, dangerous, prolonged and expensive voyage, which it was heretofore aboard the sailing packets.

The sailing packet was a small trader – a schooner or sloop – the cabin of which was usually of very limited extent, lined with berths and with but a curtain partitioning off those that were appointed to ladies. In the centre was a table, which was seldom used, since the formality of dinner was a rare event. The steward was invariably an awkward boy, whose only recommendation was the activity with which he answered the calls of unhappy sufferers, and the voyage across was a kind of purgatory to be endured only in the case of absolute necessity. But it was not alone the miserable accommodation and utter indifference to the comfort of the passengers that made the voyage an impossible evil; before the application of steam made its duration a matter of certainty, the voyage, which usually occupied but three or four days, could occupy three or four weeks. Under such circumstances it is not surprising that comparatively little intercourse existed between the two countries and that they were as much strangers to each other as if the channel that divided them had actually been impassable.

Sixteen years ago the St George Steam Company established packets between the port of Cork, and the ports of Dublin, Liverpool and Bristol, and more recently London.

The immediate result was that the value of the poor man's property was augmented. Previously he was at the mercy of agents who purchased his produce at fairs, compelling him to sell it at the prices they dictated, or to return home with it, which was frequently a distance of twenty miles. The old saying that 'the pig paid the rent' was literally true, and the fair-day was always rent day. But now the farmer is very frequently his own export agent and accompanies his half score of pigs, crate of fowl or his hamper of eggs to England.

A material change for the better has therefore taken place throughout Ireland, which is perceptible even in the remotest districts, but very apparent in the seaport towns. The peasantry are better clad than they formerly were, their cottages much more decent and their habits far less uncivilised – although the very lowest classes, perhaps, have not yet felt the full benefit of this movement. Undoubtedly the most beneficial changes may be dated from the introduction of steam into commerce inasmuch as it has largely contributed to develop and increase the resources of the country and to improve the moral and social conditions of the people.

Hitherto, although steam has so largely assisted in inducing visitors from Ireland to England, visitors from England have not, in the same ratio, increased. Happily, many of the causes that produced this evil exist no longer and others are rapidly disappearing. It will be the leading object in this publication to induce the English to see and judge for themselves a country which holds out to them every temptation the traveller can need: scenery abundant in the wild and beautiful, a people rich in original character, a cordial and hearty welcome for the stranger and a degree of safety and security in his journeyings such as he can meet with in no other portion of the globe.

In all our tours, we not only never encountered the slightest stay or insult, but we never heard of a traveller who had been subjected to either; and although we were sufficiently heedless in locking up our boxes at inns, in no instance did we ever sustain a loss by our carelessness.

We may add that travelling in Ireland and the charges connected with it are so moderate that a month at Killarney shall cost less than would be spent, during the same time, at Ramsgate or Cheltenham, including the cost of the journey from London.

The usual routes to Ireland are either from Bristol to Cork or Waterford, or from Liverpool to Dublin. The voyage across to Cork generally occupies twenty-four hours; to Waterford, twenty hours, and from Liverpool to Dublin, twelve hours – although it is frequently made in less time. The shortest sea-passage is between Holyhead and Dublin, which is usually made in six hours.

Chapter One

CORK

Our work commences with Cork.

The distant appearance of Cork harbour from the seaward approach is gloomy, rocky and inhospitable. But as the entrance between the two bold headlands – scarcely half a mile apart, and crowned by fortifications – opens upon the view, its character undergoes a complete change.

The town of Cove, with the island of Spike which forms a sort of natural breakwater, and several smaller islands, give interest and variety to a noble expanse of sea that spreads out like a luxuriant lake to welcome the visitor. The harbour is one of the most secure, capacious and beautiful in the kingdom and is said to be large enough to contain the whole navy of Great Britain. It is diversified by other islands beside that of Spike; one of which, Haulbowlin, is the depot for naval stores. Another, Rocky Island, is the government depot for gunpowder, the store rooms for which are excavated from solid rock and communicate with each other by apertures in the sides.

Passing Monkstown and Passage, two pretty and picturesque villages which, together with the town of Cove, we shall presently describe, the vessel proceeds from the latter place to the quay of Cork, which lies at a distance of about ten miles.

The moment the voyager lands, he is impressed with a conviction that the natural advantages of Cork have been turned to good use. There is bustle on the quays; carriages and carts of all classes are waiting to convey passengers or merchandise to their destination, and an air of prosperity cheers him as he disembarks.

Unhappily however, the first peculiarity that strikes a stranger upon landing here, or indeed in any part of Ireland, is the multiplicity of beggars. Their wit and wisdom are as proverbial as their rags and wretchedness, and both too frequently excite a laugh at the cost of serious reflection upon their misery and the means by which it might be lessened. Age, decrepitude, imbecility and disease surround the car the moment it stops.

'Good luck to yer ladyship's happy face this morning – sure ye'll lave a light heart in me bussom before ye go?'

'Oh then, look at the poor that can't look at you, my lady, for the dark man* can't see if yer beauty is like yer sweet voice.'

'Darling gintelman, the heavens be yer bed, and give us something?'

'Oh then, won't yer ladyship buy a dying woman's prayers – chape?'

In the small town of Macroom, about which we walked one evening, desiring to examine it undisturbed, we had refused in positive terms to relieve any applicant, but promised however to bestow a halfpenny upon each who might ask of it the following morning. Next day it cost us exactly three shillings and tenpence to redeem the pledge we had given, no fewer than ninety-two having assembled at the inn gate.

And it was in Macroom that we noted a fair-haired girl amongst a group of beggars. There was something so sad, so shy and yet so earnest in her entreaty for, 'charity, for the love of God,' that we would have at once bestowed it had not a thin, pallid woman, whose manner was evidently superior to those around her and whose tatters bore a character of old decency, made her way through the crowd and, struggling with excited feelings, forced the girl from our side.

'My name's MacSweeny,' said the woman somewhat proudly, after a few preliminary questions, 'and I am a lone widow, with five of these craythurs depending upon my four bones. God knows, 'tis hard I work for the bit and the sup to give them, and 'tis poor we are and always have been, but none of my family ever took to the road or begged from any Christian – 'til this bad girleen disgraced them.'

*blind man

The mother was by now sobbing like a child and so was her girleen.

'Mother,' said the girl, 'sure little Timsy was hungry, and the gentleman wouldn't miss it.'

Our car was waiting, we had far to go that day and we were compelled to leave without hearing what, we were sure, would have been a touching story. But we left the widow less broken-hearted than we found her.

As contrast to this let us relate an incident that occurred in Cork where, by the way, the beggars seldom appear in public until nearly mid-day.

We were sitting at the window of our hotel (The Imperial, which for elegance and comfort may vie with any hotel in the kingdom). Our attention had been frequently called from the book we were reading by the querulous whine of a beggar who uttered at intervals the customary salutation of 'Good luck to ye,' and then the usual accompaniment of, 'Lave us a ha'penny for God's sake; for the lone widdy and her five fatherless childer.' As we had heard but few blessings following the appeal, we concluded that her efforts were unsuccessful, the more especially as at times her prayer ended with an undefined growl. Still, she kept her position directly beneath our window.

We had seen her there all morning; her tattered grey cloak falling back from her long, lean throat, her dirty cap so torn as to be insufficient to conceal her tangled tresses, her right hand supported by her left so as to stand out in the most imploring posture – the sad picture of confirmed and hardened beggary.

As the evening was closing in, we were wondering how much longer she would remain in the same spot when a very loud double knock echoed from the opposite side of the street, followed almost immediately by the woman's strenuously repeated petition, with the addition of, 'Do, dear, handsome, honourable young gentleman, bestow a ha'penny on a pore lone widdy, with *seven* small starving little childer, that haven't broke their fast this blessed day.'

We looked out the window and saw that she had crossed over and was urging her request most emphatically, while the young man thundered again at the knocker.

'Why then, more power to yer elbow, and it's yerself that's strong enough in the wrist anyhow; God keep it to ye, sir, and lave the little token of a ha'penny with the lone widdy and her seven fatherless childer.'

'I really have not any silver about me,' drawled out the young man.

'Bedad,' replied the beggar, 'I did not ax ye for silver nor gold, but for one ha'penny for the broken hearted widdy and her poor naked fatherless childer.'

'I tell you I've no halfpence,' he replied, losing what people never should in Ireland – his temper – seeing that the loss is immediately taken advantage of.

'Why then, bad luck to ye,' she exclaimed, setting her arms akimbo, and looking a fury. 'Then why did ye bring me from my comfortable seat across the street wid such a knock as that, if ye hadn't any money in yer pocket – ye poor, half-starved, whey-faced gossoon.'

On the subject of beggars; the beggars in the various towns have their distinctive characters and they differ essentially from those who beg in the country. In the towns it is usually a 'profession' and they are very jealous of interlopers, unless good cause can be shown for additions to the 'craft'. In Dublin they are exceedingly insolent and repulsive; in Cork merry and good-humoured, but most provokingly clamorous; in Waterford their petitions were preferred more by looks than words and a refusal was at once taken. In Clonmel – we were there during a season of frightful want – they appeared too thoroughly depressed and heart-broken to utter even a sentence of appeal. In Killarney they seemed trusting to their utter wretchedness and filth of apparel to contrast with the surprising grace and beauty of nature all around them. And in Wicklow, where we encountered far fewer than we expected – always excepting Glendalough – they laboured to earn money by tendering something like advice as to the route that should be taken by those in search of the picturesque.

In the country, where passers-by are not numerous, the aged or bed-ridden beggar is frequently placed in a sort of handbarrow and laid at morning by the roadside, and not unfrequently their business is conducted on the backs of donkeys, often drawn about by some neighbour's child.

Cork holds rank in extent, population and commercial importance as the second city of Ireland. Its situation is low, having been originally built on marshy islands, whence its name – Corcash – signifying in Irish, 'land occasionally overflowed by the tide', but the northern and southern suburbs stand upon high ground. Scarcely a century has gone by since the river ran through its principal streets, which are arching over the stream.

In a very rare tract, so rare indeed as to be said to be unique, entitled: 'A Relation of the Most Lamentable Burning of the City of Cork by Thunder and Lightening', which was printed in London in 1622, the following graphic account of old Cork occurs.

'The cittie of Cork hath its beginning upon the side of a hill, which descendeth easily into one wide and long street; the onely principall and chiefe street of the cittie. At the first entrance there is a castle called Shandon Castle and almost over against it a church built of stone, as the castle is a kind of marble, of which the country yeildeth store. The cittie hath many houses built of the same stone and covered with slate, but the greatest number of houses are built of tymber or mudde walls and covered with thatch.'

The foundation of Cork is generally attributed to Danish adventurers in the ninth or tenth century. It is contended however that its origin was earlier and that the founder was Saint Finn Barr (the fair-headed or the white-haired, for the Irish allows both translations), whose ecclesiastical establishments contained, it is said, no fewer than seven hundred priests, monks and students.

Cork has a cheerful and pleasing aspect, the leading streets are wide and 'though the houses may be described as built with studied irregularity, the character is by no means ungraceful or unpleasing.

The quays on both sides of the Lee – here of course a river muddied by traffic – are constructed from limestone and may be said to merit the term 'grand and elegant' which is so frequently applied to them. The city is a mere mart for commerce, with the whole of the gentry and indeed a large proportion of the trading inhabitants living in the picturesque and beautiful outskirts.

To do full justice to the exceeding beauty of the river Lee is impossible. On either side, immediately after the harbour's mouth, numerous attractive objects greet the eye, and the wild and cultivated are happily mingled. From its mouth to the city quays the river, in its perpetual changes, appears as a series of lakes, from which there is no passage except over one of the surrounding hills. These hills are clad from the summit to the water's edge with every variety of foliage, and graceful villas and ornamental cottages are scattered among them in profusion, and here and there some ancient ruin recalls a story from the past. A sail from Cork to Cove is one of the rarest and richest treats the island can supply and, it is therefore not surprising, considering also the cheapness and rapidity of the passage, that a vast proportion of the citizens have dwellings, magnificent or moderate, according to their means, along the banks of their glorious and beautiful river.

The public buildings of Cork are neither numerous nor remarkable; the Court House being almost the only good example of modern architecture, if we except the offices recently erected by the St George Steam Packet Company on the quay which their vessels have made more bustling than that of the Custom House, which is an ungainly structure and stands on the opposite side of the river.

The bridges, as may be supposed, are numerous. St Patrick's Bridge had formerly a drawbridge attached to it, but, being as this is one of the most frequented thoroughfares to a new and populous district, it was removed in 1823. In 1830 Anglesey Bridge or, as it is more generally called, The Metal Bridge, was constructed by the

ST PATRICK'S BRIDGE,
CORK

eminent architect, Sir Thomas Deane, from a design by Mr Griffits. It consists of two elliptic arches, forty-four feet in span with a drawbridge to admit vessels to the quays where it crosses the south branch of the Lee.

Antiquities are rare. The Cathedral, dedicated to St Finn Barr, is built on the site of an early church, a few of the remains of which have been introduced into the modern structure, and the tower of the steeple is comparatively ancient. The building, taken as a whole, has no pretensions to Cathedral grandeur. It was erected in 1735, the expense having been defrayed by a tax of one shilling per ton on all coals and culm consumed within the city.

Institutions – charitable, scientific and literary – abound in Cork. It has been celebrated more than any other city of Ireland for the production and fosterage of genius and is the birthplace of many distinguished characters in literature, science and the arts. Among the former who are at present living, or recently were so, may be named General O'Leary, the South American Patriot; Mr Hastie, the tutor of King Radamah, and to whose exertions the present civilised state of Madagascar may be mainly attributed; and Miss Thomson, the favourite wife of Muli Mahomed, the late Emperor of Morocco.

The jails of Cork – the city and county – are models of good management, cleanliness and order. As in nearly all the jails throughout Ireland, there is in those of Cork, which are otherwise so admirably managed, a grievous want of classification, and atrocious criminals and petty offenders are mixed together in a manner sadly prejudicial. At Clonmel in particular, the evil is especially great; the prisoners were placed before us in files; among them we saw an elderly and respectable-looking man striving to hide his face with his hat and stepping back to elude observation. We found that he had been confined for drunkenness, but that the person next to whom he stood was about to be tried for sheep stealing, and had previously been in custody on suspicion of murder. This most injurious system is however rapidly giving way, and we must do the governors of the several prisons we inspected the justice to say that they are making unceasing efforts for its entire removal.

The most remarkable and, to a stranger, the most interesting of the public institutions of Cork is the lunatic asylum of the county and city. The latest return – dated March 1840 – gives the amount of patients at 406: 200 males and 206 females.

The national customs that prevail among the people of Cork are common to other parts of Ireland with one exception and, although it is partially found elsewhere – in the Isle of Man, for instance – it is certainly confined to the southern parts of Ireland.

For some weeks preceding Christmas, crowds of village boys may be seen peering into the hedges in search of the tiny wren, and when one is discovered the whole assembly eagerly give chase until they have caught and killed it. In the hunt the utmost excitement prevails: shouting, screeching and rushing, and all sorts of missiles are flung at the puny mark and, not unfrequently, they light upon the head of some less innocent being. From bush to bush, from hedge to hedge, the wren is pursued and bagged with as much pride and pleasure as the more ambitious sportsman bags the cock of the woods. The stranger is utterly at a loss to conceive the cause of this hubbub or the motive for so much energy expended in pursuit of such small game. On the anniversary of St Stephen (the 26th December) the enigma is explained.

Attached to a large holly bush, which is elevated on a pole, the bodies of several little wrens are borne about. The bush is an object of admiration in proportion to the number of dependent birds, and is carried through the streets in procession by a troop of boys, among whom may usually be found 'children of a larger growth' shouting and roaring as they proceed along, and every now and again stopping before some popular house (such as that of Mr Olden, the distinguished inventor of Evkerogenion, a liquid soap) and singing the wren boy's song.

Of course contributions are levied in many quarters and the evening is, or rather was, occupied in drinking out the sum total of the day's collection.

This is, we believe, the only Christmas gambol remaining in

Ireland of the many that in the middle ages were so numerous and so dangerous as to call for the intervention of the law. As to the origin of the whimsical, but absurd and cruel custom, we have no information, but there is a legend still current among the peasantry which may serve in some degree to elucidate it.

In a grand assembly of all the birds of the air it was determined that the sovereignty of the feathered tribe should be conferred upon the one who would fly highest. The favourite was of course the eagle, who at once commenced his flight towards the sun. When he had vastly outdistanced his competitors he proclaimed with a mighty voice his monarchy over all things that had wings. Suddenly however the wren, who had secreted himself under the feathers of the eagle's crest, popped out from his hiding place, flew a few inches upwards and chirped out as loudly as he could, 'birds, look up and behold your king.'

There is also a tradition that in 'ould ancient times' when the native Irish were about to catch their Danish enemies asleep, a wren perched upon a drum and woke the slumbering Danish sentinels with its tapping just in time to save the whole army, in consequence of which the little bird was proclaimed traitor and outlawed, with his life declared forfeit wherever he was thenceforth encountered.

Another old custom prevails to some extent. May Eve, the last day of April, is called Nettlemas Night. Boys parade the streets with large bunches of nettles, stinging their friends and occasionally bestowing a sly touch upon strangers who come in their way. Young and merry maidens too not unfrequently avail themselves of the privilege to 'sting' their lovers, and the laughter in the streets is often echoed in the drawing room. These are the only customs peculiar to Cork.

Promenades in the immediate neighbourhood of Cork are few. The oldest is the Mardyke, a walk between rows of aged, but not ungracefully lopped trees which shade a gravelled path at the side of a muddy and half stagnant canal.

The new cemetery, however, demands some notice. It was formerly a botanical garden attached to the Cork Institution, but in 1826 was sold to the Very Rev Theobald Mathew, who converted it into its present use. It is therefore perhaps unrivalled in the kingdom, being full of the rarest trees from all parts of the world. Its walls are covered with ivy, climbing roses and other shrubs and, from the nature of the soil and aspect, everything is growing in luxuriant profusion.

However, we regret to add that the cemetery is completely overgrown with weeds, and gigantic nettles and docks have been permitted absolutely to cover the graves. In such a situation and under such circumstances this is to be lamented; although Mr Mathew himself is unable to attend to the proprieties of this naturally beautiful cemetery, the care of it should be confided to someone whose time and attention might be worthily employed in improving it and keeping it in order.

Cork is the great outlet of emigrants from the south of Ireland and the Australian Emigration Society have an agent here.

In the month of June, we stood on the quay of Cork to see some emigrants embark in one of the steamers for Falmouth on their way to Australia. The band of exiles amounted to two hundred and an immense crowd had assembled to bid them a long and last adieu. The scene was very touching, and it was impossible to witness it without heart-pain and tears. Mothers clung upon the necks of their athletic sons, young girls clung to elder sisters, fathers – old, white-haired men – fell upon their knees with arms uplifted to heaven, imploring the protecting care of the Almighty on their departing children. Amid the din, the noise, the turmoil, the people pressing and rolling in vast masses towards the place of embarkation, there were many such sad episodes. Men, old men too, embracing each other and crying like little children. Several passed carefully bearing little relics of their homes: the branch of a favourite hawthorn bush or a bush of meadow-sweet. Many had a long switch of witch-hazel to encircle the ground whereon they were to sleep in the foreign land, so as, according to the universal superstition, to prevent the approach of any venomous reptile or poisonous insect.

On the deck of the steamer there was less confusion than might have been expected. The hour of departure was at hand, the police had torn asunder several who at the last would not be separated, and as many as could find room were leaning over the side of the craft speechless, yet eloquent in gesture, expressing their adieus to their friends and relatives on shore. In the midst of the agitation, a fair-haired boy and girl were sitting tranquilly, yet sadly, watching a very fine white Angora cat that was carefully packed in a basket.

'We are going out to Papa and Mama with nurse,' they said in an unmitigated brogue, 'but we are very sorry to leave dear Ireland for all that.' Their father had, we imagine, been a prosperous settler.

It is impossible to describe the final parting. Shrieks and prayers, blessings and lamentations mingled in one great cry from those on the quay and those on shipboard until a band stationed in the forecastle struck up 'St Patrick's Day'. The communicating plank was withdrawn, and the steamer moved majestically forward on her way. Some, overcome with emotion, fell down upon the deck, others waved hats, handkerchiefs and hands to their friends and the band played louder.

We left the vessel and her crowd of clean, well-dressed and perfectly sober emigrants with deep regret, reminding ourselves that while there are in Ireland so many miles of unreclaimed land, it is a sad loss that such a freight should be conveyed from her shores.

The evening that succeeded this agitating morning was calm and balmy. We desired to examine the scene of the morning's turmoil and drove along the quay which was lonely and deserted save for a few stragglers. We continued our voyage until the signs of immediate traffic were wildly scattered. We drove through the village of Douglas, once famous for its sail cloth manufacture and proceeded until the Cork river widened into a mimic sea, called

Lough Mahon. We drove slowly, enjoying the rare and exquisitely varied landscape.

To the city of Cork belongs the honour of forwarding and establishing one of the most extraordinary moral revolutions which the history of the world records: the Temperance Movement, at the head of which is the Very Rev Theobald Mathew, a Capuchin friar, and superior of the order.

For centuries past, drunkenness was the shame and bane of Ireland; an Irishman, without reference to his rank in society, from the highest to the lowest, had become proverbial for intoxication, and to picture an Irishman truly, either in words or on canvas, or to represent him accurately on the stage, it was considered indispensable that he should be drunk.

A manifest improvement has of late years taken place among the higher classes; we are ourselves old enough to recollect when a host would have been scouted as mean and inhospitable if he had suffered his guests to leave his table sober. Ingenious devices were invented for compelling intoxication: glasses and bottles so formed that they could not stand and must be emptied before they could be laid on the table – the object being to pass the wine around rapidly. If a guest were able to mount his horse unassisted in the 'good old times' he was presented with a 'deoch an durass' (drink at the door) which he was forced, seldom against his will, to drink at the door. The glass used for this occasion usually held a quart, and was terminated by a globe which of itself contained a 'drop' sufficient to complete the business of the night.

This degradation was looked upon as a distinction; an Irishman drunk was an Irishman 'in all his glory' and a strong head was considered an enviable possession. Many years ago we were acquainted with a gentleman at Ross-Carbery whose daily stint was five-and-twenty tumblers of whisky punch of the ordinary strength.

Among the gentry, however, this most pernicious practice had been latterly not only in disuse, but treated as disreputable and

THE CORK RIVER

(FROM BELOW THE GLANMIRE ROAD.)

disgraceful, and gentlemen after dinner have ceased to be disgusting in the drawing-room.

Yet the middle and humbler classes had undergone little or no change. The vigilance of the excise men and a large reduction of the tax on spirits, had indeed destroyed the illicit trade in whisky and made the private poteen still a rarity, but it was so cheap that any man might drink himself into a state of insanity for fourpence. In the towns and villages every other house was 'licensed to sell spirits' – or sold them without a licence. Fairs, wakes and funerals were scenes of frightful excess; in the former, men seldom met without a fight; at the latter, the merriment excited by the drink was unnatural and revolting, and very often the year's produce of the small farmer was consumed in a night.

In brief, wherever twenty persons assembled within reach of spirits, nineteen of them were certain to be drunk. It is unnecessary to add that nearly all the outrages that were committed were the results of intoxication, or rather that drink was the preparation for every atrocity.

All attempts to check the progress of intemperance were fruitless; it had long been the custom indeed to take oaths to abstain from drink for a season, but if kept, they produced no permanent good, and the tricks and shifts to evade them were generally successful. We recollect a man swearing that he would not drink for a month and so he soaked bread in spirits and ate; another, who swore he would not touch liquor while he stood on earth, but who got drunk amidst the branches of a tree; another, who swore he would not touch a drop in doors or out, and who therefore strode across his threshold, placing one leg inside and the other outside, and so drank until he fell; another, who bound himself not to touch liquor in the parish, but who brought a sod of turf from the distance and placed his foot upon it when he resolved to drink.

To make the Irish abstain, even to a moderate extent, was therefore considered a hopeless task.

On the 20th August, 1829, the Rev George Carr, a clergyman of the Established Church established the first Temperance Society of Ireland in the town of New Ross. He had read some American newspapers which contained encouraging accounts of the progress the principle was making in the New World, and saw at once that there was no country where it was so much needed as Ireland. For several years however, little way was made, and the advocates of temperance were exposed to contempt and laughter. A coffee tent, which they erected at fairs, was an object of ridicule, and although they had not abandoned hope their efforts were comparatively fruitless, and even the most optimistic amongst them indulged in no idea of large success.

Shortly afterwards a temperance society was formed in Cork, the example of New Ross having, by the way, been followed in many other towns. Among its leading members were the Rev Nicholas Dunscombe, Mr William Martin, a Quaker, and two tradesmen, Mr Olden, a slater and Mr Connell, a tailor. They conceived the idea of consigning the important task into the hands of the Rev Mr Mathew, then highly popular in the city and respected by all classes. He met these gentlemen, seriously pondered their plans and probabilities of succeeding, and ultimately – though not immediately – joined them, 'hand and heart'.

On the 10th April, 1838, the Cork Total Abstinence Society was formed. It is certain that Mr Mathew never for a moment anticipated the wonderful results that were to follow its establishment, and was probably as much astonished as any person in the kingdom when he found not only thousands, but millions, entering into a compact with him to 'abstain from the use of all intoxicating drinks' – and keeping it! His Cork society was joined by members from the very distant parts – from the mountains of Kerry, from the wild sea-cliffs of Clare, from the banks of the Shannon, and from places still further off. He had travelled through nearly every district of Ireland, held meetings in nearly every town, and on the 10th October, 1840, his list of members contained upwards of two millions five hundred and thirty thousand names.

In reference to the extent to which sobriety has spread, it will be almost sufficient to state that during our recent stay in Ireland, we saw but six persons intoxicated, and that for the first thirty days we encountered none. In the course of that month we had travelled from Cork to Killarney – round the coast and returning by the inland route, not along the mail-coach roads, but on a jaunting car through byways as well as highways, visiting small villages and populous towns, driving through fairs, attending wakes and funerals (returning from one of which, between Glengariff and Kenmare at nightfall, we met at least a hundred mounted farmers); in short, wherever crowds were assembled and we considered it likely that we might gather information as to the state of the country and character of its people.

We repeat, we did not meet a single individual who appeared to have tasted spirits, and we do not hesitate to express our conviction that two years ago, in the same places and during the same time, we should have encountered many thousand drunken men.

From first to last we employed about fifty car-drivers, and we never found one to accept a drink. The boatmen of Killarney, proverbial for drunkenness, insubordination and recklessness of life, declined the whisky we had taken with us, and after hours of hard labour, dipped a can into the lake and refreshed themselves from its waters.

The whisky shops are closed or converted into coffee-houses; the distillers have, for the most part, ceased to work, and the breweries are barely able to maintain a trade sufficient to prevent entire stoppage. There are but two distilleries at work in the whole county of Cork, and at the late fair of Ballinasloe – the great cattle-fair of Ireland – there were but eight gallons of whisky consumed; the average consumption heretofore being between seven and eight puncheons – 800 gallons.

The immediate outlets of Cork possess considerable interest, and their natural beauties are perhaps not exceeded by those of any city in the kingdom.

The river Lee above and below the bridges, the alternate hill and dale, the high state of cultivation, the number of fine seats and pretty cottages and the abundance of trees and evergreens are objects that meet the eye in every direction around Cork and seem to justify the title bestowed upon it by the natives, and assented to by all visitors, 'The Beautiful City'.

On one side is Sunday's Well, from the height of which there is a magnificent view of the river and the landscape for many miles around it. Sunday's Well derives its name from one of those sacred fountains which abound in every part of Ireland, where devotees assemble at particular periods under the belief that the water is blessed and cures all disorders.

On the same side of the river are the Upper and Lower Glanmire Roads – not long since solitary walks, but now a busy and populous district. The Lower conducts to the wharfs and timber yards and skirts the river, and the Upper to the barracks, and both roads terminate in scenery of great beauty.

Few places in Ireland are more familiar to English ears than Blarney; the notoriety is attributable first to the marvellous qualities of the famous stone and next to the extensive popularity of the song, 'The Groves of Blarney'.

When or how the stone obtained its singular reputation is difficult to determine, and the exact position amongst the ruins of the castle is also a matter of doubt, since the peasant-guides humour the visitor and direct him who desires to 'greet it with a holy kiss' either to the summit or the base, according to his capacity for climbing.

It is certain that to no particular stone of the ancient structure is the marvellous quality exclusively attributed; but in order to make it as difficult as possible to attain the enviable gift, it had long been the custom to point out a stone which jutted out a few feet from below the battlements and which only the very daring would run the hazard of touching with their lips. The attempt to do so was indeed so dangerous that a few years ago Mr Jeffreys, the present owner, had it removed from the wall and placed on the highest point of the building where the visitor might greet it with little risk. It is about two feet square and contains the date 1703, with a portion of the arms of the Jeffreys family, but the date at once negates its claim to be considered the true marvel of Blarney.

A few days before our visit a madman made his way to the top of the castle and, after dancing around it for some hours – his escape from death being almost miraculous – he flung this stone from the tower. It was broken by the fall and now, as the guide stated to us, the 'three halves' must receive three distinct kisses to be in any degree effective.

He who has kissed the Blarney stone is assumed to be endowed with a fluent and persuasive tongue, although it may be associated with insincerity, the term 'blarney' generally being used to characterise words that are meant neither to be 'honest nor true'.

The stronghold of Blarney was erected about the middle of the fifteenth century by Cormac MacCarthy, surnamed Laider or the Strong, whose ancestors had been chieftains in Munster from a period long before the English invasion and whose descendants, as Lords of Muskerry and Clancarty, retained a considerable portion of their power and estates until the year 1689, when their immense possessions were confiscated and the last earl became an exile, like the monarch whose cause he had supported. The castle, village, mills, fairs and customs of Blarney, with the land and park belonging thereunto, containing 1400 acres were 'set up by cant' in the year 1702, purchased by Sir Richard Pyne, Lord Chief Justice, for three thousand pounds and disposed of by him the following year to General Sir James Jeffreys, in whose family the property continues. Although the walls of the castle are still strong, many of the outworks have long since been levelled with the earth, the plough passed over their foundations and the stones of which they were built have been used in repairing the turnpike roads.

The fate of the once formidable clan of the MacCarthy is similar to that of nearly all the ancient families of Ireland. The descendants in direct line may often be found working as day labourers around the ruins of castles where their forefathers had ruled and, in many cases, a period of little more than a century and a half has passed between their grandeur and their degradation.

The small village of Blarney is about four miles north-west of Cork. A few years ago it was remarkably clean, neat and thriving, its prosperity having resulted from the establishment of several linen and cotton factories, the whole of which have now been swept away, and the hamlet is now, like the castle, an assemblage of ruins. In the vicinity however, there is yet a woollen manufactory and a paper-mill both in full work. The scenery in the neighbourhood is agreeable, but the grounds that immediately surround the castle are of exceeding beauty.

The sweet Rock-close is a small dell in which evergreens grow luxuriantly, and is completely shaded with magnificent trees. At its termination are the Witches Stairs, a series of rugged stone steps which lead down through a passage in the rock to a charming spot of greensward forming the banks of a clear rivulet and where some singular masses appear to have been the work of 'druid hands of old'.

We visisted the Rock-close during a sunny day in June, and we can never forget the fragrant shade afforded by the luxuriant evergreens which seemed rooted in the limestone rock. The little river Comane is guarded by a natural terrace, fringed by noble trees; several of the spaces between are natural grottos, some with seats where, undoubtedly, many a love tale of old has been told. It is indeed a spot of singular beauty and exceeding wildness. At some particular points you catch a glimpse of the castle, the river and the mysterious entrance to the Witches Stairs. Still, notwithstanding the variety of these objects, and a cave moreover, where some beautiful princess of old went through a long enchantment, the character of the Rock-close is one of deep shadow. Occasionally a sunbeam struggles through the gloom and points out a bed of richest moss, or a grey stone winged with waving fern.

We wandered from the shade of the Rock-close across the green and richly wooded pastures that lead to the lake, which is a fine expanse of water about a quarter of a mile from the castle. The scenery here is more English than Irish, but every step is hallowed by legend; it is implicitly believed that the last Earl of Clancarty who inhabited the castle committed the keeping of his gold plate to the deepest waters of the lake, and that it will never be recovered until a MacCarthy be lord of Blarney. On midsummer night enchanted cows dispute the pasture with those of the present possessor, and many an earthly bull has been worsted in the contest. As to fairies, their rings are upon the grass from early summer to the last week in harvest.

Our attention was somewhat drawn to the multitude of lilies that floated on the waters of the lake, rendering it near to the shore a mass of living gold. We never saw the flower in such abundance or perfection. One which we gathered contained within its calyx a small green lizard that came creeping forth, its fixed and jet-like eyes staring us out of countenance until we transferred it to another home. A most delightful day did we spend amongst those ruins of art and beauties of nature. We sat beneath the shadow of the old ward tower to partake of some refreshment, and the children of the dairy farm close to the castle brought us a plate piled with potatoes and enveloped in a warm white cloth.

Those who visit Blarney would be repaid for their trouble by extending their drive through a secluded glen in which the Awmartin descends into the valley. This neighbourhood has many circular raths and some square entrenchments with the usual subterranean cells. The road wanders through the beautiful pass almost as wildly as the river, and at its extremity the Rev Mathew Horgan is erecting a round tower close to his chapel with a view to get even with his ancestors and to puzzle posterity!

Proceeding from Cork, the object which first strikes the tourist is the castle of Black Rock – a modern structure, but which, from its position standing on the extremity of a small peninsula, commands special notice.

Passing through Lough Mahon – part of the river, but because of its peculiar character styled a lough or lake – the village of Passage, which lies five miles from Cork, is reached. Here all large vessels discharge their cargoes, for the channel is not of sufficient depth to allow their approach nearer to the city. An excellent quay has recently been built to facilitate the embarkation and disembarkation of passengers. In excavating for its foundation part of an iron cannon was discovered, and this certainly belongs to an early period of English artillery – if it be of English manufacture. If it is of Irish manufacture, it is far more difficult to conjecture the age, for we know that leathern cannon hooped with iron were used by the Anglo-Irish so late as the reign of Charles I. The one discovered at Passage may possibly be referred to the time of Henry VIII, and the warlike demonstrations then made by the citizens of Cork in favour of Perkin Warbeck may be brought forward to support the conjecture and account for the locality in which it was found.

About a mile further on is the village of Monkstown. It was formerly confined in the gorge of a deep and richly wooded glen, but has gradually extended along the shore where a row of excellent houses have sprung up; and a handsome church, an hotel with baths and some pretty villas have recently been built. The castle of Monkstown, though now a complete ruin, was in repair and used as a barrack during the last war.

It was built in the year 1636 and, according to the popular tradition, at the cost of a groat. To explain the enigma, the following story is told: Anastatia Goold had become the wife of John Archdeken, who went abroad to serve in the army of Philip of Spain. She was determined to give him evidence of her thrift on his return by surprising him with a noble residence which he might call his own. Her plan was to supply the workmen with provisions and other articles which they required and for which she charged the ordinary price, but as she had made her purchases wholesale, she found upon balancing her accounts that the retail profit had paid all the expenses of the structure – except fourpence.

Between the two villages, Passage and Monkstown, a delightful road has been lately formed along the shore a little above the high-water mark by cutting away the rock which descended abruptly to the river. The depth of the water here is very great, and it is pointed out to the stranger's notice as a place where several ships have foundered, particularly one commanded by Captain Cole, in 1758.

The foundation of this road however, has much injured a singular freak of nature called the Giant's Stairs, some of which it has entirely displaced. Fifteen or sixteen huge knobs of rock, each many tons in weight, rose from the water's edge one above the other up the face of a very steep rocky ascent with nearly the regularity of a flight of steps.

Nearer the harbour's mouth, on the west side, is a creek called Crosshaven, remarkable for the tradition that it once sheltered the gallant Admiral, Sir Francis Drake, when he was pursued into the harbour by a Spanish squadron. The spot where he anchored is still called 'Drake's Pool'. The Spaniards, after remaining some days in the bay of Cork, as its harbour was then and for some years subsequently called, sending boats up the river in vain pursuit and exploring in all other directions, stood out to sea again, completely unable to account for the mysterious disappearance of the vessels they had chased so closely and so keenly, and which, after due consideration, they gravely concluded could only have been snatched from their grasp and have disappeared in so astonishing a manner by the power of magic.

The town of Cove, as we have stated, faces the entrance to Cork harbour, from which however it is distant about five miles. It is built on the side of a steep hill and rises from the water's edge, terrace above terrace, with the more elevated parts commanding a magnificent bird's-eye view of the extensive anchorage.

Cove has a southern aspect, and the climate is consequently mild during all the seasons. From the nature of the site on which it stands, Cove is almost always clear, with a fall of rain carrying its impurities into the Atlantic. On all sides the shore is covered with villas and the trees, usually stunted on the coast, grow gracefully and majestically. The islands and fortified headlands are imposing and the gay yachts, which a tourist described a century ago as 'little vessels, that for painting and gilding exceed those of the king at Greenwich', give animation and variety to the exciting scene.

'The Yacht Club' of Cork is said to be the oldest association of the kind in the United Kingdom. The 'Rules and Orders', printed in 1765 under the name of 'The Cork Water Club', give a list of the old members of 1720, and reference is made to its 'ancient rules and constitution'. One of the early regulations provided that no long-tailed wigs, large sleeves or ruffles should be worn by any member. In 1830 it received the prefix 'Royal' and in 1831 the French Government conceded to it the privilege of free access to all the ports of France.

The club has of late years successfully laboured to improve the construction, appointments and management of vessels of all descriptions, and the commonest craft of the harbour may now vie with those belonging to any English port. The skill and hardihood of the Cove boatmen and mariners is proverbial, and if the kingdom shall again require sailors to maintain the supremacy of the British flag, and give emphasis to the almost forgotten line, 'Britannia rules the waves', the Cove of Cork, at least, will supply its quota.

Previous to the war between England and her American colonies, Cove consisted of little more than the mud cabins of a few fishermen. Dr Smith, whose history of the county was published in 1750, describes it as 'a village built under a steep hill, inhabited by seamen and revenue officers'.

So late as 1780, Cove had scarcely advanced beyond the dignity of a fishing hamlet. Soon afterwards however, the value of Cork harbour having been appreciated, Cove gradually rose in importance; houses were built, fortifications for defence constructed, government stores established and it became the naval station of an Admiral's flag. Bustle, activity and a thriving trade followed. It was no unusual sight to behold from 'Spy Hill', as the highest point of Cove was called, three hundred sail of merchant vessels assembled, waiting for convoy.

With peace however, the glory of Cove departed. Notwithstanding the arguments and remonstrances of its inhabitants, Cove was reduced from an Admiral's command to a mere naval station for the supply of water and provisions. Now-a-days, the appearance of a ship-of-war is an event of rare occurrence.

But the natural beauty of the situation of Cove, the salubrity of its sea-breezes, its vicinity to Cork and the facility for communication by means of the steam boats have averted the anticipated ruin of the place. Its present population exceeds 7,000 and its character is now that of a thriving and improving town. Moreover the mild air and warm southern aspect, added to the advantages of sea-bathing, strongly recommend it to invalids by whom it is now visited from all parts of Ireland.

On the east side of Cork harbour, and about three miles from the shore, is the small town of Cloyne – a bishop's see, founded in the sixth century, by St Colman. The cathedral is a low cruciform structure. The last bishop of Cloyne was Brinkley, the profound mathematician and eminent astronomer, who was consecrated in 1826 and died in 1835, when the see was merged into that of Cork and Ross.

At Cloyne there is one of those singular round towers which for so long a period have excited the curiosity of antiquaries; but its conical stone roof was destroyed by lightning in the year 1749. The neighbourhood of Cloyne abounds with natural caves in the limestone rock; one of which, in the episcopal grounds, is 'of unknown length and depth, branching to a great distance under the earth and sanctified by a thousand wild traditions'.

At Castle Mary, a fine seat not far from Cloyne, may be seen one of those ponderous masses of stone supported by smaller stones which are popularly termed Druid's Altars or 'cromleachs' and close to it is another, smaller one. The altar stone of the great cromleach measures fifteen feet in length and is about eight feet wide and three and a half feet thick. The position of both is inclined, from which it is conjectured the name cromleach, 'the bending stone', is derived. Similar rude monuments are found in all parts of Ireland.

The most remarkable seat in the vicinity of Cloyne is Rostellan, the mansion of the Marquis of Thomond. It is modern but occupies the site of an ancient castle of the Fitzgeralds, seneschals of

Imokilly. In 1648 the notorious Lord Inchquin – famous or infamous, according to the views of the historian – obtained a grant of the estate, which grant was further confirmed to him in the eighteenth year of Charles II.

Before we proceed further upon our journey, and describe the northern division of the country, it will be well to picture the vehicles, on one or other of which the tourist will have to travel. We shall first, however, advise him to lay in both a stock of good humour – for petty annoyance will frequently occur – and a plentiful supply of waterproof clothing, for sunny June is no more to be trusted than showery April. Someone has said that the only day on which you can be certain to escape a wetting is the 30th February – a day which never comes. This is undoubtedly a sad drawback upon pleasure; the humidity of the atmosphere is a continual affliction to those who are not used to it, and is very insufficiently compensated for by the fact that the grass in Ireland is evergreen. Yet the evil is one that can always be guarded against.

Machines for travelling in Ireland are, some of them at least, peculiar to the country. The stage-coaches are precisely similar to those in England and travel at as rapid a rate. They of course run upon all the great roads and are constructed with due regard to safety and convenience.

The public cars of Mr Bianconi have, however, to a large extent, displaced the regular coaches and are to be encountered in every district in the south of Ireland. In form they resemble the common outside jaunting car, but are calculated to hold twelve, fourteen or sixteen persons. They are well horsed, have cautious and experienced drivers, are generally driven with three horses and usually travel at the rate of seven Irish miles an hour, the fares averaging about twopence per mile. They are open cars, but a huge apron of leather affords considerable protection against rain, and they may be described in all respects as very comfortable and convenient vehicles.

Post-chaises are now very seldom used; they are to be had in the larger towns and are generally cleanly and well arranged, very different in form from what they were when the caricature pictured them as thatched with straw, and from the bottom of which the travellers' legs protruded.

The cars are of three kinds: the covered car, the inside jaunting car and the outside jaunting car – with the latter being the one most generally in use and the only one employed in posting. The two former, indeed, can seldom be procured except in large towns. The covered car is a comparatively recent introduction, its sole recommendation being that it is weather-proof, but it effectually prevents a view of the country, except through the two little peep hole windows in the front or by tying back the oil-skin curtains behind. Our longer journeys were made in this machine; it preserved us from many a wetting and we endeavoured to remedy the evil of confinement by stopping at every promising spot and either getting out or making the driver turn his vehicle around, so that from the back we might command the prospect we desired. This class of car has of late multiplied greatly in all the larger towns and they are in Ireland what the hackney-coaches and cabriolets are in England. We hired this car in Cork for twenty days at the rate of ten shillings a day, expenses of man and horse included, and for two persons it is a very desirable mode of travelling.

The inside jaunting car is not often to be hired; it is usually private property and is perhaps the most comfortable as well as the most elegant of the vehicles of the country.

The outside jaunting car is that to which especial reference is made when speaking of the 'Irish' car. It is exceedingly light, presses very little upon the horse, and is safe as well as convenient. It is always driven with a single horse. The driver occupies the front seat and the travellers sit back to back, the space between being occupied by the well, which is a sort of boot for luggage. But when there is only one passenger the driver usually places himself on the opposite seat to balance the car. The foot board is generally of iron and is made to move on hinges so that it may be turned up to protect the cushions during rain.

The private cars of this description are, of course, neatly and carefully made, and have a character of much elegance, but those which are hired are, in general, badly built, dirty and uncomfortable. Yet in nine places out of ten the traveller has no chance of obtaining a vehicle of any other description and will often find even in a populous town that if the car is out, he must wait until its return. He will never have any difficulty in procuring a horse, and as to drivers, any boy will answer for the nonce, but one car generally suffices for a town. In New Ross, for example, we were detained two hours before we could proceed on our road to Wexford.

A car therefore is usually hired for a journey, changing horses on the route. The charge for posting is sixpence a mile for two persons and eightpence a mile if the travellers exceed two. This is the rule all over the country, except in the county of Wicklow, where the rate is eightpence a mile; the consequence has been that the greater number of tourists hire a machine in Dublin and are not customers at the inns on the road.

The car, or rather cars, used by the peasantry require some notice.

Flat boards are placed across a frame and upon these straw and often a feather bed is laid. These vehicles have old-fashioned wheels cut out of a solid piece of wood and are now, however, nearly obsolete. We met but few of them on our latest journey, their unfitness having been at last understood, and they have given way before modern improvement.

The miles are now generally measured as English miles, and in posting, are charged for accordingly. The reader will bear in mind that eleven Irish miles are equivalent to fourteen English. At present this causes some confusion, the natives being as yet unable to comprehend how it is that familiar places have moved further from each other. We asked one of them the distance from Cork to Kinsale.

'Troth sir,' he answered, 'it's hard to say. Not long ago 'twas twelve miles, but they've been flinging stones at each other (fixing milestones), and Kinsale is druv a good step further from Cork. It's English roads they've made of them; wisha bad luck to them – it's everything Irish they're taking from us . . . except the poverty and the sod.'

Persons who have never travelled in Ireland can have but a very inadequate idea of the wit and humour of the Irish cab drivers. They are, for the most part, a thoughtless and reckless set of men, living upon chance, always 'taking the world aisy', having no care for the morrow and seldom being owners of a more extensive wardrobe than the nondescript mixture they carry about their persons. They are the opposites in every respect of the English postillions – the latter do their duty, but seldom familiarise their fares to the sound of their voices, and the traveller never exchanges a word with his post-boy. A touch of the hat acknowledges the gratuity when the stage is ended, and the driver, having consigned his charge to his successor, departs. He neither knows, nor cares, aught for their concerns, except that he is to advance so many miles upon such a road according to the instructions of his employer.

The Irish driver, on the contrary, will ascertain during your progress where you came from, where you are going and, very often, what you are going about. He has a hundred ways of willing himself into your confidence, and is sure to put in a word or two at every available opportunity – yet in such a manner as to render it impossible for you to subject him to the charge of impertinence.

For example, we engaged one at Closheen.

'Ah then is it to Cahir ye're going sir – and it's from Lismore ye're coming, I'll go bail?'

'You've made a good guess.'

'Maybe it's to my lord's I'll be driving ye?'

'Not so lucky this time.'

'To Mr Grubbs' then did ye say sir?'

'No.'

'Well then, it's to Mr Fennells' yer honour'll be telling me to drive ye?'

'Yes.'

'Is it Mr Joe Fennells', or Mr Jonas Fennells' or Mr Fennells of the cottage?' And then came a long history of all of the name who dwell in or near one of the prettiest and cleanest towns in Ireland.

We encountered one of the richest characters of the class on the road from Ross to Wexford, and he told us how he had got his first position.

'The master – a mighty pleasant man who loved a joke – had two beautiful English horses, and he wanted a careful man to drive them. Well there was as many as fifteen after the place and to the first that went up to him, he said, "Well my man, tell me, how near the edge of a precipice would you undertake to drive my carriage?"

'So the boy considered and he says, says he, "Within a foot, plaze yer honour, and no harm."

'So the next came up, and he says he'd be bound to carry them within a half a foot, and the next said five inches, and another – a dandified chap intirely – was so mighty nice, that he would drive it within "three inches and a half, he'd so bail."

'Well, at last my turn came and when his honour axed me how nigh I would drive his carriage to the precipice, I said, sez I, "Plaze yer honour, I'd keep as far off it as I could."

'"Very well, Mr Byrne," says he, "you're my coachman."'

We have described the principal objects of attraction on the southern bank of the river Lee, but those on the north are, however, of equal interest and beauty, and among the most conspicuous is the pretty village of Glanmire, with its small but clear and graceful river, which is one of the latest tributaries that the Lee receives.

On the north side of the great island on which Cove stands and on the direct road from Cork to Youghall, are the small towns of Middleton and Castlemartyr.

Youghall is situated at the mouth of the romantic river Blackwater, but the fine and picturesque harbour has the disadvantage of a bar by which it is often rendered dangerous, and

THE VALLEY OF THE BLACKWATER
(BETWEEN LISMORE AND YOUGHALL)

which effectually prevents competition with its safer neighbour of Cork. The town consists principally of one long street and is at the base of a steep hill. A tower stands near the entrance to the harbour, which tradition states to have been a lighthouse in ancient times, and it is more than probable that it is this building which M. Boullaye le Gouz (who toured Ireland in 1644) refers to as 'formerly part of a convent of nuns, of which there remains a tower called the Nunnery, upon which they used to light torches to enable vessels to come into harbour during the night'.

Close to this tower is the piece of land in which it is said Sir Walter Raleigh planted the first potatoes that were grown in Ireland; the honour however is disputed by the garden which adjoins the house in which he lived.

The house stands close to the church and the ancient wall of the town and is called Myrtle Grove, from the luxuriant growth of myrtles by which it is nearly covered. At present it is in the occupation of Colonel Fount who carefully preserves it from injury. It has however undergone certain 'improvements' – the character of which was described by an aged gardener with whom we conversed.

'Ah sir, this was an ould, ancient place – once!'

The house was said to have been the original residence of the wardens of the collegiate church, but was probably altered to its present character – which closely resembles that of the ordinary English manor house of the sixteenth century – by Sir George Carew or Sir Richard Boyle, both of whom resided here. The walls are of considerable thickness and the whole of the interior is wainscotted with Irish oak; the panels in the main room are black as ebony and it contains a chimney-piece of oak also, reaching from floor to ceiling and of very elaborate workmanship, but the bad taste of the former proprietors has defaced the other chambers by a coating of green paint.

In the garden there is a group of yew trees which tradition states to have been planted by Raleigh, and where it requires no great stretch of the imagination to believe that he sat there many a time, reading or dreaming of that El Dorado in the vain search for which he sacrificed his fortune and, ultimately, his life.

There is little doubt that the first potatoes grown in the British Empire were planted at Youghall – probably in 1586 – by Sir Walter Raleigh, who became a mayor of the town in 1588. For a long period however, the potato was cultivated in gardens as a rarity and did not become general food.

It is uncertain when the potato became an article of general food in Ireland, and it is more probable that, as in England, they had long been considered 'conserves, toothsome and daintie', before they were in common use. It is generally believed, however, that the potato celebrated in the Elizabethan age, is 'not the same root as that now commonly known by that name'.

It is unnecessary to state that, for above a century and a half, the potato has been almost the only food of the peasantry of Ireland. They raise corn, wheat, barley and oats in abundance, but it is for export and – although the assertion may startle many – we have no hesitation in saying that there are hundreds in the less civilised districts of the country who have never tasted bread. Whether the Irish have to bless or ban the name of Sir Walter Raleigh is a matter still in dispute, but it is generally admitted that a finer or hardier race of peasantry cannot be found in the world, and although it is considered that their strength fails them at a comparatively early age, it is impossible to deny the nutritive qualities of the root upon which so many millions have thriven and increased.

But there can be as little doubt that the ease with which the means of existence are procured has been the cause of evil; a very limited portion of land, a few days of labour, and a small amount of manure will create a stock upon which a family may exist for twelve months. Also, the periods between exhausting the old stock and digging the new are seasons of great want, if not of absolute famine. If the season is propitious the peasant digs day after day the produce of his plot of ground and, before the winter sets in, places the residue in a pit to which he has access when his wants demand a supply. Every cottage has a garden of an acre or half-acre attached, and as the cultivation requires but a very small proportion of the peasant's time and still less of his attention, his labour remains to be disposed of, or his time may be squandered in idleness. He can live if his crops do not fail, and he can pay his rent if his pig – fed like himself out of the garden – does not die, but to decency of clothing and to any of the luxuries that make life something more than mere animal existence, he is too often a stranger.

The peasant usually has three meals – one at eight in the morning, at noon, and at seven or eight in the evening when his work is done. The potatoes are boiled in an iron pot and strained in the basket from which they are thrown upon the table – seldom without a cloth – and around which the family sit on stools and bosses (the boss is a low seat made of straw). The usual drink is buttermilk when it can be had, and it goes around in a small piggin, a sort of miniature English pail.

The Collegiate Church of Youghall is one of the most interesting churches in the kingdom. Part of it is still used for service, but a larger portion is a ruin and, we fear, one of those which neglect is consigning to utter destruction. It was founded in 1224 for Franciscan friars by Maurice Fitzgerald. He was erecting a castle on the spot, and as it was the eve of some festival the workmen who were building the foundations requested a piece of money to drink his health, which he instructed his eldest son to give to them. But instead of obeying the command, he abused the men, and when this act of parsimony and disobedience came to his father's ears, he changed his plan and built the monastery instead of a castle as a punishment to his heir apparent.

Adjoining the church and indeed once forming part of the structure, is a large square tower, now used as a belfry but evidently a work originally built for defence. It is scarcely necessary to add that Youghall, having been one of the strongholds of the Geraldines, was the scene of many struggles for power.

From time to time it was attacked, defended, and taken. On the 29th May, 1650, Oliver Cromwell embarked at Youghall for England after his extraordinary conquest of Ireland.

Notwithstanding its proximity to Cork, Youghall enjoys a flourishing trade, and a narrow bridge of great length crosses the Blackwater and unites the town with the county of Waterford.

Having detained our readers so long at Youghall, we must conduct them somewhat more rapidly through the towns in the north of the county of Cork. These are Fermoy and Mallow, on the river Blackwater – the exceeding beauty of this river, we shall endeavour to describe in our treatment of the county of Waterford – Castletown-Roche, Buttevant, Doneraile, Kilworth, Glanworth, Newmarket and Kanturk and still further north, Mitchelstown on the borders of the county of Tipperary and Charleville on the borders of the county of Limerick.

Fermoy, an obscure and insignificant village nearly a hundred years ago, became an important town in the early part of this century in consequence of the exertions of Mr Anderson, who had extensive barrack and mail-coach contracts with the Government. His speculations were ultimately unsuccessful and with the prosperity of its founder, that of Fermoy in the same measure declined. Its extensive barracks however and its vicinity to the Cove of Cork make Fermoy a valuable military station.

Mallow has been styled the Bath of Ireland. It is a pretty and agreeable town, its spa has long been celebrated and is much frequented by invalid visitors.

On the banks of the Blackwater and midway between the towns of Mallow and Fermoy is the ruin of the ancient abbey of Bridgetown, which contains several monuments of the once proverbial family of Roche; about a mile distant from the abbey is Castletown-Roche. The Roches were barons of Parliament so early as the reign of Edward II and, though now fallen upon evil days, the name is still honourably conspicuous in the counties of Cork and Limerick.

Buttevant, formerly a place of note and 'a nest of abbots, priests and friars', has dwindled to a mere village with the decay of its noble abbey. The name is said to have derived from the war-cry 'Boutez-en-avant', used by David de Barry, one of the early English invaders. Buttevant was anciently called Botham and, by the Irish, Kilnemullagh. It was surrounded by a stone wall with gateways and was governed by a corporation, and scattered among wretched hovels may be detected many traces of its former consequence.

Buttevant Abbey must have been a pile of considerable magnitude and grandeur. Close to the entrance is a large heap of skulls and bones, said to be the relics of those who fell at the battle of Knockninoss in 1647, between the army of the Parliament commanded by Lord Inchquin and the Irish forces under Lord Taffe.

Buttevant and its neighbourhood – its hills, valleys and rivers, have been rendered classic by the pen of the immortal poet, Edmund Spenser, for he not only resided at Kilcoleman, but here he also composed his *Faerie Queene*, and made the surrounding objects the themes of his undying song.

Spenser first visited Ireland in the year 1580, as secretary to the Lord Deputy, Lord Grey de Wilton, and he discharged his duties of the office with ability and integrity. In 1582 he returned to England and in 1586 he obtained a grant, dated the 27th June, for 3028 acres of the fortified estates of the Earl of Desmond at the rent of seventeen pounds, thirteen shillings and sixpence. He received it on the same conditions as the other undertakers – conditions which implied a residency on the property thus acquired, the policy of the Queen being to people the province of Munster with English families.

Spenser took up his residence at the castle of Kilcoleman, and spent four years here, working upon the first three books of the *Faerie Queene.* He then journeyed to London with his friend, Sir Walter Raleigh, and published them. On his return to Ireland he married a country lass of mean birth, whose name was Elizabeth. During the following six years, he wrote the fourth, fifth and sixth books of the *Faerie Queene* and printed an able and statesmanlike view of the condition of Ireland.

In 1598 the Tyrone rebellion broke out, his estate was plundered and burned and in the flames his youngest child perished, and he was driven into England with his wife and remaining children – a wretched exile. He never recovered from this affliction and died a year later in an obscure lodging in London in extreme indigence, if not in absolute want.

Charleville is a poor town. It was so named by the Earl of Orrery, the Lord President of Munster, as a compliment to Charles II; it was formerly called Rathgogan.

Mitchelstown is the property of the Earl of Kingstown, whose magnificent seat, a modern castellated mansion, is in the immediate neighbourhood. It was erected by Mr Pain, an architect of Cork, recently deceased, to whose skill, judgement and experience the city, and indeed the country at large, is very considerably indebted.

Passing through the small and unimportant town of Millstreet, we return to Cork for the purpose of conducting the tourist through the county of Kerry – first by the inland route which runs through Macroom, and next by the longer, but more interesting route along the coast to Bantry and Glengariff.

The river Lee from the north to its source in the romantic lake of Gougane Barra – a distance of some fifty-five miles from the city of Cork – is exceedingly picturesque and beautiful. It is less rapid than most Irish rivers and its banks are frequently wooded. The Lee is interesting, however, not only from its natural advantages, but it has associations with the history of the past, and numerous castles, now in ruins, look down upon it and many monasteries and abbeys skirt its sides. Among the most striking are the castle of Carrig-a-driod and the Abbey of Kilcrea.

Carrig-a-driod castle is built on a rock in the Lee; although this pass of the river must have been one of importance, the building is comparatively modern. In 1641 however, it was a strong fortress and had the credit of baffling the army of Oliver Cromwell. The Roman Catholic Bishop of Ross had garrisoned it with an army for Charles I. Cromwell dispatched Lord Broghill with orders to attack and scatter the Irish in this quarter, and in the rout that followed the bishop was taken prisoner. A free pardon was offered to him if he would procure the surrender of the castle, which he appeared willing to do. However, when he was conducted to the walls, instead of calling upon the Irish to admit their enemies, he boldly adjured them to hold out while one stone remained upon another and then, turning to the astonished general, he yielded to his fate and was immediately hanged. The castle was soon afterwards taken by a very weak stratagem. The English drew towards it the trunks of trees yoked behind oxen which the garrison mistook for cannon and immediately parleyed.

Tradition states that the castle was erected by a MacCarthy to 'please the Lady O'Carroll, who desired a residence upon this wild and beautiful spot'.

However, a legend attributes its origin to circumstances still more romantic. A poor peasant, lame and hump-backed, fell in love with the fair daughter of his chieftain and pined in despair at the hopeless nature of his attachment. Wandering by the river-side he suddenly heard the click-click-click of the leprechaun's hammer, seized the tiny brogue-maker and compelled him to reveal the secret whereabouts of his treasure trove. The little being not only endowed him with riches, but changed his awkward and ungainly form to one of manly grace and the lovely maiden was readily wooed and won.

The friary of the castle of Kilcrea, both built by Cormac, Lord of Muskerry, one for the protection of the other, stands on the banks of the small river Bride, a mile to the south of the mail coach road between Cork and Macroom, and about twelve miles west of Cork. They are both highly interesting and picturesque, and the approach to both is over a long and narrow bridge which appears to be as old as the venerable structures to which it leads. The castle is described as a 'strong building, having an excellent staircase of dark marble from bottom to top, and about seventy feet high'. On the east side is a large field called the Bawn, which was a usual appendage to great men's castles and was formerly used for dancing, goaling and such diversions and where they also kept their cattle by night to prevent their being carried off by wolves or their more rapacious neighbours.

In the friary, or as it is usually called, 'the abbey', are interred the bodies of a host of the MacCarthys, including among them its founder who died of wounds received in battle, in 1494. A considerable portion of the edifice still remains and, as in all the ancient churches, human bones are piled in every nook and cranny and thrust into corners or gathered in heaps directly at the entrance – a site far more revolting than affecting.

The guide, a respectable elderly woman, whose shed (for outside it looked nothing more) was nestled down by the roadside close to the entrance gate, was, as usual, very anxious to ascertain the motive of our visit to Kilcrea.

Had we come to make drawings . . . a great many ladies and gentlemen came to 'make drawings', and she would get us a chair, and a table too, for that matter, if we wanted them.

We told her we only desired to look about us and, entering a little gate, proceeded down a fine avenue of ancient elm trees. The walls of mortal remains, we suggested to her, ought to be buried.

She shook her coifed head very gravely and answered, 'It would be no use – they wouldn't remain underground.'

We asked her, had she ever tried the experiment.

No, not she indeed, for she knew better than that.

Between Kilcrea and Macroom there are several ruins of castles, once the strongholds of the MacSweeneys, powerful chieftains, although feudatories to the lords of Muskerry. The family were famous for their hospitality and one member had a stone set up on the high road with an Irish inscription, signifying to all passers-by to repair to the house of Mr Edmund MacSweeney for entertainment. It may be added that until recently the stone was still to be seen lying in a ditch where it had been flung by a degenerate descendant who, according to the popular belief, never throve afterwards.

The town of Macroom, twenty-four miles west of Cork, is situated on the Sullane, a river which, for extent and beauty, rivals the Lee. The castle of Macroom is very ancient, or rather, parts of it are of very remote antiquity, for it has undergone many changes. It was converted by its late proprietor, Robert Hedges Eyre, Esq, one of the old Irish gentlemen, into a comfortable mansion and it is now easy to distinguish the ancient from the modern portions of the building. It consists of one huge square of masonry – the mere keep – with embattled parapets, but the hand of taste is not very apparent in the alterations it has undergone to convert the ancient fortalice of the O'Flynns into a dwelling house of the eighteenth century.

During the lifetime of Mr Hedges Eyre, it was impossible for the inn at Macroom to prosper, for whenever a customer arrived whose manner denoted him a gentleman, a messenger was soon in his chamber with the news that a room had been prepared for him at the castle. Since the death of the generous gentleman the inn has assumed a more stirring aspect, and is likely to have employment for both cook and housemaid.

From Macroom to Killarney, the road is by no means picturesque; it passes along the banks of the river Sullane, and through the small village of Ballyvourney, which is almost the only congregation of houses on the route. It runs, however, within a few yards of the singular castle of Carrig-a-Pooka, built by the MacCarthy of Drishane, and placed on the summit of a solitary rock which is so steep as to render caution necessary in climbing it. It is now a single tower, and never could have been much more extensive, for it almost covers the rock upon which it stands.

A visit to the castle affords us the opportunity for introducing to the reader one of the fairy legends of Ireland – the legend of the Pooka.

The Pooka belongs to the malignant class of beings which compose the Irish fairy mythology, and is pre-eminent in malice and mischief. In form he is generally a horse, often an eagle or bull, and he sometimes becomes an *ignis fatuus*. Among the great diversity of form at times assumed by him, he exhibits a mixture of the calf and the goat. Probably it is in some measure owing to the assumption of the latter form that he owes his name: *puc* being the Irish for goat.

The Pouke or Pooka means, literally, the evil one; playing the puck, a common Anglo-Irish phrase, is equivalent to playing the devil.

There are many locales which are favourite haunts of the Pooka and to which he has given his name, such as Drohid-a-Pooka, Castle Pook and Carrig-a-Pooka. The island of Melaan also, at the mouth of the Kenmare river, is a chosen site whereon this malignant spirit indulges his freaks. It is uninhabited and is dreaded by the peasantry and fishermen, not less because of its gloomy, rugged and stern aspect than for the tales of terror connected with it. The tempest wails fearfully around its spectre-haunted crags and dark objects are often seen flitting over it in the gloom of the night. Shrill noises, wild cries and moaning sounds are heard, and the fisherman benighted or forced upon its rocks may often behold in the crowding groups which flit around him the cold faces of those long dead.

The great object of the Pooka seems to be to obtain a rider, and then he is in all his most malignant glory. Headlong he dashes over mountain and valley, moor and river. He flies over and beyond them, gratified by the distress, and utterly reckless and ruthless of the cries, danger and suffering of the luckless wight who bestrides him. As the *Tinna Geolane* or Will o' the Wisp, he lures but to betray, and leads to destruction in a quagmire or pit.

The English Puck is a jolly, frolicsome, night-loving fellow, full of archness and fond of all kinds of merry tricks, but he is very probably in his origin the same as the Irish Pooka. The English adventurers imported to the Irish shores their softened version of the native Pooka under his Saxon appellation of Puck and have left his name to Puck's Rock, near Howth, and Puck Castle, a romantic ruin in the county of Dublin.

An ancient chronicler at Bantry related to us the adventures of many of his friends to support his assertion that a Pooka haunted his own neighbourhood. He knew two boys who, on their way back from midnight mass, met a horse. '"Let's get up on his back," sez one, and so they got up and och, murdher, didn't he give 'em a ride, next morning laving them twenty miles from their door.'

This however is the only instance within our knowledge of the spirit being encountered by more than one at a time. On our venturing to hint that the fact was unusual, we were met at once by the answer, 'Sure, weren't both of them brothers.'

Another friend of the old man, going through a narrow pass, heard a horse coming along at a fast gallop and drew up to let him pass, when he heard a voice by his side, say, 'Lien,' that is, lie down, 'here's the Pooka coming.' And sure enough, he saw the beast with his eyes and nose flashing out fire. So the boy turns around and says, 'Who are you?' thinking it was a fellow Christian that had given him the warning.

'I'm the Lanian Shee,' says the voice.

Now wasn't it queer that the spirit should be afeared of the Pooka, but you see, they weren't friends at all.

The highest of the Galtee mountains, called the Galtee Mor, and sometimes Dawson's Seat, rises over a gloomy lake which is said to be the residence of a Pooka, who is believed to be chained to the bottom and only permitted to make excursions upon state occasions. The lake is believed to this day to possess, in consequence of its terrible inhabitant, three properties:

First, it is unfathomable; an attempt was once made to sound it and, from the descriptions of the people, it appears that the regular process was adopted, but no line could be found that would reach the bottom.

Secondly, let the slightest breeze arise on the warmest day of summer, and the cold around the lake will be intense.

Thirdly, although the lake does not appear to be of great extent, no stone could ever be thrown across it. We have heard that a famous stone thrower from Clonmel – a man who could throw a stone from Fairy Hill to the other side of the river, which is a much greater *apparent* distance than the extent of the lake – attempted to throw a stone across the waters, but like all other stones it did not go beyond the centre and then fell into the dark waters.

To properly examine the romantic lake of Gougane Barra, the Pass of Keim-an-eigh, and the wild and singular scenery that leads to and surrounds them, the traveller must diverse from the high road and follow a route that leads 'back again', unless he is prepared to tread over mountains where a goat would scarcely find his way homewards without direction, and to encounter the perils of bogs and morasses more numerous than cottages. The adventurous pedestrian, however, will be amply repaid for his risk and labour, for in no part of Ireland has nature been left more completely to her own guidance and government.

From Macroom to Inchageela, a village midway between the town and Gougane Barra, the road becomes wilder and more rugged; huge rocks overhang it, high hills look down upon them, and over these the mountains tower.

The Lee, which for a considerable space has dwindled to a small murmuring rivulet, at length widens out into the sheet of water which forms the picturesque Lough Allua, the lake of the Lee. The road winds for about three miles along its northern margin, with the rocks on one side, and the clear, deep water on the other – and a more perfect solitude it is impossible to imagine. Not a tree is to be seen, but the rocks have assumed the most singular and fantastic shapes; and yet a century and a half ago these rocks, hills, and valleys were clothed with forests to the water's edge, and in their fastness the red deer roved.

A sudden turning in the road brings the traveller within view and almost over the lake of Gougane Barra. It is a scene of utter loneliness, stern grandeur and savage magnificence, but it is redeemed by a little island with its group of graceful ash trees and ruined chapel. Numerous streams rush down from the surrounding mountains into the lake which sends them forth again in a bountiful river – for here the Lee has its source – until they form the noble harbour of Cork and lose themselves in the broad

GOUGANE BARRA.

Atlantic. In summer these streams are gentle rills, but in winter the foaming cataracts rush over ridges of projecting rocks baring them of even the lichens that strive to cling to their sides.

The small island is nearly midway in the lake, and a rude artificial causeway leads to it from the mainland. This is the famous hermitage of Saint Finn Barr who is said to have lived here previous to his founding the cathedral of Cork. It is classed amongst the holiest places in Ireland, and has long been a favourite of devotees, who journey there in the confident expectation that its consecrated waters have the power to heal all kinds of disease. Here at certain seasons they assemble in immense crowds, bringing their sick children and ailing animals to bathe, and upon the neighbouring bushes and wooden crosses hang fragments of clothes or halters and spancels in proof that the lake had performed the anticipated miracle to the various animals, both biped and quadruped.

The greater portion of the island is covered with the ruins of the chapel and its appurtenant buildings and there is also a large court or cloister containing eight arched cells.

The sacred character of Gougane Barra has, it is said, preserved it from the pest of so many Irish lakes – the monster worm or enchanted eel. We heard stories of them in abundance. Often, but always at night, the hideous head of the serpent is raised above the surface of the water; and if a cow is missing from some neighbouring herd, there is no difficulty in ascertaining its fate – it has been made a 'toothful for the ould enemy'.

Indeed, in ancient times, the blessed isle of Saint Finn Barr was subjected to the visits of such an intruder who, having been guilty of the impudence of snatching from the very hand of the priest the *loneen* – a vessel for holding holy water – as he was in the act of sprinkling a crowd of devotees, the creature was expelled from the neighbourhood for his wickedness and has never ventured to leave his loathsome slime upon the green banks of the lake.

The Pass of Keim-an-eigh (the path of the deer) lies to the south-west of Inchageela in the direction of Bantry Bay, and the tourist will commit a grievous error if he omits to visit it. Perhaps in no part of the kingdom is there to be found a place so utterly desolate and gloomy. A mountain has been divided by some convulsion of nature and a narrow pass, about two miles in length, is overhung on either side by perpendicular masses of stone clothed in wild ivy and underwood with occasionally a stunted yew-tree or arbutus growing among them. At every step advance seems impossible, for some huge rock juts out into the path and, on sweeping around it, seems to conduct only to some barrier still more insurmountable, while wild fountains rush downwards from all sides.

As may be expected in these modern times, these rocky fastnesses have often given shelter to bands of lawless or disaffected men; and here also in some deep dell smoke might have been detected issuing from the roof of some illicit still-cabin. Among these rocks, too, smugglers had many a cave in which they deposited their goods until suspicion had been lulled on the highways, so that they might be conveyed in safety to the neighbouring towns. And here too men who had set themselves against the law often met to arrange their plans for carrying destruction into the adjoining valleys.

Still nearer to Bantry and still among the wild and almost trackless wastes is the mountain called the Priest's Leap. We asked a peasant why it was so called and received the following answer.

'Ye see sir, one time in this country there was a reward of five pounds for a wolf's head and five pounds for a priest's head, and a dale of money was made out of both of them.

'Well a holy priest was riding over the hill and he was pursued by the Tories (they called the blaggards Tories that did be hunting the priests) and just as they had their bloody hands on his robe, he prayed to Saint Fiachna to help him out of their way, and the ass he was on gave a leap and sprung seven miles over the mountain to th'other side – and there are the marks of the baste's knees in the solid rock to this day. And the people won't blast the rock even though it comes right in the way of the road for Bantry.'

There is beyond question a singular rock which greatly interferes with the road, containing two holes of a remarkable character, and while the removal of this rock seems to be necessary, it remains untouched.

This road, formerly the principal line of communication between the two most picturesque portions of Irish scenery, Glengariff and Killarney, has now been abandoned for one of the best roads in the kingdom, and to the lover of the wild and romantic we recommend this road for special enjoyment. The scenery over mountain and through glen is glorious; the broad bay of Bantry glistens far beneath and the blue shores of Ivera and Bear in the distance are noble features in the majestic panorama. Nor has the voice of tradition failed or become silent among these hills and many a wild legend and whimsical fiction may be gathered from the shrewd, inquisitive and really imaginative inhabitants.

Nearly midway in the course of the mountain road stands the ruin of one of those small ancient churches whose era, from their style, must be placed between the fifth and eleventh centuries. Only a portion of the walls remain, and the stones are large, curiously jointed and well-fashioned. We were told that it was one of the first churches 'called at Rome' – a traditional record of its high antiquity. Outside the burial ground is a natural rock of tabular form with five basin-like hollows in the surface, each of four or five inches in depth, and about a foot in diameter. These are filled with water and in each a long oval stone fits perfectly into the space. The whole forms a 'petrified dairy', with the basins being the 'keelers', and the ovals the 'rolls of butter'.

The history of this strange monument is that, in ancient times, a woman lived here who, not respecting the commandment against thieving, milked the cows of her neighbours at night and transferred the milk as well as the butter to her own dairy.

She was suspected at length and the hue and cry was raised against her, and Saint Fiachna resolved to punish her. He mounted his horse to visit her, but she fled. The saint as he followed, turned her dairy into stone as he passed, and then continued on down the hill after her. In crossing the stream his horse left its hoof-marks on a stone in the centre of it (this we did not choose to look at, but we were assured that it was there).

The saint then galloped up the opposite hillside where, about midway, he overtook the criminal and instantly turned her into stone, and there she stands still, the Irish 'Lot's Wife', – not however a pillar of salt, but a stone of about six feet in height, and still having a resemblance to the original lady.

We must now reconduct the reader to Cork in order that we may be his guide to the county of Kerry along the sea-coast through Bantry and Glengariff.

The port of Kinsale, although not on the direct route, may be visited on the way. The town is exceedingly interesting as, for a considerable period, it was the most frequented and celebrated of the southern harbours of Ireland – taking precedence over that of Cork – and it occupies a full and prominent page in Irish history.

The road to Kinsale – a distance of nineteen English miles – has little to interest the traveller, but on either side the mountain-hills are richly cultivated. The town is seen to great advantage from this approach. It is built on the side of a hill and is of a peculiarly quaint character. The streets are remarkably narrow and many of the houses have projecting windows like those of the Spaniards, by whom some of them were probably built.

The charter of incorporation is so early as Edward III. Lord Kinsale is the premier Baron of Ireland and Kinsale gives the title of Baron to the De Courcys, the descendants of Milo de Courcy, son of John, Earl of Ulster, and the Lords of Kinsale enjoy the exclusive, although vain and useless privilege of being covered in the royal presence, which privilege was granted by King John to the Earl of Ulster.

It would occupy far more space than we can afford to give even an outline of the sieges to which the town has been subjected from a very early period. It was several times in the occupation of the Spaniards, who had possession of it so far back as 1380 and who, in 1601, having been largely aided by O'Neill and other Irish chieftains, kept the English army under the Lord President, Sir George Carew, at bay for some considerable time.

On the 12th March 1689, James II landed in Kinsale (the house in which he slept is still pointed out) and then commenced his struggle to regain the throne he had abdicated. In 1690 the town was taken by the Duke of Marlborough, but only after a gallant defence, and the garrison were allowed to march out 'upon honourable conditions'.

The parish church is dedicated to a female saint – Saint Multose or Multosia, by whom it is said to have been erected in the fourteenth century.

A legend is told in connection with it. When the saint was building the church – which she did with her own hands – she desired to remove a large stone, which was however too heavy for her to lift. Seeing two men passing, one a native of the town, the other a stranger, she summoned them to her aid; the native refused to help, but the stranger laboured until her object was effected. The saint then gave her blessing to the one and her curse to the other.

It is a remarkable fact that when two inhabitants of the town marry, they will not go through the ceremony within the walls of Saint Multose, but are united at some other church in the neighbourhood, and we were supplied with proofs in support of the legend by reference to several unlucky couples who had been so unwisely sceptical as to neglect the ancient warning.

The harbour of Kinsale, although greatly inferior to that of Cork, is capacious, deep and well-sheltered. It is defended by a strong fort, called Charles Fort, in honour of Charles II and erected by the Duke of Ormond in 1681.

One of the outer forts of Charles Fort is called the Devil's Battery. The legend attached to it is that the Devil was wont to take his rounds upon the ramparts, carrying in his hand a cannon-ball and terrifying the sentinels night after night. The cause of this appearance is said to have originated in a tragic event that once occurred there.

The only son of the governor prevailed upon the sentinel on duty to convey a message from him to the town, and took his firelock and place during his absence. The young man fell asleep at his post and the governor, visiting the stations and finding, as he supposed, the sentinel betraying his trust, shot him dead; and only then discovered to his horror that he had slain his child. So great was his despair that he leaped from the ramparts into the sea and perished.

From that fatal night his Satanic majesty was a constant visitor at the fort, and a cannon is shown to this day on which he left the mark of his thumb.

The Old Head, the point nearest the sea, has a lighthouse and has been a famous landmark for mariners. Although for upwards of a century Kinsale has ceased to occupy a very prominent station among the harbours of Ireland and has lost its commercial importance, it is still a flourishing town, its prosperity being sustained chiefly by its facilities for fishing – the Cork markets are almost exclusively supplied from it – the skill of its ship and boat builders and by its convenience as an outlet for the transfer of cattle to England.

The adjoining coast is unhappily full of melancholy relics of shipwrecks and in the churchyard are numerous gravestones recording merely the facts of bodies being washed ashore and interred there.

The road from Kinsale to Innishannon passes along the banks of the river Bandon. About midway to Innishannon, a pretty village that skirts the clear and rapid river, is the ancient castle of Shippool, a structure erected by the Roches. Between Innishannon and Bandon is the castle of Dundaneere – or Downdaniel – which stands near the confluence of the rivers Brinny and Bandon. The castle is now a complete ruin, but one of the most striking and interesting that we have visited. It commands a charming point of the river; the surrounding scenery is perfectly beautiful and the neighbouring hills are covered with woods and villas. The road leads along the banks of the Bandon the whole way to the town to which it gives its name. It was formerly called Bandon-bridge, and was built by the first Earl of Cork who, in a letter to Mr Secretary Cook, dated the 13th August, 1632, describes the place in which it is situated as 'upon a great district of the country that was until lately a mere waste of bog and wood, serving for a retreat and harbour to wood-kernes, rebels, thieves and wolves'.

The town is of considerable size and is populous and flourishing, being, as it is, the great thoroughfare into Carbery and also to Killarney. It belongs partly to the Duke of Devonshire, and partly to the Earl of Bandon, whose beautiful seat, Castle Bernard, is in the immediate neighbourhood.

From Bandon to Bantry there are two roads: the northern and nearest through Ballyneed, Dunmanway and Drimoleague, and the southern and more picturesque along the coast through Clonakilty, Ross-Carbery and Skibbereen.

Ballyneed and Drimoleague are small villages, and Dunmanway is the only poor town in the district, for emigration has drained it of its most able-bodied and intelligent inhabitants. And, as their dwellings remain tenantless, and an Irish cabin is never worth pulling down, they crumble with every shower and every storm, giving to the scene an aspect of extreme dreariness and desolation.

The little inn at Dunmanway is very clean and, considering all things, comfortable. The landlord, as is usual at country inns, walks about with his hands in his pockets, evidently desiring to be thought anything rather than an innkeeper; and it is a curious thought but we do not recall ever seeing a landlady anywhere, with the exception of the hostess of the Imperial Hotel in Cork, who came often to inquire if all things in her well-managed house pleased us.

The little maid at Dunmanway did her best certainly to make up for the absence of her mistress. She was the model of a cheerful, do-everything sort of girl that, like one of the faeries of her own mountains, was in a score of places at the same moment, and, in addition to her being cheerful and active, Mary of Dunmanway was ready-witted, as the following incident will show.

The inn was certainly very clean, having been newly painted, and the little drawing-room was enriched by, as she called it, 'a bran new Kitterminister carpet,' but, notwithstanding this, a particularly active little insect left undeniable proof of its propensities upon our wrist – two large red spots.

'Mary,' we said, 'look here, this really is too bad.'

She looked with feigned or unfeigned astonishment – it was difficult to say which – and exclaimed, in a tone of mingled anger and repugnance, 'Why then, bad luck to the dirty bastes at the house ye *last* slept in!'

Of the towns on the southern or coast road, Ross-Carbery alone demands particular notice. It is one of the oldest towns in Ireland, the ancient name being Ross-Alithri, 'the field of pilgrimage', and, according to history, 'there was anciently here a famous university whereto resorted all the south-west part of Ireland for learning's sake'. It was formerly a bishop's see, but was united with that of Cork, and recently with that of Cloyne.

A glance at the map of Cork will convey some idea of the numerous bays and harbours along the coast. It is for the most part exceedingly rugged, and for mile upon mile there is not a single tree to be found. But the ocean around it is dotted with small islands, against which the breakers dash and foam.

Not only the number, but the advantageous positions of the harbours will claim attention, and the coast from Youghal to Bantry is indented by at least twelve, eight of which are perfectly calculated for merchant vessels of burthen, and not less than five would float the largest ships of the British Navy.

In former times, when temptations to illicit trade were great, and the securities against detection comparatively easy, smuggling was carried on to a large extent along the coast, which was of course so favourable for it. For some years it has been on the decline and is now nearly abandoned.

Between the towns of Ross-Carbery and Skibbereen, and at the head of the Glandore Harbour, the tourist passes along a beautiful and picturesque road where 'lakes upon lakes interminably gleam', and to one point in particular his attention should be directed; the glen called 'The Leap', the ancient boundary which divided the civilised from the uncivilised. 'Beyond the Leap, beyond the Law', was, even within our own memory, an accepted proverb.

Not far from Skibbereen is a singular salt-water lake, Lough Hyne or Ine (the deep lake). In the centre is a long island, upon which are the ruins of one of the castles of the O'Driscolls. It is surrounded by picturesque hills, some rocky and precipitous, others steep and wooded, rising from the edge of the lake. There is also a churchyard, peculiar to Ireland, devoted exclusively to the interment of children and where there was formerly a chapel dedicated to Saint Bridget.

The coast south-west of Skibbereen is dotted with islands, the most famous of which is that of Cape Clear. Innisherken, with its ruined abbey, opposite Baltimore Harbour is also full of interest. The O'Driscolls had formerly castles here which defended the entrance to the harbour.

Cape Clear, the well-known landmark for vessels outward or homeward bound, is the most southern point of Ireland. In the ancient ecclesiastical books it is called 'Insula Sancta Clara', and in the old Irish manuscripts, 'Inish Damhly'.

Many years have passed since we visited this wild and primitive district, but we learn from more recent travellers that the character of its inhabitants continues quite unchanged. They exist almost in a state of nature, depending for food upon the potato crop and the fish that swarm around their rocks; they seldom visit the mainland and are devotedly attached to their rugged strand and almost as rugged plain.

In the year 1750 there were about four hundred families on the island, and they do not appear to have increased, for the latest returns give the population at less than eleven hundred. Indeed, it is not likely that it could supply the means of existence to a larger number, for the island is only three miles long and one and a half miles in breadth. On the south side is the lighthouse which, it is said, may be distinguished in clear weather from a distance of twenty-eight nautical miles. On the north-west point of the island is the singularly picturesque ruin of the castle of Dunanore, or the Golden Fort. It stands on a rock and a very narrow passage leads to it. The path is so steep and high, with the sea dashing and foaming against it on either side, that the ascent is a somewhat perilous task.

Legends enough to make a volume are connected with this remarkable ruin: it was formerly the stronghold of the O'Driscolls, some of whom are stated to have mingled the hospitalities of the Irish chieftain with the reckless darings of the buccaneer.

To the west of Baltimore is the harbour of Crookhaven, which is separated by a narrow promontory from the beautiful Dunmanus Bay, which another promontory divides from the famous bay of Bantry.

The mail-coach road from Skibbereen to Bantry runs through a wild and uninteresting country and the traveller who desires to examine this most peculiar and picturesque portion of the Irish coast will have to pursue a route which is less easy of access, but far more certain of recompense for the expenditure of time and labour. The mountains appear to rise directly from the sea, as if they were but the continuations of mountains directly underneath the ocean, and there are small villages thickly scattered about their bases. Mount Gabriel, bleak and barren from foot to summit, looks down upon the poor village of Scull, which was once a famous collegiate town.

Lakes are to be seen in every valley, upon the mountain sides and on their summits, and streams pour down that now and then break in cataracts over precipices. On the opposite side there is the sea with its stores of green islands or black rocks, creeks, bays and harbours running into the land, and beyond all the broad Atlantic that affords no resting place for the sea-bird until he closes up his wings and stands upon the continent of America.

The ocean, with its tales of shipwrecks and piracies; the land, with its legends and traditions, both afford themes to fill volumes of interest and excitement; and every castle (of which there remain the ruins of hundreds) has its story of bold adventure.

The lakes too are rich in legends; there is that on the summit of Mount Gabriel, with its eternal serpent and depth that has never been fathomed; Loughdrine, where on a certain day of the year the islands used to dance merrily, change places and shift from one side to the other from sunrise to sunset. (Unhappily an officer thrust his sword through one of these floating sods – they are no more – and the country people will tell you that 'it limped in the water ever after'.)

There is Ballinlough where the faeries keep nightly guard, protecting the passage that leads from the ancient rath that borders it, to the bottom where *Thierna-na-oge*, the land of perpetual youth, flourishes.

In short, the stranger will find wherever he travels in this wild and entirely primitive neighbourhood, a rich abundance to interest, excite and amuse and not a little to inform and instruct.

The far-famed Bay of Bantry is perhaps unsurpassed by any harbour of the kingdom for natural advantages combined with natural beauties. As we approach it along the dreary road from Skibbereen, a sudden turn at the base of a rugged hill brings us suddenly within view of the most striking objects which make up the glorious scene. Far and away in the distance tower the lofty Mangerton and Macgillicuddy's Reeks; nearer, rises Hungry Hill, the Sugar Loaf and at long range, the Caha mountains among which it is said there are no fewer than three hundred and sixty-five lakes – the number having of course suggested a legend that some holy saint prayed for a lake to supply water for each day of the year.

Little flat and fertile islands lie at the feet of the spectator and nearly facing the town is Whiddy Island with its fierce-looking fortifications and its fields rich with promised harvest.

The road into the town – a town that has been truly described as a seaport without trade, a harbour without shipping and a coast with a failing fishery – runs immediately under the fine demesne of the Earl of Bantry, and all the way it is one continued line of beauty, where one never loses sight of the distant mountains or the foreground of green islands.

There are not many islands in this vast expanse of water; Whiddy is the largest, but there are also Hog, Horse, Coney and

Chapel flung into the glorious bay. The bay is memorable in history as having been twice entered by a French force for the invasion of Ireland: the first time in 1689 in aid of James II, the next in 1796.

To visit Glengariff, the tourist may proceed either by land or by water across the bay. It is obvious that the best mode is to go by one and return by the other, and both offer strong temptations to the lover of the picturesque. Those however who take it in their route to Killarney and do not design to make any stay at Bantry had better continue on by road, for the Bay may be seen fully from the hills above either Bantry or Glengariff, or at all events by taking a boat a mile or two from the shores of either.

The road is exceedingly wild and picturesque. A short distance from the town the Mialloch, 'the murmuring river', is crossed by a small bridge, a little way below which is the Fall of Dunamarc, a precipice of some thirty or forty feet over rocks of the most fantastic forms. Close to it we saw a water-mill in full work, driven by the diverted current from the cataract.

In this immediate vicinity, according to one of the fanciful traditions, the first human foot trod upon Irish ground, Ladra having effected a landing in Ireland exactly forty days before the flood.

After passing three or four miles of good road and comparatively cultivated land, we entered a rough and rugged district with barren hills towering over us at either side and among them rapid streams rushing over gigantic stones down into the valleys. We passed on the right an interesting object – a little chapel nestling among the barren hills, and a short way further on we passed one of those singular dwelling places that are by no means rare in this part of the country. We were startled by a human form issuing from a huge mass of rocks and, upon inquiry, learned that a family actually lived in a hole which the rocks protected and sheltered; the rocks had evidently fallen ages ago in the position which they retained, enclosing and covering a natural chamber.

On entering we found a woman with three children; the man

was at work in the adjacent 'garden' and here they contrived to exist during the summer months, for we ascertained that in winter they quitted it for some neighbouring town where they worked or begged according to their circumstances. The woman replied to our few questions with cheerfulness and civility, and to an expression approaching condolence as to the misery of her lot, replied, 'It's bad enough sure yer honour, but there's many have worse places to lay their four bones in.'

Language utterly fails to convey even a limited idea of the exceeding beauty of Glengariff – the rough glen – which merits to the full the enthusiastic praise that has been lavished on it by every traveller by whom it has been visited.

It is a deep alpine valley, enclosed by precipitous hills, about three miles in length and seldom exceeding a quarter of a mile in breadth. Black and savage rocks enclose a scene of surpassing loveliness; beyond is the magnificent bay with its numerous islands, by one of which it is so guarded and sheltered as to give it the aspect of a serene lake.

The mountains are of all forms, altitudes and outlines; the most prominent amongst them is the Sugar-loaf, Slieve-na-goil, 'the mountain of the wild people', with its conical head soaring up into the clouds and to the rear, but at a considerable distance, Hungry Hill, with its naked and meagre sides down which runs a stream from the lake on its summit, which, gathering as it goes, breaks into a tremendous cataract of eight hundred feet, and flings out a spray around it that seems to cover a third part of the hill with a thick mist.

From the road to Kenmare the surpassing loveliness of the valley and the full glory of the bay will be seen to perfection. For three or four miles the traveller winds around the side of mountain along a steep and weary road barren of interest. Suddenly he arrives on the brow of the hill; he is over the glen, many thousands of feet above the ocean which he beholds stretching out into space, while the islands appear as dots around it; the river that runs through the valley has dwindled to a white thread, the trees have gathered into masses and the hill upon which he stood a while ago now seems no bigger than a fairy mound. Midway down are scattered cottages which only the pale smoke distinguishes from mole heaps. Thin and narrow streams, like snow wreaths, are running from the mountains into the lakes that send them forth again to fertilise the valley.

The village of Glengariff consists of but a few houses; there is a little inn, happily situated at the head of the bay, and the glen is divided between two proprietors – Lord Bantry, and the widow of his brother, Colonel White. His lordship has a small lodge where he generally resides, in a valley away from a view of the sea, but the other seat skirts the left of the bay, is cultivated to the water's edge and commands a view of the principal island on which is built a Martello Tower – as if for the express purpose of giving interest and value to the demesne.

The old bridge, now a ruin, which in ancient times was on the high road to Berehaven, is called Cromwell's Bridge, and as history is silent as to the origin of the name we must have recourse to tradition.

When Oliver was passing through the glen to visit the O'Sullivans, he had so much trouble in getting across the narrow but rushing river that he told the inhabitants if they did not build him a bridge by the time he returned he would hang up a man for every hour's delay he met with.

'So the bridge was ready agin he came back,' quoth our informant, 'for they knew the ould villain to be a man of his word.'

West of Glengariff is the promontory of Berehaven, separating Bantry Bay from the Kenmare River. It is a wild and primitive district, abounding in picturesque and romantic scenery, full of legends, with historical associations of great interest and possessing the ruins of many castles of the O'Sullivans, who were for centuries the lords of the soil, although their descendants are now but the hewers of stone and the drawers of water; of the castle of Dunboy, the ancient stronghold of the O'Sullivans, only a few walls remain, barely sufficient to point out its locality.

In the parish of Berehaven is worked one of the few profitable mines of Ireland. It is situated on the property of a Mr Puxley and

GLENGARIFF INN.

was discovered some thirty years ago, by a very minute scrutiny of the estate by Colonel Hall, who was at the period working his own mines in the neighbouring districts of the county.

We are now about to quit the county of Cork and enter into that of Kerry; and although we have occupied in describing Cork a much larger space than the limits of our work will justify us in devoting to any other county, we are fully aware that we have omitted to direct the tourist's attention to many subjects connected with it that are of exceeding interest and deep importance.

The county of Cork in the province of Munster is the largest county in Ireland and larger than any English county with the exception of York; from east to west it extends above ninety English miles, with its greatest breadth being about forty. It is bounded on the north by Tipperary and Limerick; on the north-east by Waterford; on the north-west by Kerry and on the south by the ocean.

The county is divided into the East and West Ridings, the East comprising eleven baronies, with the liberties of the city of Cork and the port of Kinsale, and the West, eight baronies.

The baronies in the East Riding are: Duhallow, Orrery and Kilmore, Condons and Clongibbons, Fermoy, Kinsale, Imokilly, Kerrycurrihy, Kinnalea, Barrymore, Barretts and East Muskerry.

In the West Riding they are: Ibane and Barryroe, Bere, Bantry, West Muskerry, Kinameaky, Courcies, East and West Carbery.

The principal towns of the county, besides the city of Cork, are Youghall, Kinsale, Bandon, Mallow, Cove, Bantry, Fermoy, Skibbereen, Macroom and Dunmanway.

Chapter Two

KERRY

The entrance to the county of Kerry (the Kingdom of Kerry, as it was called in bygone times) from that of Cork is through a tunnel of about two hundred yards in length, and a very short distance from this there are two others of much more limited extent. They have been cut through the solid rock of the mountains whose peaks we have described as overlooking Glengariff. Until these tunnels were cut and the road made, travellers to Killarney were compelled to order carriages from Kenmare to meet them on the Kerry side of the mountain or, as was usually done, to hire five or six stout peasants from Glengariff to carry the car on their shoulders over rocks and along precipices that were exceedingly dangerous from the want of a protecting wall and on account of the numerous ruts on the route.

As the traveller emerges from comparative darkness, a scene of striking magnificence bursts upon him, for while his eye retains the rich and cultivated beauty of the wooded and watered glen, he is startled by the contrast of barren and frightful precipices along the brinks of which he is riding, and gazes with a shudder down into the far-off valley where a broad and angry stream is diminished by the distance into a mere line of white.

Nothing can excel the wild grandeur of the prospect which extends mile upon mile; scattered through the vale and among the hill slopes are many cottages, white always and generally slated, and lime-kilns, which are so numerous in all parts of the country, are attached to several of them.

There is a view from the road almost the whole way down to the Kenmare River, and this road has been so admirably constructed and is kept so carefully that by universal consent it is classed amongst the best in the kingdom. The whole district we believe belongs to the Marquis of Lansdowne, and a better ordered estate or more flourishing tenantry are not to be found in any mountain district of Ireland. Such was not always the case, for at one period it was proverbial for the poverty of the land and the wretchedness of its inhabitants.

We had scarcely passed through the tunnel and entered the county when we encountered a group that interested us greatly. On enquiry we learned that a wedding had taken place at a cottage which was pointed out to us in a little glen, and that the husband was bringing home his bride.

She was mounted on a white pony guided by a smart-looking and well-dressed youth whose face was absolutely radiant with joy. The parents of the bride and groom followed, and a little girl clung to the dress of a staid and sober matron, whom we at once, from her pensive and almost sorrowful aspect, guessed to be the mother of the bride.

We may take advantage of the occasion to describe the ceremonies and formalities connected with an Irish wedding.

When the match is made it becomes necessary for the bridegroom to obtain a certificate from his parish priest stating that he is free to contract marriage with any woman equally free from canonical bonds or impediments; and to this a fee of five shillings is always attached. He must also procure from the bishop or vicar-general a licence to marry, to which a fee of seven shillings and sixpence is attached. This being done, he repairs with his bride to the house of her parish priest accompanied by as many of both his and her friends that they can muster, and before he is married he lays down to the priest the marriage fee, which is according to his circumstances. The friends of both parties are called upon to pay something, and between their reluctance to meet the demand and the priest's refusal to marry them 'til he is satisfied, a scene, sometimes humorous and sometimes discreditable, often arises. If the bride's father is a 'strong' farmer who can afford to furnish a good dinner, the marriage takes place at the bride's house, the bridegroom bringing with him as many friends as choose to accompany him. The same process as to money takes place here and it is not uncommon for the collection to amount to twenty, thirty and sometimes forty or fifty pounds where the parties are comfortable and have a strong line of followers.

The ceremony is in Latin and is very nearly what the Church of England ceremony is in English, but the priest closes it by saying, 'give your wife the kiss of peace'. A struggle often ensues for his bride's kiss between some wag and the bridegroom, with the latter generally surrendering ill-humouredly. The priests in some instances discountenance and in others overlook the practice; but we have seen a priest give a young fellow who attempted to snatch the kiss a severe slap across the face.

The most favoured time for celebrating weddings is just before Lent. The guests are always numerous, and consist of all ranks from the lord and lady of the manor through the intermediate grades of gentlemen, 'squireens', farmers and down to the common labourer, and wives are, of course, included. Perfect equality prevails on this occasion and yet the natural courtesy of the Irish character prevents any disturbance of the social order, and everyone keeps his place while at the same time utmost freedom reigns.

On the first May day after the wedding it was customary for the young men and maidens of the Parish to go to the wood and cut down the tallest tree, which they dressed up with ribbons, placing in the centre a large ball decorated with variously coloured paper and gilt. They then carried this in procession to the bride's house, setting it up before the door, and commenced a dance about it which lasted all day. They were of course 'thrated' liberally by the bride on such occasions, but this custom, which appears to have been a relic of Druidism, is now nearly obsolete.

It is also worthy of remark that second marriages are very rare amongst the peasantry, and comparatively so among the higher classes. This affords strong proof of the depth of their attachment, and they do not hold it to be strictly right for either men or women to marry again.

About three or four miles west of Kenmare are the copper and lead mines of the 'Kenmare Mining Association'. The copper mines are at Ardtully with the royalty belonging to Mr D D Croker (but the property is at present in dispute); and the lead mines are on the estate of the Marquis of Lansdowne at Shonagarry. They have been at work for three years but with very limited success; however, a shipload of twenty-eight tons has just been sent off to Swansea, and we have not yet been able to ascertain the price it brought.

The road from Kenmare to Killarney, which lies nearly due north, possesses very little of interest for the first five miles. But before entering upon this road a deviation to the west will conduct the traveller to many objects of considerable interest.

A mile or two from the town are the ancient ruins of Dunkerron Castle, once the hospitable seat of the O'Sullivan Mor, and also Cappanacuss, another shattered castle of the same family.

Further on the river Blackwater flows into the bay. Its source is a small dark lake among the Dunkerron mountains, and it is crossed near its mouth by a bridge of two lofty arches which pass over a chasm of great depth.

Twelve miles to the west the visitor may see one of the rarest treats which the country supplies: the fort of Staigue, or Staigue-an-ar, 'the staired place of slaughter'. It is a circular stone structure standing on a hill within a deep hollow which is formed by the surrounding mountains and open only to the sea on the south side. The periphery is divided into ten compartments of steps or seats ascending to the top and the whole is surrounded on the outside by a moat twenty-six feet wide and six feet in depth.

The new road to Killarney is one of the best roads in the kingdom and the old road that lay between Mangerton and Torc is now completely deserted. The present course of the road leads for some miles along a range of hills which overlook the Upper Lake of Killarney.

The lakes of Killarney are three in number: the Upper Lake, the Torc or Middle Lake and the Lower Lake.

The Upper Lake is the first at which the traveller arrives if he journeys from Kenmare, but the last to be examined if his starting point is the town of Killarney. The tourist to whom time is an object should take a guide from Kenmare; he will then be made familiar with every object of interest and importance before he arrives either at Gloghreen or Killarney, and will not find it necessary to retrace his steps. He may also visit both the Torc Waterfall and Mucross Abbey on the way, and all of this may be accomplished in one day.

The Upper Lake is the smallest of the three, and much narrower than either of the others. It is situated in the midst of an amphitheatre of mountains, the effect of which is considerably heightened by the comparatively limited space which the lake occupies, and the best view of this lake will be obtained from the police station.

The tourist on approaching the lakes of Killarney is at once struck by the peculiarity and variety of the foliage in the woods that clothe the hills on all sides. The effect produced is novel, striking and beautiful, and the extreme western position, the mild and humid atmosphere and the rarity of frosts contribute to bring on an enormous growth, far surpassing that which attains in any part of Great Britain.

The exceedingly beautiful road we have described led us – after a course of five or six miles along the shores of the Upper Lake – to the pretty inn at Cloghreen, immediately facing the entrance gate to Mucross.

The Mucross Hotel, kept by Edward Roche, is a long narrow building with but one storey above the ground floor, but it is constructed with due care to comfort and convenience and contains a large number of rooms. Its situation is peculiarly eligible, lying as it does almost at the foot of Mangerton close to the Torc Waterfall, and almost adjoining the Abbey; it does not, however, command a view of the lakes from any point.

Mr Roche is unremitting in his attention to his guests, and is not unfrequently their guide or their pilot across the waters to the adjacent wonders. The servants, too, are very active and obliging; the head waiter especially merits a compliment from us, for he was ever at hand when wanted, always ready with a word of caution or a sentence of advice and, although he never intruded, he contributed largely to the many sources of enjoyment that this pretty unpretending inn supplied.

The charges at this fashionable resort for persons who have no immediate thought of economy were absolutely startling:

Two breakfasts 3s. 0d.
Two dinners 4s. 0d.
Pint of wine 2s. 0d.
Two teas 2s. 0d.
Bed 1s. 6d.

The moderate tourist will calculate his necessary expenses at Killarney at something less than seven shillings per day. The only charge at which he will complain is the hire of a boat – sixteen shillings – but it includes the dinners of five men. The charge for a pony to Mangerton or 'The Gap' is five shillings, and Mr Roche is amply supplied with good boats and sure-footed ponies with careful men and boys in abundance.

Travellers who prefer state to quiet may take up their abode in the Royal Victoria Hotel kept by Mr Finn, who was for many years the landlord of the Kenmare Arms in the town of Killarney. The charges here exceed those of the Mucross Hotel, but it is a very splendid establishment and may vie, both in its external appearance as well as the costly character of its interior, with any hotel in Brighton or Cheltenham. Its situation is perhaps unrivalled in the Kingdom; it is about a mile and a half from the town and the adjoining grounds are exceedingly beautiful. It also skirts the Lower Lake, commands a fine view of Ross and Innisfallen, the evergreen hills and the more distant mountains.

*

Our first duty after our arrival was to select a guide. Irish guides are, as our readers will imagine, the most amusing fellows in the world; always ready to do anything, explain any matter, go anywhere – and if the tourist were to propose a trip to the moon, the guide will undertake to lead the way, 'Bedad he will, wid all the pleasures in life'.

They are invariably heart-anxious to please, sparing no personal exertion and willingly enduring the extreme of fatigue, carrying as much luggage as a pack-horse, familiar but never intrusive, never out of temper, never wearied either of walking or talking and generally full of good humour. They enliven the dreariest road with their wit, and are of course rich in old stories, some of which they hear, others they coin and occasionally make a strange hodge-podge of history. If they sometimes exact more than in 'the bond', they do it with irresistible suavity. The guides of all countries extort, the Irish guide does so only by 'laving it to yer honour'.

But our especial business now is with the Killarney guides, and truly their name is legion. Every boy or girl child, from the time they are able to crawl over the door-step, seems to have a strong natural instinct to become a guide, and to climb – or rather trot – up Mangerton, round the Devil's Punch Bowl or, and what is worse for the traveller, disturb the solemnity of the Eagle's Nest with their importunities that you will drink goat's milk fresh from the cow, taste poteen or eat wild strawberries.

Immediately upon arrival at Gloghreen we proceeded to appoint our bodyguard and, when our purpose became known, a score of candidates presented themselves outside the gate of the garden of our hotel. They were, as we found, of all sizes and ages, eager to display their accomplishments and set themselves to the best advantage.

'I was the man that was with Sir Walter Scott and Misther Moore himself, yer honour.'

'I'm the boy that's mentioned in Mr Crofton Croker's books.'

'I know every spot where there's a road, and where there isn't, sir.'

'Ye can't go wrong if ye hire us all,' exclaimed a little fellow, whom his companions called 'go-by-the-ground'. 'The tall boys'll point out the beauty of the heavens and the short ones the beauties of the earth.'

We had however instituted very minute inquiries as to the qualifications of the several candidates we were likely to encounter, and in reality, our choice was already made. Our scrutiny ended with the appointment of three: Sir Richard Courtenay, Knight of Mangerton, as commander-in-chief; the second, a most kind and considerate fellow with but one arm, whose name we unfortunately forget; and Mr Lyons, the Captain of Mangerton. By what means the latter obtained his commission we cannot say, but Sir Richard at once enlightened us in regard to his distinction, by answering our question: 'How did you obtain your title?'

'Troth sir, I was be-nighted on the mountain!'

We shall now proceed to visit the Upper Lake – a scene which far surpasses in natural beauty aught that nature has supplied elsewhere in Great Britain.

The three lakes are separated by a very narrow channel and two of them have scarcely any perceptible division. They have, nevertheless, very distinctive characteristics. The Lower Lake is studded with islands, all richly clothed with evergreens, the Upper Lake is remarkable for its wild magnificence, and the Middle Lake is conspicuous for a happy mingling of both – and yet it is inferior to the one in grace and beauty and to the other in majestic splendour.

The romantic beauties of the Killarney lakes were celebrated ages ago and in a very ancient poem they are classed as the tenth wonder of Ireland. The Irish name is Loch Lene, the 'Lake of Learning', according to some authorities, and a name by which it is still recognised among the peasantry, and which is presumed to have derived from the number of bookish monks who crowded the monasteries of Innisfallen, Mucross and Aghadoe.

The lakes are formed and supplied by numerous minor lakes that exist in the surrounding mountains and they may be described as an immense reservoir for the several rivers that also flow into them. The only outlet for the waters thus collected is the narrow and rapid river Laune, which runs out into the Atlantic through the beautiful bay of Dingle. The origin of these lakes – covering an extensive valley – is therefore self-evident, but fiction has assigned to them one of a far less obvious nature, and the scene is full of wild legends and marvellous traditions. The legends all agree however that the men and women who then peopled this lovely valley did not perish when it was flooded, but continue to exist beneath the lake, where O'Donoghue continues to lord it over his people, living in his gorgeous palace, surrounded by faithful friends and devoted followers, and enjoying the delights of feasting, dancing and music.

The name of O'Donoghue is closely associated with Killarney. Wander where you will in this delicious neighbourhood, either up the mountain, along the valleys, upon the water or on any one of the islands,and you are sure to find some object connected with it. Every rock of an unusual shape is forced into an illustration of O'Donoghue's tale; the guides and boatmen will point out to the tourist O'Donoghue's horse, his prison, his stable, library, pigeon-house, table, cellar, honeycombs, pulpit, his broom and, most at the summit of lofty Mangerton, a huge stone which is described as the shaft of his jaunting-car which he broke one night returning from a revel with the Devil who, to give a fitting reception to his guest, had filled the 'Devil's Punch Bowl' with the genuine dew of the mountain for the night. The most remarkable of these rocks is O'Donoghue's horse which, from some points of view, bears a close resemblance to the form of the animal whose name it bears. We were most desirous of visiting this natural wonder, for its base is being undermined by the continual action of the water and it is not likely to remain on the comparatively slender props that now sustain it. In a few years the horse may be an inmate of the chieftain's stable under the waves.

Although its variations are numerous, the original tale may be told in a few words. In ages long past, O'Donoghue of Ross was lord of the lake, its islands and the land that surrounded it. His sway was just and generous and his reign propitious. He was brave, hospitable and wise and the sworn foe of the oppressor. And annually, since his death – or rather disappearance – he is said to revisit the pleasant places among which he lived. Every May morning he may be seen gliding over the lakes mounted on a richly caparisoned white steed, preceded and followed by youths and maidens who strew spring flowers in his way, while sounds of unearthly sweetness glide along the waters and become thunder as they make their way up the surrounding hills. Although he appears in state only on May mornings, he is seen on various other occasions, and lucky is the child of earth by whom the immortal spirit is encountered, for good fortune is sure to wait upon him.

Many living witnesses are ready to testify to the appearance of the O'Donoghue, either riding over the lake, walking on the shore or playing hurly upon the surface of the waters and, as we have conversed with so many of them of credit and repute, we have no hesitation in believing them to have actually beheld him 'with their own two eyes'.

The Upper Lake will require no very detailed description. Its length is somewhat more than two miles; it is in no place more than a mile in breadth and its circumference is around eight miles. It is narrow and straggling. The islands it contains, though small, are numerous and gracefully wooded, but its chief value derives from the mountains – the most conspicuous being the Reeks – by which it is on all sides surrounded, and which throw their dark shadows upon the water so as to give it a character of gloom in perfect keeping with the loneliness of the scene. One feels as if the sound of the human voice would disturb its solitude and wishes that the oars that row him over were muffled.

The more prominent of the islands are Oak Island or Rossburkie, Stag Island, Eagles' Island, Ronayne's Island and Arbutus Island and nearly in the centre the fine and beautiful cascade of Derricunnihy sends its abundant tribute into the lake. Its superabundant waters are discharged through the pass which commences at Colman's Eye – which is a promontory that juts into the lake and limits the passage to a breadth of about thirty feet. This promontory derives its name from a legendary personage who, it is said, leaped across the stream and left his footmarks behind, imprinted in solid rock; the guides, of course, will point them out to the curious stranger.

There are three modes of visiting the Upper Lake: by water, by the Kenmare Road and across the Old Weir Bridge, and the other by proceeding through the Gap of Dunlow. The latter is to be recommended as affording the tourist who is willing to rise early an opportunity of examining in one day the most remarkable points in the scenery, proceeding by land and returning by water through the three lakes.

The Gap of Dunlow is in itself one of the greatest, if not the greatest, of the Killarney wonders. The entrance to the Gap is between three and four miles from the town of Killarney and the pass is about four miles in extent. The pedestrian will find a pretty considerable 'bit' in addition before he arrives at the lake where arrangements will have been made – beforehand, of course – for the boat to meet him. The journey to the entrance may be in a carriage, but the remainder must be either on foot or on the back of one of the little sure-footed ponies that know every rock and stone they will have to encounter.

A slight deviation from the road will lead to the ancient walls of Aghadoe, consisting of the remnant of a round tower, the walls of a small cathedral church and the base of a round castle, called the Pulpit and sometimes the Bishop's Chair. The church is a low oblong building consisting of two distinct chapels of unequal antiquity. As usual, the church is rendered revolting by the relics of mortality that lie scattered in heaps in all directions around it. Many of the skulls have been bleached by the rains and winds of centuries and are as white as the clearest paper.

A short distance from the entrance to the Gap of Dunlow there is a singular cave which the tourist should on no account omit to visit. It is situated in a field immediately adjoining the high road, and was discovered in 1838 by some workmen who, in constructing a sunken fence, broke into a subterranean chamber of

UPPER LAKE, – KILLARNEY.

a circular form, the walls of which were of uncemented stone inclined inwards with a roof of long transverse stones. In the passages were found several human skulls and bones.

The cave of Dunlow may be regarded as an ancient Irish library lately disinterred and restored to the light. The books arc thc large impost stones which form the roof; their angles contain the writing. A library of such literature was never heard of in England before and scarcely in Ireland, and yet it is of the highest antiquity. The discovery opens a new page concerning the hitherto disputed question touching the acquaintance of the ancient Irish with letters.

The Ogham writing, as it is called, is stated to have been known and practised in Ireland long before the era of Christianity; it is to the Irish what the Runes are in the north and the Arrow-headed or Wedge character is in Babylonia and Persepolis. The scale consists of four series of scores, each series embracing five characters, and each letter ranging from one score to five. The position of these groups in reference to a main or medial line, called fleasg, constitutes their power. It has been called the Craov or Branch Ogham, because it has been assimilated to a tree: the fleasg answering to the trunk or stem, and the scores at either side, the branches.

The earliest piece of Ogham writing at present known, is in an ancient vellum manuscript of the eleventh century which is now preserved in the British Museum.

The entrance to the Gap of Dunlow is a sudden introduction to its marvels and thc singular character of the deep ravine would seem to confirm the popular tradition that it was produced by the stroke of a sword of one of the giants of old. Anywhere, and under any circumstances, this rugged and gloomy pass would be a most striking object, but its interest and importance are, no doubt, considerably enhanced by the position it occupies in the very centre of gentle and delicious beauty.

Along the banks of the river is a narrow and, of course,

circuitous path. On the right, the Reeks, with their grand-master, Carran-tuel – the inverted sickle – the highest mountain in Ireland, look down upon the dark glen, while on the left, Tomies and the Purple mountain rise above it, and with a more gracious countenance, for their sides are not so steep but that the goat finds sure footing and pleasant pasture, and the cow – if it be a Kerry cow – may also wander and ruminate at leisure. The road, or rather bridle track, often passes along the brinks of precipices and then descends into absolute pits and the roar of the rushing torrent is plainly heard all the while.

This dark stream is the Loe, and in its limited course through the Gap it expands at several points into lakes of various and unequal magnitude and again contracts itself to gather force for a new rush through the valley. The rocks along the pass are of the most grotesque forms and each has received some distinguishing name from the peasantry. One of them is christened O'Donoghue's Heart on account of its singular shape. Sir Richard, our guide, was ready as usual with the why and wherefore, but in this instance his interpretation was very Irish. 'Gad sir, we always knew his heart was a big one, but we never thought it was so hard.'

When the pass terminates and the tourist is wearied in heart and foot, he suddenly comes upon a scene of unrivalled beauty. A turning in the narrow pathway brings him just over the Upper Lake, and the Black Valley, the 'Croom Duvh'. On the side of a lofty hill is the 'Logan Stone' which is about twenty-four feet in circumference. The peasants call it the 'balance rock' and it is doubtless a druidical remain of remote antiquity.

Leaving the Black Valley with the white cataract that crowns it, the tourist passes through Lord Brandon's demesne, and, having found his boat waiting in one of the sweet and lonely creeks, of which there are so many, he takes his seat and allows the oars to rapidly convey him through the Upper Lake.

The narrow and tortuous channel – about four miles in length – that leads from the Upper to the Middle or Torc Lake, is full of interest and beauty, the water is clear and rapid and amply wooded on either side. About mid-way is the far-famed Eagles' Nest, the most perfect, exciting and glorious of the Killarney Echoes. The rock – for, in comparison with the mountains that look down upon it, it is nothing more – derives its name from the fact that for centuries it has been the favoured residence of the royal birds, by whose descendants it is still inhabited, their eyrie being secured by nature against all human trespassers. The rock is of pyramidal shape, about 1700 feet high, thickly clothed with evergreens, but bare towards the summit, where the nest of the birds is pointed out in a small crevice nearly concealed by stunted shrubs.

About a mile from the Eagles' Nest is the Old Weir Bridge, a bridge of two arches of which one affords a passage for boats, and through which the water of the Upper Lake rushes into the Torc Lake on its way through the Laune to the sea. The current is exceedingly rapid, and it is usual for tourists to disembark and walk across the isthmus, meeting the boat on the other side, for the passage is considered dangerous for persons who are either easily alarmed or indisposed to take the advice of the boatmen, which is 'plase to sit quiet'.

Mr Roche, who acted as our helmsman, was however anxious to try the strength of our nerves as well as to exhibit one of the Killarney lions in all its wrath and power. He therefore gave us no warning until we were actually within the fierce current. We shot through with frightful rapidity, and it was evident that a very small deviation either to the right or left would have flung us among the breakers, the result of which must inevitably have been fatal. The men, who had rested on their oars, were watching us with some anxiety, awoke the echoes with a loud shout the moment we were safely through, and congratulated us on our 'bowldness'. We can, however, claim but little merit for our heroism, having been perfectly unaware of the peril we encountered until it was over.

When the bridge is passed, the tourist is in Torc Lake, and immediately facing him is Dinis Island, which is the property of Mr Herbert of Mucross, who has generously built an exceedingly pretty cottage upon it for the gratuitous use of visitors. It is furnished with every requisite for their entertainment, and the housekeeper, a most attentive and obliging person, is ever ready with her friendly greeting and willing advice to those who require her attendance. A turf fire is always prepared for that necessary portion of an Irish feast – the potatoes – and the menu includes salmon which is sliced and roasted within a few minutes after he has been a free denizen of the lake.

Although Mr Roche took especial care that our dinner should not be without salmon, we suspect that it was 'fish out of water' many days. On the Shannon however we were more fortunate, having caught, landed and eaten part of our salmon within a quarter of an hour of its catch – and we can say that we never tasted anything so delicious.

At Dinis Pool the current divides, one branch turning to the right and entering Torc Lake, the other turning to the left and running between Dinis Island and Glena Mountain to join the Lower Lake at Glena Bay. There is, we think, nothing at Killarney where nature is everywhere charming to absolute fascination to equal this surpassing lovely spot. The mountain of Glena looks down upon a little vale endowed with the rarest natural gifts. The name Glena signifies the 'glen of good fortune' and is the property of Lord Kenmare, whose accomplished and excellent lady (we heard her virtues very often lauded by the tongue of humble though powerless gratitude) has built a cottage *ornée* in this delicious valley. It is happily in keeping with this beautiful scene and the walks and gardens that surround it are so formed and disposed as in no degree to deduct from its simple beauty. Here also, a pretty and convenient cottage has been erected for the accommodation of strangers. It is placed in one of the forest glades, close to the shore, and is spacious enough to afford entertainment for several parties. Glena – although we have described it here – properly belongs to our discussion of the Lower Lake.

The Torc or Middle Lake, also called Mucross Lake, is more sheltered and more crowded with islands than the other lakes. The entrance into it from the Upper Lake we have described, and that from the Lower Lake is either round by Dinis Island (which is a course seldom taken) or under Brickeen Bridge, a bridge of a single arch which connects Brickeen Island with the peninsula of Mucross. Under this peninsula is the far-famed Mucross Abbey, and the great tributary to the lake is the beautiful Torc cascade, which is supplied by the Devil's Punch Bowl in the mountains of Mangerton, and is conveyed through a narrow channel, called the 'Devil's Stream'. The cascade is a chasm between sixty and seventy feet, which at times is very great, but not unfrequently the supply is so limited that it dwindles by comparison into a mere mill stream.

The Abbey of Mucross adjoins the pretty village of Cloghreen, and is in the demesne of Henry Arthur Herbert Esq., which includes the whole of the peninsula. The site was chosen with the usual judgement and taste of the monks of old which invariably selected the pleasantest of all pleasant places. The original name was Irelough, and it appears that long prior to the erection of this now ruined structure a church existed in the same spot, which church was consumed by fire in 1192.

The Abbey was built for Franciscan monks in 1440, according to the historian Archdall, but the *Annals of the Four Masters* date it a century later: both however ascribe its foundation to one of the MacCarthys, princes of Desmond. It was several times repaired and once subsequent to the Reformation. The building consists of two principal parts, the convent and the church. The church is about one hundred feet in length and twenty-four in breadth; the steeple, which stands between the nave and the chancel rests on four high and slender pointed arches. The old bell which originally hung in this tower was found in the lake, and the *'Cork Remembrancer'* of about 1750 records 'the bell found in Killarney lake, the circumference is as big as a table that will hold eight people to dine at. The clapper was eaten away by rust and they are now making it for a steeple at Killarney'. We could not ascertain what had become of it.

The convent, as well as the church, is in a very tolerable state of preservation, and Mr Herbert has repaired the foundation in some parts and the parapets in others and so judiciously that the eye is never annoyed by the intrusion of the new among the old, for the use of ivy furnished him with the means of hiding the unhallowed brick and mortar from sight. The dormitories, the kitchen, the refectory, the cellars, the infirmary and other chambers are still in a state of comparative preservation. The upper rooms are unroofed and the coarse grass grows abundantly amongst them. The great fire-place of the refectory is curious and interesting – affording evidence that the good monks were not forgetful of the duty they owed themselves nor of the bond they had entered into, on the advice of St Paul, to 'be given to hospitality'.

The cloister, which consists of twenty-two arches, is the best preserved part of the abbey. In the centre grows a magnificent yew-tree which covers the whole area like a roof. Its circumference is thirteen feet, and its height is in proportion. It is more than probable that the tree is coeval with the abbey and that it was planted by the hands of the monks who built the sacred edifice centuries ago. It is believed that any person daring to pluck a branch or in any way attempting to injure the tree will not be alive that day twelvemonth. To such an extent has this conviction taken root in the neighbourhood that we thought our attendant would have fainted on seeing one of us pluck a small twig from the yew.

Although the monks must have lived and died in the Abbey of Mucross for a very long period of time, posterity has been puzzled to find out the places where they were interred. Time has mingled their remains with those of the tens of thousands of nameless men who have here found their homes. However, the peasantry still point out an ancient, singular and rudely constructed vault on the outside of the church, immediately under the east window where the bones of the holy fathers have become dust.

Until within the last three or four years the Abbey of Mucross and the adjacent churchyard were kept in a very revolting state. It is the custom of the Irish to inter the dead within a few feet – and sometimes a few inches – of the surface, and, as the ground becomes crowded, it is often necessary to remove the remains of one inmate before room can be found for another. The consequence is that all the old abbeys and churches are filled with decayed coffin planks, skulls and bones scattered without the remotest care to decency which is absolutely disgusting to the spectator. This reproach has been entirely removed from Mucross by the care of Mr Herbert and there is now no disagreeable object to intrude upon the sight. Mr Herbert adopted the course of digging a large pit and conveying the relics of mortality that were formerly scattered about the church into it. Mr Roche, our guide and inn-keeper, who assisted at the removal, informed us that the process occupied four men five weeks, and that between seven and eight hundred cart-loads were taken away.

A visit to Mucross Abbey may naturally suggest some account of the funeral ceremonies of the Irish, which are most peculiar, remarkable and interesting.

The most anxious thoughts of the Irish peasant all through his life are concerned with his death, and he will endure the extreme of poverty in order that he may scrape together the means of obtaining a 'fine wake' and a 'decent funeral'. He will, indeed, hoard for this purpose, although he will economise for no other, and it is by no means rare to find among a family clothed with rags and living in entire wretchedness, a few untouched garments laid aside for the day of burial.

Only a month ago we gave a poor woman, an inmate of our parish workhouse, a few shillings. On asking her soon afterwards what she had done with the money, she said she had purchased a fine calico under-garment to be kept for her shroud so that she might be buried decently.

As his end approaches, the Irish peasant's first care is to obtain the consolations of his religion; his next to arrange the order of the coming feast. To 'die without the priest' is regarded as an awful calamity, and we have heard more than once a dying man exclaim in piteous accents, mingled with moans, 'Oh, for the lord's sake, keep the life in me 'til the priest comes.'

The formalities commence almost immediately after life has

ceased. The corpse is at once laid out, and the wake begins, the priest having been first summoned to say mass for the repose of the departed soul, which he generally does in the apartment in which the body reposes. It is regarded by the friends of the deceased as a sacred duty to watch by the corpse until it is laid in the grave, and only less sacred is the duty of attending it thither.

The ceremonies differ somewhat in various districts, but only in a few minor and unimportant particulars. The body, decently laid out on a table or bed, is covered with white linen, and, not unfrequently, adorned with black ribbons if an adult; white if the party be unmarried and flowers if a child. Close by it are plates of tobacco and snuff, around it are lighted candles, and usually a quantity of salt is laid upon it also. The women of the household range themselves at either side and the keen *(caoine)* at once commences. They rise with one accord and, moving their bodies with a slow motion to and fro, their arms apart, they continue to keep up a heart-rending cry. This cry is interrupted for a while to give the *ban-caointhe*, the leading keener, an opportunity of commencing her lament. At the close of every stanza of the dirge the cry is repeated, and then dropped, and the woman then continues with the dirge, and so on to the close. The only interruption which this manner of conducting a wake allows is the entrance of some relative of the deceased who, living in a remote district, may not have been in at the commencement. In this case, the *ban-caointhe* ceases, all the women rise and begin to cry, which is continued until the newcomer has cried enough. During the pauses in the women's wailing, the men, seated in groups by the fire, or in the corners of the room, will indulge in jokes, or exchange repartee and banter with each other, some about their sweethearts, and some about their wives or talk over the affairs of the day. It is needless to observe that the merriment is in ill-keeping with the solemnity of the death chamber, and that disgraceful scenes are, or rather were, of frequent occurrence, the whiskey being always abundant and the men and women being nothing loath to partake of it to intoxication.

By-the-by, the keener is usually paid for her services, the charge varying from a crown to a pound, according to the circumstances of the employer. They truly live upon the dead.

The wake usually lasts two days; sometimes it is extended to three and occasionally four. The funerals are invariably attended by a numerous concoursc – some from affection to the deceased, others as a tribute of respect to a neighbour and a large proportion because time is of small value and a day unemployed is not looked upon in the light of money lost. No invitations are ever issued. Among the upper classes, females seldom accompany the mourners to the grave, but among the peasantry there is always a large assembly of women.

If two funerals meet at the same churchyard, a contest immediately takes place to discover which will enter first, and happily, if descrying each other at a distance, it is only a contest of speed, for it is often a contest of strength, terminating in bloodshed and sometimes in death. This arises from the belief that the last person buried in a churchyard is employed in bringing water to his fellow tenants of the 'narrow house' until he is relieved in turn by the arrival of a newcomer.

To return to the beauties of Killarney, however. The Lower Lake is, as we have said, much larger than either Torc Lake or the Upper Lake, and the tourists generally prefer it to either of its sister rivals. It is more cheerful and in parts more beautiful, but less graceful than the one and far less grand than the other.

There are islands small and large, in the Lower Lake, to the number of about thirty-five, and of all sizes and proportions. These are not merely bare rocks, and nearly all of them are luxuriantly clothed in the richest verdure and foliage. The principal ones in extent and the most distinguished for beauty are Ross, Innisfallen and Rabbit Island, but there are several smaller that far surpass their giant neighbours in natural loveliness and grace, for example Mouse Island, the tiny speck which lies between Ross and Innisfallen.

The usual place of embarkation for strangers who design to visit the various objects of attraction that must be seen by water is at the quay on Ross Island, immediately under the walls of Ross Castle, and to which there is a carriage road, crossing a small bridge from the town of Killarney. The guests at the two hotels, 'Roches' and the 'Victoria', have their own miniature piers; the former at a little creek under the banks of Mucross.

Ross is more properly a peninsula than an island, being separated from the mainland by only a narrow cut through a morass. The island, for so it must be termed, is the largest in the lakes, containing about eighty plantation acres. It is richly and luxuriantly cultivated, and a portion of it is converted into a graceful and carefully kept flower-garden, where seats are placed so as to command a more striking and picturesque view. There are the fine remains of a castle, which is much less injured by time than the majority of its co-mates in Kerry county. It is a tall, square, embattled building and contains a spiral staircase of cut stone. It was erected by one of the earlier chieftains of the O'Donoghues. It forms a conspicuous feature in the landscape from every part of the Lower Lake and, as the modern additions to the ancient structure are rapidly becoming ruins also, they will ere long increase rather than lessen its interest – more certainly if the Lord Kenmare will take some trouble to cover them with ivy.

As we have observed, from all parts of the lake and from every one of the adjacent mountains the castle of Ross is a most interesting and attractive point in the scenery, and it amply repays the honour it receives by enabling the visitor to obtain from the summit of its tower a commanding view of every important object by which it is surrounded. An hour passed walking around the island will be an hour pleasantly and profitably spent, and curiosity may be gratified by inspecting the surface of the famous copper mine, the debris of which is scattered in profusion upon the western shore. Among them are several huge portions of a steam engine, which is, we believe, the first ever introduced into Ireland.

When these mines were opened by Colonel Hall in 1804, he obtained unequivocal proof that they had been worked previously, but at a period very remote and when mining as an art was utterly

ROSS CASTLE – KILLARNEY.

unknown, and several rude hammers were discovered. We procured two of them during our recent visit to Killarney, but they are now, of course, becoming very scarce. A groove had evidently been cut, or rather rubbed around the stone so as to attach a handle by a strap, perhaps leather, to it, and the larger end, against which the blows were struck, is obviously worn by use. They are popularly called 'Dane's Hammers' and it is not unlikely that the Danes may have been the miners who left them there, although they certainly received their shape from nature and were not in themselves the work of man, for one of those we obtained had no mark of a groove upon it.

Colonel Hall's miners also found the remains of fires all along the vein; these fires must have been lit in order to consume the limestone in which the ore was bedded so as to form a natural smelting house in the quarry. Of course the mine had been loosely worked and very little of its wealth had been removed.

Ross Island is nearly in the centre of the Lower Lake, and next in importance is Innisfallen. It receives from all the tourists the distinction of being the most beautiful, as it is certainly the most interesting of the lake islands, inasmuch as here, twelve centuries ago, an abbey, of which the ruins still remain, was founded, and from which afterwards issued the *Annals of Innisfallen*, which are amongst the earliest and most authentic of the ancient Irish stories. The original work which was written, and for several centuries preserved in the Abbey of Innisfallen, is now in the Bodleian Library. It is on parchment, in medium quarto and contains fifty-seven leaves. The earlier portion consists of extracts from the Old Testament, and a history of the ancient world down to the arrival of St Patrick in Ireland in 432. From this period it treats exclusively of the affairs of Ireland, terminating with AD 1319.

It appears to have been the production of two monks; one of whom carried it to the year 1216, and the other continued it to the year 1320. There are several copies of it in existence, one of which is in the collection of His Grace the Duke of Buckingham at Stowe, part of which was translated and printed in 1825 by Dr O'Connor. The facts are narrated in the smallest compass and present a dry, but sad, 'succession of crimes, wars and rebellions'.

On approaching the island, we seem to be drawing near a thick forest, for the foliage is remarkably close and extends literally into the water, with many of the finest trees having their roots beneath the surface. On landing, however, we find that the lofty elm and magnificent ash, mingled with hollies of gigantic growth and other evergreens of prodigious height and girth, only encircle a greensward, of so pure and delicious a colour as to demand for Innisfallen, beyond every other part of Ireland, the character of being pre-eminently the 'Emerald Isle'.

Of the Abbey of Innisfallen a few broken walls alone remain. It is said to have been built in the seventh century by St Fintan the Leper, who was a descendant of one of the most renowned of the Munster kings. The abbey was subsequently appropriated for the use of the regular canons of St Augustin. A far more ancient structure, the small oratory chapel, is an object of considerable interest with its picturesque situation and, overspread as it is with ivy, it is happily in keeping with the ancient character of the island. For upwards of a century it has been desecrated to the purposes of a 'banqueting house' for visitors, but within the last few months the good taste of Lord Kenmare has caused it to be unroofed and converted into what it had been since the ejection of the monks – a ruin.

Our guide, Sir Richard, having first conducted us up and down the tiny hillocks and through the miniature vales of this delicious isle, and having listened with evident pride and pleasure to our expressions of exceeding delight, proceeded to introduce us to the two island-wonders: the Needle and the Bed of Honour. Through the former he led, or rather pushed us. It is a crab-tree with a kind of double trunk, forming an aperture which is said to have a powerful influence on the after-destiny of any of the gentler sex who venture through it.

Sir Richard then ushered us with all due ceremony and state to the Bed of Honour. This is a seat formed by the matted branches of a yew-tree, but the traditions that account for its name are confused and contradictory. Sir Richard however took advantage of our disposition to 'sit awhile and rest', for the day was very fair and the sun was sinking, and related to us some of the numerous legends of the lakes . . .

How St Patrick never came into Kerry, but only looked into it, holding his hands out to it and saying, 'I bless all beyond the Reeks.'

How Fin MacCool kept his tubs of gold in the lake under Mucross and set his dog, Bran, to watch them; this was ages ago, long before the Flood. An Englishman – a grate diver intirely – came over to try and get the gold, and when he went down the dog awoke from his slumbers and seized him, and I'll go bail, he never tried the experiment again.

How when O'Donoghue leaped out of the windy of Ross Castle, his enchanted books flew after him – and there they are! – O'Donoghue's Library, only turned to stone and, like the Killarney guide books, rather heavy.

How, under the Crebough there was a huge carbuncle that lit up the rocks under the lake of a dark night, and showed the palaces and towers of the ould city that the waters covered.

How a holy hermit fell into sin and did a hard penance for seven long years, just where the trees of Mucross dip into the water. He walked straight into the water, and stuck his holly-stick into the gravel at the bottom, and made a vow never to leave the spot until it threw out branches and leaves. And for seven years he stood there without sleep or food, 'til at last the stick blossomed, and in one night became a great tree, and then the holy hermit knew that he was pardoned, and 'twas he that did the wonderful cures from that day, 'til all the country was running after the Hermit of the Hollytree.

How, when the first O'Donoghue was a tall slip of a boy, and sitting in his nurse's cottage, she suddenly sets up a screech that the O'Sullivans were stealing the cattle. So up he gets, pulls out an ould sword from the thatch and kills every mother's son of the thieving blaggards. When the fight was over, up comes his servant and, 'didn't we do that nately?' says he.

'Were you helping me?' says O'Donoghue.

'I was,' says the gilly.

So with that O'Donoghue goes out and sticks one of the dead men again' the wall with his eyes staring open and his spear in his fist, and then he calls out to the gilly, 'Kill me that big fellow.'

But the gilly was frightened and tried to sneak off.

'I knew ye were a coward,' says O'Donoghue, and hanged him on the next tree.

How an Englishman inquired of a Kerry peasant by what means Ireland happened to have so many mountains, to which the Kerry boy made answer. 'Ye see, Ireland being the finest and best country in the world, in coorse was the last country that Nature made. And when Ireland was finished, Nature had a dale of stuff to spare, so she left it here – and that makes the mountains!'

We cannot quit the Lower Lake without requiring the reader to make with us the ascent to the summit of Mangerton, or, if he be in rude health and strength, and time be not of much value, he may attempt Carran Tuel – the highest mountain in Ireland – from the top of which he will see the magnificent panorama of the lakes at the foot, the Atlantic Ocean in the distance and, between them both, a tract of country unparalleled for grandeur and beauty.

The village of Cloghreen is a very short distance from the base of Mangerton. The tourist, however, should diverge somewhat from the direct route to examine the little church of Killaghie, which is, we believe, the smallest church in the kingdom. It is very simple in its construction, and is obviously, with the exception of the tower, of remote antiquity. Wild flowers of various hues grow from the walls and adorn its roof of stone.

The journey to the summit of Mangerton is not to be thought of lightly, although the labour may excite a smile in those who have climbed the 'Monarch of the Mountains'. For a very long period, indeed, until within the present century, Mangerton had usurped the honour of ranking as the highest of the Irish mountains. Since the improvements in surveying, however, Mangerton has been compelled to resign its throne to Carran Tuel. Still, to dwellers of the valley, and more especially to those of the city, its height is sufficient to afford a pretty correct idea of what a veritable mountain actually is.

We commenced our excursion on a morning that gave promise of a fine day, mounted upon the sure-footed ponies who are never known to stumble, and along the road that leads from Cloghreen to the base of the mountain. The sure feet of our horses were soon tired since the little rough-coated animals had to make their way over rocks, bogs and huge stones, through rushing and brawling streams and along the banks of precipices – places where it would be very difficult for persons unaccustomed to mountain travelling to move along on foot. At length we reached the Devil's Punch Bowl, a small lake in the midst of almost perpendicular rocks. The water is intensely cold, and yet in the severest winter it never freezes. The peasants, of course, attribute this peculiarity to the influence of his Satanic Majesty, but from its position it is never calm, being in a state of agitation on the mildest summer day. As it is chiefly supplied by springs that pass over the surrounding peat-bed, the water is of a very dark colour and its depth is said to be unfathomable.

A footpath marks the way to the summit of the mountain. It is perfectly level, of considerable extent and covered with a deep stratum of peat moss, into which the foot sinks some inches even in the driest weather.

The view from the mountain-top defies any attempt at description; it was the most magnificent sight we had ever witnessed, and one that greatly surpassed even the dreams of our imagination.

In the distance is the broad Atlantic, with the river of Kenmare, the bay of Dingle and the storm-beaten coast of Iveragh. Midway are mountains of all forms and altitudes. At our feet lie the three Killarney lakes, with the islands in the Upper and Lower Lakes dwindled into mere specks. The rapid river Laune winds prettily along the valley, and the Fleask-bridge, with its dozen arches, resembles a child's toy.

*

The tourist in Kerry will be most agreeably disappointed if he imagines that his sources of information and pleasure in visiting it are limited to the far-famed lakes. Kerry abounds in natural wonders, and the beauty and grandeur of the scenes to which we have more especially referred may certainly be equalled, if not surpassed in other, although less celebrated districts of the country, and above all, by the wildness of the sea-coasts. It will be in our power to do little more than direct the attention of the reader to some of the numerous bays and harbours by which it is indented from the Shannon to Bantry Bay.

However, before we direct the attention of the visitor to the sea-coast of Kerry, we shall require him to visit another of the inland lakes, although from its proximity to the sea, it appertains almost as much to the ocean as the land having, to a considerable degree, the advantages and attractions of both.

The vicinity of this lake – Lough Carah – has long been a terra incognita, partly owing to the fact that its beauties were unknown and consequently undescribed by tourists, and partly in consequence of the bad roads that lead to it, and the ill accommodation provided for strangers when there. These obstructions to its fame are now in a great degree removed. There is a small and well-conducted inn kept by an Englishman at Glenbay on the coast of Castlemain, on the high road to Iveragh and Cahirciveen, which is a tolerable centre for the sportsman and tourist.

Carah Lake lies about fifteen miles west of Killarney and is approached by the high road to Killarglin, a miserable village about four miles from the lake where there is also a small inn. The approach on this side, with the exception of the view of the Reeks, is uninteresting. It may be reached also by a new road, branching off from the former about ten miles from Killarney, and leading through a ravine in the Reeks called Glouncetane, by the very beautiful lake of Coos, and through the valley of Glencar to the upper end of the lake. This road is on the eve of completion and well deserves to be explored as there are few parts of Ireland which exceed the valley of Glencar in wild and solitary beauty.

The lake of Carah, taking its origin in this valley, runs in a northerly direction to the sea, to which it is connected by the Carah River, which is about five miles in length, and celebrated for its winter salmon fishing. The length of the lake is about seven miles and its breadth varies from two to four miles and it is divided into an Upper and Lower Lake. The lower, which is the widest and least picturesque, is however a fine sheet of water and contains many objects of interest. From this point one of the best views of the Reeks is obtained. The mountains on the eastern side terminate in that of Gortnagloron, which is almost perpendicular and luxuriantly wooded.

The Upper Lake may be classed among the grandest and most beautiful of all the lakes in Kerry, being little, if at all, inferior to its more celebrated namesake of Killarney. The mountains open here and surround Glencar like an immense amphitheatre at the distance of five or six miles, rising one above the other in endless varieties with the Reeks and Carran Tuel towering high above the rest. The lake terminates in a long river navigable for about two miles, running up into the glen between scenery of surpassing beauty. The river ceases to be navigable at a place called Blackstones where the river from the mountains rushes into it through large masses of black rock, from whence it derives its name.

If we may return to the town of Killarney. This may be dismissed in a sentence: the tourist will be satisfied with a drive through it. A short time ago, he was compelled to make it his headquarters, but the inns established on the borders of the lakes have ruined those of the streets, although there still exist many neat and convenient lodging houses for the accommodation of visitors who object either to the cost or bustle of an hotel.

In the year 1830, the number of houses exceeded 1000, and the population was about 8000; both however, have now largely increased. It has little or no trade; the only approach to which is the manufacture of toys made from Arbutus wood, which are purchased by strangers as souvenirs of the place. The best of such toys are made by a widow and her daughters who have a shop in the high street immediately opposite the Kenmare Arms.

Kerry possesses pre-eminently one distinction for which it has long been famous – the ardour with which its natives acquire and communicate knowledge. It is by no means rare to find among the humblest of the peasantry who have no prospects but that of existing by daily labour, men who can converse fluently in Latin, and have a good knowledge of Greek. However, a more general spread of information and the increased facilities for acquiring it have deprived Kerry of the honour of being exclusively the seat of peasant learning in Ireland. But its inhabitants are still remarkable for the study of dead languages, acquaintance with which has been formed by the greater proportion of them literally under a hedge.

The genuine 'hedge schools' of Kerry are rapidly disappearing, and necessarily with them the old school masters who were in some respects a meritorious, and in others, a pernicious class, for whenever there was disaffection the village school master was either the originator or the sustainer of it. He was also generally the secretary of illegal associations, the writer of threatening notices and too frequently the planner and leader in terrible outrages. The national system of education has destroyed their power by substituting in their places men who are, at all events, responsible to employers interested in their good characters and good conduct. The ancient Domines however, had their merits: they kept alive the shrivelled seed of knowledge from utterly perishing.

During our recent visit we saw but two or three hedge schools; some twenty years ago we should have encountered at least one in every parish. They received their peculiar designation from the fact that, in fine weather, the school room was always removed out-of-doors, with the Domine usually seated beside his threshold and the young urchins, his pupils, scattered about him.

In addition to the pupils who paid to the teacher as much as they could afford and in the coin most at their command, there were generally some in such establishments who paid nothing, and were not expected to pay anything. They were termed 'poor scholars' and received their education 'graatis' and were not unfrequently intended, or rather intended themselves, for the priesthood.

The only established route by which the traveller will be enabled to form any idea of the character of the coastal scenery of Kerry is that which conducts him to Killarney through Limerick and Tralee. But a journey so made will supply him with but a very limited notion of its grandeur and beauty. It will be necessary for him to make frequent excursions in order to visit the several attractions of the county, beginning with Tarbet on the banks of the Shannon and ending with the Skelligs, a group of small island rocks in the Atlantic. However, if his starting point be the lakes, he will examine the southern parts first, beginning with the huge promontory that lies between the bays of Dingle and Kenmare.

Lough Carah, which we have briefly described, is almost in the direct line to the wild and picturesque district of Cahirciveen, the southern coast of Dingle bay and the interesting harbour and island of Valentia which, with the exception of the Blaskets, is the nearest point of land in Ireland to America.

In the vicinity of Cahirciveen is Derrynane, the seat and birthplace of the late D O'Connel, Esq., MP. It was originally a farm house and has been added to from time to time according to the increase of the property or family of its possessor. It is beautifully situated, and in its immediate neighbourhood are the picturesque ruins of an abbey founded by the monks of St Finbar.

The island of Valentia belongs to the Knight of Kerry, who resides there. Although very fertile, and still maintaining the distinction of the granary of the country, its only peculiar produce is that from its slate quarries – the slabs of which are of great strength and size and find a ready market in London. The Spaniards occupied the island and harbour until expelled by Cromwell, whose lieutenant erected forts at both entrances in order to put a stop to the privateering purposes to which it was applied. A harbour lighthouse has been opened during the present year.

About twelve miles south of the harbour are the Skelligs, a

group of rocks which class among the greatest curiosities of the Atlantic. They were formerly celebrated as the resort of pilgrims, and many a weary penance has been performed upon their naked and inhospitable crags. The Great Skellig consists of two peaks which rise from the ocean so perpendicularly as to closely approximate to the shape of a sugar loaf; the larger rising in thirty-four fathoms of the ocean to 710 feet above sea-level, and with only the occasional projection being clothed with grass. The island is, at all times, nearly covered with sea-fowl.

The peasantry have numerous tales to tell in connection with these singular rocks and a whimsical tradition exists that every madman, if left to his own guidance, would make his way towards them. However, of late years they have lost much of their sacred character, and are now-a-days visited by very few penitents. A few years ago, two lighthouses were erected on the Great Skellig by the Trinity House, and the effect has been almost to put an end to wrecks on the coast.

To visit the wild peninsula, north of Dingle Bay, which runs out into the Atlantic, and which contains on the south Ventry Harbour, Dingle Harbour, Mount Eagle and Castlemain, and on the north, Smerwick, Mount Brandon and Tralee Bay, the tourist should fix his headquarters at Tralee, the principal town of the county.

Tralee contains nearly 10,000 inhabitants and the remains of several ruins are in the immediate vicinity with, among others, that of an abbey in which for several centuries the Desmonds were buried. The first occupants of the tombs were Thomas Fitzgerald, surnamed the Great, and his son, Maurice, both of whom were slain at Callan in a fight with the MacCarthy Mor.

The most interesting monastic remains in Kerry are, however, those of the abbey of Ardfert which lies about six miles to the north-west of Tralee. Ardfert is a bishop's see, held with the bishopric of Limerick. The ruins of the cathedral are still in good preservation and bear the marks of high antiquity. A round tower, 120 feet high, and built chiefly of dark marble, which formerly stood near the west front, suddenly fell down in 1771.

The cathedral is dedicated to St Brandon and contains the cemeteries of many of the old families of Kerry. In the immediate neighbourhood are the ruins of other churches of which tradition states that Ardfert formerly had seven, and the remains of four may still be traced within the cathedral enclosures. Of the strong castle, the seat of the Lords of Kerry, which formerly protected the churches of Ardfert, there are now but a few broken walls standing. It was demolished 'in the wars of 1641 by one Lawler, an Irish captain, who set it on fire'. But the building then destroyed was a recent structure, erected on the site of the ancient castle, 'built by Nicholas, the third Lord of Kerry, in 1311, and re-edified by Thomas, the eighteenth lord in 1590'.

In the village of O'Dorney are the ruins of another abbey – a shapeless pile – but the deformity of which is hidden by the ivy that covers the whole if it.

The peninsula to which we have referred that stretches out into the Atlantic is full of interesting historical associations as well as abundant natural beauties. The Spaniards had settlements in this district and the remains of the fortifications still exist. The ruins of old castles are numerous all along the coast; one of the most conspicuous of them is that called Ferriters Castle, the ancient stronghold of the Ferriters. The ruin is situated in a wild spot, almost on the verge of the Atlantic and a single tower is all that endures.

The whole of the peninsula is indented with bays and harbours from which the mountains ascend, giving a character of rude grandeur to the scene. The mail coach from Tralee to Limerick passes through the town of Listowel, and that of Tarbert, the former being inland and the latter on the south bank of the Shannon. The far-famed caves of Ballybunian are about an equal distance from both but on the coast. Listowel is a poor town with, of course, the ruins of a castle, and it is watered by the Feal.

The caves of Ballybunian are not often visited, yet they may be classed among the most remarkable of the natural wonders of Ireland. They are distinguished by names, each name bearing reference to some particular circumstance, as for example the

Hunter's Path, from the tradition that a rider once rode his horse over it; Smuggler's Bay which, for centuries, was famous as a safe shelter for free traders.

The county of Kerry is bounded on the north by the estuary of the Shannon, which separates it from the County of Clare; on the east by the counties of Limerick and Cork; and on the south and west by the Atlantic. Large districts of Kerry are, however, promontories. A mine of wealth is therefore at hand, which activity and industry, aided by a moderate capital, might easily render available, and yet the fisheries are few and we have heard of none that are extensive.

The great export trade of Kerry is in butter, a large proportion of which finds its way to Britain through the market of Cork. The Kerry cow is proverbially small but of a remarkably beautiful shape and is especialiy valuable for the quality and quantity of its milk.

Kerry in extent ranks as the fourth of Irish counties. It is divided into eight baronies: Iraghticonner, Clanmaurice, Corkaguiny, Truchanackmy, Magunihy, Iveragh, Dunkerron and Glanerough. Its only towns of note are Tralee, Listowel and Kenmare.

Chapter Three

WATERFORD

Waterford is perhaps the least interesting and certainly the least picturesque of the counties of Ireland. It is for the most part barren of trees and the soil, which is naturally poor, has had little advantage from cultivation. Its coast, moreover, is inhospitable, its bays and harbours are few and, with one great exception, neither safe nor commodious. It resembles Cornwall, not only in its rugged character and comparative poverty of its surface, but also because it is likely to rival the mineral wealth of the great mining county of England.

The mail-coach road from the borders of the county of Cork to Waterford City is through a barren tract of country, which presents few objects worthy of interest. However, by taking this route, the tourist will visit Dungarvan, the town that ranks next in importance to the capital of the shire. It is a sea-port, but with little trade, and belongs chiefly to the Duke of Devonshire who has expended a large sum on its improvement.

Persons who are not compelled to pursue the beaten track and may choose their own route, will no doubt prefer to pass through the county of Tipperary, although this journey is somewhat circuitous. However, the direct course is through Youghal and Lismore, and the road between these two towns runs along the banks of the Blackwater, which is one of the most beautiful of all Irish rivers.

At Youghal a long narrow bridge connects the counties of Cork and Waterford and over this bridge we passed for the purpose of examining the singular round tower and ruins at Ardmore. This bridge was commenced in the year 1829 and finished in 1832, at a cost of somewhat less than £18,000.The architect was Mr Nimmo, and the resident engineer during the erection was J E Jones Esq., who is now successfully pursuing his profession in London. Until the bridge was built, a dangerous ferry journey of nearly half a mile was the only means of communication at this point between the two counties except by going a distance of sixteen Irish miles to the bridge at Lismore. Youghal bridge is one of the most remarkable in the kingdom: it is 1,542 feet in length and is composed of forty-seven bays of thirty feet span. Its breadth is twenty-two feet and the height above high water is ten feet.

Ardmore is about six miles from Youghal, but the foot passenger, by crossing a ferry and steep hill, may shorten the distance and bring it within an hour's walk. It is one of the places which, for many reasons, no-one should neglect to visit. Though now a miserable village containing no house above the rank of cabin save that of the rector, there was a time when Ardmore was classed among the high places of Ireland. It was anciently an episcopal see erected by St Declan in the infancy of the Irish church and before the arrival of St Patrick. St Declan, it is said, was a native of Ireland who travelled to Rome and returned to teach his countrymen in the year 402. The ruins of two churches which, from their architecture, must be of the saint's era, are in the immediate neighbourhood, and one of them, which had been used for service until very lately, is close to the famous round tower.

The Round Tower at Ardmore differs from all the others that are still standing in Ireland inasmuch as it is divided by four beltings into as many storeys with a window to each. It is built of elaborately cut stone and is between ninety and one hundred feet high. The entrance is about thirteen feet from the ground and the circumference of the base is about forty-five feet. In the upper storey there are four opposed windows and the conical cap, which has vanished from most of the round towers, still graces that of Ardmore.

The 24th July is the patron day of St Declan, whom the Romish Calendar states to have flourished prior to the appearance of St Patrick. He is said to have landed at Ardmore and to have there preached Christianity where he also, and in one night, built the famous tower and the adjoining church. The grave in which he is supposed to be buried and a singular mass of rock on the sea-shore near the church are objects of peculiar veneration. This rock is believed to have floated over from Rome with the vestments of the saint, a bell for his tower and a lighted candle for the celebration of mass.

From Youghal to Lismore, which is a distance of about eighteen miles, the road is exceedingly picturesque and highly interesting, passing, as it does, for a considerable distance along the beautiful banks of the Blackwater, of which it commands many striking views. However, we preferred engaging a boat and making the journey by water.

From the source of this fine river in Slieve Lougher, one of the Kerry mountains, to its mouth at Youghal, it passes through a large extent of country, nearly every portion of which is closely, and often painfully, associated with the history of Ireland. The banks are for the most part wooded and at times the river runs through fine, fertile valleys, or it winds along the base of, or between, huge and barren mountains. Every now and then the interest of the scenery is enhanced by some ruin of castle or church lying broken and covered by weeds.

The most remarkable of the many ruins that will be encountered between Youghal and Lismore are Rincrew, once the property of Sir Walter Raleigh, and which originally belonged to the Knights Templar; Molana, where it is said Raymond le Gros, the friend and counsellor of Strongbow, lies buried; Strancally, a stronghold of the Desmonds, and where there was, in ancient times, a cave used as a prison 'for such persons who had fortunes in this part of the country, whom the cruel and tyrannical Earl invited to his castle to make merry and afterwards confined to this hole where he suffered them to perish'. One person, having escaped, proclaimed the treachery of the Earl and both the cave and the castle were destroyed.

One will also encounter Dromana, the reputed birth-place of

the old Countess of Desmond who, at the age of one hundred and forty years, crossed the Channel and travelled to London to demand the restoration of her jointure from James I and whose death is said to have been caused by a fall from a cherry tree.

There is Affane where in 1564, was fought a bloody battle between the Earls of Ormond and Desmond in which the leader of the Geraldines was wounded and taken prisoner by his ancient hereditary and implacable foes, the Butlers. As they were carrying the chieftain from the field on their shoulders, one of the leaders of the Ormond party rode up and enquired in a taunting tone of triumph, 'Where, is now the great Lord of Desmond?'

The faint and wounded Earl raised himself and replied, 'Where, but in his proper place – on the necks of the Butlers.'

On approaching Lismore and on the right bank of the river is the prettily situated and improving town of Cappoquin, the church spire of which can be seen from afar rising above the trees.

Among the mountains above Cappoquin is the singular settlement of Mount Melleray. In the year 1831, when the monks of La Trappe were dispersed by the French Government, a considerable number of them proceeded to Ireland and obtained from the proprietor, Sir Richard Keane, a lease of 575 acres of mountain land, for a term of ninety-nine years at a nominal rent. It was a brown, heathery, stony waste, but of this they have reclaimed some 200 acres, having been assisted by the peasantry who worked for them for several months and supplied them with horses and carts without charge. They were also greatly aided by subscriptions from the neighbouring gentry, with the Duke of Devonshire giving them £100. Soon after their arrival they circulated printed handbills recounting the different prayers they would contract to offer up to the Virgin on account of those who gave alms. The invitation to contribute was pretty generally accepted, and even now they occasionally make calls for assistance which are rarely refused.

They have built a chapel, 160 feet long, with a steeple of about

170 feet high from the stones picked off their land. The entire mason-work and carpentry was performed by eight of the brotherhood, who took three years to accomplish it.

On their arrival in Ireland their number amounted to fifty, but it is now about seventy. They are nearly all of them English or Irish, and they keep the vow of the order and are never heard to speak. Their mode of life is, of course, simple to the point of austerity, and it is certain that they are entire strangers to what the generality of mankind consider enjoyment.

The approach to Lismore is picturesque and beautiful. The river ceases to be navigable at a short distance from Cappoquin, and a canal to facilitate intercourse with the town has been cut at the expense of the Duke of Devonshire, who is one of the few absent landlords who is continually labouring to benefit and improve a country from which he derives a considerable portion of his income. The canal runs for some miles through a finely planted pleasure ground, and the castle, high above the level of the water, is kept in view nearly all the way, and crowns a landscape that is at once magnificent and graceful. The castle is situated on a steep rock which rises perpendicularly from the river. To look down from one of its chamber windows would make the clearest head dizzy, and there is a tradition that James II darted back in terror when he was conducted to a lattice to take a view of the surrounding scene; the window still bears his name.

There are no fewer than forty-two salmon weirs on the Blackwater between Youghal and Lismore; the one immediately under the castle is the last and most productive, where it is by no means rare to take 600 fish at a first haul. The fishery is rented from the Duke by Mr Foley at a rental, we were informed, of £700 per annum. The fish, being the property of the renter, are consequently preserved and the water is not free to the angler, although he may – and we believe often does – obtain the privilege to fish there by the courtesy of the renter.

It may be well to suggest that the angler should take with him to the Blackwater but a limited supply of flies, for those that may be very killing elsewhere will be found to be perfectly useless here.

There is however a sportsman resident in the neighbourhood who is an accomplished master in the art and from whom all requisite aid and information may be obtained. His name is Hallahan, and he will act as a guide.

Lismore is but a few hours from Waterford, and Waterford is but twenty hours' sail from Bristol; therefore it is classed high in the list of Ireland's natural beauties and for many centuries occupied a prominent station in its history. Though of late years it has dwindled to a rank scarcely above that of a village, time was when it could vie in importance with the most flourishing city in Ireland, having once been a university and a bishop's see. It was founded early in the seventh century by St Carthagh and, it is said, contained no fewer than twenty churches. There is a tradition that King Alfred received part of his education in the college of Lismore, and although this rests upon no good authority, it is by no means unlikely to be true. Henry II first promulgated English law in Ireland in Lismore in 1172. The see was united to that of Waterford so long ago as 1358.

As we have intimated, our journey from Lismore to Waterford city was through the county of Tipperary, a route which led us along the base of the Knockmeledown Mountains. This range divides the two counties, on the highest mountain of which lie the remains of Major Eeles, an eccentric gentleman of considerable ability who was a mighty huntsman and a close researcher into the mysteries of electricity. We were told by many that an iron grid was driven through his body upon his death by his directions, in order that it might attract the lightning to descend and thus consume him utterly.

The City of Waterford ranks among the oldest and most famous of the cities in Ireland. It was anciently called 'Cuan-na-Grioth' – the Harbour of the Sun – and its existence is said to be dated back as far as AD 155. It is certain, however, that it was a place of some note in the ninth century when it was a colony of the Danes, who retained possession of it until the invasion of Ireland in 1171. A

LISMORE CASTLE,
WATERFORD

singular round castle still stands on the quay and bears an inscription, which is signed by Sir John Newport, Bart, as Mayor, which records that it was erected by Reginald the Dane in the year 1003; was held as a fortress by Strongbow in 1171; was converted into a mint in 1146; and that in the year 1819 it was converted into a jail for refractory boys and sturdy beggars – to which purpose it is still applied.

The city is said to have received its name from the Danes: Waterford being considered a corruption of *Vader Fiord*, the Fiord of the Father or the Great Haven, for it has received both translations. In the various contests of which Ireland was the arena, Waterford has played a conspicuous part, having endured sieges from Strongbow, Cromwell and William III to say nothing of Perkin Warbeck.

It is however its fine harbour that distinguishes Waterford far more than its historic reknown. It is happily situated on the southern banks of the Suir about sixteen miles from its influx into the sea. The harbour is exceedingly beautiful; it might not be so highly planted or ornamented with villas as that of Cork, and yet it is scarcely inferior to it in the grace of its foreground and the grandeur of the mountains that look down upon it.

However, Waterford has one great advantage over its neighbour – the River Suir. This river is navigable for very large ships, having sufficient depth of water to allow vessels of from 800 to 1,000 tons burden to discharge their cargoes at the quay.

This quay is unrivalled in Ireland and perhaps in England also. It is a mile in length and in a continuous line. On the side next to the river is a slightly raised path which forms a delightful and healthful promenade for the citizens. At its western extremity, connecting the city with the county of Kilkenny, is a wooden bridge across the Suir. It is 832 feet in length and forty in breadth, supported on stone abutments and forty sets of piers of oak. The building of this bridge was undertaken in 1793 by a company who subscribed £30,000 to complete the work, including the purchase of the ferry. The money was raised by loans of £100 pounds each, the interest on which was to be paid by tolls across the bridge. The work was completed for less than what was originally estimated and only required the payment of £90 on each debenture. The present value of the shares is about £180; the tolls letting for £4,500 per annum. The architect proposed to the company to erect one stone arch for every year until the whole should be completed, and thus ultimately raise a substantial and permanent structure. Unhappily, this suggestion was not acted upon; surely a subject of blame when it is considered that the funds were ample for so desirable a purpose. The architect was a Mr Cox, of Boston, America.

Waterford City has an exceedingly cheerful appearance. The principal mercantile houses are built along the margin of the river and command a view of the opposite side (in the county of Kilkenny) where several villas have been erected and above which towers a lofty range of mountains. But the Commeragh Mountains, which occupy the centre of the county, are those which merit especial notice. They present varied and picturesque outlines from every point of view, and from the sea or southern side they are well known to mariners by whom they are called 'the high lands of Dungarvon'. They are of considerable elevation, the highest peak called Mon-a-bullach, that is 'the mount of the summit' which is a table-land about 2500 feet above the level of the sea, which is remarkable for having three lakes upon its summit well stocked with trout. In two of these lakes, called Stillogues, large black trout are found, which are very unpalatable. In the other, called Loch an Cumalig-owr, 'the Lake of the Grey Phantom' (we spell as near the pronunciation as we can), red trout and the gillaroo may be found.

But the greatest natural curiosity in these mountains is the appearance and site of a nearly circular lake by name Coom-shinawin, the 'Valley of the Ants'. This circular basin appears to have been formed at an early age by a landslip, or to have been the crater of an extinct volcano. About a fourth of the way down the almost perpendicular slope lies a cave covered by a projecting rock, called Crotty's Rock. It takes its name from a bandit of ancient days who made it his asylum when hard pressed.

The Commeragh Mountains have often afforded a secure

WATERFORD.

retreat to those unfortunate men who have set the laws of their country at defiance. Within the last few years, the mountains have been famous for harbouring two notorious outlaws, the Connollys.

These unhappy men were brothers, and had been thrice taken prisoner and as often made their escape from jail. By retiring into the fastness of the mountain districts they contrived for a long time to baffle all attempts to re-capture them by the police. They were assisted by the farmers who supplied them with necessaries, and they had made every preparation for embarking for America, when they were foolhardy enough to venture into Waterford to buy new hats and the police, being forewarned, took them prisoner.

The proximity of Waterford's port to England is no doubt of considerable advantage to it, and it is perhaps a matter of some surprise that greater results have not risen out of it. The introduction of steam seems to have benefited the city far less than might have been anticipated. Although Waterford is a mercantile city and one with advantages peculiarly eligible and accessible, there is a sad aspect of loneliness in its streets and a want of business along its quays, except on those days when the steam boats leave and the live stock assembles in huge droves to embark for the English market. The hotels, too, usually sure indications of prosperity or its opposite, have a deserted look, and it would hardly be an exaggeration to say that the grass springs up between the steps that lead to their doors.

There are no public buildings displaying any architectural skill and taste; however, a contract has been recently entered into to erect a 'Saving's Bank' at the cost of £4000. But in general the improvements that have taken place in the city in late years are neither marked nor numerous,and it has but little increased in the last quarter of a century.

The Cathedral of Waterford is reported to have been originally built by the Danes in 1096, when they first embraced Christianity.

An interesting ruined monastery of the Franciscans lies close to it, part of which is in good repair and exists as an almshouse for aged women. This is called the Holy Ghost Hospital and was founded by a Patrick Walsh in 1545. It was used as a French church for a considerable time, having been assigned by the corporation to the French protestants who settled in Ireland in consequence of the revocation of the Edict of Nantes.

Waterford abounds in schools; it has one, however, which is somewhat peculiar – and an inspection of which gave us much pleasure. It is named the School of the Christian Brothers, and was founded in 1803 by Mr Edmund Rice. He retired from business while comparatively young and devoted his entire time and talents and the property he had obtained by industry to the education of youth. At that period property was not easily obtained by any class and was almost beyond the reach of Roman Catholics. The benefit he has conferred upon his native city by nearly forty years of labour is therefore incalculable.

The River Suir ranks amongst the noblest rivers in Ireland; it is broad, deep and not too rapid and its character is highly picturesque both above and below the city. It rises out of a spring at the foot of Banduff mountain in the county of Tipperary, where the Nore has its source also, and, receiving several tributaries on its way, it flows into St George's Channel between Dunmore Point and Hook Head in the county of Wexford. About four miles from the city the Suir is united with the Nore and the Barrow, and a magnificent view of the confluence of the three rivers is obtained from the Hill of Faithlegg – a corruption of Faith-league – which rises above Creek Point, which was formerly a packet station.

There are but two towns of consideration on the banks of the Suir; Clonmel and Carrick and, although they have suburbs in Waterford, both towns are in the county of Tipperary. The river is crossed by bridges at both of these places and ruined castles abound on either side. A lofty tower which attracts notice from all points of the scenery along the river draws one's attention to

Curraghmore, which is the mansion of the Marquis of Waterford. The house is a comparatively plain structure, built in 1700 on the site of an ancient castle, part of which still exists. The park is extensive – the most entensive in Ireland and larger, perhaps, than any in England – comprising nearly 5000 statute acres of land. It has been planted with the rarest trees and commands magnificent views of the surrounding country.

In Curraghmore House there is a Murrain Stone, which, it is believed, will cure the murrain on cattle. We have heard that the stone is frequently borrowed by the country people and placed in a running brook and the cattle driven through the water to be charmed by the stone and be cured. The Murrain Stone is one of the heirlooms of the Beresfords.

In the immediate vicinity of the grounds of Curraghmore House is the small town of Portlaw which has grown from a poor and insignificant village into a place of considerable importance in consequence of having been selected by the Messrs Malcolmson of Clonmel to decide the question of whether cotton factories may or may not flourish in Ireland. The experiment has been eminently successful.

The distance from the city of Waterford to the sea-coast (across the promontory) is but five or six miles, although the harbour is of much greater length. The two most famous places on the coast are Dunmore and Tramore, which are both favourite bathing places. However, the former long enjoyed the advantage of being a government packet station and possesses both a lighthouse and a pier. The village is beautifully situated, the coast is bold and rocky and it is immediately upon the sea. The pier is 600 feet in length and the cost of the works is believed to have exceeded £100,000, a sum immensely disproportionate to their value to the public.

A druid's altar stands on a rocky eminence near Dunmore. The situation is particularly wild and beautiful, and it commands a view of the estuary of the Suir with Cremla Island and Hook Tower on one side, and the great bay of Tramore with the rugged precipices of the Cumarocks in the distance on the other. The altar consists of fourteen perpendicular stones forming a perfect circle of thirty-six yards in circumference on the outside. Across the centre, forming the diameter, are two horizontal stones which lie parallel to each other, each one of which is two yards wide and seven long. They are covered by five flat flags and form a covered passage which is closed at one end and is about two feet high. This covered way occupies the centre of the circle. One stone of the roof is raised on one side by the interposition of a block so as to resemble a cromliac or sacrificial flag, and from which the blood of the victim flowed off. A short distance away are the ruins of the ancient church at Kilma Combe.

The village of Tramore is more sheltered than that of Dunmore and appears to be in higher favour with the citizens of Waterford. Passage, the ancient 'bathing village', is now completely deserted, although it still maintains some importance as a ferry in connection with the opposite shore of Wexford. Between Passage and the sea are the ruins of a few houses that point out the locality of New Geneva, which was originally a colony of the Genevese and afterwards a barracks, and is now almost level with the pasture ground all around it.

By far the most interesting and important district of the county of Waterford at the present moment however, is that of Bonmahon, which is on the coast mid-way between Dunmore and Dungarvon, and in the immediate vicinity of which are the mines of Knockmahon, the property of the 'Mining Company of Ireland', which is now, we believe, the most prosperous and profitable of the Irish mines. This company was founded in 1824 chiefly by the exertions of Richard Purday Esq., the present secretary.

The maritime county of Waterford is in the province of Munster. It is bounded on the west by the county of Cork, from which it is divided by the river Blackwater; on the north by the counties of Kilkenny and Tipperary, from which it is separated by the Suir; and on the east by the county of Wexford, with the harbour of Waterford running between them; and on the south side by St George's Channel.

It is divided into seven baronies; Gaultier, Middlethird, Upperthird, Decies without Drun, Coshmore and Coshbride, and Glanehiry. Its only towns of size are Dungarvon and Lismore, and the extreme length of the county is about forty miles, with the greatest breadth, twenty.

Chapter Four

LIMERICK

The city of Limerick is situated on an extensive plain which is watered by the mighty Shannon, the King of Ireland's rivers. It lies about sixty Irish miles from the sea and is divided, like all the towns of note in Ireland, into English town and Irish town. However, a third diversion called Newton Pery was added to it during the last century, the work being commenced in 1769 by the Right Hon Edmond Sexton Pery.

The English town stands on the King's Island, which is an island formed by the Shannon which divides into two streams about half a mile above the city; the narrowest of these streams is called the Abbey Stream. There is also an extensive and populous suburb on the opposite bank of the river in the county of Clare. The more modern parts are remarkably handsome, the streets being wide and the houses evenly built; however, the ancient portions are narrow, confined and dirty.

Limerick may be classed as among the best cities of Ireland, and it is rapidly improving. Within the last few years, squares and crescents have been added to it and several public buildings have been erected on a plan which is at once elegant and convenient.

The most remarkable of the ancient structures of Limerick, with the exception of King John's Castle, is the Cathedral, which is dedicated to St Mary. It is a large and heavy-looking structure, built on the site of the palace of O'Brien, king of Limerick. Its tower is remarkably high, and from the summit there is a magnificent prospect of the various objects of attraction in the immediate neighbourhood. This is indeed the only place from which a view can be obtained, for there are no adjacent hills – a circumstance to which the city is considerably indebted for its natural strength.

The merchants of Limerick are active and enterprising, but their advantages are less than those in any other sea ports, and although a next-door *neighbour* to America, the long and circuitous sea voyages from English harbours has curtailed the trade that might have been looked for with the United States.

The city has long been unrivalled in Ireland for some peculiar advantages; the world is familiar with the fame of Limerick lasses, Limerick gloves, Limerick hooks and Limerick lace, but the latter is a distinction of more recent growth. The women of all ranks throughout the county are remarkably beautiful in form and feature. The gloves retained their celebrity for above a century, but the manufacture has dwindled of late, and a short time ago, a glover of the city excused his want of punctuality in discharging an order by the simple truth that he had not yet received a supply from Cork where 'Limerick gloves' are now almost exclusively made. The leather in the gloves was so delicate and the workmanship so fine that a pair was frequently passed through a wedding-ring. We purchased a pair enclosed in a walnut shell.

The hooks have long been – and still are – famous; the saying that 'every hook is worth a salmon' continuing to hold good. The hook is formed of the purest steel and each hook is separately tempered. The point is remarkably sharp, carried almost to the point of a needle; it will never bend, will rarely break and it is longer in the fang than any other hook and has no bend.

Limerick, like all the cities and towns in Ireland, abounds in charitable institutions. There are two or three of them however, that call for especial notice. The first is called the Protestant Orphan Friend's Society which was founded in 1833. Its peculiar feature is this: the children are not boarded together in one place, but are located with discreet matrons in various places. These matrons receive monthly payments and are superintended in every parish by a committee of ladies, with the average sum allowed for the support and clothing of each child being about £4 per annum. When sufficiently educated, they are apprenticed to tradesmen and farmers or articled to the gentry as servants.

Barrington's Hospital and the City of Limerick Infirmary was erected and founded by Sir Joseph Barrington, Bart, and his sons, Matthew, Daniel, Croker and Samuel, at their sole expense and for the benefit of the poor of their native city. The building was completed in the year 1829 and incorporated by Act of Parliament in 1830 by which it was deemed and considered as the City of Limerick Infirmary.

The Monte de Piete, or charitable pawn-office, which was established some years ago in the city under the auspices of Matthew Barrington Esq., was, most unhappily, not found to answer. It has been abandoned and with it we fear has perished the several branches which at one period promised a long and healthy life to the great comfort and benefit of the community.

The great attraction of Limerick, although by no means the only one, is however its majestic and beautiful river, the Shannon. It takes its rise among the mountains of Leitrim and, strange to say, the precise spot has not yet been ascertained. It runs for a few miles as an inconsiderable stream, diffuses itself into a spacious lake called Lough Allyn, pursues its course for several miles and forms another small lake, Lough Eike. Continuing, it spreads out into Lough Ree, which is a lake fifteen miles in length and four in breadth, and thence proceeds as a broad and rapid river, passing by Athlone, then narrowing again until it reaches Shannon Harbour, then widening into far-famed Lough Derg, which is eighteen miles long and four broad. Progressing onwards it arrives at Killaloe, where it ceases to be navigable until it waters Limerick City, from whence it flows in a broad and majestic volume to the ocean for about sixty miles. It runs for a distance of upwards of 200 miles from its source to its mouth, which is between Loop Head and Kerry Head; it waters ten counties in its progress, and affords facilities for commerce and internal intercourse such as are unparalleled in any other portion of the United Kingdom. Yet, unhappily, up to the present time its natural advantages have been altogether neglected.

To render the Shannon a navigable river has long been a cherished object, but the difficulties appeared insurmountable. So far back as 1638 the subject excited the earnest attention of the unfortunate Earl of Strafford, then Viceroy of Ireland, and a letter has been preserved addressed by him and signed by the Privy Council, to the Earl of Thomond and others, stating that 'heere is one that offers to make the river Shannon navigable from Lymerick to above the foord of Killalow, and hee demandes for his payment and charges therein £3000'. Until recently, however, no effort was made to improve it, and so recently as 1832 Mr Rhodes (civil engineer and member of a commission appointed in 1831) reports that the 'grand designs have in a great measure been frustrated and the river may not unaptly be compared to a sealed book'.

For a long space its course is so gentle that the ancient writers supposed its name to have derived from *Seen-awn*, the slow river, but for many miles, between O'Brien's Bridge and Limerick, it rolls so rapidly along as almost to be characterised as a series of cataracts. At the falls of Killaloe it descends twenty-one feet in a mile and above one hundred feet from Killaloe to Limerick – and yet there is scarcely a single mill at work all that way.

Nearly all along its course its banks are of surpassing beauty. As it nears Limerick, its adjacent hills are crowned with villas, and upon the sides are the ruins of many ancient castles. Castle Connell, a village about six miles from the city, is perhaps unrivalled in the kingdom for natural graces, and immediately below it are the Falls of Doonas where the river rushes over huge mountain rocks, affording a passage which only the more daring will make, for the current, narrowing to a boat's breadth, rushes along with such frightful rapidity that the deviation of a few inches would invariably result in destruction. This, although the most remarkable of the falls, is succeeded by several others between Castle Connell and Limerick.

The immediate environs of Limerick are not picturesque. The city lies in a spacious plain, the greater portion of which is scarcely above the level of the water. However, at a short distance there are some of the most interesting ruins in the kingdom which lie in the midst of scenery of surpassing beauty. Of these the tourist should first visit Carrig-o-gunnel, next Adare, and then Castle Connell, the most beautiful of the many beautiful places upon the banks of the noble Shannon.

We shall now conduct the reader along the southern shore of the mighty river to the borders of the county of Kerry, which is a distance of about thirty miles along an excellent road, constructed thirty years ago and which is the general route of travellers proceeding from Dublin through Limerick to the Lakes of Killarney. Within a mile or two of the city, attention will be drawn to the venerable ruin of Mungret Priory which is said to have been founded by St Patrick and which bears some evidence of high antiquity. Only a few broken walls remain, insufficient to bear out the testimony that it formerly gave shelter to 'one thousand, five hundred monks; five hundred of whom were devoted to preaching and instruction, five hundred more being classed and divided so as to have a perpetual full choir day and night, and the remainder being old men who devoted themselves to religious and charitable works'.

About four miles further on the singular ruin of Carrig-o-gunnel, the Rock of the Candle, will be reached, and it is one of the most striking, romantic and interesting in Ireland. Its site is remarkably commanding. It covers the summit of a huge rock overlooking the broad Shannon, the city of Limerick and miles upon miles of richly cultivated country. The castle must have been of amazing strength and the outworks evidently extended a long way down the adjacent slope, for some traces of the old walls may still be discovered. It is said to have been built by the O'Brien family, and was the seat of Donough O'Brien in 1530, having been frequently won and lost during the contests with the Earls of Desmond. It became a ruin, however, only so recently as 1689, during the siege of Limerick.

But superior in interest even to Carrig-o-gunnel are the storied remains of Askeaton, which lies about sixteen miles distant from Limerick. Askeaton is a populous and busy-looking town, situated on the river Deel near its junction with the Shannon. A waterfall of considerable elevation formed by a barrier of rock stretching across the entire bed of the river and visible from the town has given the name to the place – *As cead tinne*, the Cascade of the Hundred Fires. The fires were probably connected with the rituals of the druids in some way.

It was a holiday when we entered Askeaton, and its streets were densely crowded; business, pleasure or devotion, as well as the fineness of the day having congregated together a very numerous population. This circumstance gave the place an aspect of cheering industry which it otherwise probably had no claim to. An excellent bridge of five depressed arches connects both sides of the town, for it lies on either bank of its river. The place was formerly surrounded with a wall and other defences. At the Limerick side of the town a new church has been recently built. It partly occupies the site of a far more ancient structure, founded in 1298 by the Knights Templar and of which all that is now left is a portion of the tower, the lower part of which is a square, the upper an octagon.

The castle, an ancient residence and stronghold of the Earls of Desmond, stands at the foot of the bridge, and even in its extreme ruin shows that it had been a pile of great strength and importance.

But the object of principal interest here is the abbey. It stands at the opposite side of, and adjacent to, the river, near to the Catholic chapel and is a pile of very considerable extent, and in tolerable preservation. It was founded in 1420 by James, seventh Earl of Desmond, for conventual Franciscans, and was reformed in 1490 by the Observantine friars. James, the fifteenth Earl, died and was buried here in 1558. In 1564, a chapter of the order was held within it. At the suppression of the monasteries, towards the end of the reign of Elizabeth, after the destruction of the Desmonds' power, this structure shared the general fate, but an abortive effort at its restoration was made in 1648 by the Confederated Catholics. Since then it has gradually, though slowly, progressed to its present state. The church stands in the midst of the conventual buildings. It is a long oblong, from which a transept branches off at the north side and at the intersection of which formerly stood a tower, the ruins of which lie around in solid masses.

About two miles from Askeaton is the small village of Shanagolden which stands out on a prominent hill of considerable elevation and steepness. It should be pointed out that it is unconnected with any other eminence in its vicinity. This is the hill of Shannid – *Shanait* – the old place. It terminates in a double peak, which is evidently sacrificial, and each forming a truncated cone, which were fashioned in the remote past for the purposes of defence. The northern peak is surmounted by a castle, the area of which is 180 feet in circumference and covers the whole extent of the platform. In height this structure is something between thirty and forty feet and the walls are ten feet in thickness.

The southern peak is crowned by one of the ancient raths. This is a hill fort formed of earth and surrounded with deep fosses and ramparts. The area of this is extensive and it possesses the peculiar feature of being subdivided into four equal portions by the intersection of a rather deep cut through the centre, but with what object it is hard to determine. This structure is of course of greater antiquity than the adjacent castle; the utmost date which can be assigned to the latter is the commencement of the twelfth century, while that of the rath may be lost in the clouds and mists of the remote ages.

The purpose for which it was erected was at once of a domestic and military character. In a country so subdivided as ancient Ireland into clans or tribes of different descendants and almost perpetually harassed by internal dissensions, security of residence was not always easily attainable, but every means available was used for that purpose. The site was of course the cardinal object: a hill, the neighbourhood of a river, a wood or a morass was sought out, and this being chosen the fosse was hollowed out, the high embankment thrown up and the interior of the enclosed area was wrought into galleries and intricate mazes. The form of these forts was generally round; indeed, the circle appears to have been a favourable figure with the ancient Irish.

We are to presume that the buildings which occupied the area within the entrenchments were generally formed of the same material still used by the peasantry in the erection of their mud edifices – that is, earth intermixed with rushes or straw and the roof composed of thatch or shingle. Timber, doubtless, was also extensively used in these structures.

The ancient Irish possessed several other kinds of fortified dwellings: the Dun, the Dangion, the Lios, the Cashiol and the Cahir. These names are sometimes found combined, as Dundangion near Cork, or Lios-na-ratha, the Court of the Forts. The cashiol and cahir are generally of stone and Staigue Fort, in Kerry, is of this class.

Proceeding south-east from Askeaton, or journeying from Limerick to Kerry by another excellent road, the tourist will pass two places of great interest: Adare and Croom. The former is on the direct route and the latter a mile or two away from it, but it supplies an ample recompense to visitors who care to visit it, for it contains the only round tower that now exists in the country.

Adare is about eight miles from the city, and it is a neat and generally flourishing town. Immediately adjoining it are the remains of several monastic edifices, the greater number of them being within the walls of the Earl of Dunraven's beautiful park. One of the old abbeys has been converted into a church, and another into a chapel, and both retain traces of their original grandeur, although modern improvements have essentially changed their character.

The whole central district of Limerick is indeed studded with remains, both religious and castellated, which most emphatically speak of the former power of the Geraldines but they are mostly ruined and decayed now. A chain of towers may be traced in continuous succession from the Shannon to Kilmallock, indicating the territorial supremacy of the Fitzgeralds, whilst their numerous ecclesiastical structures tell of wealth, munificence and taste.

In the centre of an extensive valley stretching out from the eastern base of Knockfeerena, stand the remains of a small but very ancient church whose era belongs to the very earliest period of Christianity in Ireland. It is a plain oblong, about forty-six feet in length and eighteen broad. On one of the jamb stones of the door are a number of scores which is a circumstance worthy of remark, because a number of such scorings have been frequently found on or near other Romanesque remains, and are supposed to have some affinity with the Ogham character.

Ten feet north of the church stands one of those round towers so peculiar to Ireland, and so fruitful of controversy to antiquaries. It is fifty feet in height, and fifty feet in circumference at its base. The door, which has a semicircular head, is sixteen feet from the ground. Above this are three windows at different heights. One of them is round-headed, while the others are pointed. The upper portion of the tower, with its conical cap and upper windows, has been destroyed. The floors were placed on rests formed by diminishing the thickness of the walls. The peasantry call it *Clogawse-na-desart*. *Clogawse* signifies a growth of stones and bears reference to its supposed sudden growth in one night.

Lough Gur claims particular notice at our hands because it has hitherto received so little attention from previous visitors and even from the county historians. This secluded lake is about ten miles south of the city of Limerick, is irregular in form and the circumference is between four and five miles. From its bosom rise one large and three or four small islands. The principal island, which is connected with the eastern shore by a causeway, contains fifty or sixty acres, and is called Knock-a-dun, or the Fortified Knoll.

But it is the extensive assemblage of druidical remains on this island and around the lake that render it perhaps the most interesting spot in Ireland for the visitor in search of the antique, and yet, strange to say, these gigantic relics, which extend over so many miles of country, have been allowed to remain unexplored and undescribed. Three stone circles, close to the high road between Limerick and Cork, are mentioned for the first time by Mr Twiss, in his tour through Ireland, which was published in 1755.

AUGUSTINIAN ABBEY, ADARE
(WITH THE CASTLE OF THE FITZGERALDS AND THE FRANCESCAN ABBEY.)

As the three stone circles on the west side of the lake are so close to the high road, the tourist will perhaps act judiciously in making them his starting point, and proceed around the lake by a road which branches off at a place called Holy Cross. This road will lead him by the ruined church which stands on an eminence that descends to the southern shore of the lake. The roofless and deserted walls still retain the name of the 'New Church'. This was built by Lady Bath, and the chalice and patine from it are now preserved in the neighbouring church of Knockaney. From this point various stone circles and other ponderous remains may be seen and a serpentine passage of considerable length, formed by parallel lines of huge masses of stone, can be traced from the shore to the Red Bog, which is a tract of low ground some distance away. The opposite side of the road from that on which the church stands is crowded with druidical works, one of which the country people call *labig yermuddagh a Grana*, that is, 'Edward and Grace's bed'. This was probably a tomb. It had been a complete oblong chamber formed by great stones and covered with vast flags. An old woman resided in it for many years, and on her death the covering stones were thrown off and it was left in its present state by 'money diggers, who found only some burned bones in a ould jug that surely was not worth a brass farthing'.

Above this tomb stands a tabular rock, which is upwards of ten feet in circumference and which rests upon four supporters. And not far distant there is a singular natural formation called 'Carringnanahin', or the Mass Rock. It is full of chasms and hollows and is said to receive its name from the priest having regularly celebrated the ceremonies of the Roman Catholic Church within one of its recesses at the period when that religion was proscribed.

The eastern shore of Lough Gur abounds also with mighty vestiges of druidical power. One eminence particularly, called Carrickgalla, has two remarkable circular works of masonry, called Danish Forts by the country people. Branching off in all directions from the once sacred shores of this beautiful and romantic lake, evidence exists of an assemblage of altars, temples, caves and tombs, much too numerous for us to even notice in the most rapid manner. This chain of druidical works extends into the county of Tipperary, and there is a cromleach, the largest we have ever seen, on Galtee Mor, and on Cromwell Hill there is a sepulchral chamber called *Labig yermuddah*, or Edward's Bed, which is similar to the one upon the southern side of Lough Gur.

In the low ground throughout this district of ancient druidism, in swampy hollows, now surrounded by bog, which there can be little doubt was formerly richly wooded, the antlers and bones of that gigantic animal, the Moose Deer, long since extinct in Ireland, have been dug up in considerable quantities.

We may now quit the county of Limerick which is in many respects the most interesting and important county of Munster, not only in reference to the number and magnificence of its ancient remains, and its grand scenery, but also as regards those modern improvements in agriculture, manufacture and commerce, by which it is rendered honourably conspicuous among the counties of the south of Ireland.

Limerick is bounded on the north by the Shannon, which divides it from the county of Clare; on the south by Cork; on the west by Kerry; and on the east by the county of Tipperary.

The aspect of the county is generally flat and its soil is proverbially rich, with a considerable portion of it stretching from the city south-east to the border of the counties of Cork and Tipperary and being so fertile as to have received and merited the title of the 'Golden Vein', and few districts in Ireland are more abundantly supplied with rivers.

The county is divided into ten baronies: Owenybeg, Coonagh, Clanwilliam, Small County, Coshlea, Coshman, Pobble-brien, Upper Connello, Lower Connello, Kenry, and the liberties of Limerick and Kilmallock.

Its principal towns are those of Kilmallock, Askeaton, Newcastle, Rathkeale and Bruff.

Chapter Five

CARLOW

The town of Carlow is seated on the east bank of the river Barrow. It is said to have been called Bergus or Bargus by the ancients, and Bearbha by the Irish; but some writers consider its present name to be merely a slight alteration of Barragh, the boundary river, as it was for several centuries the boundary which divided the English Pale from the Irish clans. The river has its source in the Slieve Bloom mountains in the Queen's County, and, passing through the towns of Portarlington, Monastereven, Athy, Carlow, Leighlin-Bridge and Graigue-ne-managh, it forms a junction with the Nore and both join the Suir a few miles from Waterford. The Barrow is navigable for a distance of forty-three miles.

The town is modern in its general aspect, presenting a singular contrast with its neighbour, the city of Kilkenny, which is full of castellated and monastic remains. The only ancient relic in Carlow is 'the Castle'.

The Castle is situated on a gentle eminence overlooking the river, and is said to have been erected by Hugh de Lacy, who was appointed Lord Deputy of Ireland in the year 1179. It was built after the Anglo-Norman style of architecture; a square area surrounded by thick walls, fortified and strengthened at each corner by a large round tower. Until the year 1814 it had bravely withstood the attacks of time and war, but its ruin was effected by the carelessness of a medical doctor into whose hands it had come, and who designed to put it in order for the accommodation of insane patients. In the progress of his work he applied gunpowder – for some unexplained object – to the foundation, and in a moment completed its destruction, leaving but two of its towers and the wall between them.

Ireland has been termed the 'granary of Great Britain' and so it is to a considerable extent, and Carlow is one of the most fertile and best cultivated of the counties of Ireland and has been termed the Garden of Erin. It is almost exclusively an agricultural county, its soil being admirably adapted for the production of corn of every description – a fact that may account for the flour mills to be found in every district of it. The principal mills are those of Mr Alexander at Milford, and the Lodge Mills at Bagenalstown of which Mr Crossthwaite is the present proprietor. The grain raised in this county commands a high price in the markets of London and Liverpool. Its butter is also famous, competing with that of Cork and Kerry, and large tracts of rich pasture-land are occupied as dairy farms.

Mr Alexander's mill, which was established in 1790 at Milford, is one of the most extensive and celebrated in Ireland. It is situated about four miles from Carlow on the Barrow, in the centre of a lovely valley through which the river runs, and is surrounded with hills and with the magnificent mountains, Leinster, Blackstairs and Brandon in the background. Plantations of trees are growing up around it, and the aspect of the whole neighbourhood is remarkably cheering, comfortable and encouraging. Roads have been opened through several of the adjacent mountains and cultivation has naturally followed. The hedgerows in every direction are as neatly and carefully trimmed as those of England; the cottages are exceedingly clean and well-ordered, and they are frequently white-washed, the material being supplied gratis to every applicant.

The Barrow is navigable not only south to Waterford, but north to Dublin; a large quantity of flour is exported to England through the former, with a supply, which is largely for the home market, being carried to the latter along the river to Athy, and thence by the Grand Canal to the capital. There is a lock connecting both these waterways so there is no necessity for transferring the load from one boat to another during its transit.

*

The county of Carlow was made shire-ground by King John under the name of Catherlogh, which signified the Castle by the Lake, and it comprehends the ancient territories of Hy-Cabanagh and Hy-Drone, being the northern part of the principality of Hy-Kinselagh. The representatives of many of the early English settlers and some few of the descendants of the ancient Irish families still live upon their hereditary estates in the country. Among the most distinguished of the latter families is that of Kavanagh of Borris-o-kane, whilst among the English names it has been remarked that a large proportion of them begin with the letter 'B'; Bruens, Butlers, Bagenals, Bests, Browns, Bunburys, Burtons. Hence the popular saying in Carlow: 'Beware the B's' and 'the B's of Carlow carry a sting', alluding to the 'good auld times' when a 'duel at daybreak was considered necessary to procure an appetite for breakfast'.

Leighlin – Old Leighlin – although now dwindled to a small village was in ancient times a place of great importance, and is still an episcopal see, but was united, in the year 1600, to that of Ferns in the county of Wexford. The bishopric is said to have been established so early as the year 632 and it is stated that its founder, St Laserian, had, at one time, '1500 monks under his jurisdiction'. The cathedral, which is the plainest Gothic architecture, consists of a nave and chancel. The belfry tower has a mean sort of slated spire on top which, from its pigmy size and general unsuitableness to the building on which it is erected, has the worst possible effect. This tower is about sixty feet in height.

In the immediate vicinity of Leighlin is a remarkable and very picturesque rath, and close to the cathedral is the well of St Laserian. This was until a few years ago a famous resort of the peasantry on the saint's day, the 18th April. However, the patron was very properly prohibited by the parish priest and it is now no longer the scene of gambling and intoxication. Two very old ash trees and a whitethorn which formerly overshadowed the well were cut down about 1823 by the late Captain Vigors of Erindale, who leased a considerable tract of land here from the see of Leighlin. The whitethorn was formerly hung with all sorts of rags by the devotees, pilgrims or visitors to this holy spot. At present the well is almost choked with mud, and is hardly distinguishable from the marsh by which it is encompassed. About ten yards from the well stands a rude stone cross, about five feet in height and the whole is surrounded by a low straggling ditch.

The inland county of Carlow is of small extent, being about twenty-six Irish miles in length from north to south, and twenty-three miles in breadth from east to west. It is in the province of Leinster; bounded on the north and north-west by the Queen's County and the county of Kildare; on the west by the county of Kilkenny; and on the east and south-east by the counties of Wicklow and Wexford.

It contains six baronies: Carlow, Forth, Idrone east, Idrone west, Rathvilly and St Mullins. Its principal towns are Carlow, Leighlin-Bridge, Tullow, Bagenalstown and Hacketstown. The county is thickly studded with the seats of the resident gentry, and very few of its landed proprietors are absentees.

Chapter Six

KILKENNY

The general aspect of the county of Kilkenny is level but, with the soil being very fertile, the prospect is at all times cheering. To visit Kilkenny we voyaged along the beautiful river Nore, and landed at the pretty little town of Inistioge, which lies close to the far-famed Woodstock. Here the river is crossed by a bridge, a very elegant structure of ten equal arches, the southern side of which is ornamented by Ionic Pillars. Into the broad river that skirts its banks a score of tributary streams rush, now and then as miniature cataracts down the lesser precipices, occasionally forming a placid basin where a trout may be seen basking or at play, or it ripples onwards through, or beneath, overhanging boughs. Little valleys and small hills, undulating slopes and rough precipices, steps formed by the roots of aged oaks, rocks shaped by the hand of time into grotesque forms – such are a few of the varied sights with which Nature has bountifully enriched Woodstock.

On two or three of the heights, and also immediately adjoining the river, cottages have been erected; the former commanding magnificent views of the distant mountains and the adjacent valleys, while from the windows of the latter the salmon may be seen leaping – literally – in shoals.

It was evening when we quitted Woodstock and took the road to Kilkenny. Passing through Thomastown, a very old borough, so called from its founder, Thomas Fitzanthony, one of the earliest of the English settlers, we diverged somewhat from the regular route to visit the ancient abbey at Jerpoint.

The sun had gone down and the hour was in harmony with the solemn and impressive character of the scene. The ruins occupy an area of three acres and retain abundant evidence of the beauty as well as the extent of the time-honoured structure. It was founded in 1180 by Donough Fitz-patrick, king of Ossory, for Cistercian monks,and dedicated to the Virgin. The abbot was a peer of Parliament and, among the mitred abbeys of Ireland, that of Jerpoint was esteemed the fourth in the kingdom in wealth and architectural grandeur. On its suppression in 1540, it possessed 6500 acres in demesne land.

A short distance east of the road from Thomastown to Kilkenny, between Bennetsbridge and Dungarvon, is the round tower of Tulloherin, one of the five that still exists within the boundaries of the county. It is in a fair state of preservation, but without the cap. The ruins of a large church are, as usual, close beside it. The church is not very ancient, but appears to have been erected since the introduction of the pointed style of architecture. The stones – of red sandstone – that formed the doorway have been removed by the peasantry to make 'fire-stones'.

Unfortunately, in several other instances, we had occasion to remark the carelessness displayed in preserving those singular, interesting and mysterious relics of remote ages. In some cases the foundations have been undermined, and it is to be apprehended that in a few years many of them will be altogether lost.

The first object that strikes the visitor on entering Kilkenny is its famous castle, the ancient and present seat of the Ormonds, standing on a small hill that overlooks the river Nore. It is said to have been originally erected by Strongbow and soon afterwards destroyed by the Irish, and then to have been rebuilt in 1195 by William, Lord Marshal, Earl of Pembroke. In 1391 it came by purchase into the possession of James Butler, third Earl of Ormond, in the hands of whose descendants it has remained to this day.

From the turrets of the castle there is a striking view of Kilkenny and a magnificent prospect of the winding Nore and the fertile valley through which it passes. One is instantly startled by the singular effect – to be witnessed nowhere else in the world – of a large assemblage of houses with the usual chimneys, but from which no smoke rises. This is one of the marvels attributed to the

KILKENNY CASTLE,
KILKENNY

city in the old rhyme:

Fire without smoke, earth without bog,
Water without mud, air without fog,
And streets paved with marble.

The Kilkenny coal, of which we shall presently speak, gives no smoke; there are few bogs in the vicinity; the streets are literally paved with marble raised in the immediate neighbourhood; fogs are, we believe, very rare, and although the Nore is here as muddy as the Thames near Bankside, a vast number of small streams run into it that are as clear as crystal.

Kilkenny consists of English-town and Irish-town; the latter being, of course, the more ancient. The oldest part of this old borough is 'the Butts Cross' where formerly the inhabitants exercised themselves at the long bow, to which they were compelled by several Irish statutes. The present Butts Cross stands on the site of the ancient butts, and near it was a bull ring, the scene of a sport once famous in Ireland, or rather among the Anglo-Irish.

Kilkenny was, for a long period, strictly speaking the capital of the English Pale. In the year 1309 a parliament was held in the city; indeed, it is asserted, but upon doubtful authority, that the legislative assembly had previously met there. Of its proceedings in 1309, however, many records have been preserved. One of the acts provided for severe penalties against any of the English who 'affected the fashion of the Irish', but it would seem with little effect, for about a century afterwards another, and still severer, statute was enacted to 'prevent the contagion from spreading' and to punish those who 'looked on the long glibs of the natives as boasts and ornaments'.

Kilkenny was the most important of the counties which constituted the English Pale in the Anglo-Norman period, and the barons who settled in it were supposed to be more firmly attached to the supremacy of the English crown, and less liable to degeneracy than those who obtained lands in any other district. It was for this reason that Lionel, Duke of Clarence, summoned the parliament of AD 1367 to assemble in Kilkenny. He was anxious to ensure the enactment of laws which would prevent the increasing tendency of the English settlers to identify themselves with the Irish, and he had reason to fear that such a measure could not be carried in Dublin. The statute of Kilkenny is an act memorable in the sad legislation of Ireland, but it was never completely executed save in the county which gave it a name. It enacted that marriage, nurture of infants or gossip with the Irish, or submission to Irish law, should be deemed high treason. Any man of English race taking an Irish name, using the Irish language, or adopting Irish customs was to forfeit his goods and chattels, unless he gave securities that he would conform to English law and manners. Finally, it was declared highly penal to entertain an Irish bard, minstrel or story-teller, and even to admit an Irish horse to graze on English pasture. In consequence of this statute, Kilkenny was sometimes emphatically called 'the English county' but this is a distinction which it has long since lost.

There is in Ireland no city so full of striking, interesting and – notwithstanding the unseemly localities in which they are for the most part situated – picturesque ruins as Kilkenny. Our way was guided through numerous alleys and by-lanes to examine relics of the olden time. We found wretched hovels propped up by carven pillars and in several instances discovered Gothic doorways converted into entrances to pig-styes. It was a painful, indeed a revolting picture of the mingling of ancient glories with existing miseries for, at the period of our visit, poverty had forced its way into nearly every cabin and absolute starvation might be noted in many a form and face. Ruins of abbeys, castles and castellated houses are to be encountered in every quarter. Some of them, however, have been rescued from the hands of the despoiler, as in the case of the Black Abbey, which was recently converted into a Roman Catholic chapel, in which the gaudiness and glittering finery of modern taste were oddly and painfully mingled with the solemn grandeur of ancient state.

The Priory of St John in the 'Liberties' is now a parish church, but parts of it have been suffered to remain unrenovated. Its foundation is coeval with that of the castle. The character of the building is light, graceful and peculiarly elegant, so much so as at once to justify the term applied to it by the citizens (from the number of its windows) as the 'Lantern of Ireland'.

One of the most beautiful of all ruins, that of the Franciscan friary, has been put to uses far less worthy, for it is now, and has been for many years, a tennis court. The greater part of it however is in so solid and perfect a state that a comparatively small sum of money would suffice for its restoration and adaptation to the purposes of religion.

But by many degrees the most important and interesting of the ecclesiastical structures of Kilkenny is the Cathedral of St Canice. It is in the Irish town, and is an extensive and beautiful pile standing on a slight eminence. The foundation of it was laid towards the end of the reign of Henry II, by Bishop O'Dullany, who translated the old see of Ossory from Aghadow to Kilkenny. However, the cathedral would appear to have been raised by degrees and not to have been finished until two centuries later, and it is more than probable that it was erected upon the site of a building coeval with the introduction of Christianity into Ireland. It is a low cruciform shape, surmounted by a tower disproportionately low and in extent ranks next to the cathedral of St Patrick and Christ Church in Dublin.

About the year 1318, the cathedral was munificently embellished with stained glass, of so rare and valuable a character that Rinuccine, the pope's legate, offered for it no less a sum than £700. To the honour of Kilkenny, however, the offer was refused, but a very short time afterwards the fanatics of the English Parliament totally destroyed it, leaving but a few mutilated fragments that were gathered together by Bishop Pococke in 1760 and placed in two ovals over the western door.

A singular stone seat, the chair of St Kieran, stands in the north transept. The saint is believed to have preceded St Patrick in the mission by thirty years and to have been the first to preach Christianity in Ireland.

The well of St Canice, a short distance from the cathedral and dedicated to the patron saint, is still held in great repute by the common people of Ireland, and its water, even on the hottest day of summer, is said to possess an icy coldness.

A round tower, in good preservation, but without the cap, immediately adjoins the cathedral. It is one hundred and eight feet high, forty-seven feet in circumference and stands six and one half feet from the wall of the church.

There can be no doubt that a holy man, named Canice or Canicus, who was 'a person eminent for learning, sanctity and austerity of life', built a cell somewhere near the present cathedral from which the town afterwards took its name: Kilkenny being the 'cell or church of St Canice'.

The Kilkenny coal, which we have briefly mentioned, is chiefly raised in the vicinity of Castle Comer, a town about ten miles due north of the city, and not far from the borders of Carlow and the Queen's County, and in fact the 'coal field' extends into both these counties, it being fourteen miles in length and eleven in breadth. The collieries have been worked for nearly a century and a half, and they were first worked by Sir Christopher Wandesford who had purchased the township from the Brennans, the ancient proprietors, the last representative of whom died in indigent circumstances about the year 1795.

On approaching the coal district, the observer is at once struck by the abruptness of the ridges that form the outer ridge of the basin. The hills, rising eight or nine hundred feet and, in some cases, one thousand feet above the surrounding country, are cultivated nearly to their summits, which are usually flat and generally covered with a thin stratum of peat among which are frequently found the remains of huge trees that must have at one period completely clothed their surface.

Notwithstanding the numerous and very great improvements that of late years have been introduced into mining operations in this country, the collieries of Kilkenny, instead of making simultaneous advances, seem rather to be in a retrograding condition, for certainly no symptoms of radical improvement are visible. This probably arises more from an antipathy on the part of the working classes to the introduction of anything they have not previously been accustomed to and an injudicious selection of colliery agents, than to a want of spirit and liberality in the proprietors themselves.

The principal marble quarry of Kilkenny is situated about half a mile south of the city. The marble is black and some of it is remarkably pure. Mr Colles, the proprietor of the mills, annually exports to England about 100 tons of it and obtains in exchange the marble of Italy which he works up with the produce of the quarry into chimney pieces which he frequently inlays with coloured stones and adorns with sculptures in relief.

About three or four miles north of Kilkenny and in the immediate vicinity of some other quarries are the singular caves of Dunmore.

The principal cave has never been entirely explored, and there is a report current that it runs along underground until it communicates with the castle in Kilkenny. It has even been affirmed that the voices of people talking in the Thosel have been heard in the cave.

At Ballyspellan and Castle Comer, both within the limits of the coal district, are chalybeate springs, whose waters are much frequented for the medicinal qualities they are supposed to possess. Nevertheless, the strength of these springs is not so great as that of the waters which issue from the deep boreholes and mines of the collieries, owing, in part, to the surface water mixing more freely with them. However, the spa at Ballyspellan, in addition to the sulphate of iron held in solution, contains a considerable portion of carbonic acid gas, which it probably derives from its proximity to the carboniferous limestone.

A short distance north-west of Jerpoint is the Round Tower of Kilkree. Time has deprived it of its conical cap, but its height is a little less than one hundred feet, and at four feet above the ground its circumference is fifty and one half feet. Close to it is a very curious stone cross, formed of a single block of freestone, about eight feet high and ornamented with orbicular figures or rings.

Tradition states that this was erected in memory of Neill Callan, monarch of Ireland, who is said to have drowned in the river, since called Awnree – the King's River – while vainly trying to rescue one of his followers, with whom he perished in the stream. In the immediate vicinity of the round tower is, of course, a church, which is said to have been formerly an abbey, dedicated to St Gobban. At a short distance is the ancient town of Kells, which has now dwindled to a poor and insignificant village. However, its former state and importance are indicated by the ruins of many churches and castles.

The town was originally built by Geoffrey Fitz-Robert, one of the followers of Strongbow, as a garrison for a number of men to defend the county from the Tipperary clans, who used to enter and harry it by Mullmahone and the King's River, and various forts existed at one time along the river, beyond Callan, to check their approach and to give notice to the army at Kells, which was near enough to Kilkenny to render assistance there, if required. Geoffrey Fitz-Robert also founded a priory at Kells in 1183, which is said to have been filled with monks from Bodmin, in Cornwall.

The whole of the district, indeed, is rich in antiquities; many of them being in a comparatively perfect state and bearing evidence of the wealth and power of the Anglo-Norman chieftains – whose names are still to be frequently encountered, although the greater number of their descendants retain little else that once belonged to their mighty progenitors.

North-west of Kilkenny and almost on the borders of the county is the small village of Tullaroan, which now consists of a few poor cabins. In ancient times, however, it was a place of great importance, being the centre of the once extensive cantred of the Graces' country. The ancestors of the Grace family held, it is said, in this and the adjoining counties, a tract of land of about 80,000 Irish acres, extending between eleven and twelve miles in length and between four and six in breadth, of which a very small portion is still the property of Captain Percy Grace, RN, the last representative of the ancient and heroic race. Raymond Fitzwilliam de Carew, surnamed 'le Gros' for his great prowess, the founder of the family, was a friend of Strongbow, whose only sister, Basilia de Clare, he married. He received with her, as her marriage portion, the choicest district of the newly conquered country, coupled with the honour of constable and standard bearer of Leinster.

A few miles west of Kells, and bordering on the county of Tipperary, is the town of Callan. It is a place of considerable size and although not long ago justly described as one of the most miserable towns in Ireland, it has recently undergone considerable improvement and is no longer a disgrace to the noble family who are its owners. It has, however, like its neighbours, fallen from its high estate and reference must be made to its ruin for evidence of its early importance.

That Callan was formerly a walled town is proved by the records that have been preserved of various grants of murage to the local authorities, and it continued to be a parliamentary borough up to the year 1800. Attention must be drawn to the remains of St Catherine's Abbey, which retains marks of considerable splendour and extent.

Before we leave the county, we must direct attention to the beauty of the southern road along the banks of the Suir, which divides it from Waterford, and in particular to the neat and pretty village of Pilltown, the property of the Earl of Desborough which may vie with any place in Ireland for manifestations of industry and contentment. The cottages are remarkably neat and well-ordered; each is adorned with climbing roses and honeysuckle and the whole neighbourhood has an aspect of cheerfulness and prosperity too rarely to be met with in the south of Ireland.

Kilkenny is in the province of Leinster. It is an inland county bounded on the north by the Queen's County, on the south by the county of Waterford, from which it is divided by the river Suir, on the west by the county of Tipperary and on the east by the counties of Carlow and Wexford, and it is separated from nearly the whole of the latter by the Nore.

It is divided into the baronies of Gowran, Ida, Kells, Fassadineen, Galmoy, Cranagh, Iverk, Knocktopher and Shillelogher, and its principal towns, besides the city of Kilkenny, are Callan, Thomastown, Gowran, Freshford and Castle Comer.

Chapter Seven

TIPPERARY

Tipperary is an inland county in the province of Munster and, whilst it is not beautifully varied in scenery, it is one of the most fertile and productive of the counties of Ireland. Its principal river is the Suir which, taking its rise in the Banduff mountains, flows by Holy Cross, Cashel, Cahir, Clonmel and Carrick until it joins the Nore and the Barrow at Waterford.

Tipperary is said to be a corruption of the Irish *Tobar-a-neidth*, which signifies the Well of the Plains, and this comes from its position at the base of the Slieve-na-Muck hills, a portion of the Galtee mountains. However, others derive it from *Teobred-aruin*, the Fountain of Ara, an ancient chief whose name, in connection with that of another chief, Owny, is now given to one of the baronial divisions of the county.

Clonmel, the chief town of the county, stands on the north bank of the Suir. The origin of Clonmel is very ancient and the traditional account of it is fanciful. The Tuatha-de-Danann, a primitive people of Ireland, wishing to select a site for a settlement, and being skilled in augury, were guided in their choice by the following omen: they let off a swarm of bees and, observing where they settled, there they erected their baile, or circular fort, and gave the spot the significant name of *Cluain-mealla*, the Plain of Honey. This very spot is still pointed out and a castle was erected on it in later times in place of the aboriginal fort.

The town has a very business-like air and is indeed conspicuous for its prosperity, and is also the great outlet for the produce of the country, the Suir being navigable for vessels of size to within a short distance of the quays. Its population exceeds 20,000 and the number of houses are above 1,500. The surrounding scenery is remarkably beautiful, combining every variety of landscape from the Alpine to the pastoral, and the Commera mountains, which rise to the south, appear to terminate in the streets. There are several agreeable walks in the immediate vicinity of the town, the principal of which are the Wilderness, which for solemn gloom and wild grandeur is unsurpassed; the round of Heywood, a charming sylvan walk; the Green, commanding a delightful prospect of the river; Fairy-Hill Road, the fashionable promenade; and the Quay, from which there is another pleasing view of the river.

A little to the north outside Clonmel is the stream of Booleach, which is very insignificant in its general appearance but remarkable for the singular tradition connected with it that when it overflows for the third time it will drown all Clonmel. It has overflowed twice already; the second inundation happened not long ago, and its effects were very extensive and alarming, so it is not strange that such a notion should have circulated among the superstitious.

The church of St Mary in the north-western suburbs of the town is an object of considerable interest because of its picturesque antiquity. The steeple is unique in structure and seems to have originally been square; at present it has the appearance of an embattled octagon tower of great height, rising from a square base at about twenty-one feet from the ground, which is probably many centuries older than the upper part. Close to the summit of the steeple and in each of the eight sides is a large opening in the form of a Gothic window, to allow free transmission to the sound of a chime of bells placed in the tower. The principal entrance to the church is through the graveyard, and surrounding this graveyard on three sides are the remains of the old town wall, on which, with a view more effectually to protect it, are small square towers at stated intervals. At the north-west angle of the wall is a massive bomb-proof tower called the Magazine.

Notwithstanding the town's antiquity, however, ancient remains are not numerous in Clonmel, but one of the most striking is to be found in the 'Friary Chapel Yard'. It is a monumental stone belonging to the family of the Butlers, or Buttylers as the inscription that surrounds it sets forth. It is of blue limestone and measures about seven feet in length and is about four feet broad. Raised in high relief from the stone are effigies of a male and a female figure; the former in complete armour, the latter in a loose robe extending from the neck to the feet.

A few miles to the north-east of Clonmel is the ruined church of Donoghmore, one of the oldest edifices in Ireland, although it has hitherto escaped the notice of the antiquary. One is immediately struck upon approaching it by the contrast it presents to the Gothic edifices of more modern times. North-west of Donoghmore is the ancient churchyard of Clerihan, a 'lone, green and sunny spot', and admirably suited for a final resting place. A few miles eastwards the classic mountain of Slieve-na-man displays its bold outline against the clear skies.

In the immediate vicinity of Clonmel are the remains of many old castles and, unhappily, the ruins of some of more recent growth. One of these was pointed out for our particular notice as not long ago being the residence of a gentleman of large fortune, but whose immediate descendants are now actually tillers of the soil around it, while the immediate heir lives in the cabin of a poor cotter who, in former days, was a humble follower of the family.

In modern times, Clonmel is chiefly remarkable as the centre of a great corn and provision trade, which it exports through Waterford. The navigation of the river from Carrick to Clonmel is capable of being greatly improved, but as yet every effort to accomplish so desirable an object has been baffled.

Near to Clonmel is a holy well dedicated to St Patrick, and miraculous cures are ascribed to the waters. It was once a favourite resort for pilgrims, but is now quite deserted.

Clonmel has been rendered famous in modern Irish history by the successful exertions of a single individual who has done more to improve the condition of the country than any other person of our age: we refer to Mr Charles Bianconi, and the travelling cars that bear his name.

Mr Bianconi is a native of Milan and voyaged to Ireland around the year 1800, first visiting Dublin and subsequently settling in Clonmel where he carried on the trade of a picture dealer, cleaner and frame-maker, but upon a very limited scale, for his resources were at first exceedingly limited. By habits of industry, prudence and forethought, he contrived to save money and became highly respected by his neighbours. With the improvement of his resources he conceived the design of running a public car that, by conveying passengers at much less expense than the stage-coaches, might answer the purposes of the comparatively humbler classes. He ran his first car – from Clonmel to Cahir – on the 5th July, 1815, and shortly afterwards other cars to Limerick and Thurles. The experiment was very discouraging at first and frequently whole weeks went by without obtaining a passenger, but his energy and perseverance ultimately triumphed and he has succeeded in obtaining a large fortune for himself, while conferring immense benefit on the community and having preserved an irreproachable character and gained the respect of all classes.

He is now running forty-five double cars per day, that is, cars running up and down from the same places and travelling over 3,600 miles daily. The number of these cars which convey the mail are eighteen up and eighteen down. The number of horses to each car is from one to four, according to the circumstances. His cars vary in size, taking from four to sixteen passengers. He has a regular factory at Clonmel and builds all his own coaches. They travel at a rate of from six and a half to nine miles per hour. This variation of speed chiefly refers to the mail coaches, according to the necessity for an early delivery.

His charges average from one penny to twopence half-penny per mile, according to the turnpike, the quantity of business on the road, and the speed of the car; twopence per mile may be considered a fair ratio. Passengers on these cars are much more comfortable than on the outside coaches, being furnished with dry and comfortable horse-hair cushions and aprons. In wet weather they are never allowed to go more than two stages without changing the cushions.

The mode of travelling is pleasant as well as safe. Generally, the cars proceed at a rate as rapid as that of the stage-coaches, and persons of the highest respectability travel by them. They are planned precisely on the model of the common outside jaunting car peculiar to Ireland, but, as we have intimated, some of them are of sufficient size as to carry eight passengers on a side.

The cars of Mr Bianconi travel through nearly every district of the south of Ireland – passing through no fewer than 128 towns – but as yet they have not found their way into the north.

Six miles north of Clonmel, and commanding a very near view of Slieve-na-man, the small town of Fethard rises in the midst of a rich undulating plain which is thickly studded with the residences of the gentry. The town was built in the time of King John and is now remarkable for the preservation of its fortifications, with nearly all the walls and the castles remaining. Indeed, of the five entrances into the town, three are through the archways of castles.

A little to the west outside Fethard is a green hillock on which is the grass-covered ruin of an ancient fortress called Cahirdeard, or the Crimson City. Near it are the remains of the castle of Banetstown where, some sixty years ago, its owner, Ambrose Power Esq., was murdered on his own hearth by a party of Whiteboys.

Two miles eastward and surrounded by a large lawn is the castle of Knockelly, from whose top on a clear day there is one of the finest prospects imaginable, especially of the magnificent vale of St Johnstown underneath.

We shall now conduct the reader to a natural marvel – the most singular in Great Britain – the caves which are commonly known as the Caves of Mitchelstown, near the extreme south of the county where it borders Cork, and which is situated upon part of the estate of the Earl of Kingstown.

For centuries the neighbourhood has been famous for caves, and a very remarkable one exists that was for a long time an object of attraction and interest to the tourist. It is, however, very insignificant in comparison with a more recent discovery, and is now rarely visited. This new cave was discovered on the 2nd May 1833 by a man while quarrying for stones. His crowbar fell from his hands and while in search of it he found a cavity which was the gateway to a magnificent palace of nature.

The hill in which the cave exists rises nearly in the centre of a valley which separates the Galtee and Knockmeledown chains of mountains, with the former constituting the northern and the latter the southern boundaries.

Before we commenced our descent into the bowels of the earth, our first object was to engage the assistance of guides. We considered it desirable to procure several in order that, by distributing them in various parts of the caverns with lights, we might form a correct idea of their magnitude and magnificence. They took with them a large supply of candles and a box of lucifers to guard against the danger of some sudden gust of wind leaving us in darkness.

The use of torches is prohibited by the owner of the land – and very properly so, for we had ample proof of the injury they had already done in defacing the beauty of many crystallised roofs.

A narrow, gradually sloping passage of about four feet in height and between thirty and forty in length, terminates in an almost vertical precipice, about fifteen feet deep, which is descended by a ladder. For a considerable space – of nearly 250 feet – afterwards, the visitor is led through a dull and unpromising lane of grey limestone. The guides push forward and arrange themselves so that a sudden turn exhibits in an instant one of the most splendid of the caves in all its beauty and grandeur.

This is the lower-middle cave, but wonderful though it is, it is surpassed by the upper-middle cave, at which the visitor arrives through a passage varying in height from five to ten feet, and in breadth from seven to fourteen feet and sixty feet in length. Immediately upon entering the cave, the visitor will find attached to the wall on the right hand side the *Organ* – a huge calcareous growth, which is conceived to bear some resemblance in shape to the musical instrument from which its name is borrowed. Nine great pillars of carbonate of lime occur in this compartment, and the most remarkable pillars in this cave are known among the guides by the names of *Drum* and *Pyramid*. The former occurs fifteen feet south of the *Organ*, and the latter is at the eastern end of the chamber. In addition to the pillars, stalactites and stalagmites abound everywhere; the former depending from the roof and the latter springing from the floor of the cavern.

Soon after leaving the cave we were summoned by the guides to descend 'the chimney' – a work of some danger, for it is barely wide enough to allow a passage, and its sides have very few projections upon which to place the feet. It descends to a depth of at least thirty yards, and a slip would be fatal. A guide, however, goes before the visitor, directing his steps and frequently giving the foot a resting place upon his shoulder. At the bottom of the chimney is another cave which is nearly equal to the one above, and from this several galleries branch off, leading to objects only a degree less wonderful.

These are new discoveries, to which additions are continually being made, and consist of a number of minor caves to which no access has, as yet, been obtained.

Our desire was to proceed as far as possible and our guides, gratified by our ardour, rather than checked by the additional labour to which they were subjected, proceeded after allowing us a brief breathing time. They ushered us through a burrow which was so narrow that we had actually to twist ourselves along it. Yet, when we had reached the utmost limits to which the researches of the guides had as yet attained, the reader will guess our astonishment when we found pencilled on one of the white curtins at the extremity, the names of two ladies who, a few days previously, had accomplished the whole of the difficult and dangerous task.

The course we had taken – burrow, caves, chimney and all – we had to re-traverse, and upon our introduction to the daylight, we found we had been five hours underground, and we estimate that we must have paced on our progress and our return at least eight miles.

Our course from the Mitchelstown Caves lay through a wild country to the pretty town of Cahir. Passing by the prosperous and well-managed estate of Lord Glengall, we came in view of the castle, which stands on the river Suir and was, as well as the town it protected, very famous in former times. It is said however to occupy the site of a structure of the remotest antiquity – its ancient name being *Cahir-dunaascaigh* or The Circular Stone Fortress of the Fish Abounding Dun.

It is, of course, of considerable extent, but of an irregular outline, and consists of a great square keep, surrounded by extensive earthworks. These earthworks are flanked by seven towers, four of which are circular, and three are of a larger size and square. It has been put through much repair very recently, but so judiciously that its picturesque effect is in no degree injured. At a short distance from the river are the ruins of an ancient monastery built, it is said, in the reign of King John, for canons regular of the order of St Augustine.

The town of Cahir has a remarkably cheerful aspect and its prosperity is not alone upon the surface: it is derived principally from the extensive flourmills actively and continually at work in the immediate neighbourhood, and conducted almost exclusively by the people called Quakers.

There are, in several parts of the south of Ireland, towns universally known and distinguished as 'Quaker Towns', and these are remarkable for neatness and cleanliness, for the industry and sobriety of the inhabitants, and the air of comfort and good order within their dwellings.

Cahir also enjoys the advantage of an encouraging and considerate resident landlord, Lord Glengall, whose beautiful seat adjoins it.

The road from Cahir to Cashel lies through a picturesque and richly cultivated country, a considerable portion of it being part of the Golden Vale, which is so called from its exceeding fertility. About two miles to the left is the small and improving village of Golden, which is situated on both sides of the river Suir, the two divisions being connected by a stone bridge of great antiquity, upon which William III is said to have signed the Charter of Cashel. The remains of an old circular round tower which protected the pass in former times continue in a tolerable state of preservation.

The ruin of Cloughabreeda Castle, which lies about two miles from Cahir on the Cashel road, is all but obliterated, and though now inconsiderable, its name once struck terror into the surrounding countryside.

Shane Burke of Cloughabreeda, its last possessor, was a person as much dreaded as Blue Beard or Oliver Cromwell. He used, as an old man told us upon the spot, 'to hang people without jouge or jury, for he was his own magistrate'.

The old man related one of his deeds to us.

There was a widow woman who lived near the castle, and who had only one son – and a sorry reprobate he was. The poor mother, in despair at the conduct of her degenerate offspring, complained to the chief, Shane, about him, and he then ordered the mother and son to attend him at his castle on a certain day. They came and Shane, calling the lad to him, walked out into the orchard. He returned to the broken-hearted mother a few moments later and, with a satanic smile, said, 'I promise you, your son will be quiet in the future.' And so saying, he led her to a loop-hole and pointed out into the orchard, and showed the poor woman the body of her son hanging from the branch of an apple tree.

The way in which this man ended his days is not known. He was possessed of great riches (for he levied what they call 'blackmail' in Scotland) and he buried his wealth in some secret place, and then murdered the man who assisted him to prevent his disclosing the secret, and then he was summoned to England – from whence he never returned.

From the road and for nearly the whole of the way, a singular rath called the Moat of Knockgrafton can be seen. It is an artificial mound of earth rising seventy feet above the summit of the hill on which it was constructed. At its base the foundations of an extensive castle may be traced, of which one of the square towers still exists. It was built in the year 1108 and ranks amongst the oldest constructions of the kind in Ireland; tradition states that eighteen of the kings of Munster were born and reared within the walls.

About a mile from Golden Bridge, and still verging to the left from the road to Cashel, are the remains of the ancient Priory of Athassel. The site was chosen with the usual taste and judgement of the monks, although a few shrivelled trees are all that now remain of the woods by which it was formerly encompassed, and of which there is abundant evidence. A gentle, fertilising and productive river still rolls beside its shattered glories and the ruins afford ample proof of the vast extent as well as the singular beauty of the structure when the Augustinians kept state within its walls.

Athassel was founded by William Fitz Adelm de Burke about the year 1200 for canons regular of the order of St Augustine. This Fitz Adelm was steward to Henry II and ancestor to the illustrious family of De Burgo. On the king's return from Ireland, he was entrusted with the management of affairs and was interred at Athassel in 1204.

All the ecclesiastical ruins (of which there are many) in Tipperary, and indeed in Ireland, sink into insignificance compared with those that crown the far-famed Rock of Cashel. The rock, rising above the adjacent country, can be seen from a very long distance and from every direction by which it is approached. Its summit is crowned by the venerable remains that have excited the wonder and admiration of ages and will continue to do so for ages yet to come.

The city – for that is the rank that belongs to it, although it consists of little more than a thousand houses of which nearly three-quarters are thatched – has an aspect almost as time-worn as the ruins on the rock, but infinitely less picturesque. The streets

ROCK OF CASHEL.

are unlighted, unpaved and uncleaned. There is no supply of water but by pumps which are repaired at the expense of the city. The waterworks erected in the early part of the last century by Archbishop Bolton have completely gone to decay. The underground conduits, which are upwards of two miles in length, are choked up or obliterated, and the stream is diverted to supply the mills in the neighbourhood. The principal street is wide and well built, but the lanes and alleys that branch from it and the whole of the suburbs are mean and wretched.

Cashel, however, is chiefly important as having been for centuries the seat of an archbishop. The ecclesiastical province comprises the dioceses of Cashel, Emly, Limerick, Ardfert and Aghadoe, Waterford, Lismore, Cork, Ross, Cloyne, Killaloe and Kilfenora – a district which is very nearly co-extensive with the civil province of Munster.

But long before it attained ecclesiastical rank it was the favourite residence of the kings of Munster, and it is said a synod was held there about the middle of the fifth century by St Patrick, St Ailbe and St Declan in the reign of Aengus, who is supposed to have commemorated his conversion to Christianity by the erection of a church upon the rock, thus probably originating the assemblage of sacred edifices for which, in after times, it became conspicuous. There also appears to be satisfactory authority for the belief that it had been the selected site for pagan worship for ages previously.

It is curious to note how the authorised 'care-takers' of celebrated places assume the tone of the scenes they exhibit. At Killarney every guide, boatman and child speaks of fairy-land, ghosts, apparitions of all kinds that walk the waters, float i' the air, clink mannikin hammers under the broad-leaved dock, or of the still more mysterious creatures that watch golden treasures beneath the placid surface of the lake.

At the Giant's Causeway every fellow desires to be thought a geologist; he hints with a careless and dignified air at its superstitions, but dwells at length upon what Sir Humphry Davy and Doctor MacDonnel said to him. He talks of strata and basalt columns, quartz, limestone, octagons, formations, spars and the debris of the whole, all the while assuring you that he can account for the mighty and glorious wonders that make your heart pant and your temples throb, until you might wish that some giant would step forth and silence the petty praters who disturb without informing you.

On the Rock of Cashel, as well as among other ruins, the guide is an antiquary.

It was a cold misty morning when, having wandered through the dirty and miserable streets that lead to this noble relic, we summoned a conductor from his cottage fire to lead us up the steep path. He came willingly enough, expressing his regret for the softness – wetness – of the day, and his hopes that it would clear up for the view which many thought a great deal of – though to his mind, those who climbed the Rock would do better to keep to the ruins; fine views were to be had all over Ireland, but Ireland has only one Rock of Cashel.

A cow was sheltering close to the iron gateway which the guide unlocked. He saw that we did not altogether approve of her remaining there and apologised, saying that 'she could do no harm, the craythur.'

While the wind growled along the walls, and rushed with impotent fury through the vaulted passages, a story was told us of another guide, the predecessor of the one who had us under his especial charge.

This predecessor was a very old man when he took up his abode among the ruins, and he worked night and day to prevent the further trespassings of time upon the structure. The children would stand aside and whisper together when they saw this lover of ancient things bending over his staff as he climbed the rock, knowing well that they must not indulge in their noisy roisterings within the walls while he was there. He would remain for a month at a time, craving nothing beyond 'the handful of meal and potatoes', which the poor people did not fail as usual to give cheerfully from their scant store. He would pray and work and work and pray from sunrise to sunset and then sleep tranquilly, either beneath the grand entrance into Cormac's Chapel or by the side of the Archbishop's Tomb, waking only to resume his self-imposed task – piling together the precious fragments which time, or more destructive ignorance, had displaced, picking the green moss from out the inscriptions, and sweeping the hallowed floors. Sometimes, despite his age, he would creep along the walls to replace a stone, and the humbler class hinted that he held converse with the spirits of the air who supported him in his work. At last the old man died, and the stones fell and fragments of the most exquisite architecture were scattered by the storm and the glories of the place were crumbling into dust when, happily, one of equal taste and greater power laboured long and earnestly to preserve what the humble workman honoured.

On the south side of the cathedral and near the gateway by which the Rock is entered, there stands a rudely sculptured figure of St Patrick, the patron saint. It is mounted on a huge stone which is partially sculptured also, and tradition states that here the petty kings of Munster formerly paid their tribute to the superior potentate, and it is probable that from the latter circumstance the name of the place is derived: *cashi-ol* being interpreted by some as 'the stone of tribute'. Our guide pointed out to us with considerable ostentation the marks made by the rattling of the coined gold, and added emphatically, 'Ah, but there were no absentee landlords to take it from us in them days.'

If the adjacent country is seen to great advantage from the Rock, then the Rock, with its time-honoured structures, has a remarkably fine effect beheld from any point of approach.

We entered one of the wretched hovels that shelter at the base of the Rock. It consisted of a single dark room, without a window, the walls of which were thick with the gathered smoke of years, and a miserable bed, which was composed of a few boards placed a few inches above the clay floor, on which a few handfuls of dirty straw had been thinly scattered.

A few years ago the tourist was compelled to describe the Rock of Cashel as an assemblage of ruins, utterly abandoned to the attacks of time, and to be examined only by forcing a passage through nettles and rank weeds and over huge masses of stone and mortar. Recently, however, as we have intimated, this reproach has been removed by the late Archdeacon Cotton, who devoted his whole time and energy and largely expended his private means to preserve every portion of the venerable structure from further injury. He contrived to collect together a great mass of broken carved stones, which he so judiciously and skilfully joined that many of the figures in *basso relievo* now appear almost as perfect as when, centuries ago, they were placed in the building, and these he has fixed in the various walls, so as to effectually protect them against any further assaults of the despoiler.

The ruins of Hore Abbey exist in a good state of preservation in the vale directly under the Rock. It was founded for the Cistercians in 1272 by David MacCarvill, Archbishop of Cashel, and endowed with the revenues of the Benedictines, who were expelled by him out of the abbey. There exists a singular tradition connected with the building which is to be found in a record in Birmingham Tower in Dublin: 'In the time of David MacCarvill, Archbishop of Cashel, there was a certain abbey of black monks near the cathedral of St Patrick, founded in honour of the blessed Virgin Mary; and the aforesaid David, having told his mother that he was warned in a dream that the said black monks would cut off his head, he did, by the advice of his mother, remove those monks and gave their lands and possessions to the new abbey which he had founded.'

The archbishop also united to it the Hospital for Lepers, built by David le Latimer about the year 1230, and the ruins of which are still visible standing in a field on the road to Cahir.

Second only in interest and also in architectural beauty to the ruins of Cashel is the Abbey of Holy Cross which lies about seven miles distant from the city and three from the flourishing town of Thurles. It is situated on the Suir and is said to owe its origin as well as its name to the possession of a piece of the True Cross, which was sent, covered with gold and set with precious stones,

APPROACH TO CASHEL
(FROM THE NORTH)

about the year 1110 by Pope Pascal II as a present to Donough O'Brien, monarch of Ireland, and grandson of Brien Boru. The circumstance, however, is by no means improbable, for gifts of this kind were undoubtedly transmitted from Rome to some of the provincial Irish kings about the same period, and it is certain that a relic with attributes of peculiar sanctity was preserved in the abbey for centuries, and which is said to be in existence to this day. The abbey was originally found in the year 1182 for Cistercian monks by Donald O'Brien, king of Limerick, and from the earliest period it was endowed with peculiar privileges, and its charter was confirmed by the kings John, Henry III, Edward III and Richard II respectively.

The abbey, with part of the adjacent land, is now the property of the Rev Dr Wall, Fellow of Trinity College, who has so far cared for its preservation as to place an iron gate on the principal entrance – with little advantage however, for the broken walls afford easy access to intruders, and during our visit we saw a parcel of idle boys amusing themselves by pelting stones at the carved mullions and pillars, one of which must have been very recently broken by a mischievous scoundrel, who must have exerted considerable strength to deface it. As a monastic ruin, the Abbey of Holy Cross ranks in popular esteem as one of the first, if not the first, in Ireland.

Several of the family tombs contained in the abbey are of a very elegant character; the most remarkable of them, however, is that which tradition assigns to Donald More O'Brien, king of Limerick, its founder – but tradition is in error. There is no doubt that it was erected by, and to the memory of, a member of either the House of Ormond or Desmond. The monument is of exceeding beauty – it is, indeed, considered the most beautiful in Ireland – but unhappily it has been much injured by a party of recruits who, with their sergeant, were marching through the village some twenty years ago. We were informed that these idle vagabonds, having nothing better to do, employed themselves by battering the canopy, the pillars and the arches with the butt-ends of their muskets.

The only other towns of note in the county are Thurles, in the northern division, and Nenagh, in the north-west. The latter has recently been converted into an assize town – an act of tardy justice – for previously a 'summons to court' was an infliction of a grievous injury, involving as it did a journey of nearly 140 miles.

Tipperary is an inland county and its boundaries on the north are Galway and the King's County; on the south Waterford; on the east the King's and Queen's Counties; and on the west Cork, Limerick and Clare, with its separation from the latter effected by the Shannon and Lough Derg.

It is divided into the baronies of Clanwilliam, Eliogathy, Iffa and Offa, east and west, Ikerrin, Kilnemanagh, Middle-third, Lower Ormond, Upper Ormond, Owny, Arra and Slieveardagh.

The town which gave its name to the county, although very ancient, has yielded in rank, population and importance to that of Clonmel. Tipperary, however, still contains above 8,000 inhabitants and in 1831 the houses amounted to upwards of 1,000.

Chapter Eight

WEXFORD

The maritime county of Wexford holds a foremost rank amongst the more interesting of the counties of Ireland, not alone because of the fertility of its soil and its great natural advantages, but also because it was intimately associated with the career of the first English invaders of the island.

We commence our description with the very ancient town of 'New' Ross, which is situated near the confluence of the Nore and Barrow, and about six miles distant from the junction of both with the Suir. Tradition attributes its foundation to a 'Ladye called Rose who was the daughter of Crume, King of Denmark', and the surrounding of the town with walls to another 'Rose' – the sister to Strongbow. It was certainly a place of importance in the thirteenth century and enjoyed considerable trade so early as the reigns of the fourth and fifth Henrys – from the former of whom it is believed to have obtained a charter of incorporation. In 1572, it was declared an 'antient borogh towne'.

There are still many remains of its towers, battlements and gates as well as of the monasteries which 'formerly abounded here', although two centuries ago they were described as 'quite ruinated' or 'turned to dwelling houses'.

There are few towns in Ireland so auspiciously situated as that of New Ross: the Barrow is here a river of great width, the wooden bridge that connects it with Kilkenny being of prodigious length and its depth is sufficient to permit vessels of the largest burthern to moor at the quays. Yet its condition is by no means prosperous; its natural resources have not been rendered available and a heavy atmosphere of dullness and inactivity seems to have settled over and around it – and yet, the activity of a single enterprising merchant might enable it to vie in commercial importance with either of the second-grade towns in the south.

The adjacent scenery is of exceeding beauty; a majestic river runs between the two rich counties of Wexford and Kilkenny, its banks are richly planted and its surface is, almost literally, covered at low water by the cots of the salmon fishers.

These cots are of a very primitive character, being not unlike canoes. They are propelled by paddles resembling the common spade, and each boat contains two men. Their net is small and square and is drawn up the instant the fisher feels a salmon strike against it. There are no fewer than 400 boats on the river, giving profitable employment to 800 men, principally small farmers, who thus occupy their time when the seed is in the ground.

Pursuing the course of the river we arrive at the beautiful ruin of Dunbrody Abbey, which was founded by Henry de Montmatisco for Cistercian monks in 1182. It is situated just at that point where the Suir, the Nore and the Barrow enter the harbour of Waterford. The ruins are very extensive, and in a good state of preservation, although the west window, which is a remarkably fine example of its kind has been permitted to fall within the last two or three years, and for a long time previously the stones of the venerable structure were regarded as common property.

Passing through Arthurstown, formerly King's Way – a village where, it is said, James II passed his last night in Ireland – we enter the poor village of Duncannon with its singular fort situated about seven miles from the entrance to the harbour, and eleven miles south-east of the city of Waterford. The fort is built on a point of rock, which has precipitous cliffs 130 feet in height and juts out more than 300 yards into the estuary of the Suir and Barrow. The fort, which commands the entrance to the ports of Waterford and New Ross, was granted by Henry VI to John Talbot, Earl of Shrewsbury, from whom it reverted to the crown. The Castle, with some lands for keeping it in repair, were vested in trustees by Queen Elizabeth; and in what manner the lands have been alienated does not appear.

The peninsula which runs far into the sea between the harbour of Waterford and the bay of Bannow is classic ground. But before we enter it, we may briefly visit the famous tower of Hook, standing at its extremity and now converted into a lighthouse, which tradition states to have been erected by Rose Macrume, the fair foundress of New Ross. It occupies a point of land high above the ocean and is one of the many marks to mariners with which the county abounds.

The old keeper of the tower died not long ago at the age of 100. He had been superannuated many years before his death, but was suffered to remain where so large a portion of his life had passed. So strong, however, was the habit of the old man that regularly every night he awoke and took his rounds, and was one morning found dead at the post he had guarded for nearly a century.

From the summit of the tower there is a magnificent view of the coast with its numerous creeks and bays and miniature harbours, its bold barrier of rocks and the small islands that dot the surface of the ocean.

First in interest and importance is the small promontory of Bag-an-Bun where the first hostile Englishman trod upon Irish soil. Further inland is the castle and village of Fethard – a corruption of 'fought-hard' – where the Irish made their earliest stand against the onward march of the invaders. At the extremity of its broad bay is the ancient abbey of Tintern and, at the termination of the narrow creek, are the seven castles of Clonmines. On the land opposite, the old church of Bannow crowns the summit of a small hill that looks down upon a town buried long ago in the sand.

Looking seaward again, the eye falls upon the two small islands called the Keeroes, and then upon a narrow neck of land that, stretching across from one peninsula until it almost touches the other, forms the Lough of Ballyteague, and due south of which are the far-famed Saltees, famous in the sea-calendar – for to mariners the sound was for a long period a place of fear. Further west again, and passing Carnsore point is the Tuskar Rock beside which many a gallant vessel went down, the calamity being briefly noticed with the melancholy postscript, 'all hands perished'.

But Wexford county is far less perilous than of yore, for on the very spot which we have placed the reader – the tower of Hook – we may count at least half a score of lights, and wrecks are now rare upon this once merciless coast.

We have glanced at the objects of leading interest along the southern coast of Wexford, but some of them demand more particular notice, and chief in importance is the small promontory of Bag-an-Bun. The county lies directly opposite to Cardiganshire in Wales, the distance being but a few leagues, and between the natives of both countries and from the earliest period a friendly intercourse has existed.

The ancient town of Fethard, which is now dwindled to a small village, is on the western bank at the entrance to the Bay of Bannow. The town, and an exceedingly pretty village called Saltmills, is in the immediate vicinity of the fine old abbey of Tintern, which lies a few miles northwards.

The most remarkable ruin, or rather assemblage of ruins, in the county stands nearly at the extremity of the bay. The seven castles of Clonmines – for so they are termed – lie together in a field on a bank of the Scar, and have a singular and picturesque effect. A manuscript description of Wexford written in 1684 speaks of the town as a 'very ancient corporation, but now quite ruinated, there remaining only four or five ruinated castles, an old ruined church called St Nicholas and a monastery, also ruined, called St Augustine'. This account clearly makes out the seven ruins as no doubt the belfries of the church and an abbey came in time to be reckoned as 'warlike towers'.

Clonmines was a town of great antiquity, and of some extent, covering about twenty acres, and surrounded by a vallum and fosse. In the time of the Danes it had a mint for coining silver. The old manuscript we have already quoted states that it 'was a place of great trade in times past and a harbour for shipping until the sand filled up the passage near the town of Bannow, which was the destruction of both these towns', and that 'it tooke its name from the silver or royall mines formerly dug there'. On the other side of the river five or six deep pits or mines can still be seen, and some ore is cast up, but seems to contain more lead than silver. There lived in these parts a very old man who said that he remembered having seen miners at work there but that the river came in upon the workmen so fast that they were forced to quit the undertaking 'for good and all'.

A still more striking and interesting ruin, however, is the small church of Bannow which stands on the summit of a hill that overlooks a plain of limited extent undulating with hillocks, and between which are long, straight and regular depressions which clearly point out the old town of Bannow which was buried many years ago beneath the sand. The little church, a few dilapidated walls, and a square tube of masonry, believed to have been the massive chimney of the town-house, that peeps above the soil of the churchyard are the only relics of the work of man now visible in the district. But the town may be easily traced; it consisted of several wide streets crossing one another, and extending generally eighty to one hundred yards before the traces are lost. Mention is made in the rent-rolls of the following streets in this town: High Street, Weaver Street, St George's Street, Upper Street, St Tollock's Street, St Mary's Street, St Ivory Street, Lady Street and Little Street.

There are no existing data to determine the precise date at which the submersion took place. But there can be little doubt that the destruction was gradual, enabling the inhabitants to remove their goods and leaving nothing but the bare walls for the sand to cover. The process by which it was destroyed is still going on in the vicinity, and it is curious to watch the perpetually changing character of the adjacent soil as small clouds of peculiarly fine sand hover about it, now settling and now shifting and, where it meets an obstruction, forming a small nucleus around it and altering in a few hours the form of that particular spot.

The church is obviously of very remote origin. The interior is filled with sculptured ornaments of great beauty as well as antiquity, and the comparatively modern graves of the lords of the soil are mingled with those of their great English progenitors – for perhaps in no county of Ireland can there be found so many who trace their descent in a direct line from the triumphant knights of the reign of Henry II.

Bannow, so entirely isolated and so completely out of the way, enclosed by its own bay and the outstretched arm of the Scar, and being the high road to nowhere, is remarkably fertile in character. When, in our early youth, our studies were made among its people, they had little intercourse with other parts of the country. John Williams, the Bannow postman, supplied this primitive neighbourhood with news twice a week for more than thirty years, we believe. He was a right honest poor fellow, who managed to keep the accounts of some dozen families in his head and was never known to miscalculate a single penny.

The baronies of Bargy and Forth, which extend along the coast from the bay of Bannow to the bay of Wexford, form perhaps the most singular and remarkable district of Ireland, with its inhabitants being, to this day, 'a peculiar people' more distinct from the aboriginal Irish than from the Welsh, from whom they are undoubtedly descendants. Of the peculiar locality from where they came, however, there is no evidence, and they seem to have settled as colonists rather than invaders and probably preceded, by a long period, the arrival of the Anglo-Normans.

The peninsular position of these baronies – the sea on one side and the mountain of Forth on the other – contributed no doubt in a great degree to the safety and stability of the colony. Yet, had it not been for the numerous castles, or more properly speaking, fortalices, the ruins of which form so remarkable a feature in the landscape, the courage and daring of the native Irish would have caused their extermination. Over the surface of about 40,000 acres, there are the remains of fifty-nine buildings still standing, and the sites of many more can still be pointed out. The walls of solid masonry were equally secure against the arrows and javelins of the foe and the effects of fire, their roofs could not be given to the flames, nor 'their flesh to the eagles' while entrenched in these strongholds, and the castle of the chief was the rendezvous of the vassal, with his flocks and herds. A plentiful supply of pure water was never wanting where a castle was erected, and from the warder's watch-tower on the summit, at least two, and often six or more castles were in sight. The beacon fire, or other signal raised on one, spread the alarm in a short time over the entire county. These castles have, for the most part, the same character: a single tower at one corner of a square embattled courtyard.

The people of Fort and Bargy are, on average, rather above middle size, generally stouter than the native Irish and of a slower and more sober footstep. From early life they are accustomed to active habits of industry, and there were, until very recently, but few cottages of working men who had not one to three acres attached to the dwelling. The dwelling houses and the out-offices are far more convenient and comfortable than most Irish houses. They are generally clay built, but dashed within and without with lime mortar, neatly thatched and have solid chimneys of masonry. There are no native travelling beggars in the district; such as have no direct personal means of support apply to their more fortunate neighbours, and neither consider themselves, nor are they considered by others to be beggars. In every farmhouse an open sack of meal was formerly placed in the kitchen, with a plate, to be dealt out in charity to the wandering poor, whilst food and lodging was to be found wherever it was required. While the male portion is engaged in out-door work, the females are no less so within, and the winter evenings are employed in spinning, knitting and sewing. Honesty and even the absence of suspicion of theft prevailed so generally that locks were unknown and a simple bolt formed the interior fastening, while the barn and all the outhouses were left on the latch.

The erection of a lighthouse on the Tuskar Rock – the extreme south-east point of Ireland – has been one of the most valuable works ever raised on the Irish coast. The work was commenced in the summer of 1813, but on the evening of the 16th October a strong gale sprung up from the south-west and increased in fury until the 18th. The condition of the unfortunate men on the rock was frightful. The huge billows began to roll over the entire extent of the rock, which exceeds a surface of more than three acres. The summit of the building was far overtopped; the sheds and workhouses were swept away in an instant and the loss of life in a moment was thirty, and only those who clung to chains and large blocks survived the following wave. Every succeeding wave swept away some poor wretch. Some bound themselves by ropes to the chains and blocks and fortunately the tide began to lower, and yet the fury of the elements abated not. The unfortunate survivors prepared against the horrors of the next full tide which, if possible, was even more dreadfully violent. In this condition they remained for forty-eight hours, never free from the running of the sea, frequently buried at high tide many feet beneath the moving mountain of water. The building itself was demolished, and several poor creatures were hurled along with the mass of stones into the abyss. Others were torn from the chains, benumbed and exhausted, whilst several died lashed to the embrace of the iron chain which had almost cut their bodies in two. Nineteen shattered and mutilated creatures were, at length, and with great difficulty, rescued from their horrid condition.

However, on the evening of Sunday, June 4th, 1815, the light – the mariners' guiding star to the Irish Channel – was first exhibited.

The entire construction is a fine work of art, and though the furious billows have beaten to the height of fifty feet on the cone-shaped building, not the least effect or injury has been as yet sustained.

Numerous raths are dispersed throughout the baronies, but in most places the vallum, or rampart, has been partially carried away, and a more than usual fertility is the distinctive mark of the site. The most perfect one is at a place called Ballytrent, in Fort, near to the seashore. It is formed of two concentric circles, or ramparts, of clay, sand and stones, carried thither from the sea bank. It is now planted as an ornamental garden, and has a fine effect. On top of each rampart are gravel walks bordered with evergreens, and in the immediate vicinity are the remains of two others.

Nearly in the centre of this fertile barony of Fort is Johnstown Castle, the seat of Hamilton Knox Grogan Morgan, Esq., a descendant of the great Scottish reformer. The castle is modern but built on the site of a very ancient structure, and indeed, a tower of which is part of the present building. It is formed entirely of granite procured from the quarries of Carlow and when finished the mansion will rank among the most elegant and magnificent in the kingdom.

Happily, Wexford is in one respect highly privileged in that few of its landed proprietors are absentees. There are no huge estates over which several agents must, if necessary, be placed, and as very few of the gentry have involved properties, it follows as a matter of course that the tenants are in easy circumstances, and are neither rack-rented nor pressed for sudden payments. Unfortunately, few of the Irish counties are so auspiciously circumstanced. In many instances a nominal rent-roll misleads the owner into an expenditure far beyond his actual income, with the consequence naturally that the landlord and tenant are mutually embarrassed and then an air of poverty equally pervades the mansion and the cottage, and prosperity to either is totally out of the question.

From Johnstown – and still through the barony of Fort – to Wexford, which is a distance of about three miles above the rich and fertile valley, the road all along commands an extensive and beautiful prospect. On one side is the dark and rugged mountain, and on the other St George's Channel. We pass a memorable spot, still called Cromwell's Rock, where the great Irish bugbear planted his cannon to bombard the town then surrounded with strong walls, of which there are several remains. The town was betrayed by the governor who, being as Cromwell stated, 'fairly treated', surrendered just as an agreement was about to be signed for its evacuation.

Wexford is now an assemblage of remarkably narrow streets; the memorable jail is now an asylum for paupers, and the still more memorable bridge exists to this day – it was originally built entirely of wood, but of late years it has been partially rebuilt of stone. Its length is very great, crossing as it does a broad part of the

Slaney. The Court House, which is an excellent building, faces this bridge.

The town has a thriving aspect and, but that its harbour has the disadvantage of a bar – which there are good reasons for believing may be removed – its proximity to England would render it one of the most flourishing ports of the south. To displace this bar would, indeed, probably convert Wexford into the great thoroughfare between England and the south of Ireland, as its distance is no more than forty-five miles from Milfordhaven.

Giraldus Cambrensis informs us that when Henry II set sail from this town for Pembroke, on Easter Monday, 1173, the 'king took shipping with the bar'.

It is certain that its removal may be effected, although the cost of the work might be considerable, and the undertaking too great for any private enterprise. But public money could not be better spent, for, besides the advantages that would accrue to both countries, an immense tract of land might be gained from the ocean. As it is, however, Wexford carries on a considerable trade and there are steamboats to Liverpool which ply twice weekly. The quays are good, and although large ships are seldom seen, they are usually crowded with coasting vessels, many of which belong to the town.

Wexford may boast one of the best, if not the very best hotel in the south of Ireland – White's Hotel. We have never visited a better managed establishment. As it has been our good fortune to have friends in the neighbourhood we have never domiciled there, but we have received the highest testimonials from many as to the cleanliness, order and attention of the house – and especially in reference to Mr White's cuisine. The host attends his own business – a circumstance sufficient to account for the excellent character of the hotel.

There are several ruins within the old town walls, the most interesting of which is the old abbey of Selskar, and the modern parish church has been built quite close to it.

The road from Wexford to Enniscorthy – which is about thirteen miles – runs for some miles along the banks of the Slaney, but to see this river to advantage the tourist should take a boat at Wexford. Every spot is interesting, either for its natural beauty, for some historical association or for its legends of the olden time.

A little further on and we arrive at a most interesting relic of ancient days – the site of Carrick Castle, the first castle that was built by the Anglo-Normans – not the small antique tower which, situated on the pinnacle of a rock, forms one of the most strikingly picturesque objects in the kingdom, and which has long usurped the name and honour of the fortress of Fitz-Stephen. The true castle of the first Anglo-Norman 'adventurer and conquerer' was on the opposite side of the river. It was a stately pile that crowned the summit of a rugged hill, barely enough of which now remains to mark the space it occupied, for the plough has passed over nearly the whole of it.

Passing Ferry Carrig, and under its long, narrow and rickety wooden bridge, we reach a very wide part of the river, that has more the appearance of a spreading lake. The banks are richly wooded and a delicious landscape is nobly backed by the distant mountains, on the loftiest of which a fleecy cloud always seems to be resting; this is Mount Leinster. The longer and nearer range is Black-stairs, three pinnacles of which are known as 'the leaps of Ossian's greyhounds'; the lower hill to the east is the White Mountain; the singular conical hill to the north is Slievebuy; beneath it and nearer, is Vinegar Hill, and beyond again are the Wicklow Mountains and Tarah Hill. To the west is Brandon – and the four counties may be seen from this point – the rock nearer is Carrickburn, and more southerly is Slieve-kielter, or the shorn mountain. A little further on – and passing Pole Hore – we reach Glynn, a district broken by innumerable rivulets into glens and vales bordered by luxuriant wood, which in old times was famous for the lordly sports of hunting and hawking. Further on is Carrigmenan, the ancient and beautiful demesne of the family of Devereux.

A mile or two further still and we reach the pretty and prosperous town of Enniscorthy and at a distance of nine or ten miles – and still on the banks of the Slaney, where it borders upon

Carlow – the beautifully situated town of Newtown Barry. But we ourselves have nearly reached the limits to which we reluctantly confine ourselves in our description of the county of Wexford.

However, we may not part from Enniscorthy without some notice of the far-famed Vinegar Hill. In the dark year of 1798 the rebels had possession of it for several days during the early part of June, and here, having previously committed great atrocities in Enniscorthy, the most deliberate and cold blooded of the murders were perpetrated. The hill immediately overlooks the town and is of considerable height and extent, and the windmill, the ruined walls of which are still there, stood upon its summit. This mill they crowded with their prisoners, dragging them out occasionally for massacre.

The towns north of Enniscorthy are Ferns and Gorey. Ferns, although now dwindled into insignificance, was formerly a place of note. The diocese is said to have been founded by St Edin or St Mogue in AD 598, and a beautifully wrought monument to the memory of the founder occupies a niche in the present cathedral, which is a modern structure.

There are but few other remains of antiquity in the neighbourhood. We noticed however an ancient cross which bears the marks of extreme age, let into a wall that encloses the churchyard, and which is, in all probability, coeval with the foundation of the see. These crosses, as will be supposed, abound in all the old graveyards, and some of them are elaborately and beautifully carved, and the labour bestowed upon them would cost an immense sum at the present day. The custom is still kept up and crosses of plain wood are to be found in number wherever the dead are interred. Another relic, a font of very rude workmanship, lies among the broken gravestones.

The city of Ferns consists of a few poor houses, containing little more than five hundred inhabitants. It is built on the side of a hill, at the summit of which stand the ruins of an ancient castle which formerly ranked among the most famous in all Ireland, and may still be classed among the more interesting military edifices in the kingdom.

ENNISCORTHY,
WEXFORD

From Ferns to the borders of the county the road ceases to be picturesque, but a few miles from Gorey we enter the county of Wicklow, the northern boundary of Wexford.

The great feature of this county is its peculiarly English character. This is apparent not only in its external aspect – the skilfully farmed fields, the comparatively comfortable cottages, the barns attached to every farm, the well-trimmed hedge-rows, the neat gardens stocked with vegetables other than potatoes, and the acres of beans. The peasantry are better clad than we have seen them in any other county of Ireland, and have an air of sturdy independence, an independence which they really feel and to which they are justly entitled, for they owe it to their own honest industry; they rarely owe any debt to their landlord except 'good-will' and an arrear of rent is a thing seldom heard of. They are, in general, proud of their English descent, their ancient names and their advanced civilisation.

The county of Wexford cannot be termed mountainous, although it is enclosed by mountains which form a magnificent screen to it, and in savage times completely severed it from the rest of the kingdom, for these were covered with woods, and were strongholds of the Irish septs, so that, for nearly two centuries, Wexford could not send members to Parliament.

Its only great river is the Slaney, which has its source in the barony of Talbotstown in the Wicklow Mountains, and which, receiving the Banna and the Boro as tributaries on its course, enters St George's Channel at the Bay of Wexford, and is navigable for large boats only to Enniscorthy.

The county is divided into eight baronies; Fort, Bargy, Ballaghkeen, Bantry, Gorey, Scarawalsh, Shelburne and Shelmalier.

Its boundaries are, on the north, the county of Wicklow, on the west, Carlow and Kilkenny and Waterford Harbour, on the south, the Atlantic Ocean, and on the east, St George's Channel.

Chapter Nine

QUEEN'S COUNTY

Although the Queen's County is by no means among the least interesting of the Irish counties, it possesses no feature of a distinguishing character and we shall therefore be enabled to dismiss it briefly – for we are reminded of the necessity of compressing in cases where compression may be admitted, in order that we may enlarge where greater space is requisite or desirable.

The county is formed out of the extensive tracts of Leix and Ossory, the conquest of which was not accomplished by the Anglo-Normans until long after the neighbouring districts had submitted to their sway. It received its modern appellation in compliment to Queen Mary in the fifth year of her reign.

The capital town of the county is Maryborough. It is a place of little note, but distant from it about four miles is one of the most striking and interesting objects in the kingdom – the rock of Dun-a-mase. The ruins of a castle stand upon a solitary rock in the centre of a fertile plain, occupying nearly the whole of it from the base to the summit. Although from its great natural strength the castle would seem impregnable, except to the 'giants' who, we were told, leaped into it from a far distant hill, leaving the impression of their feet 'in the solid rock', the castle was taken and retaken several times by the 'ferocious Irish' and the English invaders, their brave, but merciless enemies.

It would appear that some rude fortification existed on the spot from the earliest period, and perhaps in no other part of the kingdom is there a place so completely formed by nature either for a stronghold of the aggressor or a refuge for the oppressed. It commands an uninterrupted view of the country to an almost inconceivable extent, being seen from a distance of nearly twenty miles in every direction all around it. On all sides but one an ascent is impossible, and although it may be approached from the east, even that is a task of some difficulty – as we found in our efforts to reach the top on a more than usually sultry day of summer – but in truth, the scaler's toil is well repaid, and the view is to the highest degree magnificent.

There are ruins of numerous other castles in the county, and among the most remarkable are those of Lea, at Portarlington and Stradbally, of which the ruins are now scarcely discernible, and the history of which is intimately associated with the Wars of the Pale.

Of the ruins of ecclesiastical structures, of which this county contains some of considerable beauty, the most interesting is that of Aghadoe, the ancient seat of the see of Ossory, which was founded by St Canice in the sixth century.

The principal towns of the county are Portarlington, Mountrath, Abbey-Leix and Mount-Melick – the latter being a Quaker town and remarkable for its neatness and the air of prospering industry that pervades it.

The county is generally flat; its rivers are not numerous, with the Barrow being navigable only from Portarlington to the sea at Waterford. It contains an undue proportion of bog, large tracts of which are, however, richly cultivated and its principal wealth arises from the labours of the agriculturist, although the manufacture of serges and stuffs is carried on to a limited extent in the vicinity of some of the towns.

The Queen's County is an inland county, bounded on the east by Kildare and Carlow, on the north by the King's County, on the west by the King's County and Tipperary, and on the south by Carlow and Kilkenny.

The baronies are nine in number: Ballyadams, Cullinagh, Maryborough East and West, Portnehinch, Slievemarque, Stradbally, Tinnehinch and Upper Ossory.

Chapter Ten

KING'S COUNTY

The King's County, like the Queen's County, is without any peculiar characteristic and may be described briefly. It received its comparatively modern appellation in compliment to Philip of Spain, the consort of Queen Mary.

The King's County abounds in the ruins of old castles, one of the most striking of which is Garry Castle. It stands beside the road leading from Birr to Banagher, and was the ancient fortalice of the MacCoghlans.

We visited the King's County in one of the canal boats which run from Dublin to Shannon harbour, passing through the Bog of Allen for nearly the whole distance of, perhaps, eighty miles. The boat is called a fly-boat; it is composed of iron and is drawn by two or three horses and proceeds at the rate of nine English miles an hour. The country is very flat and there are comparatively few locks and fifteen miles of the journey was made without encountering one. It is however by no means a pleasant mode of travelling, for the boat is exceedingly narrow and the passengers are painfully cramped and confined.

The bog commences at Robertstown in the county of Kildare, twenty miles from Dublin, and continues with little interruption to Shannon harbour. In the midst of this bog are the two principal towns of the county – Philipstown, the former capital, and Tullamore, the present one. They are by no means remarkable either for cleanliness or character and after visiting both one might quote, without incurring a charge of bad taste, the old rhyme:

Great bog of Allen swallow down
That odious heap call'd Philipstown,

SEVEN CHURCHES OF CLONMACNOIS

(ON THE SHANNON.)

And if thy maw can swallow more,
Pray take – and welcome – Tullamore.

The passage through the bog of Allen, although dreary and monotonous, is by no means without interest, and as the recurrence of locks enables the passenger to walk on land occasionally, the voyage will amply repay curiosity.

The aspect that surrounds him on all sides is very singular: huge clumps or stacks of turf border the canal, and here and there a cabin rears its roof a few feet away above the surface from which it can scarcely be distinguished. It is hardly possible to imagine more wretched hovels than those which the turf-cutter inhabits.

The man usually rents from two to five acres and the turf he cuts with his own hands and conveys to market as best he can. When settling, his first care is to procure shelter from the wind and rain, and he therefore selects a dry bank a little beyond the influence of the flood. Here, he digs a pit – for it is nothing more – places at the corners a few sticks of bog-wood, and covers the top with flakes of heath, leaving a small aperture to let out the smoke. Yet the inhabitants of this miserable district, existing in this deplorable manner, are by no means unhealthy, and around their huts we saw some of the finest children we have seen in Ireland.

There can be no doubt that, in ancient times, this huge tract of country was one immense forest, although its remains are less numerous here than elsewhere, the turf for the most part being peat with a little admixture of wood – a circumstance which can be accounted for by the fact that, in consequence of the many difficulties of drainage, the cutters seldom work far beneath the surface. Many attempts have been made to drain it, some with partial success, and those areas which border the canal have, in several places, been converted into good arable land. When internal peace in Ireland has been followed by prosperity, the expenditure of capital will certainly convert this immense waste, which contributes so little to the national wealth, into fertile and productive fields.

The western parts of the King's County, where it is bordered by the mighty Shannon, are infinitely more picturesque than those we have been describing which lie to the north and south, or rather occupy the centre of the county. On the banks of the Shannon, and also adjacent to a branch of the 'Bog' are the interesting ruins of Clonmacnois, the school where the nobility of Connaught had their children educated, and which was therefore called *Cluan-mac-nois,* 'the secluded recess of the sons of nobles'.

In ancient times it was also a famous cemetery of the Irish kings, and for many centuries it has continued to be a favourite burial place, with the popular belief enduring to this day that all persons interred there pass immediately from earth to heaven.

The abbey is said to have been founded by St Kieran about the middle of the sixth century, and soon became 'amazingly enriched' so that 'its landed property was so great and the number of cells and monasteries subjected to it so numerous that almost half of Ireland was said to be within the bounds of Clonmacnois'.

The ruins retain marks of exceeding splendour, and in the immediate vicinity are the ruins of two round towers.

The boundaries of King's County are, Kildare on the east, Meath and Westmeath on the north, the river Shannon on the west, which separates it from Roscommon and Galway, and part of Tipperary, and on the south the Queen's County.

Its baronies are eleven: Ballyboy, Ballybrit, Ballycowen, Clonlosh, Coolestown, Eglish, Garrycastle, Geashill, Kilcoursey Lower and Upper, Philipstown, and Warrenstown.

APPENDIX

The following stories from Hall's Ireland are presented exactly as they first appeared in the original work and, as such, their phonetic rendering of the Irish accent of the time may appear as quaint and curious. It is worth pointing out that this is how English as spoken by an Irish native would have sounded to foreign ears in the middle of the last century.

I

Our attention was some time ago directed to a very aged woman and a young girl sitting beside the wall of a half-roofed cabin. The aged crone appeared to be bent double by age; she clasped in her hand a long rough stick, which she used as a divining rod for the discovery of 'spring water'. The girl – who was remarkably handsome – was evidently watching until the oracle found voice, for it was sufficiently apparent that the consultation was one of no ordinary moment. A friend, who was our companion, knew the girl, and addressed her; she was prompt with a reply.

'I stood at her door with the rising sun,' she said, 'to know who charmed away the cow's milk, that my mother paid her to find out; and to know also about a little matther of my own – that ain't much; and sorra a thing she did but eat her breakfast and come out into the sun, like the butterflies, and I tending on her.'

And why do you not come another day?

'What! And leave my luck? Which would be all as one as turning it. Och! Sure that would never do. Maybe she'll spake at the change of the day, there'd be something in that!'

Our friend knew well the subject that had brought two such unsuitable associates together: the one was a famous dabbler in the 'hidden art'; the other was a rustic jilt as well as a rustic beauty. Our friend – who had the care of the village dispensary – easily divined the designs of the girl, and he communicated to us the secret of her purpose in telling the following anecdote of the last lover she had trifled with.

A smart lad – Aby Arnold his name – had called upon him a short time previously, with the startling request, 'Doctor, I'm come to ye, sir, to ask ye to raise my breast-bone off my heart where it's troubling me, doctor dear.'

It is a common idea that in cases of trouble the breast-bone sinks and presses against the heart. The doctor never attempts to reason with a patient under such peculiar conditions; but by complying with his whims saves time, and relieves the sufferer.

'Very well, Aby, and shall I do it with a knife?'

'No, doctor dear, iv you plaze, with a hot glass sir; and iv you plaze, iv that doesn't do – bedad, ye must turn my heart's blood the other way, sir, for its bating and boiling it do be, and all on account of that Kate Cleary, and ould Nanny Lacey for her adviser; that's the way I'm in, you see, and a dimness afore my eyes doctor, whenever she's in my sight, and every drop ov blood in my body out of it in my head, and it's then my breast-bone presses hard and fast into my very heart. So, doctor, you'll raise it, iv you plaze.'

The operation was performed to the patient's satisfaction by a cupping-glass; and the doctor hoped that Aby had chosen another love, as he had not seen him for some days. One morning, however, upon the doctor's entering the surgery – there stood Aby.

'It's worse than ever, sir, on me; bedad it is. I'm sure she's given me something not right, for sport; I'm sure she has. See doctor, I was altogether another man, quite a gay fellow until late yesterday evening. You know Barney Gallagher; well, when I went into the dance-house, what should I see but her covering the buckle and heel on toe on the flure opposite him, and he, the ugly frosty-faced thief, flinging and rattling like murder. Well, whin I looked on the shine of her hair, and the shine of her eyes – you would not b'lieve it, but it's thruth I'm tellin ye – my breast-bone wint down upon my heart, worse than ever! and staid there! Ah, yarra! It never rose since; and doctor, sir, if ye can't give me something to make her *uneasy*, the Lord love ye, and take her charrum off me. Sure I was obligated to lave the dance-house with the wakeness she put on me; and then to see her and that flattering deceiver coming out together for a breath of fresh air, and she having the impudence to ask me "how I felt"; and such a skit of a laugh upon her purty mouth – bad luck to it – the Lord forgive me, but sure it's hard for me to be wastin' into my grave for a slip of a girl like that.

'So, doctor, if ye'd bleed me this turn, may be that some of the charrum would come away with the blood; and, anyhow, I know one that can punish her with it, so, iv you plaze, you raise it again for me.'

The doctor did not argue with the man, for he knew that if he did he would immediately go to some 'wise man or woman' and so lose both his time and money; but he forthwith complied with his request. Several weeks elapsed and Aby did not return; but at last one morning he made his appearance with a basket of eggs.

'Long life and success to yer honour, doctor, dear, and it's fine health I have sir, praised be the Lord and yer honour – that's finished it, yer honour – Kate Cleary missed the boy she was afther, and thought to put the comether of her shining hair and her shining eyes on me, no later than last night; but sure a little colleen-das, little brown-eyed Shelah Nevil, that I'm under a promise to next Monday for the priest to spake the words, she was with me, and though I felt my blood going a little faster – and asthray like – sorra a taste of harrum it done me; and "Good evenin' to you Miss Cleary," says I; and "I'll be happy of the pleasure of seein' you at my place," says Shelah; and the craythur hadn't power to say more, on account of the blushes; and so doctor, dear, I'm cured now, and hope the eggs will prove fresh; and sure if I know any boys with the same ailment, I'll recommend them to yer honour.'

II

There is little more in this story than a development of the strength and durability of female affection – proof of reckless daring on one hand, and pure devotedness on the other.

Old Jacob Bobenezer had commenced with that rigid discipline towards his daughter Rachel which he imagined would fortify her against all the Irish Whiteboys that ever galloped beneath the moonlight; and, moreover, every Sabbath day he invited to his table a young man, in whose sober manners, discreet conduct, and great worldymindness he exceedingly rejoiced. Adam Switzer, the only son of his most esteemed friend, had, upon being told by his father that Rachel would be a fitting bride for him in every respect, resolved to marry her; and her father contemplated the fast-growing crops, the plentiful increase, the well-fed kine of the Switzers, as if they had already been added to his stock. Rachel did not smile nor frown upon the youth: if she had done either, there might have been hopes that his suit would prosper; but of all things, indifference is the most fatal to love. Young Adam did not know this – or if he did, he did not heed it.

How Rachel became acquainted with James Hennessey is not upon record; they never frequented the same places of worship or of amusement. James was known to be a fierce and restless fellow, full of those wild notions of liberty which eventually render a man either a hero or a slave; he was of a good but sinking family, handsome, and better educated than most young men of his time and station. Of all the youths in the neighbourhood, he was the most frequently spoken of in terms of strong disapprobation by the Bobenezers and the Switzers.

'Any news to-day, good Adam?' the wife would inquire; 'for truly Jacob grows so deaf that he hears but little, and Rachel and I never visit but amongst our own people.'

'Nothing,' Adam would answer, 'but that James Hennessey grows worse than ever; he told a magistrate of his own people that he lied!'

'Oh! To a burgomaster!' exclaimed the old lady.

'Perhaps it was true,' suggested the maiden.

'And even if it was! – but such a thing could not be true. I wonder you do not see how impossible it must be, Rachel,' continued the dame.

'It would be a great blessing if he were out of the country,' said Adam; 'he turns the heads of the men and the hearts of the women.'

'I do not see what that is to thee,' answered the dame, 'as long as thy own head is steady, and this maiden's heart is true.'

Rachel looked one way, and Adam another, but neither seemed pleased.

That very night, beneath the waning beams of the harvest moon, the Palatine girl was weeping on the shoulder of James Hennessey – weeping as if her heart would break – weeping, not loudly, for her grief was heavy-hearted, so that its demonstration could hardly make way. She had met him that night, and too often before, in her own bower, over the trellis of which the aged hands of her father had trained woodbine and roses, that she might sew, and spin, and knit, and read her bible in the free and fragrant air – there she had frequently met her lover, and listened to the deep and passionate declarations of an affection which, to do him justice, he really felt.

'I daren't come again into the valley, darling of my heart, my own cushla machree! It would be as much as my life is worth. I daren't do it, by night or day,' he continued; 'the storm may blow over, as storms have done before, or as people say they do, forgetting what they rive and wrack in their passing; and if it does, why, Rachel, I'll ask you boldly from your father, and if he refuse, we must take the leave he will not give; if the storm does not pass, why then, mavourneen, I must leave the country, that's all.'

'And I with you – I with you,' said Rachel, suddenly changing from the calm, cold, patient girl, to the wildly enthusiastic and devoted woman; 'I will never leave you, James; the greater the shame, the harder the fate; but the more truly will I cleave to you.'

James Hennessey was indeed, as the country people express it, 'on his keeping'; his connection with Whiteboyism had become notorious, and he could no longer walk abroad with impunity; he was a marked man among the marked – for he was well known to possess the hardy daring, and the rude but powerful eloquence that enters at once into, and masters, Irish hearts.

Rachel clung to the hope that brighter times would come. She could not comprehend why her father would oppose her union with James when he was made aware how (according to her belief) the youth was maligned and persecuted. She had often implored him to tell the truth to the Palatine; but James knew better than the girl, the horror that such a man as Jacob must feel at the idea of his child being the wife of a proscribed outlaw – for so in reality he was. He therefore trusted to his own influences over the affectionate creature who had so confidingly launched her heart upon a stormy and perilous sea; and well he might have trusted one so pure and so devoted. After many vows and little consideration, Rachel agreed to meet her lover under the ash-tree amid the ruins of Carrig-o-Gunnel the next Sunday, at midnight; he could know, he said, by that time whether it was likely he should be obliged to leave the country altogether; or, if his former errors were overlooked or forgotten, he swore to the weeping girl that he would enter upon a new life, and become anything, everything she desired. With men like James Hennessey, such resolutions are broken almost before they are fully expressed.

'I wish, Jacob,' said Rachel's mother to her husband, on the following morning, 'I wish you would come into our child's room; it is near ten of the clock, and she is still sleeping. I do not like to wake her, but she is so disturbed, that I cannot bear to look on her. She is little more than half undressed, her arms tossed over the coverlet, and her beautiful hair clings in heavy wreaths to her damp brow.'

The Palatine moved, with a lighter tread than was his wont, to the door, through which his worthy wife had passed; she pointed to their child, while the old man lingered on the threshold, gazing with a troubled countenance upon his fair daughter. 'Leave her alone,' said the confiding father, 'leave her alone; even now her head has fallen from her pillow upon the bible that was half-placed beneath it – the child tarried too long at her prayers.' If Rachel could have but heard the words, how bitter would have been the reproaches of her conscience!

The next Sabbath brought her common-place lover, and even he observed that 'the maid Rachel seemed disturbed'. She had received in the morning from the hand of a mountain-boy a feather from a wild bird's wing – 'Sich birdeens,' said the urchin, 'fly far but remember where they build their nests.'

Rachel had not forgotten. She did not, however, meditate a far flight, for she took nothing with her, save the national cloak of their Irish serving girl, and enfolding herself in its ample screen, she threaded her way across the meadows which lay between her dwelling and the Rock of the Candle. She was a fearless girl, and yet many things contributed, that night, to make her shudder, despite her confiding love. She knew she was doing wrong, and, as she flew past the gloomy spots that tradition had invested with a peculiar or fearful interest, she paused and trembled every now and then; the ruins of the magnificent rock loomed in the distance, and frowned in mysterious grandeur over the moonlit meadows. At last, panting and breathless, she achieved the trysting-tree, and stood with her hands clasped over her panting bosom beneath its shadow; the breeze sighing through the leaves, the rustle of the rabbit as it cropped the clover, the beating of the bat's wings upon the air, the heavy whirr of the broad-faced owl – even the half murmured bleat of a kid, as it nestled more closely to its mother's side, increased her fears; nor was it until she was clasped in her lover's arms, and felt his warm breath upon her cheek, that she again forgot all the world in him. Whatever were his plans, he had not time to develop them – for the rolling first of one stone, then of another, down the ravine, told James Hennessey that footsteps unaccustomed to the rocky passes were approaching.

In an instant, before she had time to remonstrate, or even to ask why or how, James had lifted her in his arms, and passed with her into the depths of one of the caves known only to the disaffected. It was the action of an instant; and the girl brought up with so much care, and in so much piety, was clinging to the most daring of the

Whiteboys, in the midst of twelve or fourteen fellows, as daring and more desperate than he. She heard the sharp, quick click of their pistols, and was nearly suffocated by the smell of the ardent spirits that stimulated them to so much evil; the light of one bogwood torch, shaded as it was, was sufficient to show her the glitter of pikes, and the more horrid expressions of fiend-like faces that glared upon her; suddenly, even this light was extinguished, and James murmured she 'was safe', for she was with him. Rude and harsh words were exchanged in whispers, which the firm authority of Hennessey suppressed. Rachel heard the heavy tramp of a strong man near her; it was the tread but of one man – yet what child does not recognise a parent's footstep? A horrid conviction that her father had tracked her flight came upon her; for a moment she could not speak, but at last terror lest any harm might come to him forced a word or two from her clammy lips.

'Stand here!' muttered Hennessey, 'if you cling to me I cannot save him, if it be he. Rachel, his life will answer for this rashness, for he cannot live and we be discovered.' Still, although fainting, she clung feebly to her lover: the footsteps passed away, but the girl was roused from her insensibility by a voice calling her sternly and heavily by name, far above where she lay.

'Rachel! – my child! – Rachel!' She felt that James had quitted her, and she struggled in the darkness with those who would have held her back; it was a faint struggle – a feeble girl against strong-armed men.

'Father, I am here,' she cried, but her tones were weak – a pause – and then came a distant rush, and blows, desperate and determined. 'They won't fire if they can help it,' said one fellow to another, in the same suppressed tone. She heard no more; utterly exhausted, she lost all consciousness, not did she revive until aroused by the rapid motion of a horse, and again a well-known voice whispered, 'Darling mavourneen, you are safe with me.'

Several months had elapsed after this occurrence; the old Palatine's garden bore a neglected aspect; the trees were untrimmed, the path overgrown with weeds; a light gleamed without its walls, for the night was dark; and through one or two apertures in the window the glimmer of a candle flickered over the flower bed that had been Rachel's. Within sat the Palatine and his wife; his hair was now white, his fingers lean and dwindled; his eyes were weak and dim as he bent over his bible – but the eyes of his wife were fixed on him. 'We have heard God's word again and again,' he said, 'and we must be comforted. It was a memorable mercy on that night no blood was shed, though mine was thirsted for; do not look so sad, wife – God is a wise God.'

'I do not look sad,' she answered, 'for you are with me Jacob; but when I realise that you will not be so long – if –'

There was a slight knocking at the door.

'Who's there?' inquired the Palatine. The sound was repeated.

'Friends know it is not safe to open doors to a tongueless man,' he answered; and then came a reply that sent him staggering against the wall, while his wife, with a speed that marred her intention, endeavoured to undo the fastening. At last, Rachel crawled, rather than walked, to her father's feet; but he would not look upon her: she then took refuge on her mother's bosom, who parted the hair upon her brow, while large, heavy tears dropped like hail upon the wasted features of her child.

'I have you here for ever now,' said the poor woman; 'here you will remain – no one will rive a crushed and faded flower – for ever now.'

'For one hour,' answered Rachel, 'for one hour and then I quit you, my mother, for a long, long time. Mother, in heaven's sight I declare I had no thought of leaving you that night; and he saved my father's life, and will carry to the grave the mark he received in defending it.'

Her mother declared she should not leave her.

'Let her go to her keeper,' said the old man, sternly.

But Rachel arose and answered, 'Father, before the day was done, he was my husband; he has worked me no wrong, for the choice was my own; and I am thankful to bear shame with him, if it can lighten his heavy load. Mother, you would have done as much for my father.'

'There is a curse, strong as well as deep, that sooner or later will overwhelm the children of disobedience,' said her father bitterly.

'I know it – I believe it – I feel it – but even so, I submit.'

'The time will come,' continued the old man, 'sooner or later – the time will come, when he in whom you trusted will fail you in your uttermost need; when he will pour into the core of your breaking heart the poison you gave your parents. Oh, what fools are those who put faith in their own children! He will spurn you and desert you.'

'He may do so,' she replied, weeping, 'he may do so; but I will never desert him.'

'Jacob,' interposed his aged wife, 'Jacob, our child – she – given to our prayers after long months of expectation – she says she has but one hour to stay with us; do not let it pass thus. She is still our child, Jacob; but one hour to stay,' repeated the mother, wringing her hands, 'but one hour!'

'Not an hour now,' said Rachel, 'not much more than half; you, Mother, will listen to me; people spoke falsehoods of him, decoyed away he was: but he is not what they say; they will not hear him, will not pardon him; if he remained in Ireland, he must be as he is, outlawed and wretched. He has yielded to my prayers; and in a foreign land, where we are going, he may still be what the Almighty intended he should be – great and good; he gave me one hour to bid you farewell, to pray for your forgiveness; only one hour, and the minutes are flying by while I speak.'

'Will he come for you?' inquired her father.

'Oh no, he cannot, he dare not venture here, nor would the others let him,' she replied.

The old man rose steadily from his seat, and before either mother or daughter was aware of his intention, he had seized Rachel in his iron grip. 'As the lord liveth,' he exclaimed, 'you go not hence; I will bind you to the horns of the altar; I will not suffer even a tainted sheep of the true fold to become the prey of the ravening wolf: here you remain; vain will be your cries for aid; all vain: here will I stand; and whoever enters shall have the recompense he comes for, who would rob an old man of his child.'

Rachel implored, conjured, entreated, wept; even her mother's tears were added to hers; but all in vain. The Palatine shouldered one of the heavy muskets of his own country; and paced backwards and forwards, opposite to where he had bound his child with cords which her mother dared not loosen. His eyes scowled upon the unhappy girl, while ever and anon he muttered between his clenched teeth such texts of Scripture as seemed to him to bear hardest upon her case – threats against disobedient children and denouncements against the associates of the ungodly. When the first gleams of morning broke through the crevice of the window, Rachel spoke again.

'If harm come to my husband, his blood be upon your head!' It seemed after that as if a portion of her father's sternness had entered into her gentle nature. She would neither taste food nor drink; but sat with clasped hands, and eyes turned towards the mountains, the sun-lit tops of which were seen through the latticed window.

'She will die, she will die,' said her mother.

'Pray God she may,' was the father's harsh reply, 'that I may lay her in the grave and then be gathered to my fathers.'

She did not die; but a desperate and very dangerous fever came to her relief, for it took away her mind from present thoughts; weeks and months elapsed ere she was able to sit at the cottage door. But the lapse of time had wrought changes in many ways: the country was more tranquil; and people said that since James Hennessey had disappeared matters were become altogether different. The Palatine relaxed but little of his severity, except that, thinking himself secure in Rachel's weakness, he suffered her mother to move her from place to place in her arms. She took no interest in anything. Nothing amused, nothing drew from her a word or even a look of intelligence. All blessed her as they passed along the road, and the little children used to heap her lap with wild flowers. Her mother reconciled herself to the violence with which her husband had practised when she found that no letter, no token arrived from James; that he had gone into exile was certain – but had he forgotten Rachel?

Months rolled into years; two years had passed and Rachel was still the same. Usually the Palatine preserved the most rigid silence towards his daughter, but sometimes he would give vent to bitter feelings, and reproach her in strong language; it was all the same, her features remained unmoved, and she seldom shed tears. Once, indeed, when they were alone, and her mother wept over her, she desired her to be comforted, as she should be happy yet.

People wondered how she lived, how anything so heartbroken could remain so long in a torturing world.

One morning she told her mother she would lie down; and her father at the noonday dinner, looking into the room (where he had once been deceived), laid his hand upon her shoulder, as if to assure himself that she was there 'in the flesh'. Suddenly she opened her eyes, and raising her head, kissed his cheek; he was so unprepared for the act that he had no time for consideration, and, as if by instinct, a blessing fell from his lips. When her mother came to her with some food, she said, 'Father has blessed me at last; you do so too, then let me sleep.'

When the evening meal was prepared, and her mother again sought her, she was gone; if the neighbours had seen her, they stoutly denied it, and declared that she was spirited away by the 'good people'. The old Palatine traversed the country like one demented, bending his way at last to the ruins of Carrig-o-Gunnel, not with any distinct hope of finding her there, but from the natural desire of seeking in every possible and impossible place for a thing cherished and lost.

There, under the ash-tree, he saw his child, her head reclining against its trunk; he called to her, in a voice tremulous from an emotion he would fain have suppressed; it was vain; he fell on his knees by her side; he turned her face towards him; the cheek upon which he had impressed the kiss of returning affection was cold, her heart had ceased to beat, her eyes to weep for ever! Then, indeed, the strong pent-up current of parental love, that had been so long congealed within his bosom, burst forth. He wept as only strong men weep; he lifted up his voice, exclaiming like the Royal Poet-Prophet of old – 'Oh, Rachel, my child! My child! Would that I had died for thee!'

People say that the spirit of the Palatine girl wanders amid the ruins of the Rock of the Candle to this day; and there are few bold enough to approach the ash-tree after night-fall. 'But sure, your honours,' said our guide, when he had closed the story, the leading points of which we have preserved, 'a spirit so good as hers could harm no living mortal.'

III

An itinerant apple-dealer was applying to the magistrate for 'justice against a jackeen*', who had given her some cause for complaint.

'If yer honour plazes to hear me,' she said, curtseying respectfully; 'if yer honour's so good as to hear me, and let me tell mee story – just from the beginning to the end – and not mind the jackeen that murdered me, yer reverence will understand the rights of it from a poor heart-broken widdy woman with nine soft childer as good as my own, for two of them's my sister's – God be good to her in her grave.'

Having opened her case, addressed a few words of the 'mother's language' to the baby in her arms, and warned two imps at her feet 'to mind their manners, or his worship would put them in the law', she hitched up her cloak on one shoulder, tucked a few of her straggling locks under a wide mob-cap, and rubbing the back of her hand once or twice across her lips, curtseyed, and began again.

'My name, plaze yer honour, is what I go by, Mary Brady – I mean that's not what I go by, though it's my name – there's some call me Poll, and more "College Poll", because I do be about the University betimes; and twice seven years I've been in the beautiful city, and never was forenint yer honour, or any of yer sort (glory be to God for all his mercies!) but twice – counting this one as nothing – and the other time, sure it was on account of the flaking poor Dan gave me, and the murder of his own lawful babby, which he marked for life through the whiskey. Hould up

* unemployed layabout.

yer face, littly Danny, my man, and let his reverence see "daddy's mark" on ye, my child! – God help ye, he spiled yer beauty anyhow. Well sure, we little know what's good for us,' she added wiping a genuine tear from her worn eye; 'as long as my back was sore with the flaking, I was mad enough with him; but now – wouldn't I say, "Flake away, my jewil, and welcome", so I had you once out of the cowld dirty grave – and love heals all blows. It's little ye thought, Dan darling, yer lawful wife would have to be cheated and insulted by nothing but a bit of a jackeen!'

'Not cheated, if ye come to that, Poll,' was the faded looking young man's comment; 'not cheated – and if yer worship will listen to me–'

'Listen to you!' repeated Poll. 'His honour listen to you! Bedad, it's sowld I'd be altogether if you war to begin on yer justification. My lord, the tongue ov him would coax King William off his stand, if he could hear it – that it would! Indeed, his honour is too much of a gintleman to listen to a word out of yer curly head; sure it's justice he's there for, and ain't I a poor widdy of a plaintiff, with no-one to spake for me?'

In vain the magistrate endeavoured to bring her to the point – an attempt on such occasions seldom successfully made. At last she seemed inclined to proceed a little faster.

'Yer honour's in a hurry, and I'd be sorry to inconvenience ye; but there's many of the college-boys, born gintlemen, would be here to-day, to stand for me. "But," says I, "no," I says, "I can trust to his noble justice," I says, "bould as a lion and bright as a star, that won't let the fatherless and the widdy be put upon by a Dublin jackeen."'

'Well, but what has he done to you?'

'Is it done to me? – Oh, then, by Saint Patrick, everything he could; in one day – last Friday – God bless it, he had five oranges and three apples ov me, and promised to pay me the next day. Well, the next day I met him, and axed him for the money. "The oranges war sour," he says (that was only one of his lies, saving yer presence); "but I'll pay you like a man," he says, and offers me a glass on it – it was such a cold morning. Well, I laid down my basket, and left Jimmy and Johny, these two innocent childer, to watch it, because, though sometimes obligated to go into such a place meeself just for a drop to keep the wakeness off my heart, I'de scorn to bring up mee childer in low company.

'Well, in I goes, in all innocence, and he takes a glass, and I a taste, and while I was turning the babby in my arms, to give it a drain to keep the cowld out, he whips off like a flash o' lightning, and laves me, God help me, to pay for it. Well, you know, that wasn't all, but he makes off with my pipe and tabaccy, as good as what cost me a bender, barring one smoke, out of the basket from the little boys, and a new handkercher.'

'Oh, Poll!' exclaimed the defendant, 'the handkerchief was my own – my name's on it – oh, honour and decency, Poll!'

'That's no proff, yer lordship; his name's on many a thing he has no call to.'

'Have ye done now, my good woman?' sighed the exhausted magistrate.

'Plaze yer honour, noble gintleman, I am as good as done, anyhow.'

'And now, what have you to say for yourself?' he inquired of the threadbare defendant, who managed to get as far away as possible from his fair accuser, and had occupied himself with running his finger round his stock in search of a collar, and then running the whole five into what Poll had aptly termed his 'curly head'.

'Sure, it isn't misdoubting my word, yer lordship would be?' inquired the widdy, bridling and jolting the peevish infant a little higher on her arm; 'sorra a word but the bare truth I've told ye, and where's the good o' wasting time with him?'

'What! You want to have it all to yourself, I suppose?' said the patient dispenser of the law, and repeating his question to the man, added an inquiry as to 'what he was'. It was then that College Poll burst forth into a torrent that stunned the court; holding forth her arm at its full stretch, she swept the cloak that had fallen from her shoulder to her side with the other hand, thus leaving her right arm free for the illustration of her eloquence:

'Plaze yer worship,' she commenced with a satiric smile, 'I'd be sorry to see a modest young man like himself wid a blush on his cheek; so I'll tell ye what he is. He had for his mother a half-lady, who'd spend her husband's week's wages on a feather for her bonnet, coax the holes in her stockings under heel, and pull down the bill in her windy with "lodgings to let", whenever a visitor turned the corner; he had a father, whose blood was so thick you could cut it with a blunt knife, and who hung like a cobweb at a government office whin they were plinty, until it dropped off; and at last took to his relations until they dropped off too; and then, out of rivings to those who owed him nothing, he advertised for the nearest relations to Ned Murphy, late living in Aungier Street, who would hear of something to his advantage by applying at 7, Liffey Street, at twelve o'clock the next day; and sure enough above twinty came, and, dying as he was, he had himself lifted to the windy to see how eager those who had refused him another sixpence, and denied their own blood, would hurry to make what they could out of his bones! The windy was pushed up, and findin' himself too wake to speak to them, he threw the last drop of whisky he had down his throat, and died.'

The unfortunate offspring of such parents had wound his features into a smirk expressive of derision during the painting of this extraordinary picture; but his lips quivered as it was concluded. Nature moved within him, as it does more or less to the last hour of existence in every human being.

'Sure I ought to know it!' she added, after pausing a moment for breath; 'wasn't I helping to mind him, for God's sake, at the same time? What he is – why, there he is! A half-sire he was – sometimes dipping his rod in the wather, sometimes poaching, sometimes hanging afther the heels of anyone who wanted a turn done too dirty for themselves to do; and all because he was too fine for a trade, and too poor in board and breed for a gentleman! And afther awhile, grown in everything but the Lord's grace, he's fixed as a low jackeen for the rest of his days – scorned by the rich – hated by the poor, hard-working, industrious, God-fearing craythurs like meeself – the first to twist a knocker, break a window or a lamp, or rob one who (and let him deny it if he can) often took the bit of bread or half-potato out of mee own mouth to give it to him – just because of a wakeness not to see the child I lifted out of the measles, when his mother died, lost intirely. And, oh, ye poor brainless spalpeen, to think of yer sarving me such a thrick at the end!'

'Oh then,' said the magistrate, 'after all, you are old acquaintances?'

'Yer worship may say that! Havn't I often washed his bits of rags to send him decent to the Park or Zoologies of a Sunday, because he had no friend but ould Poll, and pledged my basket for a new shirt-collar! The Lord gave him his wits to live by, and the divil stole them from him, and left him enough to be wicked, but not enough to hide his wickedness: there's too many of his sort, but not half as many as there used to be!

'Ah, you dirty snake!' quoth Poll, shaking her fist at the fellow, while a relenting aspect stole over her features; 'I could forgive ye anything but the tabaccy, and laving one who often did you a good turn in pledge in such a disgraceful place.'

'Do you mean to swear he stole the tobacco?' inquired the magistrate, whose patience was nearly gone.

'Is it swear agin him! Faix I won't; but I'll trust to yer honour to see me right; that's what I'll do. I'm asier now, the Lord be praised, since I gave him the weight of my tongue.'

IV

It was with anything but a pleasant feeling that we entered the ruined windmill; and when we stood within its walls, we found we were not alone; a stern-looking man, whose long grey hair played around his bald uncovered head, was walking round and round the walls inside, somewhat in the way of a wild animal, caged, pacing about its den. He paused and looked at us; we felt that he was there from some higher motive than mere curiosity, and turned to withdraw.

'Don't, don't,' he said; 'I'm long enough in it – quite long enough – God knows!'

He went out, and a few moments after we saw him moving rapidly backward and forward over the top of the hill, in the same half-unconscious manner. He was dressed like a farmer of the better class. At last he sat down, rested his elbows on his knees, and covered his face with his hands so as to shut out the scene altogether. We were about to descend the hill, when a very old gentleman of our party, who had known the country for more than fifty years, fancying he recognised the stranger, whose peculiar manner and appearance had attracted our attention, walked up and laid his hand upon his shoulder, calling him by a name. It was alarming to witness the effect the action produced: he started up – looked earnestly in his face.

'Good Lord of mercy,' he exclaimed, 'who is it that knows me? Below there in the town, nobody bid "God speed me!" The old inn is filled with new faces; and yet it seems but yesterday that I stood where we all stand now. I'm free long ago to walk through my own country wherever I please to set my foot; but God help us – sure isn't it Master Ned I'm speaking with! Oh then, dear sir, but the change has come over you very soon. I ask your pardon, but I should not have known you at your own hall door! You're not like the same Master Ned I tended duck shooting over the slobs; you took the cares of the world early upon yourself – and the young mistress – your honour's handsome bride.'

Our old friend's wife had been dead more than twelve years, but his love was alive as ever, and the exile noted his changed countenance.

'I'm sorry for your trouble – I didn't think she could have died so soon; sure that can't be her daughter; she's like, but older than her mother – there's nothing so handsome as it used to be. Ah, but I ought to mind how sudden death comes! Sure my father and my two fine brothers were alive, and yet buried like dogs in a few hours – buried in that glen. I could hardly bear to cross it a while ago, for fear of walking over their bones.' The poor man, deeply affected, passed his sleeve several times across his brow, in the effort to hide his tears; at last, unable to conquer his emotion, he turned to the valley, and wringing his hands in bitter anguish of heart, repeated, 'Oh, that day, that day.'

After a while he continued. 'I couldn't rest any longer away from the place, for I know I'm dying, and I thought I'd like to lay my bones under the sod of my native land; and somehow I thought I'd care more about the people here than I do; but I can't steady my mind upon anything present; only keep going back, going back, until my eyes see everyone dead long ago. Two or three to whom I've talked think my head's not right; may be so; God knows best.' There was a melancholy cadence in his voice when he said this that was very touching; and the stern expression of his strongly-marked features relaxed into almost childish weakness.

'I was,' he continued, 'as you know, Master Ned, forced to fly – though six years younger than your honour – a mere boy, hardly able to shoot a crow; not but I was ready and willing to do my best; I'll not deny that. My father brought his three sons – all he had – to the cause. His three sons and his heart's blood.'

It was next to impossible to imagine the man who said this, the same who, a few moments before, had confessed his brain was turned. He was, he told us, standing beside his father in yon gap when he fell, and as he stepped forward to take his place, his eldest brother said, 'It's my turn, not yours,' and then he stood beside his eldest brother, as he had stood beside his father; he looked across the valley, and it was smoking with blood and fire; just one minute he took his eyes off his brother, and when he turned there was no-one there; he was lying a corpse on his father's body.

'Then,' he continued, while his eyes gleamed and the summer wind tossed his grey hair about, 'then I stood in the gap myself, proud of their death, and longing to meet such another; but the second boy forced his way and pushed me aside – he was my mother's darling – and though he had a better right there than I had, being older, I strove to get on the spot, for death was over it; but he would not give in. The soldiers came on, and he fell.

'I never knew how I escaped, until I found myself at my mother's door. She asked first for my father, and I told her the truth; then for John, that was the eldest. I saw she dreaded asking after her *white-haired boy* – her darling darling! – and no tears came to her eyes, only she stood erect as a spirit before me in the moonlight, and at last she laid her hands on me and looked straight in my face.

'Mother,' I said, 'I stood in the gap beside my father, and beside John, and beside him, and I would have taken his place, but he would not let me!' She made no cry nor moan, but fell flat on the grass. I raised her in my arms – the mother that bore me – for she was a small, delicate woman; and I ran down with her to a brook that used to come welling up out of the earth, and laid her beside it, and bathed her face, and called to her; but she did not hear me, and my grief was greater about her than about those I had lost on the hill; and while I was there, along with my dead mother (for she was dead), I heard a shout and a tramp. Where I carried her was beside a shroud of bushes that had gathered over and about the well, not two hundred yards from the house, yet overhung in such a way that nothing could be seen of the water from the house. I heard, as I tell you now, Master Ned, the tramp and shout, and I knew the soldiers had got sight of the house, and would be on us; so I took up my dead mother in my arms and crept with her into the heart of the bush, keeping the brambles from touching her, and trying, God help me, to warm her face in my bosom. I lay there while they fired the house; I heard their curses, and returned them in the depth and bitterness of my silence; I heard the crackling of the fire and the howls of our dog; the blaze made light the bush, and I could see the death-glaze in my mother's eyes. They found out the well when the burning ceased, and stabbed at the bushes when they passed, and yet I escaped, though they drank and washed in the stream.

'I stole away in the night, which darkened when the moon went down, and before the morning came in; but still I carried my mother with me: she seemed the last thing left to me in the whole world. I got into the wood yonder, and sheltered about two days, until, meeting one or two more, who were hunted like myself, we carried her into holy ground, and buried her in the silent night.'

V

Jack Casey was a prosperous and wealthy farmer, but his neighbours called him 'hard and honest', and certainly, whatever were his claims to the latter distinction, there could be no doubt as to his meriting the former. He had two daughters, Anty and Honor; the eldest, a cheerful, sunny-hearted creature, the youngest, a gentle, beautiful girl, four years younger. Anty had mirth and mischief enough in her composition to enliven half-a-dozen farms; she was the very consolation of her mother, who, by some unexplained obtuseness of female intellect, had never been able to discover her husband's weak points so as to turn them to domestic advantage. Though married to him for twenty years, the poor woman had only become thoroughly acquainted with his obstinate ones, which she unfortunately strengthened by opposition.

Anty, though afraid of her father, was the bird of his bosom – the peacemaker – the joy-giver – the harmony of the house, taking off the rough edges of unkindness by her sweet words and kindly manners, and being withal the gayest at the rustic dance, as well as the most devout at the parish chapel. Her nature was warm and enthusiastic, and her mother, doubtless remembering her own young days, importuned the Virgin with many a prayer to 'overlook' her beloved Anastasia, and keep her from trouble. The poor woman believed for a long time her prayers were answered; but it so happened that a young farmer of a neighbouring parish was so captivated by Anty, that he took every opportunity of meeting her whenever her father was absent, well-knowing that a sort of faction feud which had existed for many years between the Coynes of Ballyduff and the Caseys of Ballyran, of which each was a member, added to the impossibility of his telling down guinea for guinea with 'hard Jack Casey', would effectually prevent the old man's favouring the suit; he trusted, however, to time – and chance – and his 'luck' – the old man's love for his daughter – to all and everything in fact which lovers trust to, without looking closely to the future. To HOPE he trusted, believing it would do all for them both.

Anty did not care whether her lover was a Casey or a Coyne; she loved him with all the enthusiasm of a young warm heart, and without enquiring of herself why she did so. From her mother, hitherto, she had never had a secret, but she cherished a dangerous habit of evasion and concealment with her father, a habit which extreme sternness invariably originates, and the only person in her perfect confidence was her little sister, Honor. Still, the knowledge she was carrying on a clandestine courtship dampened her spirits; instead of her voice echoing through the house in merry laughter, her very footsteps descended upon the floor as though she would not have them heard. If this absence and care of manner was at all noticed, she would atone for it by a burst of merriment too boisterous to be natural even in an Irish woman, or break into some of those wild snatches of song so characteristic of a people whose feelings are easily excited.

One clear moonlit night, Anty met her lover at the old Tryst – a tree near to the holy well, under the shadow of which they had spent many hours together, talking over the various 'nothings' which time out of mind have made up the sum of lovers' 'somethings'.

'My heart misgives me, John,' she said, 'not so much on account of my father, for sure it wouldn't be possible to do anything with him – but my mother, John dear – my kind, gentle mother, that I never told a lie to about any but you – that's what's grieving me and making my heart heavy; and I'm thinking John dear, no blessing will be over us this way; and the last time I was with the priest, he told me as much; and that's another thing, it has kept me from my duty (confession) lately; and John agra, maybe it would be better we unsaid the words that –'

Her lover would not permit her to finish the sentence. 'Unsaid the words!' he repeated; 'do you mean, Anty Casey, that we should unsay the promise we made kneeling by that blessed well, to each other, in the sight of God, with his stars looking down upon us; haven't we the same hearts in our breasts, the same feelings towards each other? The Coynes and the Caseys are not further off than they were. At the very last fair day, though hurling Casey dragged his coat through the fair green, daring a Coyne to touch it, did I lift a finger to him? And for whose sake did I stand back, with the eyes of all my people on me, but for yours? And this is my thanks? Oh, Anty, I never thought it would come to this!' and he dashed himself passionately on the ground; while poor Anty, terrified at his vehemence, stood by trembling, not knowing how to appease his anger.

'John, dear, sure I hope for the best,' she said at last, while kneeling by his side, 'it was for the best, I spoke, only to unsay the words, until such time as I could tell my mother the truth, and maybe bring my father to rason; he's bitther intirely lately on account of Jim Coyne of the mill's boast, that you heard of, and that stirred up all the bad blood of the family. And my mother, that seldom takes part in anything, joined my father last night against every Coyne that ever broke the world's bread.'

'And you agreed with her,' again interrupted the impetuous young man, springing up, 'you know you did, Anty, or you would not be for unsaying the words; it's all because hardship has weighed heavy on the Coynes, while the Caseys have got up in the world; but I care no more than you.'

'But I do care John; God, he sees my heart, for its light to him; and he knows I would rather beg my bread with you through Ireland's ground this minute, than live in a palace with any other – and that's more,' she added turning away her face, upon which the moon shone brightly, as if ashamed of the confession – 'that's more almost than I ever dare own to myself before.'

Her lover pressed her to his bosom, and instead of 'unsaying the words', they repeated their vows of mutual affection, kneeling before the cross which some pilgrim had carved ages ago upon the south side of the well; and which was regarded with extreme veneration by the peasants – who mingle religion with the business of their lives; some call it superstition, and so it is, to a certain extent, but still it proceeds from a 'looking upwards' at all times and under all circumstances – a firm belief in the omnipotence and omnipresence of the Creator; and a trust in Him, which never fails them, is never shaken and seems to grow stronger the more they prove the instability of all worldly promises. And yet, when Anty returned home, her spirits were heavier than ever, and though her father was in excellent humour, she could hardly prevent tears from rising to, and overflowing her eyelids.

'Anty, mavourneen,' he said, 'put a brighter colour in yer cheek, and a finer polish on yer hair against this time tomorrow night – there's one will be here then that will be proud of ye, as well he may be – and you of him; Anty, a cushla, I'm not going to keep my daughters moulding at home; hould up yer heads girls, there's money bid for ye; the best in the counthry know there's something in Jack Casey's house besides smoke. Come, Honor, take the plate from yer sister, and get supper; we can't have her always, nor you either, little Honor, when yer time comes; a cushla macree, we'll have a bright house this time tomorrow, when Alick Cotter and his father's to the fore –'

'Anty, what ails you, agra!' inquired her mother. 'Anty, my jewel; Anty honey! – Oh, John, the life has left her; she's both cowld and heavy in my arms! Anty! Mother's blessing! Spake to me darlint!' Anty had fainted on her mother's bosom.

'What ails her?' inquired her father, sternly, when she had somewhat recovered, 'what ails her?'

'A wakeness came over her,' said Honor, trembling.

'I'll have no such wakeness come over my girls,' observed the old man, in a determined tone; 'I'm not going to give them what I earned by the labour of my hands and the sweat of my brow, unless they plaze me in the only thing I want them to plaze me in.'

'I want nothing from you, Father dear,' exclaimed Anty, falling at her father's feet; 'I ask nothing but to be let remain here, to slave for you and my mother to the day of my death, if you'll not ask me to marry Alick Cotter – that's all – but I'll die first – I'll never say the words for him before Priest or Bishop. Oh, Father, sure you'll never crush the heart of your poor Anty.'

A loud and angry scene followed, but Anty lacked courage to confess the truth: errors in domestic management acquire fearful strength as they grow – and the first harshness – the first equivocation – the first duplicity – if not stifled in its birth, is certain to produce a base and powerful progeny.

The farmer was not to be turned from his determination. The next evening Alexander and his father arrived at Ballyran, where all was made ready to receive them, and Anty, in obedience to commands she had not the power to dispute, moved silently about the house, more changed in her appearance within twenty-four hours, than if ten years of ordinary existence had passed over her head.

After supper, the two fathers sat at the table with the punch 'screeching hot' between them, arguing stock against stock, advantage against advantage, guinea against guinea; while the lover, not consulted in any way in the transaction, was left, as was supposed, to make the best progress he could in the affections of his intended bride; in accordance with this design, he seated himself by her side on the 'settle' which was close to a wall that projects in Irish cottages before the door, so as to form a sort of screen to protect those who sit round the fire from draughts. He addressed the poor girl in the rural jargon of prescribed love-making, while her mother and sister were busied about the house. She listened to all he said as one who heard not; but on his endeavouring to kiss her, she sprang from her seat, and, casting a look of horror and disgust on the perplexed youth, rushed from the room; while the fathers were so intent on their traffic as not to notice the occurrence. Alick was sufficiently astonished to remain with his eyes fixed on the fire for some minutes, and then endeavoured to keep himself awake by setting the cat and the dog to fight; a pastime they sometimes indulged in after the fashion of the master and mistress of the house, reversing, however, the finale, as the cat usually came off conqueror. This, however, was put an end to by 'the misthress' throwing a pitcher of water over the combatants; and, being informed by Honor that 'Anty was in the room above and would not come down,' the lover, imagining his duty ended, folded his arms, and fell asleep.

'And now, children,' said John Casey, rising at last, 'and now children, having settled this business to our entire satisfaction, it only remains for us to give ye our blessing and fix the day for his reverence to spake the words – but thunder and ages, Mr Cotter, why, yer boy's fast asleep – Mitty – Honor – where's Anty? – where's Anty, I say.' He continued furiously, stamping while Honor and her mother, after telling what they believed, that 'she was above in the room', shrank in affright before him, and young Cotter, roused at last, looked stupid and astonished, as sleepy-headed people do when suddenly awakened.

Anty was nowhere to be found; she had taken nothing with her – even her bonnet and cloak were in their accustomed places. Honor, as much terrified as her mother at her absence, flew towards the well, the trysting place, where she thought she might find her sister. She was followed by her father and young Cotter; it was a fine clear night, but the moon hardly showed above the horizon.

'Ye needn't run so fast, Honor,' said her father; 'I found only this morning who she had fixed her mind on, and the message she sent to one who I'd rather see a corpse at my feet than married to. And I fastened her pretty messenger in until this night was over, for he wouldn't tell me the rights of what she entrusted to him. No need to hurry, she'll be met at the well, but not by him she expected.'

'Here she is, Father, like a silver rod in the starlight; for the love of God, don't terrify the life out of her. Anty, I'm here,' shouted Honor.

'To disgrace her family this way,' muttered the old man between his clenched teeth, grasping his shillelah more tightly in his rigid hand, 'to disgrace me and mine.'

It would appear that Anty, not meeting her lover as she expected, saw who was coming, and knowing the stern violence of her father's nature, resolved, in a moment of desperation, that he should not overtake her. She flew like an antelope across the field.

'Father, Father,' cried Honor, in irrepressible agony, 'she's making for my aunt's house, and the foot-bridge is broke. Oh Father, the narrow stream is deep enough to drown ten men. Stand back Father, let me call.' And she did – but in vain; Anty unconsciously ran forward to her doom. They saw her on the very edge of the bank – and then she disappeared. Honor and the young man arrived almost together at the fatal spot; nor was old Cleary far behind; in an instant both men had plunged into the dark water, from the broken edge of the frail bridge, which they had often talked about repairing.

Once, while they were striving with the rapid stream, Honor saw, or fancied she saw, her sister far below where she stood. It might have been she, or the sudden brightness of the moon, she could not tell which. Had not her screams not brought help, and speedily, Casey would have shared his daughter's fate; Alick's arms were strong – and he was a good swimmer; he dived moreover, and well, but brought nothing from below save the broad leaves of the water lilies, which clung around him like a shroud. The next morning, the once light-hearted and joy-giving girl was found about three hundred yards from where the accident occurred, in a pool into which the eddy of the stream must have hurried her, even while the voices of her father and sister were ringing in her ears. There she lay – as if asleep – one hand grasping a bunch of rushes, the other tangled in her hair. In death she was even more beautiful than in life; and no-one who looked upon her ever forgot her; bitter were the lamentations at her untimely end. The most celebrated keener in the country composed a keen expressly for her, calling her 'The fair-haired girl of the clear stream', 'The white dove of the valley', 'The early blossom shaken from the branch by the north wind', 'The music of the waters', and other epithets equally gentle and endearing. Her young companions kissed her in her shroud, and her broken-hearted lover presented himself at her wake; and after pouring a torrent of bitter reproaches upon the grey-haired old man, demanded the privilege of carrying her head, ie walking under the head of her coffin to the grave. The Coynes mingled with the Caseys at this mournful funeral.

The people call the pool the Grave of the Maid or the Maiden's Grave to this day. The village boy will not ply his idle business of angling in its waters, but will cross himself, and pass on to another spot. Nor do the young men even now deem it lucky to meet their sweethearts under the shadow of the well-tree. Coyne emigrated after that, and a long, long time elapsed before the bereaved parents were observed to go about their usual occupations.

Time, however, though it does not obliterate, disperses sorrow.

2

Honor grew in status and in beauty, and the love of both father and mother twined closely, and more closely, round their surviving child.

'I'm thinking,' said the old man to his wife, 'I'm thinking – don't let the little colour that the throuble has left there quit your ould face intirely, agra, whenever I'm going to spake to ye; but I am thinking that Honor has more than a mind to take up with young Lawrence Coyne.'

'Lord save us!' muttered the old woman, laying down her knitting, and looking over her spectacles at her husband, while she trembled violently at what might follow.

'I'm sure of it; my ears hear nothing but her step and her voice, and the study of my life is to try and see into her heart' – he paused – 'if it is so,' he continued, 'and I know it is, I'll not put against it,' (his wife clasped her hands in silent thankfulness) 'and I'll never put against it, even if it broke my heart; though the spirit's going out of the factions, and the boys are forgetting their ould ways, and born foes are dying friends, still a Coyne's a Coyne, and a Casey's a Casey; but I'll not put against it, for the sake of the dead or the living; if Jack Casey's heart was hard, it has had enough to soften it; and you, my poor woman,' he added, with the touching emotion of a stern man, the more powerful from being so seldom excited, 'you have had enough to break yours, poor Mitty! You war young and handsome – so like HER when I had you first – and you bore that thrial without ever throwing one reproach in my face or meetin' me once, even once, with a cowld look, though I murthered your child!' The old man laid his furrowed brow upon the faded cheek of his loving wife, and their tears mingled together.

'It was her hard fortune, John dear; it was the will of God; and she's one of the bright angels long ago. I often think, and I lay awake in the night, I often think what a time it will be when we see her in glory! And she may be the angel sent by the Lord's goodness to give us the first insight into the ways of heaven! But don't give way, John, agra. Sure it was the will of God.'

'Not it,' he exclaimed starting up. 'It was the wilfulness of man that flew in God's face.'

'Whisht, whisht, alana machree, and don't be talking such wild words, that's enough to lift the roof off the house – it was the will of God, mavourneen, and that's my great comfort – His holy will be done!' and she covered her face with her hands and rocked herself backwards and forwards, while her husband paced up and down to subdue his emotion.

'Well,' he said at last, 'but about Honor. Lawrence isn't a bad lad for a Coyne, though he has nothing but his hands and his heart.'

'Many an Irish boy has made great way intirely in the world with no more.'

'I can't take what we got out of the world,' said the man, his old hardness dictating an apology for his present liberality.

'And if you could, dear, sure, it wouldn't be any use! There's a dale of differ betwixt the riches of earth and the riches of heaven.'

'You may tell Honor – that – she may ask Lawrence Coyne here – or do you do it; that will be better – he's a good boy, though a Coyne; one can't go past luck, and so – a Coyne must be in the family – that's sartin – his house can be mended with the thrifle she'll have at first, and in God's name, let him take home his bride – better he should take her home, than death, dear Mitty. We know that the ould man must part with his money – better his money than his child, you know; and they'll be convanient, not far from us in our ould age – there's no going past luck – a Coyne and a Casey in these times!' And so he muttered to himself, and walked up and down long after his wife had hastened to communicate the tidings to Honor, who could hardly believe it possible that the good news was true, and that she was at liberty to make her own choice.

In the early part of the next spring, a group was seen passing along the road leading from Ballyran to Ballyduff; the bride was 'bringing home' to her husband's house, followed by her aged parents and the blessings of her people.

VI

The most touching and sad, though interesting funeral we ever attended was at Mucross, during our recent visit. It was a damp and somewhat gloomy morning, and the waiter, who entered fully into our desire, told us, with evident pleasure, that 'we were in great luck, for two widows' sons were to be buried that day', adding, 'I'm sorry for their trouble, but sure it was before them; and as they could not get over it, and as you had the curiosity to see it, I'm glad they're to come today.'

We walked about a quarter of a mile away, as it were, from the Cloghreen entrance to Mucross, to arrive at the gate appropriated for the passage of the dead to their last homes. Long before we could see any portion of the crowd, we heard the *keen* swelling on the ear, now loud and tremulous, anon low and dying, dying away. Keening has fallen into disuse into this district; but the Kerry keen was more like what we imagine the wild wail of the Banshee to be, than a demonstration of human sorrow.

The body had been put in a plain coffin – what, in England, would be called a shell; and this was put upon a very common hearse, not unlike a four-post bed, drawn by an active, but miserable-looking horse. The widowed mother, shrouded in her blue cloak, sat beside the coffin; and when the keeners cried the loudest, she rocked her body to and fro, and clasped her hands, as if to mark the beatings of her stricken heart. Those who followed were evidently of the poorer class of artisans from the town of Killarney, and peasants of the neighbourhood; yet they were orderly and well-behaved – no drunken man disturbed the mournful ceremony. The humble grave was dug, not by any appointed sexton, but by a 'neighbour', and before it was half-finished, the other funeral we had been told of had filled another corner of the churchyard.

This one had no hired keeners, yet there was no lack of tears and sighs, and bitter wailings. To us it was a wild and singular scene. While the narrow and shallow graves were preparing, the mothers were crouching at the head of each coffin. The deep blue hoods completely concealed each countenance; and so alike in attitude was one to the other, that they could not have been distinguished apart. Groups of men and boys were scattered throughout the churchyard. In the distance a young girl was kneeling beside a grave; sometimes she wept, and then threw herself upon the greensward with every demonstration of agony.

Not heeding the crowd who waited patiently for the lowering of the coffins, two aged women were seated, midway between the two funeral parties, on a broad flat stone, intent on observing both, and they discoursed upon the departed.

'And which of the two widdy women do you pity most, Ally?'

'Och, and trot, by dis and by dat, I can't tell. Sure I saw Mary O'Sullivan's boy alive and well yesterday morning, an' he said – it was mighty quare – "Mother" he says to her, and he goin' out the door –'

'Did he turn back to say it, alana?' interrupted the first speaker.

'He did.'

'Inugh! Inugh! See that now. I wonder he hadn't better sinse than to turn back of a Saturday mornin'.'

'Mother,' says he, 'what a handful you'll have of white silver to-night, and I in work all the week!'

'God bless you, my darlint, Amin!' she answered, and then he came about and kissed her. Oh, wasn't she turned intirely from life, when, in less than an hour after, he was brought in a corpse and he her only comfort and help! I remember her a fine brave-looking woman, and see what she is now. Well, God look down upon us all!'

'Yarra! Amen – there's Betsey Doolan out there, showing her

bran-new shawl at a funeral! Well, the consate of some people! Do you know where the up funeral is from?'

'T'other side of Mangerton, they say – an only son too!'

'Oh, Peggy, you ain't in airnest, are ye?'

'Fait, it's as thrue as gospel, Ally! Or may I never light another pipe – two lone women's only sons: ain't it a sorrowful sight? But her boy was going off in a consumption this many a day: and sure that was some comfort to her, to have him left in the sight of her eyes, and left to do what she could for him till the last; that was some comfort. Holy Mary! Did ye hear that cry from Widdy O'Sullivan? What ails her? I –'

'Yah! They've got down on her husband's coffin, and she can't abide his bones being disturbed, and small blame to her; he was a decent man. Yah! yah! Hear to that screetch, it bates the head-keener of them all – the strength of the trouble of the widdy's heart was in it; poor craythur! The Lord above look down and comfort ye.'

'I wonder will any of the quality in Killarney look to her? It's a pity my Lady Kenmare's not in it; sure she looks to every poor craythur that wants. Oh, thin, sure the power of the blessings she resaves from the poor will carry her soul to heaven! It's a comfortable blanket I had from her last frost. May she have all her heart's delight to the end of her days.'

'Some people have grate luck,' said the other woman with a sneer; 'but by dis and by dat, I never made a poor mouth to the quality.'

'And the dickons thank ye for her perliteness, and the man that owns ye in constant work; not like a poor craythur such as me, who has no head, God help us, these ten years to think for the childer – only our own two hands to gather for them and ourselves the scrapings of the earth.'

At last we saw the coffin lowered but a little way beneath the turf, and the humble grave quickly filled. There was no priest of any description present, nor do the Catholic priests in general attend the humble funerals. This we think exceedingly improper; it is distinctly and positively his duty – a duty he owes to the poor as well as the rich; and yet the victim of sudden death had prayers, many and sincere, offered over his grave!

When the coffin was completely covered, and the friendly gravedigger threw down his spade, every person in the churchyard knelt down; the men covered their heads, the females clasped their hands; the very children crowded to the spot, and knelt silently and reverently under the canopy of heaven; there was no word spoken – no sentence uttered; the desolate widow even suppressed the sobbings of her broken heart; and thus the people remained prostrate, perhaps for several minutes. When they arose, the funeral howl broke forth afresh, in all its powerful and painful modulations.

The other funeral was soon over; the people from beyond the mountain exchanged greetings with those who dwelt in the town. After a little while, their immediate friends – for the poor are the friends of the poor – persuaded the widows to rise from the earth, and their tottering limbs were supported with the most tender care, while every epithet to soften and cheer was used towards them. Much that was said was in the native Irish, and of that we understood little; but it was impossible to mistake the eager looks and sympathising tears of many who were present.

It so happened that the two widows met when they were leaving the place, where their last earthly blessings were consigned to the earth. 'I'm very sorry for your trouble, my poor woman,' said the mountain widow to the townswoman.

'Thank ye, and kindly too; the Lord's hand is heavy on us both;' she replied, looking earnestly, and yet with an almost meaningless gaze on the widow who addressed her, and who was a much younger woman. 'Two only sons!' she added – 'they tell me, two only boys, yours and mine, and we to be left! But not for long. Tell me, mavourneen,' and she laid her hand on her arm, and peered into her face – 'did your boy die hard?'

'God be praised, he did not; he wasted away without any pain or trouble. Long summer days and winter nights I watched and prayed for him – my *gra* boy! But the Lord took him for the best, if I could only think so.' She paused to weep, while the people around her – some in Irish, some in English – exclaimed, 'God comfort her!' – 'the Lord look down on her!' – 'Holy Mary pity her!' 'Well, she has grate strength intirely.'

'The last breath left him,' she added, 'as easy as the down of the wild rush leaves its stem.'

'Then thank God always,' said the old woman – 'thank God that he did not die hard! The neighbours will tell you how I lost mine. He was alive yesterday; ay, he was as full of strength as the finest deer on Glena, and what is he now? Oh, but death was hard on him: I didn't know his face when I looked on it! Think of that, my poor woman, think of that; the mother that bore him didn't know his face! Oh, it's a fine thing to have an easy death, and time to make our souls. Holy Mary,' and she commenced repeating the litany to the Virgin with inconceivable rapidity, while her face wore the cadaverous hue of death, and her eyes gleamed like lamps in a sepulchre.

'She's turning light-headed,' said a man in the crowd. 'Get her home, Peggy, the trouble is too strong for her intirely.'

VII

Of the communications that have taken place between the fairies and the denizens of earth, we have heard many stories. One of the most remarkable of them we print.

There lived some years ago near Tramore, in the county Waterford, a man called, from his reputed intercourse with the invisible world and the situation of his dwelling, *Sheevra Enuic am Aithean*, ie 'the Fairy of the Hill of Furze'. This individual might be termed the Hibernian Swedenborg, for he asserted that his eyes had been opened to see the spiritual world, and that he held constant communication with it. Our informant (a man of intelligence and veracity) affirmed that he had often seen him in the fields gathering herbs (by means of which he wrought extraordinary cures), and that, while so engaged, he would suddenly fall to the ground, as if struck down by some invisible power, and at other times would stagger over and hither in the field, as if pulled about by invisible hands. On being questioned as to the cause of this he would reply, that it arose from the attempts of the fairies to prevent him from pulling the herbs, of whose virtues they had (as if by some necessity connected with their intercourse) informed him. He was also often known to rise from his bed in the night and go out – no-one knew where. On his return in the morning, he would inform his family that he had been summoned by the fairy host to accompany them on certain errands (the nature of which he would never disclose), and that, mounted on enchanted horses, he and his aerial companions would fly over the fields like 'the winged breeze' in execution of their mysterious commission, and clear in the course of the night a space of ground to which no steed of 'earthly mould' was adequate, bounding over in their course a very wide stream, to attempt crossing which, in ordinary circumstances, would be madness. On one of those excursions the seer, having remained away for several days, assigned as the reason for not returning at the usual hour, that at this time his phantom visitants placed him, not on a horse, but on a bullock; which, however, bounded away with equal speed, but on arriving at the wonted stream, the seer felt a momentary apprehension lest the unwieldy animal would not carry him safely over; but, to his astonishment, he cleared it in such admirable style that the seer, who had expected a ducking, broke the silence (which we should mention had been strictly enjoined and as strictly observed), and exclaimed, '*Taoir slan, a bhulean baun*!' ie 'We are safe, oh white bullock!' He had no sooner uttered these words, than the bullock, the horses and their riders all vanished into 'thin air', and the seer found himself alone by the margin of a stream in the midst of the Cumera Mountains.

VIII

The most remarkable quality possessed by the fairies is that of changing their own offspring for the offspring of mortal women –

and to this 'fact', a few years ago, every cabin in the south and west of Ireland could have furnished 'sure' testimony.

'There's not as many of them now as there used to be in ancient times,' said an old man, who had been introduced to us because of his knowledge of the 'good people'. He was a tall, thin, white-headed person, and would have been the beau-ideal for a patriarch, but for the merry twinkle in his clear blue eyes.

'My father used to see them now and again,' he continued, 'just about midsummer, or maybe in harvest; but my grandfather! Bless you – he was hand in glove with them all his life, and his own mother was away with them for five or six years, more or less – I can't be particular as to a month – and her sister had the eldest boy changed by them, through her own fault; for it's a foolish thing to go against the likes of them, or to make game of them, or dare them.

'She, poor thing, wouldn't put up a horse-shoe on the door post, or cross a plate of salt, or put a prayer-book under her pillow, or peel the seven rods of hazel in her first pain, or cut a notch in a black cat's tail, or pour a sup of sweet milk out of the pail when milking, or break a new potato on the hearth stone, or bite her baby's nails instead of cutting them, or toss the first lock of hay in haymaking, first in a cross, that is, first north then south, you see – criss-cross we call it – nor own that flies always light on a body for death, nor offer a cock to St Martin – not she!

'But I'll tell you what she'd do: she'd go wandering on a St John's Eve in the moonlight, she'd think no more of crossing a fairy ring betwixt twelve and three than of kissing her hand, she'd cross a stream without crossing herself, and carry a cat over it without a taste of dread coming over her. If she saw the very print of the "good people's" feet on the silver sand on the sea-shore, instead of saying, "Wave, wave, wash out!" she'd kick the marks into nothing with her ten toes. She was a fearless, careless devil of a girl; and sure enough, instead of the purty, soft-faced rosy child, that was the moral of its own people, she had a poor, puny, wish-wash brat put in its place, that was neither fit to live or die; everyone said it wasn't a right child at all, at all. Some wanted her to put it out on a hot shovel; others, to make egg-broth before it, that is, to boil egg-shells, and offer it the water they were boiled in for its dinner, which would make it speak at once; others, to keep its head under water for five-and-twenty minutes, when, if it was a right child, it would be drowned; if it was not, why it would be alive in the face of the country.

'But the sorra a thing she'd do that had any sense in it, only declare that the child was a right child enough when it would get sense and good advice; and, in spite of all they could say, she rolled the poor scrag of a craythur into her flannel petticoat, and strapping it on her back, put her cloak over all, and set off with it to Dublin to consult some fine doctor she heard tell of, that had a great name; and when her mother-in-law got her out of the house – maybe she didn't make an alteration in the place: she nailed horse-shoes to all the doors, and a fine one, of great virtue intirely, to the head of the bed-post; then she sent for a fairyman, and whatever he bid her do, she did; and the upshot of it was that everyone said, if the poor unbelieving craythur brought her fairy-boy back with her, he'd never be able to cross the threshold.

'Well, as sure as fate, after the woman was away as good as six months, home she comes, and the husband runs out to meet her; and "Stop" she cries, "don't set eyes on the babby until we're on our own floor; and let me show you what, through the grace of God, I've saved." They all looked at each other when she said this; and in two or three minutes she sets him down – as fine a poulter of a boy as ever came into the world – round and red, and rosy, with eyes the moral of a grandmother, and a fist the image of his father's, that could grip a shillelah with e'er a man in the Barony. As to the granny, she had like to lose her life with the joy, for she knew it was their own was in it.

'"And do you mean to tell me," she says to the mother, "that that's the child you took from this?"

'"God bless it," answered the poor blinded girl, "sure that it is, and no other. My own *bouchaleen* darlin' – the grace of God be about it! – my own, own darlin', that I carried when the cry of pain, and the whimper was never away from it night or day – my own! That after dying down like the flowers in winter, came out afresh, and that the great Dublin doctor wasn't above curing. A fairy boy they called you, did they, a *cushla machree*?"

'"Whist, whist!" says the granny, very sensibly, "that's enough about it;" for she knew that the child was returned crossing the threshold, and didn't care to say anything to vex the mother, who knew no better, only thought she was doing her best – God help her foolishness!'

IX

The old superstition of witchcraft is, or rather was, common among the peasantry. We remember some years ago talking to an old man on this subject, when we received from him the following statement:

'Well, God brake hard fortune before any woman's child, but parents have a dale to answer for! Sure, I said to the boy's mother myself, "Whatever you do," says I, "don't cut his nails before he's six months old," says I; "for if you do, as sure as the sun shines in the heavens, if he's a rich man he'll be a fiddler; if he's a poor one, he'll be a thief, and now God help us."

'Believe it? Why, haven't I the sight of my eyes for it, and what can go beyond that? Sure I tell you I was out thracking hares meeself, and I seen a fine puss of a thing hopping, hopping in the moonlight, and whacking her ears about, now up, now down, and winking her great eyes, and – "Here I go!" says I, and the thing was so close to me that she turned around and looked at me, and then bounced back, as well as to say "Do yer worst!", so I had the least grain in life of blessed powder left, and I put it in the gun – and bang at her! My jewel, the scritch she gave would frighten a regiment, and a mist like came betwixt me and her, and I seen her no more; but when the mist wint off, I saw blood on the spot where she had been, and I followed its track, and at last it led me – whist! whisper!' exclaimed our narrator, 'right up to Katey MacShane's door, and when I was at the threshold, I heerd a murnin' within, a great murnin' and groanin', and I opened up the door, and there she was herself sittin' quite content in the shape of a woman, and the black cat that was sittin' by her rose up on its back and spit at me; but I went on never heedin', and axed the ould woman how she was, and what ailed her.

'"Nothing," sis she.

'"What's that on the floor?" sis I.

'"Oh," she says, "I was cuttin' that billet o' wood," she says, "wid the reaping-hook," she says, "and I wounded myself in the leg," she says, "and that's drops of me precious blood," she says.

'Now wasn't that proof?'

'Of what?'

'Why, that she was the hare I shot to be sure, and took back her own form when it sooted her convaynience.'

X

One more story we select from our gatherings; it concerns a party who, having lived with the fairies, gave some account of their 'coort'.

In our youth we had once the privilege of being shown a woman who, it was believed, had really lived with the fairies for a number of years. She was then small, old, and decrepit, with remarkably light blue eyes, which, light as they were, had a wild wandering look about them, enough to convey an idea of much mystery to the superstitious, among whom she wandered.

Superstition is by no means, even now, confined to the lower class – the imaginative faculty is ever at work with high and low; and we know several fair ladies – highly born and highly bred – who would rather not see a winding sheet in the candle, and would turn pale at the ticking of the death-watch.

'Molly the Wise' – as she was called – never wanted for food or reception; but though the food was abundant, the reception was never a hearty one, for Molly was more feared than loved. She was rather an object of dread, for they imagined she knew all that passed; it was in vain the poor little, old thing denied this – they were certain of it, and if she persisted in her denial, they persisted in their assertion, declaring it was only her 'cuteness' that made her silent. Yet her presence was considered particularly 'lucky', and she was often forced to do what she would have avoided. She was always pleased to attend weddings and funerals, but she had no particular fancy for being dragged out of her bed to be in at a birth; it was no uncommon occurrence to send for the midwife and 'Molly the Wise' at the same time; and many a poor horse has felt the weight of the midwife on the pillion, while the good man, trusting to the strength of 'the baste's' back, made no scruple of lifting Molly up before, as you would a child, for Molly would not walk.

She hated everything belonging to the sea with a determined hatred, yet every new boat must first go to sea with 'Molly the Wise' to insure it against wreck.

Molly did not much like talking of 'when she was with the good people', yet she could be persuaded to do so occasionally, particularly if bribed by a 'quarter of tobacco' or an 'ounch of tay'; these were sure to draw forth her eloquence. She would crouch close into the capacious corner of a cottage chimney, like an old cat, her back hunched up, her arms clinging round her knees, upon which she rested her chin, and then, without fixing her eyes upon any one or any place, she would wander on in her story, which she told in a faint, low monotonous sort of wail. Sometimes her eyes would fix for a moment on a particular spot; and if they rested on any of the young ones who crowded round her, you were certain to see that person grow nervous and uncomfortable and fidgety, until he or she got another seat.

'The way of it,' she would say, 'you see, was this: it was when we lived by the Slaney – God bless it – near the Enniscorthy road, where the Fitzstevens' ould tower is, that was built by King John, and battered down by Oliver Cromwell; and my father and brothers would be always out in the little cobble, earning their bread; and there's a spot there, where, long ever ago, the people say a boy was drowned – drowned, oh yah!'

'And wasn't he drowned, Molly?'

'A yah – how innocent you are! – not he indeed! He was taken by the "good people", dear – it isn't all of them that have power to take through the wather – only when they make marriages with them other spirits that live among the things at the bottom of the many wathers, and then one helps the other – tit for tat, you see, yah! So I used to be, then, a *coleen das*, not all out fifteen, in the boat with them, sometimes minding one thing and sometimes another, with plenty of heart, that kept my eyes and my feet dancing the length of a summer day. And so, it was of a Midsummer's night, and we crossing over in the cobble just to be in time for the divarshun of the bonfires; and my father and my uncle, out of respect to the poor boy that was drowned in it, raised their oars as they passed over the place where he was lost, as every other Christian does in coorse; and if I had done what I ought to do (mind this, girls, for it's Molly the Wise that's talking to ye) – if I had done what I ought at the same time, no harm could have come to me; but I didn't, for instead of a prayer, or the sign of the cross, it was lilting a song I was; and my father and uncle paused just while the boat was gliding over the place, and they said they were looking at me that minute, and thinking how purty the moonlight was settling on my face, and the next I was gone! Oh, then it was themselves that took on, and the first they thought I was struggling at this side of the boat, and then at that; there was a sort of foam, like silver, and though the blue river was so clear that they could see down-a-down into it, they couldn't see me.'

'And where were you, Molly dear? – tell us that, tell us all about it.'

'Isn't it where I was? – why, then, is it a common informer ye're wanting to make of me? I'll tell you what's fittin' without questions. I was away then, in the knowledge of the whole country – every fool knows that – and I'm here now, and fools as ye are, ye understand that much any way, don't ye? Because if ye don't, there's no use in my talking to ye at all, at all.' So, of course, her audience immediately understood everything she desired.

'I was away with them for seven years and more, and they kept me night and day; and what I had most to do was to mind the childer, and dress the queen.'

'Oh, Molly, what sort of dress did you put on her?'

'What sort of dress? Why, ye don't suppose it's trusting to one sort of dress she'd be of a day; no, nor ten sometimes, when it's a coort she'd be houlding. One day she'd be dressed all in diamonds in the morning, and in spiders' webs in the evening; and indeed, like the rest of the quality, when she'd be full dressed, it's half naked she'd be, saving yer presence.'

'Molly, avick – is it green satin and gold she'd wear?'

'Ay.'

'And Molly, what would she do wid all the gold she has – would she ate it?'

'Ate it! Bedad no – she'd put it in her pocket, I suppose. But what foolish questions you do be asking! Oh, dear me, girls *agra*, when will ye get sense? Sure, it's like an earthly queen she is in her little ways, and all – only a *weeshy* thing – and full up of all kinds of love of divarshun; and faix I a'most danced the ten toes off myself, striving to plase herself and the childer!

'Oh, then, it's them that was the childer! Talk of edication! Bless ye, they were born larned; and it's never a wink of sleep they'd get at all in the night time, nor let any one else have, only dancing on the sands of the sea, or in a ring on the softest of grass, and then take to flying on rushes, which they turn into horses, and whisk through a latch-hole or a key-hole – hundreds of them. Many an hour I spent on a beam at a dance, and many a cheek I pinched, and many a kiss I spiled, and many a pail of milk and glass of scalding-hot whiskey punch I turned over, and many a shindy I caused in a fair – Ah, yah! soh! oh! – now he's down, hit him hard, there's no one to take his part.' And then she would shout, and clap her hands and grind her teeth, in a way that left no doubt as to the occasional malignity of her insane nature.

At other times, she would describe the fairies as the most benevolent 'little craythurs' in the world, and lament bitterly that she had ever left them. 'I had,' she would say, while with them, 'white bread and fresh butter, and cruddy cream and beautiful flowers, and loads of sweet-hearts, and everything but the grace of God.'

And the manner of her getting away was this:

'The spirits' and 'the fairies' are always having feuds together, and both have strong factions; sometimes one faction beats, and sometimes another, but the spirits being the 'most God-fearing' have the best 'luck'. And one night she was by herself, the queen having gone upon some 'divarshun'. And she was very lonesome, and began thinking of her own people and her own country, and how she never had the power to say so much as a *Pater* or an *Ave* since she came into the place; and how she had no chance at all of her soul being saved, for whenever she turned her thoughts to prayer, she fell off in a sleep. And all this came over her, and as it did she dropped down on her knees to strive and pray; and the very minute she did this, who should come to her but her own uncle who had been in the boat the night she was taken, and who had been dead four years! And so he gave her a blessed herb, and as she had it in her fingers, back came the queen and all her 'coort' like a flash o' lightning. And as they did, the queen made a grab at the herb, and her uncle, who was fading away before her eyes, said 'Pray'; and the holy power was given to her, and she did pray at once, and as she did, where should she find herself but back at the door of her father's house! And he wasn't in it, but in his grave – only a week, and no grass on it yet. So she sat on the loose clay of his new-made grave, and told him all; and then she went back to the house, and there was no flax on the wheel, nor turf in the rick, nor potato in the garden. Nothing – only a wild swallow with its young in a hole in the wall; and her heart was near bursting, but she kept it whole; and she'd tried to get back to the 'good people', for the world was hard, and she had no friends; but still, if she went back, she'd have no power to pray, and what would become of her soul?

TIME AFTER TIME

Molly Keane

Bestselling author of Booker Prize runner-up
GOOD BEHAVIOUR

The ageing, one-eyed Jasper Swift and his three grotesque, elderly sisters, April, May and Baby June, have been waging quiet guerilla warfare against one another for years. They live together in damp, decaying Durraghglass, the country estate left to them all by darling Mummie.

Then, suddenly, their long-lost cousin returns from Vienna. Exotic Leda, whom Daddy had been so funny about all those years ago; and within days, the uneasy existence of the Swifts has been dramatically overturned, when desires, dormant for so long, flame fierce and bright as ever . . .

Poignant and hilarious, controlled yet outrageous, TIME AFTER TIME brilliantly captures the graceless setting of the sun on the eccentric Anglo-Irish aristocracy, emulating the classic comedy of Molly Keane's acclaimed novel GOOD BEHAVIOUR.

'Vivid and graceful . . . it is a joy to read.' *Spectator.*
'Sharp, deadly and irresistibly funny.' *Daily Telegraph.*
'The pleasure in grotesqueries is as gleeful as ever.' *Observer.*

FICTION 0 349 12076 5 £2.95

SILVER'S CITY

Maurice Leitch

Winner of the 1981 Whitbread Prize

It is a desolate city, a ruined landscape carved into sectors by slogan-covered walls, barbed wire barricades and khaki checkpoints. Ten years ago when Silver was put away for firing the first historic shot in the bloody sectarian war, Belfast was bitter and brutal. But violent as it was, it was still a real city, a city a man could rule. It was Silver's city.

Silver is a hero, his name a household name spelled out on gabled walls and carved forever in the unforgiving chronicles of the Loyalist movement. Sprung from behind the wire by the cold, professional new breed of gunmen, Silver is thrown into an utterly changed city ruled by assassins who kill not for the cause but for the thrill of killing. Silver turns against the tide of blood he loosed on Belfast, but it is a city ruled by mercenaries – it is no longer Silver's city.

Fiction 0 349 12179 6 £2.50

HALL'S IRELAND

MR & MRS HALL'S TOUR OF 1840

EDITED BY

Michael Scott

VOLUME 2

SPHERE BOOKS LIMITED

London and Sydney

First published in Great Britain by
Hall, Virtue, and Co., 1841 in three volumes
Condensed edition published by Sphere Books Ltd 1984
30–32 Gray's Inn Road, London WC1X 8JL

Set in Bembo

Printed and bound in Great Britain by
Cox & Wyman Ltd, Reading

CONTENTS

LIST OF ILLUSTRATIONS

IRELAND
0 10 20 30 40
(English miles)
NORTH CHANNEL
Ballycastle
Londonderry
LONDONDERRY
ANTRIM
DONEGAL
Larne
Strabane
Carrickfergus
Bangor
Donegal
Belfast
Antrim
Donaghadee
TYRONE
L. Neagh
Ballyshannon
Donegal Bay
Lisburn
Enniskillen
Strangford
Sligo Bay
FERMANAGH
Armagh
ARMAGH
DOWN
Downpatrick
Sligo
Monaghan
Ballina
SLIGO
MONAGHAN
Newry
Belturbet
Dundalk
Cavan
MAYO
LEITRIM
Boyle
Carrick-on-Shannon
CAVAN
IRISH SEA
Castlebar
LOUTH
Longford
ROSCOMMON
Drogheda
Roscommon
LONGFORD
Navan
MEATH
L. Mask
Tuam
Mullingar
Trim
Clifden
L. Carrib
WESTMEATH
Athlone
Howth
GALWAY
Maynooth
Galway
Leixlip
Dublin
Dublin Bay
DUBLIN
KINGS COUNTY
Galway Bay
KILDARE
Bray
Enniskerry
QUEENS COUNTY
Kildare
Glandalough
ATLANTIC OCEAN
Wicklow
WICKLOW
CLARE
Ennis
Killaloe
Arklow
TIPPERARY
CARLOW
KILKENNY
River Shannon
LIMERICK
WEXFORD
Wexford Haven
WATERFORD
KERRY
Waterford Harbour
ST GEORGE'S CHANNEL
CORK
Bantry Bay
Cork Harbour

Chapter One

WICKLOW

To depict adequately half the delights of beautiful Wicklow would require a large and full volume. We must be content to stimulate the appetite of the tourist so that he may long for the rich banquet which nature has provided for him.

Wicklow is indeed the garden of Ireland; its prominent feature is, indeed, healthful and refreshing sublimity and wild grandeur. But among its high and bleak mountains there are numerous rich and fertile valleys, luxuriantly wooded and with the noblest of magnificent rivers running through them, forming, in their course, a number of cataracts. Its natural graces are enhanced in value because they are invariably encountered after the eye and mind have wearied of gazing upon rude and uncultivated districts covered with peat, upon the scanty herbage on which small sheep can scarcely find pasture.

The inducements to tour Wicklow are in fact very strong and numerous. A journey of twenty-four hours may place one in the centre of it – a journey by no means tedious, troublesome or costly. A railway carriage conveys one to Liverpool; the steam-boats – the largest, safest and best in the kingdom, which ply twice a day – take little more than ten hours to Dublin, and Dublin is within an hour's drive of the country. The charges are so low at all the inns on the route as to astonish strangers.

The chief attractions of Wicklow are its glens – splits, as it were, in the mountains through which the hill torrents have burst, with every one of them falling repeatedly from immense heights, often for a considerable space without encountering a single break. Down the sides of each, the perpetual dripping of moisture has nourished the growth of trees and undergrowth. Some of these glens, as in the Vale of Avoca, are valleys of miles in extent;

others, as in the Devil's Glen, are little more than graceful passages and in other cases, as in the Scalp, the cuts are barren and covered only by the debris that has fallen from above or has been shaken from the sides.

The natural graces have ample scope and time to fix themselves in memory, for, as we have intimated, they are situated in the midst of arid plains or utterly barren mountains, which is land that yields but little, and that reluctantly, to the industry and enterprise of the husbandsman.

The vicinity of the county of Wicklow to the Irish metropolis is of prodigious advantage to those who require occasional intercourse with nature, either as a means of relaxation or of enjoyment. And perhaps there are few crowded streets in the world so auspiciously situated, so immediately within reach of such a concourse of natural beauties. Consequently, numerous splendid mansions and cottages *ornées* have been built in happily chosen sites, and they are for the most part in the midst of foliage, and rarely or never mar the effect of the adjacent scenery.

The principal roads from Dublin into the county are: first, that to the east through Bray, Wicklow and Arklow; second, that to the west through Blessington on to Baltinglass; the great military road between and nearly parallel to both; and the Enniskerry road.

We shall conduct the tourist by the eastern routes, upon which lie several objects of attraction that he will have to visit; the one leading through Dundrum to Enniskerry and so on to Roundwood; and that which, passing through the Black Rock, enters the county at Bray. We shall leave unnoticed nearly the whole of the western district, through which there is but one road, a wild and cheerless one, bordering upon Kildare and Carlow. This region is comparatively barren of interest except to those who admire nature in a form that has been scarcely altered since the creation.

The two routes which we shall therefore more immediately refer to and more particularly describe, may be said to join at the entrance to the Vale of Avoca, where the waters – the Avonmore and the Avonbeg – have their meeting. The obvious plan of the tourist will be to proceed by the one and return by the other. This is the plan we will adopt, but we beseech the tourist to arrange matters so that he will not be compelled to rush through the valleys and race over the hills. A mile or two of wandering off the beaten track will often repay him largely. Let him make up his mind to loiter, for his idle time will not be idly spent.

We must not, however, mislead the tourist into the notion that a great expenditure of time is necessary to examine Wicklow. The whole of its leading attractions may be visited within three days – long summer days – but a week will amply suffice to introduce him to every one of its beauties. The most desirable mode of travelling is by one of the outside jaunting cars, changing both car and horse at several stages. Posting, however, is unreasonably high in Wicklow, being 10d a mile for the car and 1s 3d for a post-chaise – and the driver will expostulate if he receives for his fee less than 2d a mile.

By the Enniskerry road – we shall proceed by that – the county is entered at the Scalp, a chasm in the mountain which separates it from Dublin. The mountain appears to have been divided by some sudden shock of nature. The sides are not precipitous, although the ascent is difficult in consequence of the huge masses of granite that prevent the semblance of a path, and not unfrequently jut out so as to suggest the idea of exceeding danger. The road runs through these overhanging cliffs; enormous granite blocks of many tons in weight having been rolled back out of the path of the traveller. The sides are perfectly naked, and so similar are both in nature and appearance as to lead the spectator to imagine that the disruption has but recently occurred and that another earthquake might reunite them without leaving a fissure between.

The Scalp is eight miles from Dublin and two from Enniskerry. The reader will bear in mind that we are speaking of Irish miles, and that eleven Irish miles are equivalent to fourteen English.

The road from Enniskerry gradually slopes until the pretty little town, which is entered by a bridge over the river Kerry, is seen in a deep valley beneath, which is especially cheering to the eye after the rugged Scalp and the barren district through which the traveller has passed.

Before we proceed onwards we must direct the tourist to make a detour to the west, for in the hills of the barony of Rathdown are many objects of surpassing interest – among others the source of the Liffy, and the dark Lough Bray.

Lough Bray is situated in the centre of a peculiarly lonely district. The lake – or more correctly, the lakes, for there are two, the Upper and the Lower, with the Lower being the more remarkable and the one to which especial mention is made – is almost circular, near the summit of a mountain, from one side of which protrudes a huge crag, dark and bare, called the Eagle's Nest. It is walled in on three sides by lofty and precipitous hills and is open on the fourth at the lowest point, from which its waters are poured through a narrow opening into the valley of Glencree, forming the Glencree River, which, joining with the Glenislorane in Powerscourt demesne, passes through the Dargle and finally flows into the sea, under the name of the Bray River. The waters of Lough Bray are very deeply coloured by the peat which covers the surrounding hills, through which the water permeates, and the deep and gloomy tint is increased by the shadow into which the lake is thrown by the overhanging mountain to the south and west.

There is one object connected with Lough Bray that looks like the work of enchantment: the Swiss cottage and grounds belonging to Sir P Crampton, Bart, the surgeon-general. The cottage was erected for Sir Philip at the expense of his grace the Duke of Northumberland who, while Viceroy in Ireland, had spent some happy days with Sir Philip in this romantic spot, in a cottage of humbler pretensions which had occupied the site and which was accidentally burned.

The view, looking north from the road, a little way below the lake is most glorious. To the right the mountains of Douce and War stand out in bold relief; to the left the Kippure mountains; before us the valley of Glencree and the demesne of Powerscourt, and further on an apparently illimitable succession of hill and valley, wood and grove, town and village as far as the eye can reach.

Several miles further to the west – and more easily visited by the direct Blessington road from Dublin – is the solemn and dreary solitude out of which rushes the waterfall of Phoul-a-Phooka, which terminates in a whirlpool of unfathomed depth and where, it is said, the famous spirit horse holds its nightly revels, luring unhappy wayfarers into the frightful vortex formed by the waters of the cataract. Its summit is crossed by a bridge of a single arch, with a span of sixty-five feet.

Phoul-a-Phooka is the name given to a succession of cataracts one hundred and fifty feet in height and forty in breadth, over which the waters of the Liffy are precipitated. This river rises to the north-east in the Kippure mountains and here, at one bound, as it were, springs from the hills to the valley. The spectacle from the bridge is sublime to a degree; looking over one side we see only the river hurrying on to take its fearful leap, but on the opposite side we gaze down one hundred and fifty feet upon the foaming waters that have passed under us. The falls are seen to great advantage by passing the bridge and entering the grounds of Lord Miltown's side of the river which are planted and laid out in exceedingly good taste.

The tourist, after visiting Lough Bray, will have to return to Enniskerry and ascend a steep hill on which the village is built, to visit both the Dargle and Powerscourt – with the former to the left and the latter to the right of the main road to Roundwood.

The demesne of Powerscourt contains 1400 acres and there is a road to Roundwood through the whole of the demesne. Moreover, as the public road is cheerless and uninteresting, the tourist should pursue that – if he can. But it will be necessary for him to procure a written permission from the agent of Lord Powerscourt – otherwise he will find the gate at the extreme end closed against him. Pedestrians, however, will have no difficulty in obtaining an exit, and should undoubtedly take this course to Roundwood – but visit the Dargle first.

The far-famed Powerscourt waterfall is between two and three miles distant from the house, and is perhaps the most magnificent waterfall in the county of Wicklow. It is nearly perpendicular; its entire height being, it is said, about 300 feet, but it is only in winter or in very wet seasons that the water is precipitated the entire distance at a single bound, and then it seems an immense arch of foam. The cataract is formed by the Dargle – or Glenislorane – river, an obscure mountain stream which is part of the Douce mountain, from which it falls, making its way through the glen of the Dargle and meeting the sea at Bray, having been united in the Deer Park with the river Glencree.

The Dargle commences, as we have intimated, on the side opposite the gate to Powerscourt, but more correctly speaking the glen terminates here, the authorised entrance being through a gateway at the opposite end near the Bray road. Before treading the lonely path that leads through it, the tourist will do well to visit a small hillock just over Tinahinch and then to climb a steep hill that arises immediately above it on the south. As the Dargle is usually the first beauty of Wicklow to be introduced to visitors and, in consequence of its short distance from Dublin, many travellers examine no other portions of the county, the glen has attained greater celebrity than others which are more picturesque, magnificent and solemn.

Nearly in the centre of the glen is a large crag covered with herbage called the Lover's Leap; it hangs over the torrent and from this spot the best view of the valley is to be obtained. Yet for the glen of the Dargle to be estimated justly, it should be seen from one or both of the adjacent hills we have referred to. The first, which forms part of the demesne of Tinahinch, rises but a little above it, and is almost on a level with the topmost branches of the trees and near enough to the river for its subdued murmur to fall upon the ear. The view, although limited in extent, is of exceeding beauty. From the higher hill the prospect is infinitely extensive: immediately beneath us was the dark ravine – a line of trees let in, as it were, between the mountains, and these are surrounded on all sides but one, and here they are left open to the sea where, beyond Bray-Head, the island of Dalky gladdened the bosom of the old ocean. To our left was Powerscourt House, but the waterfall was hidden from us by an intervening hill. Nearer, and almost buried in a corner of the romantic dell, was Tinahinch with the smoke from the chimneys curling gracefully up the rocks and through the underwood, producing a singular effect, for it seemed as if a vapour were issuing from the clefts. This prospect reaches to the mountains above Dublin, and in an opposite direction the Paps and

THE DARGLE.

the Sugar-Loaf look down upon us as if they are the guardians of the glen.

The latter, with its peaked top, seemed to invite a visit, and we paid it. But in our mode of ascending the Sugar-Loaf we committed a serious error, against the danger of which we warn our readers. While overlooking the Dargle from a mole-heap – for in comparison to the giant mountain, it is little more – and ignorant that we must ascend 2000 feet above the valley, with the summit in our sight and without a guide to direct us, we imagined the straightest line to be the shortest at least, and so we took, in effect, the most rugged and difficult path, achieving our purpose at length, but only by a large sacrifice of time and labour.

We commenced our labour on the northern side, before which there is a small hill, like an outwork, and after we had surmounted this, the goal of our ambition was not a whit nearer to us, for between the lesser and greater Sugar-Loaf there intervenes a deep valley, from which the sides arise like walls down the one and up the other. We had therefore to climb with slow and toilsome steps until we arrived at the base of the conical hill that gives the mountain its name. The sides of this cone are covered with heath which grows from a surface of peat of variable depth, with huge masses of rock being scattered at intervals among it. Our way was lost and we were forced to follow the gullies or water courses as our guides. After a weary tramp, ankle-deep in bog, one of them conducted us to the summit. The top of the mountain, which from a distance appears so small and peaked, is a level space of several yards and is sheltered on the west side by a number of very large stones which are probably the remains of a Druidic temple.

And here we had evidence of the number of air currents and their different degrees of velocity at different heights. In the plain we had scarcely felt a breeze, but when near the summit the wind grew boisterous even to annoyance, and when we had reached the top it had assumed the character of a hurricane. The day was clear and the prospect was indeed magnificent – with the views being numerous, beautiful and varied.

We again return to the village of Enniskerry, where the tourist, if he will follow our steps, will find refreshment necessary, and he will then take the road to Roundwood, but verging to the right in order to visit Luggelaw.

This is a dreary and uninteresting road running nearly all the way through an arid and unproductive common. There are a few miserable hovels now and then skirting the wayside with wretched patches of shrivelled potatoes planted in bits of land, the forcing of which into comparative cultivation can scarcely recompense the very extreme poverty.

Within two miles of Roundwood a turn to the right leads for about three miles up the mountain, or more correctly up a long hill. The winding road is looked down upon on either side by the mountains that rise above it, with the Douce on the north and Ballinrush on the south. This road leads on to the great lion of the county – Luggelaw.

It was early morning when we commenced the ascent. The clouds were dense and heavy above and around us and our view was limited to the huge masses of granite that skirted our path, which were scattered among the slopes to our right and abundantly strewn among those to our left that led to the valley through which we heard the river rushing.

Suddenly we paused, for the mists were vanishing and almost with the rapidity of thought a most glorious and magnificent scene burst upon our sight. We beheld the whole of the beautiful vale, with Lough Tay immediately below us and, stretching to the east, the wild grandeur of Lough Dan connected by a long stream of white, and the broad river Killough that runs between them diminished by the distance almost to a thread.

Luggelaw or Lough Tay is a small dark lake in the midst of perpendicular mountains, utterly naked on one side, and richly clad on the other from base to summit with trees which have been nourished to a gigantic size.

Let no-one who visits Luggelaw leave without striving to make the acquaintance of Charley Carr, the guide, whose cottage is at the entrance to the domain. Charley is, of course, very jealous for the honour and glory of Luggelaw, and very envious of the superior attractions of Glendalough – which he abuses with a right good will, affirming that it is unnatural not to love nature better than ould stone and mortar, and at times he cannot conceal his anger at the holy saint – St Kevin – for not having carried out his intention of building his churches around Lough Tay.

From here we return to the main road and journey to the small town of Roundwood, but the pedestrian will seek it by a less easy though far pleasanter route – by walking four miles, crossing Lough Dan in a boat (which is always kept at hand for that purpose) and passing through one of the wildest of wild districts. If he be an angler, he will have an additional inducement to this course, for the ferryman throws a fly and carries his tackle with him, and Charley Carr is unrivalled as an auxiliary on such occasions.

The village of Togha, or Roundwood, is small and unimportant. It is, however, situated in the midst of mountains and the neighbouring scenery is remarkably grand. As it lies on the road to Glendalough by this route, and is usually the resting place of tourists to the Seven Churches, it is much frequented, more especially as the river Vantrey which runs by it is famous for an abundance of fine trout. The village is twenty-two miles from Dublin. There are two good inns at Roundwood – Heatley's and Murphy's – and we passed a day and a night at each of them and found them exceedingly clean and comfortable. The hostess at the latter was very kind and attentive, absolutely loading our car with cloaks and wrappers, for the rain was descending when we left her door.

At Heatley's Hotel we encountered an interesting person – a blind hostler. His meek, mild countenance attracted our notice. The morning was cloudy and, as he assisted in arranging our harness, we, ignorant of his privation, asked him if the day would be fine. He turned his face to the wind and, after keeping it upturned for nearly a minute, assured us that we would have both rain and sunshine.

'You'll have a fine day for Wicklow, for there will be more sunshine than rain, and I think tomorrow will be very fine, but I'm not certain.'

From Roundwood, passing the church of Derrylossery, we reached the village of Anamoe where the bridge crosses a river of the same name which flows from Lough Dan. The village consists of a few thatched houses, but its situation is highly picturesque, and in its immediate vicinity there still exists a ruined water-mill.

Passing the deserted and half-ruined barrack of Laragh, which is built in the midst of an arid common, with which its broken walls and desolate aspect are in keeping, we cross a small bridge and enter a narrow road that leads between the hills to the dark valley in which are the long and far-famed ruins of the Seven Churches of Glendalough.

The round tower first takes the eye, and as we advance the several points of interest, one after another, come in sight. It is impossible to imagine aught in nature more awefully grand than the lake in the midst of the mountains that surround it on all sides save the east. Except along the borders of the lower lake and on the heights that divide the mountains of Lugduff and Derrybawn not a tree is to be seen, and there is scarcely a shrub large enough to shelter a lamb – nothing, indeed, to humanise its utter loneliness. It is hard to fancy that a few centuries ago the now barren district was a huge forest – a den for wolves and a nest for outlaws – or that, in our own day, the lesser hills were covered with foliage.

We are first introduced to the ruins within about a mile of the 'city' on the road from Laragh Bridge, but on the opposite side of the river. The remains are those of a church which the peasantry call the monastery, but which is more correctly referred to as the Priory of St Saviour, and which is so marked on the ordnance map. It seems to have escaped the notice of travellers, although it is, beyond doubt, the most elaborately finished of the structures. Two of its round pillars still endure in a good state, one of them being nearly perfect and containing several sculptured ornaments, with the one which originated the legend of the dog and the serpent being very prominent. The ruin is overgrown with brambles and a flourishing mountain-ash has forced its way through a crevice in the wall.

The remains of another church, the Trinity, are also to be inspected before entering 'the city'.

'The city of Glendalough', a name which signifies the 'glen of the two lakes', owes its origin to St Kevin, by whom the abbey was founded early in the sixth century, and where he is believed to have died on 3rd June, AD 619, the anniversary of which is still commemorated by the peasantry who, until very recently, honoured the memory of the patron saint by assembling in the churchyard to drink and fight, but this custom was put to an end by the parish priest who, a few days before one of our visits, had actually turned the whiskey into a stream, gathered the shillelaghs into a huge bonfire and made wrathful and brutal men, who had been enemies for centuries, embrace each other in peace and good will over Kevin's grave.

Here, in this solitude, the saint laid the foundation of his monastic establishment. It grew rapidly, became a crowded city, a school for learning, a college for religion, a receptacle for holy men, a sanctuary for the oppressed, an asylum for the poor, a hospital for the sick, and here Kevin lived to superintend it for nearly a century, having, according to history, 'completed the uncommon and venerable age of one hundred and twenty years'.

The ruins are stated by the authorities to consist of the Priory, the Cathedral, St Kevin's Kitchen, Teampull-na-skellig, Our Lady's Church, the Rhefeart Church, and the Ivy Church, thus making the mystical number of seven, with the other sacred edifices appearing to be later constructions.

We had scarcely arrived within sight of the holy ground when our car was surrounded by a most vociferous group of all ages and sizes, each eagerly laying claim to the 'honour and glory' of being our guide. A brief scrutiny and a short examination ended in our retaining the services of George Wynder, a wild and picturesque-looking fellow, with loose drapery and a long beard, whom we at once ascertained to be 'a wit', for on asking him how he could accompany us with bare feet, he replied, 'Ah, these are the soles that never wear out, and one set of nails lasts for a life.'

So we engaged him, and a capital companion he was – and is – for he has inexhaustible humour, an exhaustless store of stories and is a poet in his way.

As second in command, we commissioned an infinitely more

sober and sedate personage, who will do very well when Wynder is away, for he has contrived to pick up most of his legends, and is cherishing the growth of his locks in humble imitation of his superior.

We set out on a voyage of discovery guided by these two, but with a concourse of followers, for, as there chanced to be no other visitors on that day, they could lose nothing by becoming volunteers.

We were first conducted over a bridge of planks laid upon gigantic 'pebbles' that crosses the Avonmore, the beautiful river whose source lies in the lake, and which runs, or rather rushes, through a fair country as far as the eye can look upon, 'meets' the waters in the Vale of Avoca, and joins the sea at Arklow.

The entrance to the city is through two Saxon arches, kept together by the embraces of ivy, and up a steep and narrow paved pathway, with a wall at either side enclosing the whole of the area in which the chief ruins are contained. We were led at once to St Kevin's Kitchen – its ancient name is lost – which is the most perfect of the churches, with its stone roof, its steeple, and a round tower in miniature, with its conical cap uninjured. Near it is a great round tower, with the usual number of seven windows, and a height of one hundred and ten feet; the cap fell to the ground in the year 1804. The Cathedral, the Abbey, or the Church of St Peter and Paul, Our Lady's Chapel, and the Ivy Church are also within this enclosure.

Among the superstitions of the churchyard is one common to other places – that any person buried here will inevitably be saved at the day of judgement, St Kevin having prayed that this privilege might be accorded to his favourite church. We were here shown the base of a cross, which weighs about 3 cwt, and the legend is that those who contrive to carry it between their teeth thrice round the ground without pausing to take breath will never afterwards have a toothache – this is one of Mr Wynder's stories to which he may, at least, attach credit.

The churches of Rhefeart and Teampull-na-skellig are some distance on the borders of the Upper Lake. With the exception of the kitchen, 'decay's defacing fingers' have been very busy with them. Traces of their natural beauty are nearly all but lost, and that of Rhefeart is a heap of stones, while Teampull-na-skellig can scarcely be distinguished from the rocks that surround it. The entrance to Our Lady's Church is composed of stones of immense size. We should point out that in this churchyard there are none of the finely sculptured crosses such as we have met with elsewhere.

Our next duty was to visit the famous 'bed' of St Kevin. It is on the south side of the lake and, as it is far more easy to climb up than down to it, a boat is always at hand to convey the curious to this especial object of curiosity. When comfortably seated, and the boatmen had taken their oars, we were at leisure and certainly inclined to listen to the legends of our guide, Wynder. Some of the most original of them, as well as a few that are to be found in 'veritable histories', we preserve for our readers. First the story was told to illustrate the piety and humanity of the saint:

'He retired to the keep for the forty days of Lent in fasting, meditation and prayer and as he held his hand out of the window, a blackbird came and laid her four eggs in it – and the saint, pitying the bird and unwilling to disturb her, never drew in his hand, but kept it stretched out until she brought forth her young and they were fully fledged, and flew off with a chirruping quartette of thanks to the holy man.

'Next, how the stone – called the deer-stone – was turned into a dairy by the saint. A poor widdy-man was left with a baby and what to do with it he didn't know in the wide world. So he went to his holiness, and his holiness says, says he, "Did ye never hear tell of the lilies of the field, and who clothes them? Come to this stone my good man every morning after airly mass, and I'll go bail ye'll get a drop for the baby." And sure enough, at daybreak, the poor fellow saw a deer come and lave a quart of new milk in the stone, and that fed the craythur until the child grew big and strong and learned enough to be the saint's coadjutor, but the stone is there to speak of this miracle to this day.

'How, one day in spring, before the blossoms were on the trees, a young man, grievously afflicted with the falling sickness, fancied that an apple would cure him, but there was ne'er an apple about the place. But what mattered that to the saint. He ordered a score of fine yellow pippins to grow upon a willow, and the boy gathered and ate, and was cured.

'How the saint was one day going up Derrybawn, and he meets a woman that carried five loaves in her apron. "What have ye got there, good woman?" says the saint.

' "I have five stones," says the woman.

' "If they are stones," says the saint, "I pray that they may be bread; and if they are bread," said he, "I pray that they may be stones."

'So with that the woman lets 'em fall, and sure enough, stones they were – and are to this day.

'How a vagabond from Connaught stole the saint's mare and her foal, and the saint overtook him and struck him dead on the spot wid the look he gave him; immediately he ris a cross in the place as a warning to all marrauders – and the cross stands there still with the marks of the mare's feet on the one side and the foal's feet on the other.

'How the saint banished the larks, but not, as the foolish imagine, because they disturbed his orisons, but because the workmen who built his churches "struck", complaining that the larks woke them early. So the saint said, "Do your duty for this day and they shall trouble you no more." And ever since then no lark floats above the holy waters.'

Of other 'haros' besides St Kevin, our guide had a store of tales. He told us of Fin Mac Cuol's Cut, which is a singular gap in the mountain. 'One day Fin met a countryman, and axed him what news of the battle.

'"Bad," says he, "we're bet into smithereens."

'"Och murder," says Fin, "why wasn't I there. I'll show ye what I'd have done." So he made a blow with his sword and cut a piece out of the hill. We call it the giant's cut; and himself and another giant used to shake hands across the lake.'

St Kevin's Bed is a hole in the rock on the side of the mountain of Lugduff, about thirty feet above the surface of the lake. The hollow, we were informed, was scooped out of the rock with no other chisel than the saint's nails. The ascent is exceedingly difficult and somewhat dangerous, for a slip would inevitably precipitate the adventurer into the lake below.

The Bed is about four feet square and the saint must have slept in a very uncomfortable position. At one end is a large though shallow cavity, big enough, quoth our guide, for the saint's head, if it were a thousand times bigger than his heart. The bottom, top and sides are literally tattooed with the names and initials of daring pilgrims who have ventured there. Among the rest is the venerated signature of Walter Scott (W. S.) carved by his son when he visited there with Maria Edgeworth in 1825.

Midway up the cliff is a small jutting rock, called St Kevin's Chair, where the wayfarer may take his rest.

Teampull-na-skellig is a ruin on the edge of the lake, close to the Bed, but so little of it now remains that a sturdy labourer might carry the whole of it away on his shoulders. At the extreme end of the lake and seen to great advantage from this spot is a fine and graceful waterfall that carries the collected streams of the adjacent mountain into it, which are again poured out at the eastern extremity into the lovely river, Avonmore.

There is another waterfall – the Pollanass – of considerable extent, but hidden among the shrubs and trees between the mountains of Derrybawn and Lugduff, a little above the church of Rhefeart. The fall is very narrow and a person may easily step across it. The rush of waters and the scattered spray, however, are apt to make the head dizzy.

Not long ago, a young bride and bridegroom, spending their honeymoon in the vicinity, were very near meeting a watery grave in one of the deep basins into which the cataract falls. The lady slipped and fell in and her husband, in attempting her rescue, followed her. They were carried down a considerable extent by the descending waters, when the two guides, Wynder and Brough, with admirable presence of mind, rushed down the valley, met them where the passage narrowed and drew them both out, without injury except for bruises. They were handsomely rewarded, each receiving a new coat, the pockets of which were well lined.

At the Church of Rhefeart or, as it is usually called, 'the sepulchre of the kings', in which generations of the O'Tooles lie interred, there is found perhaps the most interesting and striking of the ancient remains – although time has left barely enough of it to indicate the extent of its consecrated ground. It stands south of the glen that separates the two lakes and bears tokens of very remote antiquity. The interior is thronged with briars and underwood which, in many instances, completely conceal the graves of which it is full. On one of the most remarkable – a much broken oblong slab – may still be traced the letters which indicate that it once bore this inscription, in Irish characters:

Jesus Christ
Behold the resting-place of the body of King Mac Toole
Who died in Jesus Christ, 1010.

Near to the Rhefeart Church is another piece of ruin – a circle of stones; but the most singular relic of this description is just between the two mountains of Lugduff and Derrybawn. It is known as St Kevin's Cell, and consists of masses of flat stones, heaped one above the other and forming a circle, in the centre of which is a rude cross – or rather the relics of one, for time has mouldered it to an almost shapeless mass. It is situated on a rock which juts forward and exhibits to great advantage the whole of the surrounding scenery in all directions, and from this point there is a magnificent view of the valley.

From this part of the lake too we have a splendid view of the overhanging mountains – Derrybawn, Lugduff, Comaderry and Broccagh.

Glendalough is twenty-two Irish miles by the direct road from Dublin, and five from Roundwood, where a car is generally hired by tourists, who usually return to Roundwood to pass the night. A visit to the holy lake and ruined city, although they may be examined in a couple of hours, ought to occupy a day. For those who are not over-particular about creature comforts there is a tolerable inn at Glendalough, with very decent rooms and beds, a landlady exceedingly civil and attentive, and accommodation for horses.

About a mile above Glendalough there are the lead mines of Luganure, worked by the Mining Company of Ireland, under the superintendance of Captain Richards, a Cornish miner of great experience, and who possesses considerable knowledge and skill.

A still wilder part of this district is Glenmalure, through which runs the military road to the Vale of Avoca, by the side of the Avonbeg. The more picturesque road, however, is to the east, passing through the vale of Clara, the town of Rathdrum and the valley of Avondale. We may proceed rapidly over this ground, for its leading features are common to the county – wild, barren grandeur, relieved by touches of gentle beauty.

The 'meeting of the waters' commences the Vale of Avoca, which extends a distance of about seven miles almost into Arklow. It is the opening of a scene of exceeding loveliness. The visitor will pause awhile at the pretty and picturesque bridge under which roll the blended waters of the Avonmore and Avonbeg, forming here a placid lake – in the centre of which is a small island covered with underwood – before they cease their separate existence and rush together into the sea under a new name, the Avoca.

The road leads along the west bank of the Avoca. On both sides the hills are clad with forest trees, the opposite being especially rich. Nearly midway in the valley are the copper-mines of Cronbane and Ballymurtagh, the former to the left and the latter to the right, at the opposite ends of the river. A prettily situated inn, 'The Avoca Head', is upon its margin. Scenery similar in character, yet perpetually varied, continues until the 'second meeting' is reached, where the river is crossed by a handsome bridge of stone, although the locality is still recognised by the ancient name, 'the Wooden Bridge'. And here is another bridge which the tourist will do well to ascend, for nowhere is the valley seen to such advantage.

The Wooden Bridge Inn is exceedingly comfortable and the charges for entertainment remarkably moderate. Two coaches pass by it, to and from Wexford, every day. The hotel, however, is generally so crowded with visitors in the season that it will be necessary for those who design to locate here to order rooms by letter a few days before their arrival. It is thirty-six miles from

Dublin, and cars are, of course, to be had in abundance.

From the Wooden Bridge to Arklow the river narrows and deepens, and the trees being more directly over it, a darker shadow is thrown upon the waters. The woods of Glenart, the seat of Lord Carysfort, are to the right, and on the other side of the Avoca is Shelton Abbey, the mansion of the Earl of Wicklow. It is a very elegant structure, situated almost on the margin of the river. But the district through which we are now passing, although a continuation of the Vale of Avoca, is properly the Vale of Arklow, and it leads almost into the town, where we are again introduced to the arid and coarse features of the county which continue until its borders are reached, and we enter the county of Wexford.

Arklow has the aspect of a thriving town, but, like all the harbours between Dublin and Waterford, it has the disadvantage of a bar. The remains of an ancient castle still exist, but of its once famous abbey there are now scarcely any traces left. Here, the Avoca passes under a bridge of thirteen arches.

We must retrace our steps through the valley, and proceed up the mountains – the Croghan mountains – a chain that separates Wicklow from Wexford, for about four miles from the Wooden Bridge. Passing a prettily situated chapel on the side of a hill and looking down upon one of the loveliest of all the valleys, we enter a remarkably wild district in which are situated the 'Wicklow Gold Mines'. Until the period of our visit, we confess we had considered the stories in circulation concerning the discoveries here as little more than seductive fictions. We were, as our readers will learn, greatly mistaken, for we actually saw 'gold, yellow and glittering, precious gold', dug from the bowels of the earth. Weighed in our palm, we were satisfied of its veritable existence, and readily confided in the truth of the statements that gold, to the value of many thousands of pounds, has been, from time to time, collected by the peasantry, and that two months after its discovery no less than £10,000 was made by the sale of what had been gathered.

The origin of the discovery of the gold is variously told. Tradition attributes it to a schoolmaster who, in consequence of his perpetually wandering about the adjacent streams, was considered by his neighbours to be insane. He grew gradually rich, however, but at length the secret of his wealth became known, and a similar madness seized upon the whole population for miles around the place where nature had deposited her treasure.

We once again retrace our steps – through the Vale of Avoca – and ascending the hill that looks down upon the bridge which crosses the meeting, enter the road to Rathnew, leaving on the left and at about two miles distant the town of Wicklow, the capital of the county, but inferior in size and population to both Arklow and Bray.

For several miles around Rathnew the scenery is especially beautiful, but it is, however, a poor village. There are two inns of note in the immediate neighbourhood – one at Ashford, and one at Newarth Bridge.

The inn at Newarth bridge is, according to our experience, one of the most comfortable inns in the country. The landlord, Mr Hunter, was for many years butler to Mr Tottenham, in whose establishment his wife was housekeeper. They have therefore been trained in good habits and all matters about their hotel are neat, clean and well-ordered, and nothing can exceed their attention to their guests – a circumstance unhappily rare at places of this description. Also, their charges for entertainment are exceedingly moderate, and we strongly recommend the Newarth Bridge as a most pleasant resting place, from which excursions may be made to Wicklow-town, Rosanna, Dunran, and above all the Devil's Glen, where a day may be well spent.

About two miles from the inn at Newarth Bridge and one from the village of Ashford, commences the entrance to the Devil's Glen – or rather to that side of it which is the property of Charles Tottenham, Esq., for the river divides it, with the opposite land belonging to F. Single, Esq. Mr Tottenham requires that all visitors shall leave their names at his lodge where an order for admission into the glen is given by the lodge-keeper, a kindly and gossiping dame in whose company the stranger may pass a few minutes very profitably.

A narrow road, but not too narrow for ordinary carriages, shadowed all the way by luxuriant trees, runs for nearly a mile to the iron gate that bars the passage of all intruders, but where a call for admission is at once answered. We enter through a tunnel and are at once between two huge mountains where, at a prodigious depth below their summits, rushes the rapid river, brawling so loudly as to drown the music of the birds. The glen is little more than a mile in length, and midway a small moss-house has been erected – but to our minds the simple structure disturbs the perfect solitude of the place. However, this evil is an insignificant one compared to one of very recent origin, against which we may justly enter our protest: a wide carriage road has been constructed all through the glen!

Nothing in the county astonished or gratified us so much as the Devil's Glen with its roaring river, huge precipices, its circuitous paths, and the noble and graceful fall that seems as a crown of glory to its head. It is impossible for language to convey a notion of our delight when we had climbed the mountain slope by the tangled footway that ascends from the moss-house and gazed below and around us. It is perhaps one of the most graceful if not *the* most graceful and stupendous of the Wicklow cataracts. It comes rushing and roaring down from the heights above, dashing aside every impediment that would bar its progress to the sea.

And reader, to reach it is but a day's journey from London!

Dunran, another of the wonders of Wicklow, is but a short distance from the Devil's Glen, and a very short distance to those who go on foot. It is a creation of art rather than nature, for half a century ago it was almost as barren of verdure as the Scalp. The defile is a narrow pass between lofty hills, in the several interstices of which trees have been planted, where there is apparently scarcely enough soil to cover their roots. As Dunran lies upon very high ground, no water flows through it, but the views from this point are most magnificent.

Newton-Mount-Kennedy, a large village, which lies seventeen miles distant from Dublin, is also surrounded by beautiful scenery. Within a mile and a half of it is the small glen called 'the Hermitage', for which nature has done so much and art more. And here is another of the magnificent waterfalls for which the county is so famous. It is but one of the many attractions in this

BRAY.

delicious spot. The grounds have been laid out in exceeding good taste and the walks through it are very varied, and considerable skill and judgement have been exhibited in so planting and trimming as to obtain a new and striking view at almost every step.

A mile or two further on is the rich Vale of Delgany, which is seen to great perfection from the main road where a small bridge passes over a ravine. Delgany is the property of the family La Touche. From Delgany to the commencement, or more correctly, the termination of the Glen of the Downs, the distance is but a mile or two, and the public road runs through it. The glen is formed by two abrupt hills which are between twelve and thirteen hundred feet high and which are clothed by the most luxuriant vegetation from the base to the summit of each.

The glen is of considerable extent and in leaving it we enter once more a comparatively barren district, although, as we approach Dublin, the influence of cultivation is more apparent in changing the arid character of the soil, and giving the wild common the aspect of civilisation. As we advance from any of the heights, there is a glorious and cheering prospect of the sea, and mansions and cottages are more thickly scattered about the landscape and the lofty mountains take the eye from every point of view.

Leaving to the left the romantic Dargle, we draw near the northern border of the county – and before we quit it altogether, we must visit the town of Bray. Here the scenery assumes a new character, and a few steps from the main road and we are upon the shore of St George's Channel.

Bray is the largest town in the county, and from its proximity to Dublin is extensively visited by persons either in search of the sea-air or the enjoyment to be derived from beautiful scenery, and here, in consequence, is one of the most splendid hotels in the kingdom.

A large number of fishermen live in the neighbourhood of Bray, but unfortunately the want of a quay for shelter greatly militates against them – an evil for which, we believe, a remedy will be ere long provided for by the generosity of Mr and Mrs Putland, and we were greatly interested while at Bray-Head to visit a very pretty and well-managed school and a cluster of cottages built by them for the fishermen and their families.

And here we must leave this lovely county of Wicklow; passing unnoticed innumerable objects, which, to describe any of them, might occupy pages. As we have said, 'to depict adequately half its beauties would require a large and full volume'. We trust, however, we have written enough, notwithstanding our limited space, to direct the attention of the tourist towards it.

Wicklow is bounded on the north by Dublin, on the south by Wexford, on the west by the counties of Kildare and Carlow, and on the east by St George's Channel. It is divided into the baronies of Arklow, Ballinacor, Newcastle, Half-Rathdown, Shillelagh, and Upper and Lower Talbotstown.

Chapter Two

KILDARE

Kildare is a corruption of Chille-dara, or the Wood of the Oaks. It was also called Kill-dara, from the cell of St Bridget, which was first placed under a large oak, and was also known as Kill-drag, Caelan or Galen, that is, *the woody country*, for in early ages it was one continuous wood, the decay of which produced the great bogs which still cover so much of the country.

The bishopric of Kildare is said to have been founded by St Conloeth about the middle of the fifth century. The saint, however, was assisted in his labours by the famous St Bridget, who established a nunnery here in 484 AD. Her nuns were long celebrated as the guardians of an 'inextinguishable flame', which history relates was so called because the 'religious women were so careful and diligent in supplying it with fuel that from the time of St Bridget it hath remained unextinguished through so many successions of years, and though so vast a quantity of wood has been in such a time consumed in it, yet the ashes are never increased.' A low and narrow stone cell in which the fire was kept burning is still pointed out near the round tower. The fire was extinguished in 1220 by the order of Henry de Loundres, Archbishop of Dublin who, no doubt, had his own reasons for quenching the flames. The fire was, however, subsequently rekindled, and remained burning until the suppression of the monasteries by Henry VIII.

Within a short distance of the town is the far-famed Curragh of Kildare, the principal race-ground in Ireland. It is a fine undulating down, about six miles in length and two in breadth, and is perhaps unequalled in the world for the exceeding softness and elasticity of the turf, the verdure of which is evergreen and the occasional irregularities of which are very attractive to the eye.

The land is the property of the Crown and includes above 6000 acres, where numerous flocks of sheep find rich and abundant pasture.

Naas is a very ancient town and was formerly the residence of the kings of Leinster. In its immediate neighbourhood, and forming a singular and striking object, are the remains of Jigginstown, a building commenced upon an enormous scale by the unfortunate Earl of Stafford.

Athy, jointly with Naas, is the assize town for the county. Few towns in Ireland are more auspiciously sited; it is surrounded by a fertile country and the grand canal and the great southern road to Cork connect it with the metropolis from which it is thirty-two miles distant. The Barrow, on which it is situated, is navigable to Ross, and thence to the harbour of Waterford. Yet Athy is by no means flourishing, its fame being derived exclusively from its early history.

It was a frontier town of the Pale, and the neighbourhood abounds with relics of former greatness: castellated and monastic, and one of them, White's Castle, close to the bridge, consists of a massive square tower and is now used as a police barrack. The county is, indeed, full of interesting ruins, for its proximity to Dublin kept it the 'Seat of War' for centuries, and from the earliest invasions of the Danes, who scarcely left one of its towns unvisited, down to the almost as merciless soldiers of the Commonwealth, Kildare has seldom had leisure to reap a single harvest in peace.

The bog of Allen occupies a very considerable portion of the county of Kildare. The hill of Allen – Dun Almhain – whence the bog is said to have its name, is remarkable as the stated residence of Fin Mac Cual. Fin is properly said to have been general of the Irish Militia, but such an appellation has no warrant from any original records of those people. He is simply termed in Irish, *Ri'Feine* and *Flaith Feine*, that is, the king or chief of the Fians or Feinans.

The word Fian denotes a hunter or man of chase, and seems to have been used to designate those tribes who followed hunting in contradistinction to those who pursued pasturage and agriculture. These wild and hardy tribes, comprising different races, appear to have formed into a kind of natural guard whose special duty was to guard the coasts against foreign invasion.

The Feinans often affected independent authority, and at length engaged in war with the Irish monarch, Cairhe, which ended in their defeat and overthrow at the battle of Gabhra towards the close of the third century. The most remarkable amongst the Feinans were Fin, the son of Cual, their chief, Ossian (Oisin), Fergus and Dara, their chief bards; Oscar of the sharp swords, son of Ossian; Gaul the son of Morni of the golden shield; Brown-haired Dearmid, and Blue-eyed Ryno. Their deeds are celebrated in the Feinan tales and poems still extant.

Those who visit the county of Kildare in search of the picturesque will do wisely to pursue the course of the Liffey – indeed, it would be almost criminal to have sojourned in Dublin without examining Leixlip, one of the most beautiful bits of scenery in the kingdom, and within a distance of ten miles from the metropolis.

The village is neat and pretty, but the leading object of attraction is the Salmon Leap, which is about half a mile from the road. After passing along two or three green fields, through which a footpath has been generously made, the roar of the waterfall greets the ear, and through some skilfully formed breaks among the foliage that skirts the river occasional glimpses of it are caught. The cataract is of great width and very picturesque in character. The waters glide onwards in a smooth but rapid current and dash down the rocky steep. The whole neighbourhood is beautiful – the river is lined with graceful trees from its borders up the slopes of the hills that ascend on either side.

In this neighbourhood and on the road to Maynooth we pass several ruins of the olden times: relics of the former power of the Kildare branch of the Geraldines. The Castle of Maynooth was, for a very long period, their chief seat, the stronghold from whence they hurled defiance at their enemies by whom they were at all periods more or less threatened.

Maynooth consists of one long and broad street, with the dwellings of a class between houses and cabins on either side and having an air of exceeding discomfort. The hotel is a long and rambling building, the rooms of which remind one of a house in the sixth stage and seem utterly unused to the intrusion of guests. At one end of the town is the entrance to Carton, the seat of Ireland's only Duke, and at the other are the ruins of an ancient castle, the stronghold of the Earls of Kildare, and the Royal College of St Patrick. The college is a peculiarly ungainly and ungraceful structure; it appears to have been a mansion of moderate size to which additions have been made from time to time, and where elegance and uniformity have been sacrificed to convenience.

The college was founded in the year 1795. Previously youths intended for the Roman Catholic Church were compelled to enter foreign universities and to graduate there – having first received the rudiments of learning where and how they could in their own country. Towards the close of the eighteenth century, however, the war with the Continent in which Great Britain was engaged rendered the transmission of students dangerous as well as difficult, and, the more liberal spirit of the age favouring the project, application was made to the Irish Parliament by several leading members of the Roman Catholic Church for leave to establish a college, under charter, for the education of priests at home. Permission was granted and the act for its incorporation received the royal assent on the 5th June 1795.

In the following October the college was opened for the reception of fifty students and the Rev. Dr Hussey was appointed its first president. Since that period candidates for orders in the Roman Catholic Church have been educated chiefly at Maynooth, but there are now other colleges from which they have also been ordained: Kilkenny, Carlow, Tuam, Wexford and Waterford, but many youths, the sons of persons of comparatively higher stations, continue to graduate at Continental universities.

The number of students at Maynooth is now about four hundred and fifty. The number of free students is two hundred and fifty, and they are supplied gratuitously with lodging, commons and instruction. Besides the free students, there are pensioners and half-pensioners; the former paying twenty-one pounds and the latter ten pounds, ten shillings annually. Each fee student pays an entrance fee of eight guineas, and for each pensioner the entrance fee is four guineas.

There are consequently three classes of students: senior students, pensioners and free students, all of whom wear caps and gowns. Very few of the students ever leave the college for a single day from the time they enter it to their final departure from its walls; they are permitted to walk without the gates once a week, but on such occasions they are always accompanied by the dean.

At Maynooth there is an excellent and rather extensive library, formed chiefly by presents and bequests, containing the choicest works in History, Belles Lettres, the Arts and Sciences, et cetera. But the books are closed to the students! The assistant librarian, who conducted us through it, stated frankly that even he was not permitted to peruse any volume he was pleased to select, and that the majority of the students were not even allowed to enter the room, and that those who have the entrée must apply for express leave to read any particular book, and explain for what object they desire to consult it. And this restriction, as we understood it, applies to every general history.

The county of Kildare, an inland county in the province of Leinster, is bounded on the north by Meath, on the east by Dublin and Wicklow, on the south by Carlow, and on the west by the King's and Queen's Counties.

It is divided into the baronies of Carbery, Clane-Connell, Ikeathy and Oughterany, Kilcullen, Kilkea and Moone, East Narragh and Rheban, West Narragh and Rheban, East Ophaly, West Ophaly, North and South Naas, and North and South Salt. The principal towns are Nass, Athy and Kildare; the latter, although famous for centuries as a 'city renowned for saints', has dwindled into comparative insignificance. However, some remains of grandeur still exist: the ruined cathedral retains marks of its original beauty, and the round tower, one of the tallest in the kingdom, still attracts the attention of the curious.

Chapter Three

DUBLIN

There are few cities in the world, and perhaps none in Great Britain, so auspiciously situated as the city of Dublin. The ocean rolls its waves within ten miles of the quays, the bay is at once safe, commodious and magnificent, with a variety of coast from the soft beach of sand to the rough sea promontory, from the undulating slope to the terrific rock, and there are several lighthouses to guide vessels into harbour.

On one side is the rich pasture-land of Meath, and on the other the mountains and valleys of Wicklow. A noble river, the Liffey, flows through it, and breezes from the ocean and hills both contribute to keep it healthy. Scenery of surpassing beauty is within an hour's walk of its crowded streets.

Dublin is, in population and extent, the second city of the British Empire, and ranks as the seventh in Europe. It is somewhat above three miles long in a direct line from east to west, and of nearly equal breadth from north to south. It is encompassed by a circular road which is about nine Irish miles in extent. It contains above 800 streets, 22,000 houses, and the population in 1841 amounted to 232,726. It is situated at the western extremity of Dublin Bay, and the river Liffey, which rises among the Wicklow mountains, runs through it, increased by the King's River, the Dodder, and the Tolkan, but these are of small importance. Originally it was confined by walls to the hill upon which the Castle now stands, but it now occupies a space of 1264 acres.

The noble and beautiful bay of Dublin is, indeed, inexpressibly lovely, and on entering it after a weary voyage the heart bounds with enthusiasm at the sight of it enclosed, as it is, by huge rocks, encompassed in turn by high and picturesque mountains. To the

DUBLIN BAY

(FROM KINGSTOWN QUARRIES.)

south, varied into innumerable forms are the Wicklow Hills, but nearer, rising as it were out from the surface of the water, is the ever-green island of Dalky. To the north, a bolder coast is commenced with the Hill of Howth on a leading pinnacle of which stands the most picturesque of the Irish beacons. At the other side of the promontory is seen a village with another lighthouse, a martello tower, an ancient abbey, and a calm, though now deserted harbour which was for so long a period the landing place upon Irish ground.

This harbour was for a series of years the station for the Dublin packets. It was constructed at a cost to the country of nearly half a million sterling. It was commenced in 1807 and completed in two years under the superintendence of the late John Rennie, Esq., but since the construction of Kingstown Harbour that of Howth has been entirely deserted.

However, if the tourist will 'step ashore' at Howth, he may, before he is half an hour in Ireland, visit some of the most striking and interesting objects in the country – a ruined church, a very ancient castle, some druidic remains, a village which is dignified with the name of 'town' and which is essentially Irish in its desolated character. Standing beside the wall of the Baily lighthouse – erected in 1814 – the tourist may gaze over the wide ocean or, looking to the right, he may admire the beautiful scenery that borders Dublin Bay, and on the left, the famous little island called Ireland's Eye, and beyond it the renowned island of Lambay, and some forty miles north of the spot on which he stands the bold outlines of the Mourne Mountains are clearly defined.

Let us first enter the ancient abbey of Howth and postpone our progress up the Liffey awhile. The abbey – or rather church, for of its monastic rank there are no authentic proofs – is dedicated to the Virgin, and is said to have been erected by the St Lawrences early in the thirteenth century. Here, from time to time, the mortal remains of the bold barons have been laid and the aisles are crowded with relics that bear records of their prowess.

The original name of the family is said to have been Tristram – and its great founder a knight of the Round Table. The name was changed in consequence of the vow of one of its members who fought with the Danes at Clontarf, to assume that of his patron saint if he obtained the victory – this he did, and was thence called St Lawrence.

The church, like many of the sacred edifices erected in troublous times, was constructed for defence as well as for the purpose of religion. It is defended by a battlemented rampart which on one side impends over the sea, and on the other over a deep fosse.

Of the ancient college there are some remains – a hall, a kitchen, and a few cells, which until lately afforded shelter to several poor families.

The ruins of another building – a small oratory dedicated to St Fenton – still exist a little to the west of the castle. And the castle itself, which was for so many ages the residence of the noble family, retains but little of its original character. It has been altered at various periods according to the wishes or wants of its proprietors and with far more regard to convenience than to architectural skill and beauty. It does, however, contain several interesting relics of antiquity, with, among others, the sword with which Sir Tristram is said to have won the victory at Clontarf, and the bells which formerly belonged to the abbey.

A singular and romantic legend is attached to Howth Castle. The celebrated Grana Uille, or Grace O'Malley, who was noted for her piratical depredations in the reign of Elizabeth, returned a certain time from England where she had paid a visit to the Virgin Queen, landed at Howth, and proceeded to the castle. It was the hour of dinner – but the gates were shut. Shocked at the exclusion so repugnant to her notions of Irish hospitality, she immediately proceeded to the shore where the young lord of the castle was with his nurse and, seizing the child, she embarked with him and sailed to Connaught, where her own castle stood. After a time, however, she restored the child, with the express stipulation that the gates of the castle should be thrown open when the family went to dinner – a practice which is observed to this day.

Ireland's Eye is a small island about a mile from the northern shore of Howth, in the centre of which stands the ruin of a church dedicated to St Nessan. The church is very small – about twelve feet by twenty-four – and the walls, which were composed of rough pebbles and rough fragments of flint, give evidence of the most remote antiquity. There are no traces of windows and a great peculiarity in its structure is that the porch and bell tower are at the east end.

Returning to the bay, we leave the pretty island of Dalky and enter the channel between two huge sandbanks which are called – from the perpetual roaring of the sea over them – 'the Bulls', north and south. But the place of ordinary debarkation is Kingstown formerly called Dunleary, but which received its modern name in honour of His Majesty George IV who took shipboard there on leaving Ireland in 1821. To commemorate the event of the king's visit, an obelisk was erected on the spot where he last stood with an inscription setting forth the fact.

The harbour of Kingstown is safe, commodious and exceedingly picturesque. From the quay – the first stone of which was laid in 1817 by Lord Whitworth, the Viceroy of Ireland – the railway carriages start, and convey passengers a distance of seven miles in about twenty minutes to the terminus within a few hundred yards of the centre of the city. This is the Dublin and Kingstown Railway which was opened for the public on 17 December 1834, but the entire distance was not finished until the year 1837.

The stranger cannot fail to receive a most agreeable impression of Dublin, for its principal streets and leading attractions lie within a comparatively narrow compass, and his attention is sure to be fixed upon some object worthy of observation – to be succeeded, almost immediately, by some other of equal note.

If he arrives sea-ward he will have fully established the magnificence of the approach, and there is scarcely one road that conducts to it on which he will not have journeyed through beautiful scenery and obtained a fine view of the city as he nears it.

But we must place him at once nearly in the centre of the city upon Carlisle Bridge, and perhaps from no single spot can the eye command so great a number of interesting points.

He turns to the north, and looks upon a noble street – Sackville

Street. Midway is Nelson's Pillar, a fine Ionic column surmounted by a statue of the hero. Directly opposite this is the Post Office, a modern structure built in pure taste. Beyond is the Lying-In hospital and the Rotunda and, ascending a steep hill, one of the many fine squares.

To the south he has within his ken the far-famed Bank of Ireland and the University.

To the west the Four Courts – the courts of law – and the several bridges.

To the east the Custom House, a superb, though lonesome building, and the quays.

Towering above all, and within his ken wherever he is directed, are numerous steeples, of which no city, except the metropolis of England, can boast so many. In fact, nearly all the great attractions of Dublin may be seen from this bridge.

These buildings we shall proceed to describe, but we must do so briefly. First, the College:

The Dublin University differs from the universities of Oxford and Cambridge in being limited to a single college, but the distinction between the university and the college is very rarely noticed, and in common parlance they are confounded together.

The College was founded in 1591 by Elizabeth; its charter was confirmed and extended by James I who conferred upon it the privilege of returning two members to the Irish Parliament. Additional privileges were granted by Charles I, George IV and Queen Victoria. The fellows are indebted to the present queen for the liberty to marry without being deprived of their fellowships, and the advantage taken of the boon proves how earnestly it was desired.

The front of the College faces Dame Street, and by its architectural beauty it is harmonised with the magnificent structure formerly occupied by the Irish Parliament.

Trinity College was honoured by the inspection of Her Majesty and Prince Albert on the occasion of the royal visit to Dublin in 1849. The august party were received by the provost and senior fellows and conducted to the magnificent library, which excited their admiration by its extent and excellent adaptation to the

SACKVILLE STREET,
DUBLIN

purpose to which it is applied. The number of volumes is about 150,000. The present librarian has zealously exerted himself to render the collection complete, especially in foreign literature. In the eastern pavilion there is another collection of books called the Fagel Library which amounts to 20,000 volumes. It was the property of the Fagel family and was removed to London from Holland in 1784, upon the invasion of that country by the French. The Manuscript Room contains many valuable manuscripts.

The Bank of Ireland – which was the Parliament House before the Union – is universally classed among the most perfect examples of British architecture in the kingdom, and indeed it is perhaps unsurpassed in Europe. Yet, strange to say, little or nothing is known of the architect, and the history of this graceful and beautiful structure is wrapped in obscurity almost approaching mystery.

The historians of Dublin are singularly unsatisfactory upon this head. We learn from them only that the 'Parliament House was begun to be built during the administration of John, Lord Carteret, in the year 1729, and was executed under the inspection of Sir Edward Lovel Pearce, engineer and surveyor-general, but completed by Arthur Dobbs, Esq., his successor, about the year 1729.' Dr Walsh, the historian, who is usually so searching in his inquiries and so minute as to facts, tells us no more than Harris, the historian who preceded him, and who makes no mention of Mr Cassell or Castell, the architect to whom the building is usually attributed, but of whom very little is known. Mr Brewer states, but does not give upon authority, that Mr Cassell did not visit Ireland until the year 1773, nearly fifty years after the structure was commenced.

However, whomever it was, it is clear that he was content with supplying the designs and instructions without superintending the work in its progress. Perhaps it was some needy man who, oppressed by poverty, was tempted to remain in the background and sell both his genius and his glory to the engineer and surveyor-general.

In 1785, Mr James Gandon, architect, was employed in order to effect a more convenient entrance for the peers, and to add an east front to the building, and a noble portico of six Corinthian columns was erected. The old portico, however, was of Ionic columns – and for this very indefensible incongruity the architect was said to have accounted thus:

'A gentleman passing when the workmen were placing the Corinthian capitals on the columns, struck by the injudicious mixture of orders, inquired, "What order is that?" upon which Mr Gandon replied, "A very substantial order, for it was by the order of the House of Lords."'

The Exchange may perhaps rank next in beauty to the Bank. It was commenced in 1769 and finished in 1779 under the immediate direction of Mr Thomas Cooley, an artist to whom Dublin is indebted for other fine structures. Its form is nearly a square of one hundred feet and crowned with a dome in the centre of the building. The interior is a happy combination of elegance and convenience.

The Custom House was designed and erected by Mr James Gandon, the foundation stone of which was laid in 1781. It is worthy of comment that although the cost of building the Bank amounted to no more than £40,000, the expense of the Custom House exceeded £546,000. The building is three hundred and seventy-five feet in length and two hundred and five in depth, and exhibits four decorated fronts, answering almost directly to the four cardinal points of the compass, with the south being the principal front. The effect of this spacious and superb structure is now inexpressibly lonely, for time has produced changes that have rendered it almost useless, and unhappily, the paucity of Dublin's commerce is such that a cottage might suffice to transact its business in lieu of a palace, and the rooms of the Custom House are therefore deserted.

Very different in aspect is the Four Courts, in the hall of which there is a perpetual buzz. The building, which contains several Irish courts of law, was commenced by the architect Mr Cooley in 1786 and, in consequence of his death, was continued by Mr James Gandon. It is situated on the north side of the Liffey and is an exceedingly beautiful and attractive object, seen either from an adjacent point or from a distance. The ruinous houses of Pill Lane,

THE FOUR COURTS,

DUBLIN

which heretofore deformed the back of this structure, have been thrown down within the last few years, and magnificent and spacious additions have been built. The principal of these are the Rolls Court, the Nisi Prius Court and the Court of the Commissioners of Bankrupts; there is also a library for the use of the bar, and two large rooms for the convenience of the attorneys for a coffee room.

Of the other buildings the most important is the Post Office, the first stone of which was laid in 1815. It was built after a design by Mr Francis Johnson, and is one of the finest and most convenient public buildings in the kingdom. It is two hundred and twenty-three feet in front, one hundred and fifty feet in depth and fifty feet (three storeys) in height to the top of the cornice. It is surmounted by three finely executed statues representing Hibernia resting on her spear and harped shield; Mercury, with his caduceus and purse; and Fidelity, with her finger on her lips and a key in her other hand.

The College of Surgeons may be ranked next, and then the Lying-In Hospital. There are many other public buildings of great architectural beauty in the city besides those we have mentioned, but we must be content with a reference, and a slight one at that, to the more remarkable.

It will be observed that of all these edifices there are none, except the college, much above a century old. The Castle, however, is of great antiquity, and its history is, in fact, the history of Dublin. To trace the progress of the city from the period when a band of invaders destroyed it by tying matches to the tails of swallows and so communicating fire to the thatched roofs of the houses, to its present extensive size would be a task that would far exceed our limits.

The period of the foundation of the city and the etymology of its name are both involved in obscurity. The city is known in history by various names; the Irish called it Drom-coll-coil, that is, the brow of the hazel wood. Another ancient name by which it is known to the Irish to this day is Bally-athlcleath, that is, the town of the ford of hurdles, and this comes from a common practice of the Irish who used to make muddy rivers – such as the Liffey was near its junction with the sea, and near bogs and marshes – fordable by means of hurdles laid down where they desired to pass: it was a rude substitute for a bridge.

The geographer Ptolemy, who flourished in 140 AD, places a town under nearly the same parallel, and calls it Civitas Eblana, and towards the close of the second century there are records of conflicts between certain Irish kings for its possession, as a place 'commodious for traffic and fishing'. It is more than probable, however, that its commerce and fortifications were both derived from the Danish sea-kings by whom it was settled and strengthened prior to the Anglo-Norman invasion. By the year 964 it had assumed some importance, as evidenced by the preface to King Edward's Charter, where it is styled 'the most noble city of Dublin'. In the year 1014, the Danish power in Ireland was for a time effectually destroyed by a league of the native Irish princes, headed by the famous king, Brien Boru, Borome or Boroimhe. It is said that during his reign the laws were so strictly administered that a fair lady might travel from one end of the kingdom to the other with a gold ring on the top of a wand in perfect security.

The decisive contest with the Danes was fought at Clontarf, a village near Dublin which skirts the harbour. The 'strangers' were assisted by several of the native chieftains, at the head of whom was the king of Leinster. The battle was fought on Good Friday, and although the outcome was doubtful for a long time, the Irish were at length conquerors, but the victory was saddened by the loss of Brien and nearly all the Irish leaders.

However, the 'strangers' continued to keep possession of Dublin, of which they were sovereigns, for above a century afterwards. The city was conquered by the English in 1170, who forced the Danish monarch and his followers to abandon the kingdom, and with this event the dominion of the sea-kings was terminated in Ireland. The Oastmen were never afterwards enabled to regain their Irish possessions, and those who remained in the country became 'quiet subjects of the English and one people with them'. In 1173 Henry II, having received the submission of the Irish chieftains and their king – Roderick O'Connor, the last king of Ireland – granted, by charter, the city of Dublin to his subjects of Bristol to 'hold it of him and his heirs, well and in peace, freely and quietly, fully and amply and honourably, with all the liberties and free customs which the men of Bristol have at Bristol'.

The building of Dublin Castle for the residence of the viceroys was commenced by Meiler Fitzhenry, Lord Justice of Ireland, in 1205, and finished fifteen years afterwards by Henry de Loundres, Archbishop of Dublin. It was occupied as a strong fortress only until the reign of Elizabeth, when it became the seat of the Irish government, the court being previously held at various palaces in the city or its suburbs, and in the seventeenth century Terms and Parliaments were both held within its walls. The Castle, however, has undergone so many and such various changes from time to time as circumstances justified the withdrawal of its defences, that the only portion of it that now bears a character of antiquity is the Birmingham Tower, and even that has been almost entirely rebuilt although it still retains its ancient form.

The Castle is situated on very high ground nearly in the centre of the city, and the principal entrance is by a handsome gateway. The several buildings, surrounding two squares, have a dull and heavy character, for no effort has been made at elegance or display, and however well calculated they may seem for business, the whole has more the aspect of a prison than a court. There is, indeed, one building which contributes somewhat to redeem the sombre appearance of the Castle, and that is the chapel. It is a fine Gothic edifice, richly decorated both within and without. The walls by which it was formerly surrounded and the fortifications for its defence have nearly all vanished.

Nor is Dublin rich in the remains of antiquity, and one of the few that appertains to its ancient history is a picturesque gateway, but not one of a very remote date, called Marsh's Gate. It stands in Kevin's Street, near the Cathedral of Saint Patrick, and is the entrance to a large court which is now occupied by the horse-police, and at one end of which is the Barrack, which was formerly, we believe, the Deanery and Marsh's Library.

But if few of the public structures of Dublin possess the beauty of age, many of its churches may be classed with the ancient of days. Chief among them is the Cathedral of St Patrick, which is interesting not alone for its antiquity, but for its association with several events and remarkable people by which and by whom Ireland has been made famous. The Cathedral was built in 1190 AD by John Comyn, Archbishop of Dublin, by whom it was dedicated to the patron saint of Ireland. But it is said that the site on which it stands was formerly occupied by a church erected by the saint himself in 448 AD.

It is situated in a very old part of Dublin in the midst of low streets and alleys, with the houses being close to the small open yard by which the venerable structure is encompassed. Its condition too is very wretched, and although various suggestions have been made from time to time for its repair and renovation, it continues in a state by no means creditable either to the church or the city.

The Cathedral of Christ Church was, it is said, originally erected in the year 1038 by Sitricus, the son of Amlave, king of the Oastmen of Dublin and Donat or Dunan, the first Oastman bishop, who was buried in the choir, at the right hand side of the communion table, in 1074. Its architectural beauties are even less than those of its rival, although it contains some good examples of Saxon ornaments. Christ Church is, however, in better condition than St Patrick's, having recently undergone repairs and improvements. Its walls entomb the dust of Strongbow, the great Anglo-Norman conqueror of Ireland. He died in Dublin 'about the kalends of June' 1177 AD, of mortification of the foot, and his remains were interred in the cathedral. Two centuries after his death a monument to his memory was erected by Sir Henry Sidney, Lord President.

Here also, in 1487, Lambert Simnell, the imposter, was crowned with the title of Edward VI. The crown used on the occasion was borrowed from the statue of Our Lady which stood in the church of St Mary les Dames, and shortly thereafter the imposter received the homage of the citizens in the Castle.

Of the other churches in Dublin, the only one that demands particular notice is that of St Michan.

St Michan's Church has no claim to attention for any

architectural beauty. It is, like most other old churches in Ireland, merely a plain cruciform building of dark-coloured stone, its only ornament being a large square tower containing the belfry, through which is the principal entrance.

But the church is remarkable for its vaults, which possess the extraordinary property of preserving the bodies deposited there from decay, and, what is nearly as singular, the vaults are not infested with rats – a fact to which the bodies alone in the absence of other evidence would sufficiently testify. The bodies in the best state of preservation are in a small vault under the right angle of the transept, one of which is said to be the body of St Michan, laid there two hundred years ago. It is that of a man of short stature, and is still quite perfect. The nails continue on the hands and feet, and the entire flesh and skin remain on the bones. From the process of drying, the flesh is considerably shrunken on the limbs and abdomen, and the parts below the chest are sunken, so that in shape the body resembles that of a person very much wasted away by sickness. The flesh is tough to the touch but not so hard as that of a mummy, nor is the skin black like a mummy's, but rather brown and leathery, much resembling the cover of an old book in the species of binding called law-calf.

The covering and ornaments – if there ever were any – of the coffin in which it lies have long since mouldered away, and the whole has certainly the appearance of being very old. In one corner of this vault there are about twenty bodies and parts of bodies, bones, and covers and sides of coffins in a confused heap. There are also several entire coffins, some new and perfect, a few old and broken. But notwithstanding the mass of corpses in this little chamber, which is not more than about twelve feet square, and very low, there is not the least offensive odour, and from the great dryness of the soil not even the disagreeable smell usual in underground vaults. The principal vaults are in a long corridor under the centre of the church, of which there are thirteen chambers, and most of these are the burying places of particular families.

From the public buildings of Dublin, we pass on to the people.

*

There is a district of Dublin that possesses many remarkable and peculiar features. It is still called the Liberties and derives its name from certain privileges and immunities enjoyed by the inhabitants, having manor courts of their own and seneschals to preside in them; but that of Thomas Court and Donore is properly confined to the liberties, and is that from which it takes its name; this court is of very ancient foundation, being held under the charter of King John.

This area is to be found in a spacious western tract in the most elevated and airy part of the city, and contains within its precincts forty streets and lanes, called the Earl of Meath's Liberties, and a population of about 40,000 souls lives within its boundaries. It has no criminal jurisdiction, but its authorities in civil matters and the amounts of sums to be collected are unlimited. In all cases under forty shillings the seneschal decides alone, but where the sum is greater he is assisted by a jury. He has a court house to sit in and a prison in which to confine debtors.

The present state of this once flourishing region forms a strong contrast with its former condition, but it still retains many evidences of what it has been. In passing along the desolate streets, large houses of costly structure present themselves everywhere, but they are now the abode of only the most miserable. As they were deserted by the rich, they were filled by the poor, and as they decayed, they became the resort of the more abject who could find no other shelter. So crowded were they at one time that 108 persons were found in one house, lying on bare boards, and in one room seven out of twelve were found to be labouring under typhus fever.

The artisans who have made the Irish tabbinet famous throughout the world reside almost entirely in the Liberties. This beautiful fabric is everywhere esteemed and admired and its supremacy has survived all attempts at rivalry. The manufacture, which is exclusively confined to Dublin, was introduced into Ireland by certain French refugees who settled there after the revocation of the Edict of Nantes. There are, as nearly as we could ascertain, between six and seven hundred persons employed in its production, but this estimate includes weavers, warpers, winders and dyers. They are principally heads of families, and earn from ten to twenty-five shillings a week – the high wages being obtained by the weavers employed in producing brocaded or figured poplins and who are necessarily the most skilful and ingenious workmen. There are not more than two hundred looms at work in the city and neighbourhood of Dublin, and the average production of each loom is four yards per day of the plain tabbinet, and each loom employs three persons. The trade and profits derived from it are consequently limited, yet it is, strictly speaking, the only national manufacture if we except that of linens.

It is not easy to picture the 'genuine' Irish tabbinet in London, and we were given to understand that about four-fifths of the articles sold as Irish was never, either as raw or wrought material, in Ireland. As this evil is very prejudicial to the manufacture which ought to be encouraged and which deserves encouragement, we may be allowed to direct the attention of the searcher after this graceful, beautiful and durable article of dress to Miss Elliot's Irish Tabbinet Warehouse, 43 Pall Mall, where the purchaser may be assured of obtaining it without the danger of an inferior commodity being substituted for the Irish article.

The other manufactures which flourish in Dublin unhappily require but a very brief notice. In woollen cloths, the produce is of great excellence; several iron works are prosperous; the manufacture of glass is carried on to a considerable extent. In several minor articles also, the artisans of Dublin have manifested great skill, such as boots, shoes and cutlery. There is also much trade in tanning, in guns and rifles, with the establishment of Messrs Rigby having a European fame, as have the carriages of Messrs Hutton; and the porter, if we may class it under this head, of Messrs Guinness is preferred to that of any other brewery in all parts of the world, with the amount consumed in London being immense.

It is a singular fact that little more than thirty years ago London supplied the whole of Ireland with porter, and it would be scarcely an exaggeration to say that Ireland is now returning the compliment. Porter was first produced in Ireland by, we believe,

Messrs Beamish and Crawford of Cork, and its manufacture was the result of an accident. These gentlemen were agents for the sale of English porter in the south of Ireland, but on one occasion the prevalence of westerly winds kept them without a supply for so long a period that after their store was exhausted, they resolved upon an effort to avoid a similar mischance in future by endeavouring to produce it themselves. They tried the experiment; it was successful and very little London porter was afterwards imported.

The public charities of Dublin are very numerous and almost as varied as the ailments and wants of human-kind. There are hospitals for the aged and diseased; asylums for the blind, the insane, the destitute; societies to assist 'the stranger', the industrious and the 'unfortunate'; fever hospitals, lying-in hospitals, dispensaries, schools for the instruction of the deaf and dumb – in short: benevolent and charitable institutions are almost as numerous as the streets, and nearly the whole of them are supported by voluntary contributions. We have frequently had occasion to observe that nothing renders a native of Ireland, of any grade, more wretched than having nothing to give. The people are essentially charitable, and one can hardly enter a house where the ladies, young and old, are not engaged in some plan for the relief of their fellow creatures. They bestow quantities of food and clothing and are truely zealous of good works. The sums expended in private charities, considering the limited means of the expenders, is astonishing, for they are ever anxious to relieve the wants of others – even beyond their means.

Institutions for promoting science, literature and the arts are far more limited. First in rank and utility is the Dublin Society occupying Kildare House, which was purchased in 1815 from the Duke of Leinster for £20,000; it is a noble mansion, long celebrated as one of the most splendid private residences in Europe. The society originated in the meeting of a few eminent men in 1731. In 1749 it received a charter of incorporation as 'the Dublin Society for promoting Husbandry and other useful arts'. The great benefits Ireland has derived from the exertions of this institution are undeniable,and we shall refer to the Botanic Garden presently. Its museum contains a rare and almost perfect collection of the natural productions of the country; its schools have been rendered valuable auxiliaries for the spread of information and it has been eminently successful in carrying out the object for which it was established: to promote husbandry and the useful arts.

Next in importance is the Royal Irish Academy, which was incorporated in 1786 to 'promote the study of science, polite literature and antiquities'. The society possesses an extensive library, consisting chiefly of 'transactions' of foreign societies and the books relative to Ireland – a subject to which, very properly, its attention is principally directed. Premiums are occasionally given for successful essays, and the volumes of the transactions contain a vast mass of important and valuable information upon a variety of subjects. A museum is attached to the institution, which contains a collection of rare and interesting Irish relics.

The Natural History Society, which consists chiefly of the younger gentlemen labouring for the acquisition of knowledge, has already formed a museum of great value.

The Royal Hibernian Academy was chartered in 1823 for the promotion of the fine arts. It consists of fourteen academicians and ten associates. The members possess a noble and spacious building in Abbey Street erected for them by the late Francis Johnston Esq., architect, with the munificent artist having given them a lease of it for ever at the annual rent of five shillings; but notwithstanding these advantages, the Academy appears to have effected very little for the fine arts in Ireland.

The Royal Irish Academy and the Royal Hibernian Academy each receive a grant of £300 per annum from the Parliament, but in Ireland the fine arts have made but little progress; indeed, until of late, there was no effort to extend their influence, and for recent beneficial changes Ireland is not indebted to the Royal Hibernian Academy.

Hotels are to be encountered in all the fashionable streets, and the majority of them are upon a very liberal scale and exceedingly well conducted. The most popular, perhaps, is Gresham's in Sackville Street, but the old establishment of Morrisons sustains its reputation for comfort, attention and moderation of charges.

The Theatre in Hawkins Street is, and has long been, under the able and efficient management of Mr Calcraft. It is an elegant building, erected in 1820 by Samuel Beasley Esq. The earliest Dublin theatre was built in 1635 under the patronage of Lord Stafford, by John Ogilby. The next was erected in Smock Alley, then Orange Street, but it fell during representation and several persons were killed. It was subsequently repaired and F Farquhar, a native of Londonderry, made his first appearance there, as did 'Peg Woffington' Early in the last century there were no fewer than five theatres in the city, and the Crow Street Theatre was opened in the year 1758.

The Liffey is crossed by no fewer than nine bridges, and all of them are within a distance of little more than three miles. One of the most remarkable of these, the 'Barrack Bridge' was formerly called the 'Bloody Bridge', and tradition traces its ancient title to a bloody conflict fought in its vicinity in 1408 AD between the native Irish, led by a chieftain of the O'Kavanaghs, and the army of the Pale, under the command of the Duke of Lancaster, who was mortally wounded in the encounter. The erection of a grand Gothic gateway – the entrance to the Military Road – gives the bridge a peculiarly striking character, and, in a picture at least, restores it to the olden time.

The immediate vicinity of Dublin in all directions around the city is of great interest and beauty. The banks of the Liffey from the quays to a considerable distance beyond Leixlip and into the county of Kildare are highly picturesque. The Phoenix Park will be taken in by this route, for the public road runs directly under it.

In the park is the residence of the Viceroy, where of late years the representative of the sovereign in Ireland has constantly resided, being more healthful, agreeable and convenient than the Castle. The Lodge, as it is called, has no pretensions to magnificence. The park contains 1000 acres, which are admirably laid out; the trees are finely grown, and it is kept with exceeding care, and is deservedly classed as foremost among the public promenades of Great Britain.

Nearly at the entrance to the park from the city is a huge heap of stones, which are dignified by the title of the 'Wellington Testimonial', which is as ungainly and ungraceful an example of bad taste as the kingdom could supply. The cost of this absurdity exceeded £20,000, the amount having been raised by subscription. On the summit of a flight of steps stands a square pedestal, on the four sides of which are panels, with figures in *basso-relievo,* emblematic of the principal victories won by the noble Duke. From this rises the massive obelisk, which is truncated and of thick and heavy proportions. On the side of the obelisk, from the top to the base, are inscribed the names of all the places in which victories were gained by the Duke, from his first career in India to the battle of Waterloo. Opposite too, is an insulated panel on which it is intended to place an equestrian statue of the hero after his decease.

On the Kildare side of the park is an erection equally unmeaning – a tall Corinthian column surmounted by a Phoenix, which was erected in 1745 by the then Lord Lieutenant, Philip Dormer Stanhope, Earl of Chesterfield. It has contributed to the popular error which derives the title of the park from the bird fable. The origin of the name, however, is far more natural.

In the Irish vernacular, *Fionn-uisge*, which is pronounced Finnisk, signified clear, or fair water, and, articulated in the English manner, exactly resembles the word 'Phoenix'. At length the park became known, even at an early period, by no other name. The spring or well still exists, and is situated in a glen beside the lower lake beside the grand entrance to the Viceregal Lodge.

The Zoological Society have their gardens within the park, a portion of it having been allotted to them in 1830, by the then Lord Lieutenant, the Duke of Northumberland.

About four miles south-west of the city is the village of Clondalkin, with its round tower in a perfect state of preservation. Its height is about ninety feet, and it measures fifteen feet in diameter. However, the base was encased with strong mason-work in order to protect it from the assaults of time about sixty years ago – and luckily so, for, some few years after it was so judiciously guarded, a catastrophe occurred that would otherwise have levelled it with the earth. Extensive powder-mills in the neighbourhood blew up, and yet the tower withstood the shock, although, and to quote from the newspapers of the day, 'the earth seemed to shake from its very centre, and ponderous masses of many tons in weight were cast to the distance of five or six fields'.

Immediately adjoining the round tower are, as usual, the ruins of an ancient church, and it is certain that an abbey was founded here at a very early period.

The southern suburbs and vicinity of Dublin are less interesting than those of the north, but there is one district that immediately adjoins the city concerning which some remarks are necessary.

The far-famed Donnybrook is now but a shadow of its former self, but we had indeed had 'the luck to see the Donnybrook fair' before – and fortunately for the inhabitants of Dublin – it had 'fallen from high estate'. Donnybrook – the little brook – is so called from a mountain stream, the Dodder, which runs through the suburb. The Donnybrook Fair lasted for eight whole days of the month of August, and although the Irishman is no longer there in 'his glory', tents are still pitched annually on the sodden sward where they have been erected for centuries; itinerant play actors continue to gather there once a year; lads and lasses still assemble to dance under roofs of canvas; the beggars yet make it a place of rendezvous, and the din and harsh music from the shows mingles with the almost equally discordant squeakings of a score or two of bagpipes.

In the autumn of last year we were curious to ascertain the difference between the Donnybrook of yesterday and that of today, and, as prepared as we have been for the wonderful changes which a few eventful years have wrought in the habits of the people, it was with utter astonishment that we noted the contrast between the reckless devilry of a former time and the decent hilarity of the present.

Heretofore, every fair in Ireland was bad enough, but that of

Dublin surpassed them all for dissipation and vice, and a large proportion of the lower classes had to endure the penalties of want or the punishment of crime for many months after the saturnalia. To the disgrace of the country these evils were tolerated for centuries, but at length they were to some extent checked by a more efficient police, and the work of the Temperance Movement.

We entered the fair twice – at mid-day and again in the evening, a short time before the sports terminated by order of the magistrates. We saw indeed crowds of people amusing themselves. The merry-go-round and the hobby-horses were crammed, the shows thronged, and several tents were filled with dancers and gossipers, but we heard nothing and noticed nothing that could offend the most scrupulous; there was no quarrel approaching to a brawl, we did not encounter a single intoxicated person of either sex, and the next day our inquiries from a competent authority as to the amount of charges at the police-offices incident to the fair were answered by the expressive word – 'Nil.'

The Botanic Garden is situated on the north side of Dublin, at Glasnevin, about two miles from the centre of the city. A more admirable site could not have been selected. A clear stream – the Tolka – runs through a miniature valley, to which the ground gradually slopes, the tall and finely grown trees are sheltered from the north and east winds by the adjacent hills and the neighbourhood has long been celebrated for its salubrity and mild temperature.

The garden contains about twenty-eight acres and is, we believe, the largest in Great Britain. It originated in the year 1790 when Dr Wade presented a petition to the Irish Parliament by the hands of Toler, afterwards Lord Norbury, the result of which was the annual grant for its establishment and support.

Adjoining the garden is a public cemetery.

The village of Finglas stands about three miles west of Dublin. It was early distinguished for its salubrity and acquired the name of

Fionn Glas, the fair or pleasant green. It was the favoured residence of St Patrick, who predicted that it would be the future capital of Ireland, and conferred various gifts upon it, among them a well of many spiritual and physical virtues. Its waters were particularly miraculous in restoring sight to the blind, and the quantity of rags that hung about it attested to the number of its cures.

Finglas is distinguished as the scene of many historic events. Here it was that O'Connor, paramount king of Ireland, awaited the coming of the Anglo-Normans to decide the fate of Ireland. Thus the battle of Finglas attached Ireland for ever as an appendage to England. It was hither that James fled after the battle of the Boyne – 'stopping to take breath at Finglas wood'. He was speedily followed by William who encamped here with an army of 30,000 men. Hence he despatched the Duke of Ormond to take Dublin, and in the meantime strongly fortified his camp against any enemy. Part of these works form one side of the garden of the glebe-house and part is still in very perfect condition in an adjoining meadow, which is called the King's Field to this day, and which overlooks and commands the then high road leading to the capital by Cardiff's Bridge.

Among other remnants of antiquity is a ponderous stone cross of rude, but curious sculpture. The parish stands in the barony of Nethercross, so called, it is said, from a cross of great antiquity which stood there, but which had disappeared. The tradition was that a detachment of Cromwell's soldiers going to the siege of Drogheda had dashed it down as an emblem of superstition in passing by, intending to break it into pieces on their return. But the inhabitants, to protect it from further profanation, buried it and, when the soldiers came back, it was not to be found. The rumour of the circumstance induced the Rev. Dr Walsh, the curate of the parish, to search for it. After a long and fruitless search, he met with an aged man who told him that his grandfather had pointed out to his father the place where it had been buried. Taking the old man as his guide, and some labourers to assist him, he began to dig, and actually found the cross where it had been buried some two hundred years ago. It now stands in the old churchyard, but it is the intention of the discoverer to have it erected in the area in front of the new church, which he is now building, as an appropriate ornament.

About four miles north of Finglas and on the road to Drogheda, is the ancient town of Swords, with its ruined castle, round tower and its monastic remains. The castle is very picturesque, standing on the banks of a clear and rapid river. It was formerly a palace of the Archbishop of Dublin, and must have been a strong as well as an extensive pile. It consists of ranges of embattled walls flanked with towers. Swords was formerly a place of considerable importance, having had the honour to be repeatedly plundered by the Danes, who destroyed it no fewer than four times during the eleventh and twelfth centuries. But like most of the ancient towns in Ireland, Swords was of ecclesiastical origin. A monastery appears to have been erected here as early as the year 512 by the famous St Columbkill, who appointed St Finian Lobhair, or the Leper, as its abbot, and to whom he gave a missal, or copy of the gospels, which was then, of course, a rare treasure – and which had been written by himself. St Finian died before the close of the sixth century.

Some further miles north is the small town of Lusk, and here too, in the earliest age of Christianity, an abbey was erected with its attendant chapel and cells, and here also the church was castellated for the defence of the monastic establishment.

Returning towards Dublin, but along the coast, about a mile to the left of the road is one of the most venerable and interesting castles of Ireland: the Castle of Malahide, the old fortified Mansion of the Talbots – and happily not a ruin, for it is still the residence of the representative of the Anglo-Norman who won the land with his sword in the reign of the second Henry. It retains many marks of antiquity. It is an extensive square building, flanked by circular towers, having received considerable additions of late years, but they have been made in keeping with its ancient character – and a very slight effort of the imagination will link its existing state with the history of the olden time.

The mansion is beautifully furnished and in admirable taste, and the collection of paintings, although not extensive, is unsurpassed in value. Among them are choice specimens of the old Dutch and Italian masters in an excellent state of preservation, but the assemblage of portraits is, indeed, of even greater interest.

Close to the castle are the ruins of an ancient church, surrounded by chestnut trees of magnificent growth, which adds greatly to the impressive character of the whole scene, associated as it is with the memories of its heroic founders.

Some three or four miles nearer to Dublin is the singular church of St Douglough, forming, with its holy well and its stone cross, an assemblage of relics of antiquity which rank amongst the most interesting and remarkable in Ireland, for the church is one of the few remaining stone-roofed structures.

As we alighted to visit this old church, on our road from Malahide Castle, where we had enjoyed the hospitality of its noble lord and his estimable lady, the carriage was surrounded by a troop of beggars – three women, two men and a due proportion of children, but a halfpenny to each sent them cheerfully away and left us free to examine the churchyard without interruption.

You may journey many a mile in England, and the people you will meet are in their manner and deportment so much alike that they appear, if not members of the one family, then to have all been educated in the same school. It is otherwise in Ireland; everywhere there is some national characteristic, the ramifications of which are various and numerous. The English pauper is at once bowed down by misery and murmurs and complains under its endurance from first to last. The Irish beggar wrestles with distress; he can exist upon so little food as to seem almost to be able to live without it, but he cannot do without his jest – there are moments when the heart beats lightly even in his starving bosom. The poverty of the English, except at stated times, is sullen, but the Irishman is garrulous; the Englishman takes relief as a right, but the Irishman accepts it as a boon. You may aid half a dozen English paupers without receiving thanks, but you cannot relieve an Irish beggar without being paid in blessings.

We have – as we intimated we should be compelled to do –

taken but a very superficial glance at the objects of interest with which the vicinity of the city and county of Dublin so largely abound.

The county of Dublin is bounded on the north and north-west by the county of Meath; on the west and south by that of Kildare; on the south side by that of Wicklow; and on the east by the Irish sea.

It is divided into six baronies – Balrothery, Castleknock, Coolock, Nethercross, Newcastle, Half Rathdown and Upper Cross.

We cannot bring our notice of Dublin to a close without mentioning, however briefly, an event which will long be remembered in its annals: we allude, of course, to the royal visit of August 1849.

Her Majesty's sojourn in the Irish metropolis was limited to a few days, but with her accustomed activity, she so well employed her hours that ample time was found to see the principal objects of interest in Dublin and its vicinity, to render her Irish subjects happy by her frequent appearance in public, and to exercise one of the most pleasing, if not the most important functions of royalty – the holding of a drawing-room and levee in the Castle of Dublin.

Illuminations and fireworks by night, decorated arches and waving banners, bands of music and triumphal processions by day rendered Dublin the noisiest and gayest of capitals and its inhabitants the happiest of Irishmen.

From the 2000 ladies and gentlemen who were honoured with admissions to the royal presence at the castle, to the 100,000 of high and low degree who thronged the Phoenix Park on the day of the review, all were gratified by Her Majesty's affable and condescending behaviour, and we believe every one returned to his home, not only proud of his Queen and his country, but feeling his own dignity increased by his participation in the national holiday.

Let us hope that we are now rapidly approaching a brighter and calmer day, and that ere long Dublin may again take that rank among metropolitan cities which its natural beauties and artificial advantages so well deserve.

Chapter Four

MEATH

The county of Meath is the great grazing ground of Ireland and consists almost entirely of pastureland, and vies in its external aspect with the richest of the English counties, perhaps surpassing any of them in fertility. The hedges are remarkably luxuriant, and the trees – of which there are an unusual abundance – are of extraordinary growth, and the fields have at all times and seasons the brilliant green so refreshing to the eye and so cheering to the mind. There is, indeed, no part of Ireland where the Englishman will find himself so completely at home, for added to the natural beauty, he will see on all sides the beneficial results of careful cultivation, and he will mark in every direction the ordinary consequences of industry directed by science, while the poverty and wretchedness that are elsewhere forced upon his attention are seldom perceptible here, and the clamorous voice of woe rarely intrudes upon his ear. Much of this apparently prosperous character, is however, hollow and insubstantial, for while the larger farmers are indeed wealthy, there are few or no small farmers.

We shall place the tourist first in the town of Trim, which lies twenty-two miles distant from Dublin and is situated in the south-west division of the county, of which it is the assize town, although it is inferior both in extent and population to Navan. It borders the Boyne water which divides Meath into nearly two equal parts, running from south-west to north-east. At the entrance to Trim from the south stands a Corinthian column of granite erected by subscription in 1817 to commemorate the military achievements of his Grace, the Duke of Wellington, to whose connection with this country we shall presently advert.

To the right stands a county jail – one of the best built and best conducted prisons in Ireland – and the ancient castle of the De Lacys, the Anglo-Normans to whom Henry II gave a large share of the kingdom of the O'Melaghlins, who were the monarchs of Meath, and which was formerly one of the five provinces into which Ireland was divided. Hugh De Lacy, to whom Meath was granted, and who was one of the most conspicuous of the Anglo-Norman invaders, was treacherously killed at Durrow in the Queen's County by a labouring man who, with his axe, struck off the head of the great soldier as he was stooping to give him some directions concerning the hewing of a block of timber.

The castle is now a mass of highly picturesque ruins lining the banks of the splendid river, and recalls the memory of its days of almost regal splendour. The walls are nearly four hundred and eighty-six yards in circumference, and are defended by ten flanking towers at nearly equal distance – including those at the gates, one of which is in a good state of preservation, as well as the arches over the ditch and the barbican beyond it. The castle is by no means the only interesting relic of antiquity in the town of Trim. The Yellow Tower, which is part of a tall steeple, marks the site of a famous abbey, said to have been founded by St Patrick and dedicated to the Virgin.

In the school-house it is generally, but erroneously, imagined that the Marquis of Wellesley and the Duke of Wellington received their early education, but neither of them were educated here. Yet it would be difficult to convince the good people of Trim that they can lay no claim to this honour, and it is with regret that we destroy so pleasant a delusion.

However, the Duke, while representing the borough in the Irish Parliament, and serving as aide-de-camp to the Lord Lieutenant, seems to have taken an active part in the affairs of the town, for his signature, 'A Wesley', is affixed to all the leading acts of the corporation from June 1789 to September 1793.

Dangan, the former seat of the Wellesleys, is about seven miles distant from Trim and about twenty from Dublin. On the death of Lord Mornington it became the property of the Marquis of Wellesley, from whom it was purchased by a gentleman named Boroughs who, after residing there for some time, and adding many improvements to it, let it on a lease to Mr Roger O'Connor – a person whose name is sufficiently notorious, not only in the county of Meath, but throughout the south of Ireland. While in his possession, the house and demesne were dismantled of every article that could be converted into money. The trees – of which there was an immense variety of prodigious height and girth – rapidly fell beneath the axe, the gardens were permitted to run waste, and an application to the Lord Chancellor proved utterly ineffective, and at length, the premises being largely insured, the house was found to be on fire and was, of course, consumed before any assistance could be obtained to extinguish it. Most unhappily, therefore, one of the most interesting mansions in the kingdom is now but a collection of bared and broken walls – a mere shell.

The wreck of the house is inhabited by a farmer and his family, and a very pretty young woman was feeding a calf in a shed erected under the shelter of the ruins.

'Many strangers,' she said, 'visited Dangan, and it was a lonesome place in the winter time,' but she never minded, 'if there were any spirits, as people said about the house, they had too much nobility to hurt the poor that, when they were in it, gave them all they had to give – their blessing.'

She gave us something more than that – milk, fresh, warm and frothing, and after going with us from place to place, refused with a half-indignant air the money we tendered as remuneration for the trouble we had caused. In England we never have any difficulty in prevailing upon this class of persons to accept a silver token of thanks, but in Ireland, although sometimes repeated offers will overcome their repugnance, they invariably refuse, and if they do take it, apologise for so doing: 'Sure, I wasn't thinking of the like,' or 'Thank ye kindly ma'am, and sure I wouldn't let on to have it at all – only out of a remembrance.' Indeed, we have generally found it necessary when we had given trouble to, or incurred an obligation from a peasant, to present our donation to one of the children as the only way to avoid hurting very sensitive feelings. This girl, so pretty and so kind, would not barter kindness for anything save thanks. Though we shall in all probability never meet her again, we cannot forget her bland smile, and the gentle tones of her cheerfully confiding voice which clung like a strain of half-forgotten music to the honoured walls of Dangan.

The caretaker of Dangan seemed poor in all things save of 'livestock' or rosy, romping children, whose wild laughter and repeated shouts we heard through the still evening air, long before we returned to the lodge.

The entrance gates to the park of Dangan still exist, one of the gates that is to say, for another is placed before a Roman Catholic chapel recently erected at Navan. The gate that remains is of wrought iron, of very costly workmanship and great beauty; the lodge yet stands beside it, and is an exquisite example of architecture.

A short distance from the Yellow Tower of Trim, and still upon the banks of the Boyne, are the ruins of another abbey – the Abbey of Newtown. It is said to have been founded in 1206 AD by Simon Rochfort, the first Englishman who sat as Bishop of Meath, abandoning the cathedral church of his Irish predecessor in the see for his new structure, the Church of Clonard. It was a priory of regular canons and the prior was a peer in parliament.

Indeed, in all directions about Trim the remains of monastic establishments are to be encountered, and various public buildings have been erected on the foundations of several. The sites of others are indicated by but a few ivied walls; of yet others – the records of which are preserved – not the slightest remnant endures to determine their existence. The old church, part of which is still used for service, is very curious. The tower or belfry is unimpaired and affords ample proof that the building was resorted to not alone for the purposes of worship, but as a stronghold for defence in cases of danger from the inroads of the native chieftains.

But even a list of the ruined abbeys, monasteries and churches in this at all times rich and prosperous county would occupy many pages. The most majestic of them all is that of Bective, which lies nearly midway between Trim and Navan and is also on the banks of the Boyne. The abbey was richly endowed and the abbot, who was a peer of parliament, appears to have lived in considerable splendour. Under the arch of this abbey tradition affixes the interment of the body of Hugh De Lacy, the first Lord Palatine of Meath, his head having been buried in Dublin in the church of St Thomas in 1195 AD.

The ruins comprise some beautiful specimens of pointed arches and cloisters with a tower. In the centre is a square space that seems to have been roofed at one period, and in the south front is a tower with projecting angles, and access is obtained from the gallery to the cells under the chapel.

The county contains two round towers – that of Kells and that of Donaghmore.

On our way to Navan we visited Ardbraccan, the palace of the Bishops of Meath, and paid our respects to the estimable prelate who now resides over the see. The building is a very handsome one, and has been recently put into thorough repair. The gardens are nobly planted and admirably kept, and perhaps nowhere in the British dominions do we find loftier or more luxuriantly grown trees.

From Navan we proceeded about four miles on the Dublin road to visit the renowned Hill of Tara. From the main road there is a considerable ascent for about a mile before we arrive at the commencement of the mounds, which are evidently artificial. It then seems to the superficial observer a mere assemblage of hillocks, the largest of which is about thirty yards long, and of equal breadth; and nearly in the centre upon this stands the marvellous pillar stone.

This hillock is now known as the 'Croppy Hill' from the fact that a number of insurgents were buried there in 1798. The pillar originally stood upon another and smaller hillock, and it was moved to its present place to mark the spot – and to dignify it – in which so many slaughtered patriots were buried.

Tara is a place celebrated in Irish history as having been the chief seat of the monarchs of Ireland for ages. This was where their laws were promulgated, the resort of its druids and musicians and the great stronghold of druidism for centuries, having become the residence of its kings on the first establishment of a monarchical government, under Slainge, ruler of the Fir Bolgs, or Belgae, and so continuing until the middle of the sixth century – a period during which one hundred and forty-two monarchs reigned, of which six were Christian.

The principal earthen work still existing on the Hill of Tara is Rath Riogh, the next are Rath Laoghaire, Rath na Seanadh, Rath Eachhor,and the next Rath Grannia. Within the enclosure of Rath Riogh are the ruins of the House of Cormac, the Mound of the Hostages and the *teach miodhchuarta* or banqueting house, *tober finn*, the well, and the two *clann-ferts*, and of those the northern was famous for the slaughter of the virgins by the Laegenians of Smana's Day, and the southern for a false sentence pronounced there by a king named Lughardh MacCon, for which he was afterwards destroyed.

The most singular of all these ancient monuments, however, is that which still exists and is comparatively uninjured by time, and that is the pillar stone of which we have already made mention. This is the Lia Fail, the celebrated coronation stone of the ancient Irish kings. It is composed of granular limestone and is at present about six feet above the ground, and its real height is said to be twelve feet. At its base it is perhaps four feet in circumference, but it tapers somewhat towards the top, not unlike the round towers. Some remarkable relics of antiquity are also to be found in the graveyard of a church near the summit of the hill. It is modern but occupies the site of a very ancient structure, which was also built upon the spot on which it is said there formerly existed a pagan temple.

And so we part from Tara; we shall not easily forget the morning we passed upon the hill, nor the magnificent prospect of a fair country we beheld from its summit – although immediately around us we could see only high barrows, without marble or a name.

We have been seduced by the exceeding interest of the subject into describing Tara at greater length than we designed, and therefore we must be concise in our description of a scene still more singular and with claims to remote antiquity even less questionable.

The tumulus of New Grange is situated on the banks of the

Boyne, between Drogheda and Slane. It is one of four tumuli in the neighbourhood all of which, it is conjectured, cover remains equally wonderful, for all are nearly similar in appearance and supply the same external evidence of artificial origin. Of their druidical character no one can entertain even the remotest doubt.

The mound is said to cover two acres of ground. Its elevation is about seventy feet, but its original height was considerably greater, because for centuries it has been resorted to as a quarry. It is composed of small stones, heaped one atop the other above the plain, and time has covered it with a coating of earth which in some places is not many inches in depth.

At the base the hill was formerly surrounded by shapeless masses of rock, supposed to weigh from ten to twelve tons each, of which some still exist, partly sunken into the mould, with the parts that are above ground covered with lichen. The single one at the top has vanished altogether. These stones, as well as those of which the interior is constructed, are not to be found in the vicinity, and must have been conveyed to the place from a distance of at least seven miles.

The interior was first explored in the year 1699 by a neighbouring gentleman who, while carrying away some of the stones to repair a road, came at last to a very broad, flat, rudely carved stone placed edgewise at the bottom of the mound, which, he found, led into a long and very narrow gallery which in turn led to the druidic chamber.

We crept, or rather crawled, along a distance of about sixty feet, with the height being no more than eighteen inches and the breadth somewhat less than twenty-four feet. The passage is roofed and the sides are supported by enormous slabs. About midway there is a stone which appears to have fallen from the perpendicular and seems to forbid further progress, but this was passed, however, by twisting the body onwards, and the avenue gradually expands and the Dome is entered.

Here we were compelled to remain in darkness until the arrival of a supply of candles. The effect of the light upon this wonderful cave was startling and exciting in the highest degree, and we stood where, above two thousand years ago, the druids offered sacrifices, or at least where they held their solemn meetings, for of its origins there is no doubt, and almost as little that it was the Inner Temple of their secret rites.

Opposite the entrance and at the sides to the right and left are three cavities, each of which formerly contained oval basins, and in one of them – to the right – the basin is still perfect. There can be no question that the stone has been scooped into this form by art, and the other, although much broken, completely tallies with it, and many parts of the cave contain sculptured marks that are, beyond all possibility of doubt, the productions of human hands. There are various forms: spiral, lozenge, diamond, zig-zag and circular, and similar signs occur in the narrow gallery. They bear tokens of good and even refined workmanship. We found, however, nothing that bore the remotest resemblance to letters – nothing that reminded us of the ancient Ogham character, which is so frequently encountered in the south.

Of a later date, but in its way no less remarkable than Tara, New Grange and the many other curious remains and antiquities of Meath, is that extraordinary collection of bones and antiquities recently discovered near the village of Dunshaughlin.

Dunshaughlin lies on the mail road from Navan to Dublin, nine miles from the former and fourteen from the latter, and about four miles east of Tara. The place where the bones were dug up is the townland of Lagore, at the north-eastern extremity of a bog called, from the colour of the peat, the Black Bog. There is another town skirting the north side of the bog which is called Bones-Town, and both Kileen Castle and Dunsany Castle are within a short distance of Dunshaughlin, to the west.

The county of Meath adjoins that of Dublin; its boundaries on the east are with the Irish Sea; on the south it is bounded by Kildare and the King's County; on the west by Westmeath; and on the north by Louth, Monaghan and Cavan.

Its principal towns are Trim, Navan, Kells, Slane and Athboy. It is divided into the baronies of Upper and Lower Deece, Demifore, Upper and Lower Duleek, Dunboyne, Upper and Lower Kells,

Lune, Morgallion, Upper and Lower Moyfenrath, Upper and Lower Navan, Ratoath, Skreen, Upper and Lower Slane.

Chapter Five

WESTMEATH

The history of this county very closely resembles that of Meath. It was settled under the same circumstances; it is as full of the ancient remains of the Anglo-Normans and the earlier inhabitants, but it is far more abundant in natural attractions, and some of its lakes – Lough Ree in particular – may vie in interest and beauty with those of the south.

The limits of our work will not permit us to describe at length those counties which have no very remarkable or peculiar features and we must move on.

The inland county of Westmeath is bounded on the east by Meath, on the south by the King's County, on the west by Roscommon, from which it is separated by the river Shannon, on the north-west by Longford, and on the north by the county of Cavan.

It is divided into the baronies of Brawney, Clonlonan, Corkaree, Delvin, Demifore, Farbill, Fartullagh, Kilkenny West, Moyashel and Magheradernan, Moycashel, Moygoish and Rathconrath. Part of Athlone is also in Westmeath. The principal towns are Mullingar, the assize town, Moate, Rathowen, Ballymore, Castletown-Delvin and Ballynacaragh.

Chapter Six

LOUTH

Many circumstances contribute to render the maritime county of Louth, although it is the smallest county in Ireland, exceedingly interesting – either in reference to its existing remains or to the prominent station it occupies in Irish history. The Siege of Drogheda is scarcely paralleled for atrocity on the part of the besiegers, and the memory of the Battle of the Boyne-water is, as it must ever be, 'glorious and immortal'.

The county abounds in vestiges of very remote antiquity, and some of these we shall describe briefly, limiting ourselves, however, to the monastic remains.

First in interest and importance is the round tower – with its usual accompaniments of ruins – at Monasterboice, which is about four miles distant from Drogheda, and lying in the centre of a small valley a short distance from the main road. Seen from this road the effect is singularly striking; the group of sacred glories is comprised within the boundary of a small churchyard, and consists of the shells of two chapels, two perfect stone crosses of very beautiful and elaborate workmanship, and the round tower. The tower is one hundred and ten feet high, and yet the height must have been considerably greater, for the cap and upper parts were destroyed some years ago by lightning. The religious establishment of Monasterboice was for a long period ranked among the most celebrated of Ireland; its origin has been traced to St Buite, or Boetius, who was a disciple of St Patrick, about the close of the fifth century.

The Abbey of Mellifont is on the little river Mattock, near the banks of the Boyne and on the borders of Meath. The ruins are not extensive, but in architectural beauty they are surpassed by few in Ireland. The chapel of St Bernard seems partly embedded in the rock, with the floor being considerably lower than the outer surface, and the ruins consist of a crypt or underground chapel and an upper apartment. In this chapel were interred the remains of the founder of the abbey, Donough McCorvoill, or O'Carroll, who, it is said, undertook the work at the solicitation of St Malachy, and it was the first Cistercian abbey erected in Ireland.

An object of equal interest is the remains of an octagonal building, which is conjectured to have been the bapistry, on the top of which was a reservoir for water which was conveyed by pipes to the several offices of the abbey. The ruins are situated in a secluded little valley, and are highly picturesque, and their present lonely and desolate character singularly contrasts with the tokens of ancient grandeur which are apparent everywhere.

Before we visit Drogheda and the Boyne-water – subjects which will demand no inconsiderable space – we must entreat the reader to 'step across the county' from the extreme south to the far north and, passing through the poor town of Louth and the neat, clean and apparently prosperous town of Dundalk – which is famous in history as the place where Edward Bruce was 'solemnly crowned' king of Ireland in 1315 – examine awhile the beautiful seaport of Carlingford with its fine castellated and monastic remains. As with so many of the 'stone houses' of Ireland, the building of this structure is attributed to King John, whose name it continues to bear. The town was situated on the frontier of the Pale, and therefore became of importance soon after the Anglo-Norman invasion, and fortifications as well as religious establishments rapidly sprang up within its precincts. On the southern side are the ruins of a Dominican monastery. This still extensive and picturesque ruin exhibits, in the long aisle and central belfry, traces of the pointed architecture of the fourteenth century. About mid-way between it and King John's Castle are the ruins of a square building with windows which, although of an ecclesiastical character, are curiously ornamented with carvings of animals, human heads and sundry fancy wreathings. Near this, on an adjoining eminence is a church of ancient foundation.

The bay of Carlingford and the adjacent scenery are of exceeding beauty, with both its north and south borders lined with

CARLINGFORD,
LOUTH

villas and small white villages. It is surrounded by magnificent mountains and a few small green islands, nearly at the entrance to the bay, give interest and variety to the scene.

One of the most remarkable and picturesque of the ruined castles of Louth is Castle Roche. It stands on the summit of a rocky hill and was formerly one of the frontier castles of the English Pale. The area within its walls bears the form of a triangle, but is more inclined to a semi-circle as it follows the uneven form of the hill, taking advantage of the rock on which it stands. At the opposite corner to the main dwelling there has been a tower of defence and under it a sally-port. It is reported to have been constructed by a Rose Verdun, who was of an ancient English family of large possessions, and from her it was therefore called Rose Castle, which was corrupted to Roche Castle. In the year 1649 it held out for King Charles and was demolished by Oliver Cromwell.

We must now request the reader to return with us to Drogheda, a town very rich in historical associations and memorable as the scene of a massacre hardly equalled for atrocity in the records of human-kind.

At present the character of Drogheda is that of a 'compact' town; the suburbs indeed are sufficiently wretched, but the leading streets present an appearance of bustle and business; the quays look as if they were trodden by the foot of commerce and the exhibition of a coarse kind of linen on stalls in various places gives token of an approach towards the manufacturing north. The sea is close at hand and vessels of burthen may discharge their cargoes at the bridge – a bridge which divides the town, part of which, as we have intimated, is in the county of Meath. Few towns are more advantageously circumstanced for trade with England: it lies nearly opposite Liverpool; is the great outlet for the produce of the rich counties adjacent; the river Boyne runs through it to the ocean, and a navigable canal facilitates intercourse with several districts of Meath. These advantages will be considerably enhanced when the railway, which is now in progress, is completed to Dublin, so that a journey to the capital, from which it is distant about twenty-two miles, will be made in less than an hour.

At a very early period Drogheda was a fortified town, and in the fourteenth century it had attained considerable commercial importance. But until the year 1641 – the year of the famous rebellion – its annals contain no records of stirring events. A fearful and disastrous visitation, however, awaited Drogheda in 1649 when Oliver Cromwell commenced, by his assault upon that town, a ruthless and bloody career in Ireland, the remembrance of which is still freshly preserved in the expressive execration so common in the mouths of the Irish peasantry – 'The curse of Cromwell be upon you.'

Cromwell landed in Dublin early in August, with an army consisting of '8,000 foot, 4,000 horse, £20,000 in money, a formidable train of artillery and all other necessaries of war'. At the head of his forces, he at once proceeded to Tredagh – the ancient name of Drogheda – then garrisoned by 2,500 foot and 300 horse under the command of Sir Arthur Aston, the governor, 'a brave and experienced officer'.

'A resolution being taken to besiege that place, our army sat down before it and the Lieutenant-General caused a battery to be erected, by which he made a breach in the wall.'

The spot from which he first assaulted the town is still known by the name of 'Cromwell's Fort'. It stands on the summit of a hill that completely commands the town, but the fortifications which now crown it are of comparatively recent erection.

'The garrison was not dismayed' – they expected succour from Ormond – 'and seemed to be unanimous in their resolution rather than deliver up the town to expire with it – which they did not long after.'

Twice they repulsed the enemy, but a third assault, led by the Lieutenant-General in person, was successful.

'Our men entered pell-mell with the enemy, but Aston's men fought bravely and desperately disputed every corner of the streets, making the conquerors win what they had by inches.' Indeed, Cromwell himself, in his despatch to the parliament, admits that the enemy 'disputed very stiffly with us'.

Some historians assert, and it is borne out in the assertion by various safe authorities, that 'safe quarter had been promised to all who should lay down their arms', but the moment the town was completely reduced, Cromwell issued his order for a general and indiscriminate massacre.

The storming of Drogheda was but the first act of a terrible tragedy; every step which Cromwell took through Ireland was marked with blood and his frightful example was too closely imitated by his generals.

Of the old walls and fortifications of Drogheda there are still some interesting remains, the most perfect of which is the Gate of St Lawrence. Ancient monastic relics are also of very frequent occurrence within the boundary of the town. Among the more remarkable is the ruin of St Mary's Church, 'founded by the citizens of Drogheda under Edward I'. It was originally a convent of Carmelites and called St Mary's of Mount Carmel, a name which is very expressive of its situation, as it is erected on the most elevated part of the southern division of the town and occupies the south-east angle of the town-wall.

But Drogheda fills a far less dismal page in Irish history, for the name is associated with a triumph stained by no atrocities, and within sight of towers which were blackened by the ruthless soldiery of Cromwell, a victory was gained which had more beneficial results to Great Britain than all her conquests before or since achieved, and the Battle of the Boyne must be regarded as the key-stone of the temple of civil and religious liberty in these kingdoms.

The Boyne is a very beautiful and picturesque river; it winds through the fertile valleys of Meath and from its richly wooded banks the hills rise gradually, and there are no lofty mountains in the immediate neighbourhood. The depth is in nearly all parts considerable, and consequently the current is not very rapid. Its width near the field of battle varies little and is seldom less than fifty or sixty yards.

Louth is bounded on the east by the Irish Sea, on the north by the

Bay of Carlingford, and the county of Armagh, on the south by the county of Meath, and on the west by the counties of Meath and Monaghan.

It is divided into the baronies of Ardee, Ferrard, Louth, and Upper and Lower Dundalk. The only towns of note are Drogheda and Dundalk, if we except the once famous but now decayed port of Carlingford.

Chapter Seven

CAVAN

The county of Cavan possesses no feature of striking or peculiar character, and in natural beauty it is far surpassed by the adjoining counties of Meath, Fermanagh and Armagh.

This inland county is bounded on the north by the county of Fermanagh, on the west by that of Leitrim, on the east and north-east by Monaghan and on the south by parts of the counties of Longford, Meath and Westmeath.

It is divided into the baronies of Castleraghan, Clonmahon, Clonkee, Upper and Lower Loughtee, Tullagarvey, Tullaghonoho and Tullaghagh. Cavan and Belturbet are the only towns of size.

Chapter Eight

ARMAGH

Few of the Irish counties fill so prominent a page in ancient Irish history as that of the county of Armagh. And while it may be surpassed by many in picturesque beauty, it is surpassed by none in the sturdy, independent character of its peasantry. Along the high roads and also among the by-ways very little poverty is encountered; the cottages are for the most part neat, clean and comfortable, and few of them are without orchards added to the ordinary garden, and the continual click-clack of the shuttle betokens the industry that is securing humble luxuries within, and the whole of its inmates, from the very aged to the very young, are made useful in some degree.

The city of Armagh, from whatever side it is approached, is an object of considerable interest and beauty. It lines the sides of a steep hill which stands almost in the centre of a remarkably fertile valley. The new houses are, for the most part, built of marble, and the streets are literally paved with the same material. From its high position therefore, and the solid character of the buildings, its appearance is singularly pure and clear and even the lowest alleys have a character of decent and orderly arrangement.

Several public structures have of late years been erected and in every instance due regard has been given to elegance as well as durability; walks have been laid out in various directions around the city to which the public have free access and great exertions have been made by many of its citizens to render modern Armagh worthy of its ancient fame. This ancient fame is derived mainly from its cathedral which crowns the summit of a hill – Druimsaileach – and which is seen from all points within a great distance of the long-celebrated City of the Saints.

The original name was Druin-sao-each, 'the hill of swallows', which was afterwards changed into Ardsailech, 'the height of the swallows', and still later to Ard-macha, which comes from either Eamhuin-macha, the regal residence of the kings of Ulster which stood in its vicinity or, as is more probable, from its characteristic situation: Ard-macha signifying the 'high place or field', and hence Armagh. In the charter by which James I incorporated the inhabitants of the city into a borough, it is called Ardmagh.

The foundation of the city and cathedral has been ascribed to St Patrick on grounds which are sufficiently satisfactory. Patrick arrived in Ireland in 432 AD and made such rapid progress in the conversion of its inhabitants that about three years afterwards, in 435, he founded this city, built his cathedral and surrounded it with various ecclesiastical edifices.

Various opinions exist as to the birth-place of the saint. He was probably born at Tours on the 5th April 372 or 373, and his family were of Roman origin. In the sixteenth year of his age he was stolen by some adventurers and sold into slavery in Ireland. From hence he made his escape and he is said to have cherished the idea of converting the Irish; he had attained his sixtieth year before he commenced his mission into that country. However, he lived to complete his work. 'After having established 365 churches, ordained a like number of bishops and 3000 presbyters, he died in the Abbey of Saul or Sabhal, on the 17th March 493, at the patriarchal age of one hundred and twenty years.'

The schools and colleges founded at Armagh became famous throughout Europe, and are said to have furnished England with its earliest teachers, having been, in fact, the small spring which supplied the healing waters of Christianity to the other British Isles.

The comparatively humble church of St Patrick vanished centuries ago, but time after time and upon the same site sacred edifices have been erected. Early in the ninth century the city and its cathedral were destroyed by the Danes and as often as the inhabitants attempted to rebuild them, they received visits from their implacable enemies. There are records to prove that between the ninth and twelfth centuries the city was, either partially or wholly, burned no fewer than seventeen times. The cathedral having been restored was once again consumed by fire in 1404 and again, by Shane O'Neil, in 1566, 'upon which occasion the city shared the same fate and was reduced to a parcel of wattled cottages with the ruinous walls of a monastery, priory and the Primate's palace'.

In 1642 it underwent a similar fate, 'Sir Phelim O'Neil having burned it'. After that catastrophe, however, it was subjected to frequent repairs or rather 'restorations' by successive Primates. The repairs were however effected piecemeal, and the structure presented an heterogeneous mass until the present Archbishop, Lord John Beresford, was promoted to the see of Armagh to which he was translated from Dublin on 22nd June 1822. His Grace immediately applied himself to the work of its complete restoration. A public meeting was held on 14th March 1835 and subscriptions, headed by the Primate, were entered into and on so munificent a scale that the work was rapidly proceeded with. Upwards of £12,000 was at once contributed and the restoration was entrusted to Mr Cottingham, the accomplished architect whose reputation had been previously established by his successful restorations of Rochester Cathedral and the Abbey of St Albans.

In its present state, no ecclesiastical structure in Great Britain of similar extent, surpasses the Cathedral of Armagh in grace and beauty, which, crowning the summit of the hill, overlooks a wide expanse of rich country.

Although the relics of ancient times are remarkably rare within the city of Armagh, they are very abundant in its immediate vicinity; indeed, of Norman castles there are few or none, but of ages far more remote there exist some of the most striking in Ireland.

The Rath of Navan, which lies about two miles distant from the cathedral, resembles the Hill of Tara in its general character, and it is more picturesque, though less extensive. It is said to have been the site of the Palace of Eamhain, erected in AM 3603, and adjoining it was a House of the Red-Branch Knights, and to this day every place in the neighbourhood retains a name similar to that which it might have borne before the Christian era. Thus for example, a townland close beside the hill is still denominated

Creeve Roe, a name which in English letters expresses the very sound designated in the Irish characters by the words *Craobh Ruadh*, the red branch. It is impossible to examine the rath without being fully convinced that, huge as it is, it was the product of human labour.

Various relics of antiquity are dug up from time to time in its vicinity; indeed, so numerously are they found that a cottager seldom occupies a day in delving a field without striking his spade against some record of long ages past – arrow-heads continually, sometimes a spear-head or skene, and now and then a brooch or ring of costly workmanship.

In driving to the magnificent Lough Neagh from our headquarters in the neighbourhood of Portadown, we passed through a singular district called the 'Munches'. Let the reader imagine a tract of bog stretching far and away; carriage and cart roads have been formed through it at great expense, and yet the only change of soil is from bad bog to good bog, from turf so black and hard that its very sight gladdens the housewife's heart, to poor pale brown crumbling stuff, which the poor burn because they can afford no better. Squatters are numerous, but they have managed to cultivate patches of this arid common into productive land.

At the termination of this outspread bog we came in sight of Lough Neagh and, standing upon its banks, we saw, as it were, a sea encompassed by land. However, of its peculiar features, and they are many, we shall hereafter have occasion to speak in a later chapter.

Our visits to the towns of Armagh afforded us much enjoyment. Portadown, Lurgan and Tanderagee have each a thriving look; their large markets suggest the notion of abundance and the warehouses for the sale of linen bore testimony to the industry that produces wealth.

The principal proprietor of Tanderagee is Lord Manderville, who, with his neighbours, Lords Farnham and Roden, Colonel Blacker and the Marquis of Downshire, have contributed largely to the present cheering condition of the county of Armagh. Lord Manderville has established no fewer than sixteen district schools on his estate in this neighbourhood, for the support of which he devotes £1000 per annum, out of an income which is by no means large. In the schools there are twenty-two teachers and the average daily attendance of scholars is 2000, and these are maintained independently of aid from any society.

Armagh is an inland county in the province of Ulster; its boundaries are the county of Down on the east, Louth on the south-east, Monaghan on the south-west, Tyrone on the north and north-west and the great inland sea of Ireland, Lough Neagh, on the north.

It is divided into the baronies of Armagh, Turaney, O'Neilland East and West, Upper and Lower Fews and Upper and Lower Orier. Besides the city of Armagh, the county contains the towns of Lurgan, Portadown, Tanderagee, Market-Hill and Newtown-Hamilton, with all of them being comparatively large and prosperous and presenting appearances of cleanliness and comfort very cheering to the tourist who has made his way upwards from the south.

Chapter Nine

DOWN

The county of Down is remarkable for the inequality of its surface, for, although the mountains are chiefly confined to the southern district, where they are magnificent, the lesser hills are abundant in all parts; hence it is said to have derived its name, Dunum, which signifies 'a hill or a hilly country'. This peculiar characteristic – a perpetual rise and fall in the landscape – renders it highly picturesque; moreover, it is not ill-wooded, it contains many rivers, the ocean is its boundary on three sides and the huge inland sea, Strangford Lough, forms another striking and interesting feature of the county.

The tourist proceeding northwards to Belfast or, if he is en route to the Causeway, will pass through the pleasant and flourishing town of Newry, which lies about fifty miles distant from Dublin. However, the tourist in search of the picturesque must verge about seven miles to the right along the banks of the Newry-water to visit the beautiful village of Rosstrevor, which is not inaptly named the 'Montpelier of Ireland'.

The ruined castle of Narrow-water lies about two miles from Newry, but its date is no more remote than the reign of the second Charles, having been built after the restoration by the great Duke of Ormond as a protection to the river. However, a modern castle has been erected upon the rising ground above it by Roger Hall, Esq., a principal proprietor of the district. A little further on is the village of Warrens-point, which is backed by the mountains and faces the broad bay, and some three miles to the east is beautiful Rosstrevor, which is esteemed as one of the best and most frequented bathing-places in all the north of Ireland. In 1827 a small neat church was erected here, and immediately adjoining it there is a Presbyterian meeting-house and also a Roman Catholic church. Although but a few years since this was a very inconsiderable village, at present it contains a thousand inhabitants. A large windmill stands nearly in its centre, and there was formerly a very extensive rabbit-warren here, from which circumstances the place derives its name.

Newry, which is derived from Na yur, 'the yew-tree', owes its importance to Sir Nicholas Bagnal, Marshal of Ireland, by whom it was surrounded by walls and converted into a fortified town during the reign of Elizabeth. Its monastic establishments had been celebrated many centuries before. Its ancient abbey is said to have been founded by MacLoughlin, king of Ireland, in 1157 AD, and is styled in the charter Ibar-cyn-tracta, 'the flourishing head of the yew trees', from the number of large and venerable yews that formerly flourished here – one of which tradition reports to have been planted by the hand of St Patrick. The town was destroyed by the Irish in 1641, and again by the Duke of Berwick in 1689, with 'a square castle or two, and five or six houses only escaping'. It recovered rapidly however and is now exceedingly prosperous, being very advantageously situated for commerce on the borders of the counties of Armagh, Louth and Down, with a river rendered navigable by a canal which continues to Lough Neagh. The houses are well-built, the streets remarkably clean and the suburbs in all directions are of great beauty.

It was early on a Sabbath morning when we set out to climb that great hill of Clough Mor, one of the Mourne range, and the one that hangs directly over Rosstrevor, sheltering it from all unkindly winds. High as it looked – soaring above us as we stood at the door of a very comfortable inn – it is one of the smallest of the chain to which it belongs, which are said to be upwards of thirty-six miles in circumference; the loftiest, Slieve Donard, being, according to the Ordnance Survey, 2796 feet above the level of the sea. Clough Mor, 'the great stone', is so called from a huge mass of granite weighing perhaps thirty tons which stands upon the summit of a projecting cliff nearly half-way up the mountain. How it got there is one of the buried secrets of the past; if it was placed there by

NARROW WATER CASTLE,
(NEWRY-RIVER.)

human labour, or indeed, the 'work of druid hands of old' it would sanction the belief that they had the assistance of fallen spirits. There are, nevertheless, several circumstances which encourage the idea that its singular situation was not the result of chance. It stands upon the brow of a small hill, and under it are the remains of oblong stones, such as we commonly find supporting the cap-stones of cairns. It is hollowed beneath and gradually slopes to a pivot. It is almost impossible to conceive that it could have been dropped into place from one of the adjacent mountains, for those of greater elevation are at a considerable distance and a valley of some depth and space intervenes between its side and the heights that look down upon it.

When we had reached this singular summit and spent some time in its examination, we found that little more than a third of the mountain had been climbed, and that time had passed far more rapidly than we had imagined, for the chimes of the Sabbath bell came up the mountain from the valley below with a clear, sharp and shrill sound, and we saw groups assembling down in the distance on their way to church.

We made our way to the mountain's top. That which had seemed from the valley a peak, was a large flat of several acres, covered with wet moss. Immediately below us was the bay with its innumerable tiny creeks, in one of which, just under the shelter of the mountain opposite, lies the pretty town of Carlingford, and to the north, on the other side of a flat that stretches out into the sea is the bay, behind which lies the town of Dundrum. Behind us were the everlasting hills, and oceanward the sight was arrested for a moment by a shadow upon the waters; this was the Isle of Man which could dimly be seen, and to the south, the Hill of Howth appeared distinctly.

Looking inland, the mountains rose one atop the other above the bay, which seemed so directly under us. Opening among the hills was a most rich valley, which continued all the way to Lough Neagh, which is a distance of forty miles, and the lake, or rather the haze which indicated it, is clearly perceptible. In the foreground, carrying the eye beyond Rosstrevor with the tall spire of its pretty church, we traced the course of the river winding up to Newry, with the village of Warrens-point lying mid-way.

The day was drawing to a close when, pleasantly and profitably wearied, we returned to the inn, and that day will endure as one of the happiest of our memories, and we long to visit the lovely village of Rosstrevor once again.

Some fourteen or fifteen miles from Rosstrevor and a short distance from the town of Newcastle on the northern side of the Mourne Mountains is the beautiful seat of the Earl of Roden, Tullamore Park. It is situated in the midst of the most sublime scenery with the wide expanse of ocean before it, and it lies at the foot of Slieve Donard.

Slieve Donard is the highest of the Mourne Mountains, and is supposed to rise nearly four miles in gradual ascent, while the perpendicular height is estimated at nearly three thousand feet. St Donard, a disciple of St Patrick, is said to have spent the life of a hermit on this mountain and to have built a cell or oratory on the top of it towards the close of the fifth century.

Still keeping along the coast the tourist reaches Dundrum Bay, which is very beautiful, though less so than the Bay of Carlingford. Here also are the remains of an ancient castle standing on a high rock which commands an extensive prospect. The ruins consist of a circular keep or tower, surrounded by fragments of smaller towers and other outer works, of which the barbican is the most striking and picturesque object. To the south of the castle there are the remains of a large mansion or dwelling house in the style of domestic architecture usual in the sixteenth century. On the south side of Dundrum Bay is the favourite watering place of Newcastle, which was formerly called Black Rock, and adjoining it is the residence of the Earl of Annesley. The bay is noted for its sandbanks upon which many a good ship has struck. Such catastrophes are, however, likely to be averted in future, for a lighthouse is now in the course of erection.

A few miles further north and we arrive at the very ancient and venerable town of Downpatrick; venerable not only because of its antiquity, for here were interred the mortal remains of the great patron saint of Ireland, St Patrick. The grave of St Patrick is still a favourite spot for devotees, especially near mid-summer. It is said that no plant but grass and shamrock will grow on it, but this is probably because it is kept in the state of red earth by the removal of mould.

About a mile and a half east of Downpatrick in a rugged district which is perhaps more suited for melancholy than devotion, there is the favourite 'station', the Struel Well, but, notwithstanding the cures said to have been performed here, the annual assembly is nearly abandoned.

Struel is derived from Strath fuile, 'the stream of blood', and tradition accounts for the origin of the name thus: St Patrick and St Bridget were coming over the ground, and the younger saint, feeling thirsty, doubted the capability of Patrick to procure her a drink as miraculously as Moses did for the Israelites. The latter then struck her on the foot with a wand which he held in his hand and a stream of blood issued forth, which was converted into water – which has remained so ever since.

Downpatrick is built upon a group of small hills, on the south-east shore of Strangford Lough. Its corporate rank was recognised as far back as 1403, but its date is probably much more remote. It is said to have been the residence of the native kings of Ulidia, its ancient name having been 'Aras Keltair and Rath Keltair Mac Duach', which signified the fortification of Keltair, the son of Duach.

The leading object of attraction is the cathedral, which is a modern structure. It is situated on an eminence to the west of the town, and is a stately embattled edifice, chiefly of unhewn stone, and supported by external buttresses. Its site, however, is that of one of the most ancient edifices in Ireland. In the old cathedral church were the tombs of St Patrick, the founder, St Bridget and St Columba. Their tombs had, it is said, this piece of monkish verse writ over them:

One tomb three saints contain, one vault below,
Does Bridget, Patrick and Columba show.

Strangford Lough, which stretches from Downpatrick almost to the northern border of the county is, in reality, an arm of the sea, the entrance to which is, however, remarkably narrow, being somewhat less than a mile, although the breadth of the lake is in most parts above five miles. It contains a vast number of islands, some of which are so small as to be mere dots, while others comprise above one hundred acres. Indeed, the lake is popularly said to be studded by three hundred and sixty-five islands, one for each day of the year. Six of these islands are inhabited: Castle, Rea, Wood, Tagart, Maghea and Islandbawn.

Strangford Lough is a safe and deep harbour, but its entrance is dangerous from the rapidity of its tides and the number of rocks. The town of Strangford stands on its southern border and the lake was anciently called Lough Coine. Along the whole of its borders, north, south, east and west, are the ruins of numerous castles.

At the south-western end of the lake and adjacent to the small town of Killclief are the remains of another ancient castle.

Our visit to this singular and interesting part of the county of Down was made from Belfast. Passing through a peculiarly fertile country, we first reached the town of Newtownards, which is beautifully situated on the northern extremity of the lough, and where the barony of Ards commences. The town is very ancient and retains its primitive character. Nearly in the centre stands a handsome octagonal building of hewn stone, which is decorated with canopied niches, and it was, no doubt, formerly surmounted by a cross, of which however there are no remains. Adjoining this somewhat singular, although picturesque structure, are the ruins of a mansion in which the late Marquis of Londonderry is said to have been born. Until lately it had been used as a yarn mill, but it is now completely dilapidated. Another interesting structure, and one of a very olden time, has also been permitted to fall into decay. It is the church built in Newton by the first of the Montgomerys. We were given to understand that, although a fine and beautiful example of architecture, no attempt whatever has been made to preserve it from sinking into ruin.

The town of Newtownards, and the country adjacent to it along the banks of Strangford Lough, is the property of the Marquis of Londonderry, and it would be difficult to find more flourishing farmers or a better-managed estate in the most prosperous of English counties. We passed his beautiful seat, Mount-Stuart, on the road to Grey Abbey.

Grey Abbey was founded for Cistercian monks by Africa, the wife of Sir John de Courcy and the daughter of Godfred, king of the Isle of Man, in 1193 AD. It was destroyed by the army of the O'Neil in the great rebellion of 1641 and was never repaired afterwards. The vicinity of these ruins is beautiful and picturesque, and immediately adjoining them is the residence of the heir of the Montgomerys. A pretty little temple has been erected on the grounds in order to afford accommodation to visitors, and the place is in high favour with the townspeople of Belfast who occasionally luxuriate in the delicious neighbourhood.

From Grey Abbey we took the main road to Donaghadee, a neat and prosperous little town which only lies twenty-two miles distant from Portpatrick in Scotland. Its natural harbour is enclosed by piers and furnished with a lighthouse.

From Donaghadee we proceeded to Bangor, which was a famous city of the saints in old times. It is said to have been founded in 555 AD by Comgall who established an abbey of regular canons here. The fame of its learning was spread throughout Europe and its school – which St Carthagus directed – became so celebrated that it was resorted to by many students from all parts of the world and, according to some writers, it was the germ out of which arose Oxford, for when King Alfred 'founded or restored that university, he sent to the great school of Bangor for professors'.

The old castle of Bangor stands upon the quay; it is in good condition and retains tokens of huge strength.

Through the whole of this district – the barony of Ards and that of Castlereagh – a large proportion of the peasantry is employed in what is technically termed 'flowering' – which is embroidering muslin, chiefly for the Glasgow manufacturers who supply the unwrought material and pay fixed sums for the workmanship. The workers generally earn about three shillings a week – a small sum, but as the majority of the inmates of a cottage are similarly employed, sufficient is obtained to procure the necessaries of life and, indeed, some of the luxuries, for the interiors of many of the cabins presented an aspect of cheerfulness and comfort.

We found upon inquiry that the number of girls occupied in this branch of industry may be stated thus:

Between 2000-3000 girls, from 5-12 years of age, employed at veining, at weekly wages averaging from 1s 6d to 2s 6d.

Between 2000-3000 sewers employed at needle-work for Belfast houses at weekly wages averaging 3s.

And about 10,000 employed as needle-workers for Glasgow houses at weekly wages averaging 4s.

Thus, upwards of £3000 are paid out weekly in the north of Ireland for the manufacture of needle-work. Nearly the whole of the work sent from Glasgow to London and other parts of England is produced in this district, but it is bleached in Scotland and sold as 'Scotch work'. The manufacture is chiefly of collars, cuffs and like items.

From Bangor to Belfast the road passes along Belfast Lough, or Carrickfergus Bay. The banks on the Down-side are extensively wooded and all along the scenery is very charming, and now and then the high hills on the Antrim borders can be seen to great advantage, and the beauty of the country through which we pass is enhanced by the aspect of industry producing improvements that presents itself everywhere.

As we near Belfast on this road there are many interesting objects. The ruined church of Knockbreda forms an exceedingly picturesque object, being considerably elevated above the valley of the Lagan and commanding a fine view of the town and lough. The church is rapidly mouldering to decay and little of it now remains.

Our tour thus far through the county of Down has been limited to its coast, nor will the interior call for very particular notice. The towns of Dromore – the ancient episcopal see – Hillsborough and Banbridge are populous and extensive, and are supported chiefly by the produce of linen in the various branches of the manufacture.

The people of county Down are, as a whole, of Scotch origin. There are, of course, numerous exceptions, but so small a proportion do they bear to the whole that the lowland or Ayrshire dialect was commonly spoken all over the county until about the middle or towards the end of the last century. At this moment a sort of mongrel Scotch is spoken in and near Ballynahinch, Dromara, Saintfield, Combe, Killinchy, Holywood, Bangor, Newtownards, Donaghadee, Kirkcubbin and Portaferry. The nearness of this county to the Mull of Galloway has made the districts on the two sides scarcely distinguishable, and the stream of Scottish population can be traced most distinctly from Donaghadee and Bangor upwards to the interior.

Soon after entering the county of Down we began to feel we were in another country; in a district at least where the habits as well as the looks of the people were altogether different from those to which we had been accustomed. We encountered neither the sallow countenance, illuminated by brilliant black eyes and shadowed by the long, dark, silken hair of the Irish, nor those of the round, rosy, soft Munster beauties who seem the very pictures of roguish good humour, and are always ready to laugh with you or at you as the occasion serves.

The faces we met had a square, stolid, 'look-forward' sort of expression, the cheek bones were high and broad, the eyes somewhat sunk and blue rather than either black or grey, the complexions were what they call 'sandy' in Ireland, with several of the heads of the children being decidedly red. Both the men and women wore neat, well-mended clothes and tartan shawls, ribands and even waistcoats, and again intimated our close approximation to the Scottish coast.

The maritime county of Down, in the province of Ulster, is bounded on the east and south by the Irish Sea, with Carlingford Bay separating it from Louth. It is bounded on the north by the county of Antrim, and Belfast Lough, and on the west by the county of Armagh.

It is divided into the baronies of Ards, Castlereagh, Dufferin, Lower and Upper Iveagh, Kinealearty, Lecale and Mourne. Its principal towns are Newry (part of which is in the county of Armagh), the assize town of Downpatrick, one of the most ancient boroughs of Ireland, Newtownards, Hillsborough, Castlewellan, Banbridge, Warrens-point, Bangor, Strangford and Donaghadee.

Chapter Ten

MONAGHAN

The county of Monaghan was anciently called MacMahon's County, from the powerful sept who ruled there and who proved very troublesome neighbours to the early English settlers, and who manifested a strong indisposition to part with their lands at the command of the Anglo-Norman intruders.

The county is described by the old writers as being not only mountainous, but covered with wood, and while the mountains endure, the forests have long since vanished. The lakes, of which there are many, are, however, of considerable beauty.

The principal town of the county is called Monaghan, from which indeed the county is said to have taken its name, deriving it from Muinechan, the dwelling of the monks, although all traces of monastic establishments have disappeared from its vicinity. Vestiges of ancient structures, either of religious houses or castellated mansions, are indeed rare throughout the county, and in this respect it forms a singular contrast with its immediate neighbours, Armagh, Louth and Down.

The abbey at Cloynes is perhaps the only ecclesiastical building of which any remains exist and these are of small account. But adjoining them is one of the far-famed and long-famed round towers. The cap is gone and the doorway is nearer to the ground than usual, and it possesses another somewhat peculiar feature, being composed of rough stones without the smooth stones within. Of relics of more remote antiquity Monaghan has its full share, with druidical temples and raths being found in nearly every part of it.

The inland county of Monaghan in the province of Ulster is

bounded on the north by the county of Tyrone, on the south by that of Meath, on the east by the counties of Louth and Armagh, and on the west by those of Fermanagh and Cavan.

Its baronies are five: Cremorne, Dartree, Farney, Monaghan and Trough.

Chapter Eleven

TYRONE

The county of Tyrone is conspicuous in Irish history, for it was the principal arena of the contests which are recognised as the Tyrone rebellion of Hugh O'Neil, in 1597.

The O'Neils were kings in Ireland antecedent to Christianity, 'tyrannising it in Ulster before the coming of St Patrick'. The great rebel was the son of an illegitimate son of Con O'Neil, who was slain by his legitimate brother, Shane O'Neil, and Shane was, in his turn, assassinated by McDonnell, the leader of the Scots in Ulster, to whom he had fled for refuge from the English. The chieftainry was claimed by Tirlogh O'Neil, to whose daughter Hugh was married, but Tirlogh, being old, was persuaded to relinquish his right in favour of Hugh. Hugh had previously been a frequent visitor at the English court and at one time stood high in favour with Elizabeth.

In the county of Tyrone and within a distance of little more than three miles from Strabane, is to be found one of the most interesting establishments it has ever been our good fortune to visit in any country. We have inspected manufactories of much greater extent than the 'Sion Mills', but have never witnessed with greater gratification the practical and efficient working of a fine moral system.

The mills are situated on the river Mourne, which rushes along with a rapid and continued current and is about one of the best water-powers in Great Britain, with the supply being not only large but constant. About eighty horse-power is now employed to drive eight thousand spindles, and yet it is but a small portion of the water that is necessary for the purpose. Instead of the hot furnace, long chimneys and dense smoke, rendering still more unhealthy the necessary close air of manufactories devoted exclusively to the spinning of flax and tow into linen yarn, there is a clear handsome, well-ventilated building. Here nearly seven hundred of a peasantry which, before the establishment of this manufactory, were starving and idle, not from choice but from necessity, are now constantly employed, and the air is as pure and fresh as on the borders of the wildest prairie or the boldest coast. The bare fact of such a population being taught industrious habits and receiving full remuneration for their time and labour is a blessing, but not the only one enjoyed by this favoured peasantry. Agricultural labour is not neglected, for five out of the seven hundred employed are women and girls, creatures who, but for the spirit and enterprise of the Messrs Herdman (to whom, and to the Mulhollands of Belfast, Tyrone is indebted for this establishment), would be found cowering over the embers of their turf fires or begging along the waysides for morsels of food. But this system of social order and social industry is not, as we have said, the only advantage enjoyed at Sion Mills. Cottages of simple construction, but sound and comfortable, have been built for the workmen and their families; a school has been established and the Messrs Herdman themselves attend to the Sunday School, and take the greatest interest in the educational progress of their workpeople.

We visited several of the factory dwellings, and found that in many instances they combined the small comfort of town rooms with the peculiar advantages of the country cottages. We never saw a more healthy population, and the watchful eye of the proprietors has effectually prevented the growth of the immorality supposed to be inseparable from the 'factory system'.

Tyrone is an island county in the province of Ulster. Its boundaries are: on the north Londonderry, on the south the counties of Fermanagh and Monaghan, on the west the counties of Donegal and Fermanagh, and on the east the county of Armagh and Lough Neagh.

It is divided into four baronies: Clogher, Dungannon, Strabane and Omagh. The towns of size are Omagh, Strabane, Clogher and Dungannon.

Chapter Twelve

ANTRIM

We entered the county of Antrim at Lisburn, a pretty and flourishing town on the Antrim side of the river Lagan. It consists principally of one long street, at the eastern end of which is the picturesque and interesting church containing two very remarkable monuments, one to the memory of Lieut. Dobbs who was killed in an engagement off Carrickfergus Bay with the famous Paul Jones, and the other to that of the great and good Jeremy Taylor, sometime Bishop of Down and Connor, who died here in the year 1667.

The ancient name of Lisburn was Linsley Garvin (probably from the founder) and until 1641, when the town was burned by the Irish, it was called Lisengarvy, but since that time it has been named Lisburn.

There is probably no town in Ireland where the happy effects of English taste and industry are more conspicuous than at Lisburn. From the Drum Bridge and the banks of the Lagan, on one side, to the shores of Lough Neagh, on the other, the people are almost exclusively the descendants of English settlers. Those in the immediate neighbourhood of the town are chiefly Welsh, but great numbers arrived from the northern shires and from the neighbourhood of the Bristol Channel. In the village of Lambeg, which is situated only a few perches from the Belfast road, the old English games and pastimes were regularly celebrated on Easter Monday within the last twenty years. The English language is perhaps spoken more purely by the populace in this district than by the same class in any other part of Ireland.

The names of the places are modern: Solders-town, English-town, the Half-town, Stonyford, and the people of all ranks have high ideals of domestic comfort for their stations. The neatness of the cottages, and the good taste displayed in many of the farms are little, if at all, inferior to aught that we find in England, and the tourist who visits Lough Neagh – after passing through Ballinderry – will consider it to have been justly designated the 'garden of the north'.

The multitude of pretty little villages scattered over the landscape, each announcing itself by the tapering spire of a church, could almost beguile the traveller into believing that he is passing through a rural district in one of the midland counties of England.

A few miles from Lisburn, on the road to Moira, stands the comfortable farmhouse of Trummery. The ruin of an abbey is close to it and its vicinity to the celebrated 'Pass of Kilwarlin' often attracts tourists and sketchers.

From Lisburn we proceeded by railway a distance of eight English miles to Belfast. The line passes through or near the towns of Lisburn, Moira, Lurgan, Portadown and Richill to Armagh. There is also water communication from Portadown by the Ulster Canal (which joins Lough Neagh and Lough Erne) to Enniskillen and Sligo to the west.

As we drew near to Ireland's only manufacturing town, its peculiar character became apparent. It was something new to perceive rising above the houses numerous tall and thin chimneys which are indicative of industry, occupation, commerce and prosperity, with the volumes of smoke that issued from them giving unquestionable tokens of full employment, while its vicinity to the ocean removed at once all idea that the labour was unwholesome or the labourers unhealthy.

Belfast is a 'new town', but it would appear that some importance was attached to it at a very remote period, for it is mentioned as among the 'good towns and strongholds' destroyed in 1315 by Edward Bruce, and the 'castle of Belfast' was twice converted to a ruin in 1503 and 1512 by the Lord Deputy Kildare. In 1708 the castle was also destroyed by fire by the carelessness of a servant, and three daughters of Arthur, third earl of Donegal, perished in the flames. Till lately some vestiges of the castle were to be seen, but now all trace of it has vanished and the site is chiefly occupied by a fish and vegetable market.

A map of the town published in 1660 gives the names of but five streets and five rows which consisted of one hundred and fifty houses and, so late as 1720, all the houses in one of the principal streets were thatched with straw. In 1816 the town contained 5578 houses and 30,720 inhabitants, and the population at present, including the suburbs of Ballymacarret, is not less than 100,000.

As may be expected, society in Belfast is almost exclusively of a 'commercial character'. There are few resident gentry, that is to say, gentry independent of commerce in the town, although many reside in the immediate neighbourhood.

The clean and bustling appearance of Belfast is decidedly unnational. That it is in Ireland, but not of it, is a remark often on the lips of visitors from the south or west. Like most other Irish towns, the character of its streets is by no means uniform, with the commercial quarter differing much from those to the south in the neighbourhood of College and Donegal Squares, where the houses are large and handsome, although most invariably constructed of brick. But the business portion of the town also contains excellent streets. High Street is broad and spacious, and reaches upwards from the river and is terminated by the Northern Bank, a lofty brick building occupying the further end. Donegal Street, Bridge Street and Warren Street are well-built and regular streets in the immediate neighbourhood of the Commercial Buildings or Exchange. The northern district and the suburbs of Ballymacarret on the Down side of the Lagan are the poorer and meaner parts of the town.

The public buildings are sufficiently numerous, though certainly possessing but few architectural claims to consideration. The want of steeples has often been noted, with the wooden tower of the church of St Anne's being the only approach to that form of construction, if we except the somewhat paltry spire of the Poor-House. One of the most important public edifices is the Commercial Buildings, erected by an incorporated company at the cost of £20,000. It contains an excellent news-room, frequented by the most respectable merchants, an assembly room and several offices and the exchange is held here. The structure terminates on one end of Donegal Street, and nearly opposite, at the divergence of North Street and Donegal Street, stands the Old Exchange, which is a heavy building, but which is now little used, and is the property of the Donegal family.

The Royal Academical Institution is a massive brick edifice, forming one side of College Square, and surrounded by a grass enclosure of several acres in extent. It is wholly occupied by schools and class rooms and residences for two of the masters. The Theatre, a mean building with a very neat interior, has been long neglected. A handsome music-hall for concerts and similar entertainments has been recently erected, which is a sufficient indication of the taste of the town.

Although a plain building, the Linen Hall is, beyond question, the most interesting structure in Belfast. It is cheering in the highest degree to note the bustle and business that prevail here and in the adjacent warehouses.

The churches of Belfast are St Anne's, St George's and Christ's, the last a partly free church built a few years ago. The Roman Catholics have but two chapels, one large and commodious situated in Donegal Street, and the other a dingy brick building in Chapel Lane. Of Presbyterian meeting-houses there are no fewer than thirteen – ten, we believe, in connection with the General Assembly and three belonging to congregations professing Unitarianism. Of the remaining places of worship, five belong to the Methodists, and one each to the Independents, the Covenanters or Reformed Presbyters and the Society of Friends.

Belfast is honourably distinguished by the number of its charitable institutions, and these are mostly wholly supported by voluntary contributions. The Poor-House of the Belfast Charitable Society, incorporated in 1774, is an extensive structure, situated at the north end of Donegal Street and fronting the Commercial Buildings. The Fever-Hospital, opened in 1817, and capable of supporting above two hundred patients, is partially maintained by the county. A Lying-In Hospital, two female penitentiaries, a House of Refuge and an institution for the instruction of the deaf, dumb and blind are entirely supported by voluntary subscriptions. A loan-fund has been recently established with every prospect of success, and the Savings Bank has been hitherto highly prosperous.

Among the other advantages of Belfast we may not omit to notice the hotels, of which there are several that may vie in all respects with the best in Great Britain. We resided at the 'Donegal Arms' which is situated in the principal street, High Street. Its exterior is very elegant, having indeed the character of a grand edifice. It is impossible to praise too highly the whole of the well-ordered ménage, a courteous and inquiring landlord, exceedingly attentive servants, good posting – everything, in short, connected with the establishment is creditable to the excellent and flourishing town. However, we cannot say as much for the hotels of the north generally.

The scenery in the neighbourhood of Belfast is varied and picturesque. The bold range of mountains, stretching northwards from the town and skirting the western side of the valley of the Lagan contrasts strongly with the fertility of the valley itself, and the rich cultivation of the opposite sides of the county Down. The views from these mountains are, for the most part, strikingly beautiful, and in particular that from MacArt's Fort on the summit of Cave Hill, the most eastern of the chain, which almost overhangs the town, and towers, with imposing effect, over the road to Carrickfergus. A singular peculiarity connected with Cave Hill was pointed out to us: seen from nearly every part of the southern suburbs, the outline resembles in a very remarkable manner the profile of Napoleon. Almost at its foot is the town, and beyond stretches the fertile county of Down which is intersected by the Lough of Strangford, with its numerous islets; to the right lies the valley of the Lagan, bordered by the other members of the chain, with the horizon being bounded by the mountains of Mourne. In the opposite direction the eye rests on the waters of the Lough, the Carrickfergus district of Antrim, and the northern shores of Down, while, in the extreme distance, the hills of Scotland are dimly visible. To the north-west of the mountains – though unseen from this point – lies the vast sheet of Lough Neagh.

From Belfast – previous to our tour along the 'northern coast' to the Giant's Causeway – we proceeded to Antrim town in order to examine several interesting objects in its neighbourhood.

The town of Antrim is about fifteen miles north-west of Belfast on the north-east border of Lough Neagh. It is small and not of particular note. One of the most perfect round towers stands in its immediate vicinity in the grounds of G J Clarks, Esq. It is ninety-three feet in height and about fifty-three feet in circumference at the base. The cap was shattered by lightning in the year 1822 and was replaced by another which was built upon the precise model of the ancient one, the broken pieces of which are carefully preserved. The tower is built of rough stones and above the doorway is a sculpture in *basso-relievo* resembling a Maltese cross.

Jutting out into the lake is Shane's Castle, the seat of Lord O'Neil, the representative of a family whose origin is of a most remote age, and whose name is intimately associated with every remarkable event that has occurred in Ulster, and indeed in Ireland for many centuries. The present peer is unmarried and likely to be the last of the ancient and heroic race, and with him probably *The* O'Neil will cease to exist.

Tradition attributes the origin of the famous crest of the O'Neils – the red hand – to the following circumstance: in an ancient expedition for the conquest of Ireland, the leader of it declared that whomever of his followers first touched the shore would possess the territory. One of them, coveting the reward, and seeing that another boat was likely to reach it before him, seized an axe and with it cut off his left hand, which he flung on shore, and so was the first to 'touch' it. Hence, *a sinister hand, gules,* became the armorial ensign of the province.

Shane's Castle is a comparatively modern building, which is now in ruins, having been burned by an accidental fire in the year 1816, and the noble proprietor resides in a temporary dwelling formed out of one of the outhouses. From the ruins which remain it is evident that it was a fine and spacious building: the vaults, which are still entire and extend to the very verge of the lake, merit particular notice, both for their spaciousness and rather extraordinary construction. Several turrets and towers are still standing, and from their tops a fine view of the interesting scenery amid which the ruins lie may be obtained. A number of cannons are still mounted on the boldly situated fort.

Shane's Castle has been the chosen realm of the banshee for centuries. The literal meaning of the word is a 'female fairy' or spirit, and she was supposed to come always for the purpose of forewarning death, which she did by melancholy wailings. Most of the old families in Ireland were believed to have one of these spirits attending to them. The banshee sometimes appeared in the form of a young and beautiful woman arrayed in white, but more frequently as a frightful hag. Night was the season generally chosen by the banshee for her visits, but she was sometimes supposed to be heard at noon, 'when mid-day is silent around', and then the voices of several of them were heard together. Maobh, pronounced Maov, is the queen of the Irish *sidhe* or fairies. Maoveen, the little Mab, is the name of the O'Neil banshee.

Lough Neagh is the largest lake in Great Britain, and few lakes in Europe exceed it in size. It is formed by the confluence of the Blackwater, the Upper Ban and five other rivers, and the only outlet is the Lower Ban. It is beautiful only upon its north-eastern borders, being generally bare of trees elsewhere. In the immediate neighbourhood of Antrim town it may vie in parts with the fairest of the southern lakes, while it possesses a grandeur exclusively its own. In this vicinity it is richly wooded, and here are its islands – the only islands it contains, excepting a very small one off the Armagh shore – one of them, Ram's Island, consisting of no more than six acres, the other, Bird Island, being somewhat less.

Lough Neagh has abundant attractions for the tourist. Its scenery is beautiful and interesting and the lake becomes truly magnificent when influenced by storms – its waves rolling and foaming like those of the ocean in a tempest; it abounds in fish, with the eels found here being unequalled for size and delicacy of flavour, and the pollan or 'freshwater herring' being procured here in astonishing quantities.

From Antrim we pursued our route to Carrickfergus, passing through the ancient town of Temple Patrick.

Carrickfergus is one of the oldest towns in Ireland and has held a prominent place in the annals of the country for centuries. Its history is full of interest, for it has been made to play a conspicuous part in all the wars of ages. There still exist some interesting remains of the ancient fortifications: the walls may be distinctly traced and the North Gate is almost perfect. The town is said to have derived its name from *Carrig*, a rock and *Feargus*, an Irish king 'famous for his skill in blazoning of armes', who was lost in a storm off the coast some three or four hundred years before the coming of Christ. 'The Castle' is said to have been erected by John de Courcy, the 'Conqueror of Ulidia', and became celebrated very soon after it was raised in consequence of its proximity to 'those troublesome neighbours', the Scots.

The Castle of Carrickfergus is one of the most perfect castles in Ireland, and time has indeed added to its picturesque character without impairing its strength. It stands on a rock that projects into the sea and, at ordinary tides, is surrounded on three sides by water. Towards the town there are two towers, called half-moons from their shape, and between them is the only entrance which is defended by a strait passage with embrasures for fire-arms. The walls of the keep are nine feet thick and from the top there is a magnificent view of the bay and the adjacent scenery.

The old church of St Nicholas is also an interesting structure. It is kept in good repair and is used for service, although in all probability its origin may be dated back to the earlier part of the twelfth century. The aisles are full of monuments of the house of Chichester.

The town of Carrickfergus is neat and clean and more than usually straggling. A considerable part of it is called the Scottish quarter and, as will be supposed, the majority of its population is of Scottish descent.

The drive from Carrickfergus to Larne, a distance of nine miles, may be considered the second stage along the coast from Belfast to the Giant's Causeway. There is also an inland road to Larne through the commons of Carrickfergus, passing Lough Mourne, over the mountains and through the little village of Glenoe. This road, although two miles shorter than the coach road, is seldom used, for part of it is very rugged and steep and the descent into

Glenoe is all but impracticable for ordinary conveyances. The former road, however, passes through the village of Eden to Kilroot, a parish which was once held for a short while by Dean Swift, and where the now ruined church in which he is said to have preached can be found. A still more interesting object, however, is the dilapidated remains of the ancient church of Templecoran in the village of Ballycarry. Here the first Presbyterian Church of Ireland was planted under the ministry of the Rev. Edward Brice, in the year 1613, and here he remained until his death in the year 1636.

A short distance from Ballycarry is a small dell which skirts the road, which has long been called the Salt-hole, the origin of the name having been recently ascertained by the discovery of a bed of rock-salt, and in the immediate vicinity are the most extensive lime-works in Ireland, with the produce being chiefly for export to Scotland from the port of Larne.

Larne Lough extends about five miles from the mouth of the harbour, dividing Island Magee and the district of Magheramorne. In this situation the water is shallow with mud banks appearing at low tide to a great extent. A surface of about two thousand acres was surveyed two years ago by Mr Irving MP for the purposes of reclaiming and making land, which was considered quite practical and would have been beneficial in many ways, but especially to the Island Magee estate and inhabitants – and yet the project was opposed and certainly not upon good grounds.

Passing through the beautiful and interesting village of Glynn, near which are perceptible the effects of a singular land-slip, we arrived at the town of Larne. On one side of the creek the long and narrow peninsula of Island Magee runs for a distance of several miles. It extends about seven miles from the north to the south, along the coast opposite to Ayrshire, and is in few places more than two miles in breadth. The inhabitants are all of Scottish descent and are still thoroughly Scottish in dialect, manners and customs. The island is one property, forming part of the extensive estate of the Marquis of Donegal, but it is held under lease by the Viscount Dungannon.

Because it is off the high road or coast road from Belfast to the

Giant's Causeway, few tourists turn aside to examine it, the approaches being in some degree inconvenient, and the situation insular. Yet, in its scenery, bays, headlands and caves it is highly interesting, independently of the objects it presents in great variety to the geologist, naturalist and in some degree to the antiquary. On the east side are 'the Gobbins', one of the loftiest headlands on the north coast, which extend nearly two miles from north to south, and here in the interior the columnar pillars – so remarkable at the Causeway – are occasionally seen. It is full of natural wonders; the cliffs are remarkably precipitous and the coast abounds in caves, many of which were excavated by smugglers in old times.

In Brown's Bay, which is beautifully situated in the northern extremity, there is a large Rocking Stone on the sea-side. This bay is named after women called Brown who were reported to have been witches who frequented the bay at night to celebrate their orgies. So late as the beginning of the eighteenth century four women from Island Magee were tried for witchcraft and sentenced for punishment to confinement and exposure in the pillory, and the house in which these women are said to have exercised their craft is still standing and is presently inhabited.

The town of Larne has little to recommend it. In its immediate vicinity however are the remains of the castle of Oldfleet, which is situated on the extremity of the Curran, a small and narrow peninsula, so called from the Irish word, *carran*, a reaping hook, which it resembles in form. It was on this spot that Edward Bruce landed in 1315. Although at present it is of small importance, Larne is not unlikely to occupy a prominent station hereafter. Its harbour is good and completely sheltered, and supplies a convenient outlet for the produce of Island Magee. Even now it carries on some trade with Scotland, to which it furnishes an enormous quantity of lime for manure.

The Larne coast is remarkable for fine herrings, and it surprised us to perceive fishermen angling for them with artificial flies – the fly being a very rude imitation of nature – nothing more, indeed, than one of the feathers of a sea-gull tied to a large and coarse hook.

Here may be said to commence the magnificent coach-road to the Causeway. To the town of Glenarm the distance is ten miles, but we must pass along a 'rough road up hill and down dale' for about two miles before entering the 'new line', which continues all along the way to Glenarm and for a long distance beyond it.

The town of Glenarm, the seat of the Antrim family, is beautifully situated. The small bay affords a safe and convenient shelter for shipping, and the mountains look down upon it. The Castle of Glenarm became the residence of the McDonnels – Earls of Antrim – soon after an accident at their ancient fortalice of Dunluce compelled a removal to some safer spot. The Gateway to the Castle, a lofty barbican, is approached by a bridge that crosses a river. Passing beneath its arch, a fine carriage drive sweeps round to the entrance hall. The Castle is spacious and replete with elegance and comfort.

From Glenarm to the Causeway, the next stage is to Cushendall, passing through the small village of Cairnlough, and leaving to the left a rich valley which is open on the east to the sea, but is completely surrounded on three sides by the mountains. About half-way we reach Garron Point, a promontory that runs out into the ocean and from which the view, north or south, is magnificent in the highest degree. The road here is also of very recent origin, having, we believe, originated with Mr Turnley, whose name it bears and who is a principal proprietor in the district. The old road, known as the Forarn Path, leads over the mountains and, although nearly impassable, it formerly supplied the only mode of progress through the country. Nearer to Red Bay to which we are now advancing is another of the singular limestone rocks, called Clough-i-stookan, formed by the gradual operation of time and the flow of the ocean. Seen from a distance it bears something of a human shape and has been long regarded with superstitious feeling by the peasantry, for when the winds beat upon it and roam through its many crevices, a sound is emitted not unlike the calls of mariners in distress.

The valley of Glenariff stretches into the interior of the country, and a road through it leads to Ballymena. The vale is very beautiful with the eastern entrance of it being open to the sea and from the main road it presents a view at once grand and graceful.

Red Bay therefore has on one side this charming valley and on the other the wide ocean. By passing through a natural tunnel near its northern extremity we reach the far-famed caves, which are a series of three excavations in the soft red sand-stone, from where the bay derives its name. We entered into one of these caves, having previously made a brief examination of an old and very time-worn ruin that still stands upon the cliff immediately above the tunnel.

The pretty village of Cushendall lies in a hollow among the mountains and at every step we take in its vicinity we meet some spot commemorated by 'old tradition': ruins of castles rich in legends, and hills that are truly classic.

Leaving Cushendall we enter a wild country surrounded on all sides by barren but magnificent mountains, down which run innumerable streams, marked in the distance by white lines of foam, and after a few miles we ascend a steep hill road above the graceful sea-village of Cushendun at the head of a small bay into which runs the rapid river of Glendun, which is crossed by a picturesque bridge. A most extended and most beautiful prospect is presented from every part of this road, with a lovely valley on one hand and the open sea on the other.

From the summit of the mountains there is a level road until we approach the town of Ballycastle. It passes over a barren heath in which there are numerous fissures crossed by strong bridges, each bridge bearing a name, and generally also the name of the engineer by whom it was erected. The descent into Ballycastle is very rapid, leaving about three miles to the right two objects which imperatively demand a visit: Tor Head and Murlough Bay, to which objects we shall presently conduct the reader.

Ballycastle is a good town with a good inn, and the tourist will do well to rest here awhile, proceeding hence to the Causeway to examine, both by sea and land, the grandest object along this beautiful coast, the Promontory of Fairhead. A little to the left before entering Ballycastle are the remains of the ancient abbey of Bona-Margy, founded, it is said, for monks of the Franciscan order in 1509 by Somarle M'Donnel, commonly called Sorley Buy or

GLENARM.

Yellow Sorley. From that period to the present it has been used as a burial place of the famous family of the M'Donnels of Antrim.

Ballycastle consists of two parts, upper and lower; the lower usually being termed the quay, and the two are joined by an avenue of fine trees. The town was almost entirely the creation of one energetic gentleman, Hugh Boyd, Esq., to whom Alexander, Earl of Antrim, granted in 1736 a lease in perpetuity of all coals, mines, etc from Bona-Margy to Fairhead. He built a church, erected coal-furnaces, iron-foundries, salt-pans, glass-furnaces, breweries, tanyards and, in short, obtained for the infant settlement within a singularly short space of time the reputation of being the most flourishing town in Ireland. Its fall however was almost as rapid as its rise.

Acting upon the advice of some experienced guides, we resolved to visit the several objects of interest east of Fairhead by land, taking a boat at Murlough Bay and returning to Ballycastle by water. Soon after we turned from the main road towards the coast we entered a wild district, walked upon a barren heath, looked upon Tor Point, stood above the several headlands, gazed, until we became dizzy, upon giant rocks from summits of terrific cliffs and commenced a descent to the bay of Murlough.

There are spots – small unrecorded places, nooks hid beneath cliff or mountain, mere corners of the Island – that altogether escape the tourist, who bowls along the splendid roads which render the great leading features of the scenery of the county of Antrim so easy of examination. But let the visitor on no account omit to inspect this bay, which is a scene of unspeakable grandeur and beauty.

The bold and majestic promontory of Benmore, or Fairhead, underneath which the voyager passes between the two bays of Murlough and Ballycastle is grand in the extreme and sublime beyond conception. Standing upon the brink of one of the huge precipices of which it is composed, the prospect was so terrific as to have been appalling; a rapid glance was sufficient to satisfy our curiosity and we shrank back with natural dread. However, if viewed upwards, from the ocean, the extent and magnificence may be fully seen and thoroughly appreciated.

Fhir Leith or the Grey Man's Path (a fissure in the precipice), viewed either from land or sea is never to be forgotten. It seems as though some supernatural power, determined to hew out for itself a pathway through the wonderful formations that tower along the road, had willed the fearful chasm that divides the rocky promontory in two. The singular passage in its most narrow part is barred across by a fragment of pillar, hurled, as it were, over the fissure, and supported on both sides at a considerable elevation. If you descend you perceive the passage widens and becomes more important; its dark sides assume greater height and more wild and sombre magnificence, and at last they extend upwards above two hundred and twenty feet through which the tourist arrives at the massive debris which crowd the base of the mighty promontory.

Before we return to Ballycastle, we must direct the reader's attention to the singular, picturesque and interesting island of Rathlin or Raghery. The state of the weather prevented our visiting it, and we are indebted to a friend for our information on the subject.

From the striking similitude existing between the island of Rathlin and the adjoining continent, it is the general opinion that the island had at one time formed a part of the county of Antrim, from which it has been separated by some violent convulsion of nature. The nearest point of Rathlin lies about three miles from the promontory of Fairhead on the mainland, but from Ballycastle it is nearly five and one half miles.

To visit the Giant's Causeway from Ballycastle the tourist proceeds westward; the road is uninteresting, but he will have to turn off now and then and walk to examine the several headlands along the coast. First is Kenbane, the White Head, a singular promontory which derives its name from a remarkable chalk formation occuring in the midst of basalt. It is crowned by the ruins of an ancient castle of which little remains. The castle is commonly known by the name of M'Allister's Castle, and is one of the most picturesque objects on the coast of Antrim.

Near the village of Ballintoy will be visited one of the principal 'Lions' of the district – the hanging bridge of Carrick-a-rede. The day on which we examined it was very stormy and we declined to cross it. One of our attendant guides ran over it with as much indifference as if he had been walking along a guarded balcony, scarcely condescending to place his hand upon the slender rope that answered the purpose of protector – the 'bridge' all the while swinging to and fro as the wind rushed about and under it. The chasm beneath is sixty feet wide, the rock on either side rising about eighty feet above the level of the water. This chasm divides the island-rock from the mainland. The visitor will do well to ascend to a hill just above it for the prospect from here is magnificent, commanding a full view of the whole line of coast, from Fairhead to the Causeway. The whole neighbourhood abounds in natural caves; one of the most remarkable of which, Grace Staple's Cave, will be examined in the vicinity of Kenbane.

Between this singular vicinity and the town of Bushmills the tourist will have little delay, for his excursion along the headlands will be made more at leisure. A short walk however will enable him to examine the picturesque remains of Dunseverick Castle, which stands upon an isolated rock which they must formerly have covered. As this point is about three miles from the Causeway, it is usual to proceed by land and, taking a boat in the small adjoining bay, return by water. This was the plan we adopted and therefore by this route we shall conduct the reader, taking him first to the pretty town of Bushmills and leaving him for rest at the neat, well-ordered and comfortable inn kept by Miss Henry, immediately above the footway that leads to the Causeway.

The town of Bushmills, standing on the river Bush, derives its name from an ancient water mill, said to have been the oldest in the north of Ireland, the picturesque ruins of which existed until a recent period. The tourist however will not now, as a few years ago he must have done, be compelled to make the town of Bushmills his abiding place during the period of his visit to the Causeway for, as we have intimated, there is an hotel which immediately adjoins it and we can speak from experience as to its advantage in all respects – its neatness, cleanliness and good order, the attention, zeal and kindliness of its landlady and the exceeding moderation of her charges. We may recommend the hotel of Miss Henry in the strongest terms, although our residence there was but a brief one.

We will suppose the less fortunate tourist to be safely located under the roof of Miss Henry, just above the rugged pathway that leads down to the Causeway. He is preparing to inspect this great marvel of Ireland – one of the wonders of the world – and walks to the door to ascertain if the weather is friendly or unfriendly to the scene of grandeur he is about to examine. The instant he shows himself, he is surrounded by THE GUIDES!

They are of all ages and sizes, from the octogenarian to the boy who can hardly go alone; each has some promise of a treat to be seen, and all are prepared with small boxes of specimens of the natural productions of the neighbourhood.

The guides are quite as numerous and almost as ragged as those at Killarney and Glendalough, but their character is entirely different. The Kerry and Wicklow guides delight in legends of fays and fairies, and they greet you with a jest and bid you farewell with a tear. Not so the northern guides; they are, from Neil MacMullen, the protector of the Causeway – being so appointed by the noble family of Antrim – down to the smallest cragsman, people of knowledge – geologists learned in the names of stones and conversant with stratas and basalts and minutiae of their details; and when they excite an exclamation of wonder they never sympathise with it, but treat it as a matter of course that you should be the astonished and they the astonishers. The Causeway guides are of the earth – *earthy*; of the stone – *stony*; they have the mystified look of philosophers, and the youngest and most ragged has a certain affectation of learning that is very amusing. They are, however, attentive and obliging.

Neil MacMullen, be it known to all future tourists, considers himself the chief, as he has been appointed the caretaker of all the wonders of this wonderful spot, and he is very careful and intelligent.

Daniel MacWilliam has excited Miss Henry's kind sympathy because he has a large family; we found him also very attentive and informed with the old giant tales of the Causeway.

CARRICK A REDE.

Then young James King volunteered as guide because his father had been a guide and, by the laws of primogeniture, the right was his.

Although as a less prominent wonder the tourist will be called upon to visit Port Coon Cave after he has seen the Causeway, we shall take him there first. The cave may be visited either by sea or by land, but we preferred the latter. Boats may row into it to the distance of a hundred yards or so, but the swell is sometimes dangerous, and although the land entrance to the cave is slippery and a fair proportion of climbing is necessary to achieve the object, still the magnificence of the excavation, its length and the formation of the interior would repay even greater exertion.

Having already deviated from a strict topographical accuracy by the introduction of the visit to the Port Coon Cave, we shall avail ourselves of the same privilege to say a few words upon the no less celebrated cave of Dunkerry. The situation of this cave is westward of the Causeway, and is accessible only by water, with the entrance assuming the appearance of a pointed arch which is remarkably regular. The depth of Dunkerry Cave has not been ascertained, for the extremity is so constructed as to render the management of a boat there impracticable and dangerous. Besides, from the greasy character of the sides of the cave, the hand cannot be serviceable in forwarding or retarding the boat. Along its sides is a bordering of marine plants of considerable breadth. The roaring of waves in the interior is distinctly heard, and it is said that the inhabitants of some cottages a mile distant from the shore have their slumbers frequently interrupted in the winter's nights by the subterranean sounds of Dunkerry Cave.

The visits to Port Coon and Dunkerry Caves are but episodes in the tour; the tourist will return to the inn and select his guide to whom he will pay half a crown for his day's labours, attention and information. The descent to the coast is then commenced. Below him and to the left he sees the graceful miniature Bay of Portnablaw; nearer the singular formation called the Weir's Snoot, and after a brief progress still sea-ward, he beholds the two guardians of the place, the Steucans, great and little. These are hill promontories which separate the bay of Portnablaw from Port

Ganniay at the eastern extremity of which is the Causeway, dividing Port Ganniay from Port Noffer. A rugged road has been constructed at the foot of the hills along the coast. In the midst of broken columns among which we now tread is a small well – the Giant's Well – of purest spring water, beside which an aged crone sits to welcome visitors and supply them with a refreshing drink. As yet, however, although the Causeway is within a stone's throw, nothing of its extraordinary character is seen.

However, we proceed a few steps onward and, standing upon the Causeway, elevated but a few yards above the level coast we look about us. Upon the side of the hill immediately over us is the 'Giant's Organ', a magnificent colonnade of pillars, laid open as it were by a land slip in the centre of a cliff, and reaching to the height of one hundred and twenty feet. The derivation of its name is sufficiently obvious. When the eye has dwelt sufficiently long upon this singular structure, it is directed further east and then another variety in the scene is presented: 'the Chimney Tops' – three pillars, the tallest of which reaches to a height of forty-five feet, and which stand upon an isolated rock some distance from the cliff.

So far – as far as the rock surmounted by the Chimney Tops, which stands over Port na Spania between it and Port Reostan – the eye traverses along the coast from the summit of the Causeway. Looking sea-ward from this point we perceive only a rock which seems to be a continuation of the structure, but which, we understand, is not formed of basalt. Between it and the Causeway there are ten fathoms of water. Beyond it, to the east, is Seagull Island, a broad and high rock, which is almost literally covered by the birds which have given to it a name.

The tourist will now demand leisure to examine more minutely the wonderful work of Nature upon which he is now standing. The Causeway consists of three 'piers' or 'moles', the Little Causeway, the Middle Causeway, and the Great Causeway, each jutting out to the sea, the greater mole being visible to the extent of about three hundred yards at low water, the other two not more than half that distance. The parts which the sea passes over are black

SCENE ON THE GIANTS CAUSEWAY.
(COUNTY ANTRIM)

from the sea-weed, the upper portions being principally grey from the short, close lichen.

The Little Causeway is first approached from the west; next is the Middle Causeway, to which the guides have given the name of the 'Honey Comb', a name which aptly explains its character. Here is the 'Lady Chair', a group of pillars gathered around a single pillar which is depressed and so arranged as to form a comfortable seat. The Great Causeway is, however, the leading object of attraction. The visitor usually ascends it from the west and descends it to the east. On the west side he is first shown 'Lord Antrim's Parlour,' which is a space surrounded by columns where tourists usually carve their names, and the remotest date is 1717. On the east side he leaves the Causeway by what is called the 'Giant's Gateway', the columns here presenting somewhat the character of a series of steps.

Immediately upon leaving the Causeway the guide will point out the 'Giant's Loom', a colonnade thirty-one feet, two inches in height. Besides the points we have enumerated, there are the 'Giant's Theatre', 'Ball-alley', 'Pulpit', 'Bagpipes' and 'Granny'. But as we have observed, and shall find it necessary to note again, every peculiarity in this marvellous neighbourhood is assigned to the giants, either as 'articles of their manufacture' or objects formed for their special accommodation. Indeed, the Causeway itself was the production of one of them as the guides will be sure to tell every traveller; for when the Irish Giant, Fin Mac Cual, was 'wishing' to fight the Scotch giant Benandonner, and invited him over to receive the beating intended for him, the Irish giant thought it only polite to prevent the stranger wetting the 'sole of his foot' and so built a bridge for him across the sea all the way from Straffa, over which the kilted Goliath came to 'get broken bones'.

The tourist, having gratified his curiosity and satisfied his mind, will proceed along the headlands to Dunseverick, returning, as we have intimated, by water. Passing Port na Spania, where there is also a stone organ, 'the Spanish Organ', a group of pillars will be pointed out to him called 'the Priest and his Flock', next 'the Nursing child', next 'the Scholar', a white pillar in a black crevice, likened to a student, book in hand, and next the 'King and his Nobles' – these are in Port na Callian: the latter is a singular assemblage of pillars which stands at the extremity of a narrow neck of land that separates this port from Port na Tober, above which is the 'Lover's Leap', a perpendicular precipice from the summit to the shore. When this is passed, we reach Port na Pleaskin, the most famous and by far the most majestic and beautiful of the bays.

The wonders of the Causeway, the grandeur of Fairhead, the dells and glens, the changing yet perpetual beauty of Cushendall and Cushendun, of Glenarm and Red Bay, of all the Antrim coast and scenery sink into comparative insignificance before the combined grandeur and loveliness of the Pleaskin.

East of the Pleaskin, and fronting Horse-shoe Harbour – a small creek named for the object it resembles – is a singular formation of rock called the 'Lion's Head', which is formed of red sandstone. Off Kenbane Head – which is another magnificent headland – are the 'Twins', two pillars standing alone, then comes the 'Giant's Ball-alley', a perpendicular rock of prodigious height; next the 'Giant's pulpit', projecting out over the ocean and then, passing Port na Truin, we arrive at Bengore Head, which is scarcely inferior in grandeur, although it is more limited in extent, to the promontory of Fairhead. In Port na Truin, which is between Benbane and Bengore, sounds resembling human lamentations are sometimes said to be heard issuing from cavities in the rocks, and it has been suggested that the name is hence derived: *truan* or *truin* signifying woe or lamentation in the Irish language. The ebbing and flowing of the tide acting on confined air may produce them.

At Bengore Head also stands a remarkable pillar to which the guides have given the name of 'the Giant's Granny'. To the east are four columns known as the 'Four Sisters'. At the other extremity of Port Fad is a single rock named the 'Priest'. Then we enter Port Moon, a calm and beautiful bay, into which rushes a river from the Feigh Mountains, which forms a noble cataract as it reaches the coast. Here occurs one of the most striking and picturesque of all the basaltic formations, which is called the 'Stack'.

Soon after passing this the tourist reaches Dunseverick, and here

DUNLUCE CASTLE.

he may consider he has achieved his purpose, so far as to examine the coast adjoining the Causeway. His journey has been entirely east of it, for to the west it presents but few objects of attraction between the Causeway and Dunluce, a distance of some three or four miles.

From Bushmills, or from the hotel of Miss Henry, there is yet another excursion to be made – to the ruins of Dunluce Castle, and from there to the White Rocks, which lie mid-way between Dunluce and the pretty and thriving sea-port of Portrush. The White Rocks are formed of limestone, and abound in caves, of which there are no fewer than twenty-seven, some of them extending far under the hills within a distance of about two miles. The largest and most picturesque of them is called the 'Priest's Hole'.

The views from all parts of this vicinity are most magnificent; to the west is the narrow promontory upon which stands Portrush; immediately before us is a picturesque group of islands which are called the Skerries; to the east is Dunluce, and beyond it are the gigantic cliffs that hang above the Causeway.

There are few ruins in Ireland so remarkable and interesting as that of Dunluce. It stands on an insulated rock that rises one hundred feet above the level of the sea; the perpendicular sides of which appear as if forming part of the walls, while its base, by the continual action of the waves, has been formed into spacious and rather curious caverns. It is separated from the mainland by a chasm twenty feet broad and one hundred feet deep, the only approach to it being by a kind of self-supporting arch of wall about eighteen inches wide and below which the foaming waves dash with considerable violence, even in calm weather. Across this narrow and dangerous footway the adventurous tourist must pass if disposed to examine this interesting ruin. The castle on the rock contained a small courtyard and several apartments of considerable dimensions.

The maritime county of Antrim in the province of Ulster is bounded on the north by the Northern Ocean; on the east and north-east by the North Channel; on the south-east by Belfast Lough and the river Lagan, which separates it from the county of Down; on the south by the county of Down; on the south-west by Lough Neagh; and on the west by the county of Londonderry, with the river Bann, which issues from Lough Beg, dividing the two counties, but leaving the Liberties of Coleraine as the north-west boundary of Antrim. It is therefore encompassed by water and hence its name, Endruim, 'the habitation upon the waters', which was corrupted into Antrim.

It is divided into the baronies of Upper and Lower Belfast, Upper and Lower Mazzareene, Upper and Lower Antrim, Upper and Lower Toome, Upper and Lower Glenarm, Upper and Lower Dunluce, Kilconway and Cary. The principal towns are Belfast, Carrickfergus, Lisburn, Antrim, Larne, Ballycastle, Portrush, Glenarm, Ballymoney, Ballymena, Bushmills and Cushendall.

Chapter Thirteen

FERMANAGH

The county of Fermanagh abounds in lakes and hence it was called in Irish, Feor magh eanagh, the county of the lakes. We entered Fermanagh by way of Ballyshannon, for a bridge passes over the Erne river which divides the county from that of Donegal, and close to it is the far-famed Salmon-Leap, which is confessedly the grandest in all Ireland. The navigation of the river is abruptly stopped here by this magnificent fall – a fall of nearly twenty feet – which extends the whole breadth of the river, a length of above one hundred and fifty yards.

The Basin which forms the head of Ballyshannon harbour into which it falls is literally alive with salmon, and it is scarcely credible that the fish are able to spring up 'the Leap' and make their way into the comparatively placid lake. Yet, at the usual season of their voyaging, they may be counted in thousands, overcoming the great natural barrier to their passage. This, although the most extensive, is not the only fall between Lough Erne and the sea; there are, we believe, four others, one of them – and it is the most graceful we have ever seen – is near the pretty little village of Balleek, about four miles from Ballyshannon. And here the beauty of the scenery may be said to commence.

The road to Enniskillen, a distance of eighteen miles, runs the whole way along the southern borders of the lake. With the lake to the left and to the right, and almost into the town, the drive is under the shadow of lofty hills. Between the road and the water extends a fertile valley, thick with trees and undergrowth, and beyond it stretches the long and narrow lough with its multitude of islands. These islands are said to equal the number of days of the year; they are very numerous and of all sizes from the smallest dot to the plain of many acres. All of them are green, and most of them are very productive. Along the whole of the route the opposite shore is kept in view – for the lake has in no part a greater breadth than nine miles, and is so wide only in one vicinity – and this is the neighbourhood of Tully Castle, which is on the southern shore. From this ancient castle, which stands upon a promontory that juts out into the lake, the prospect is extensive and inconceivably beautiful.

The ruins of another ancient castle – the Castle of Monea – which possesses the same general characteristics, stand a few miles to the south-east of Tully.

The town of Enniskillen, independently of its picturesque and highly advantageous situation on an island between the two lakes, ranks among the most interesting towns in the kingdom. It is long and narrow, but neat and clean, and has a cheering air of prosperity. The public establishments are well conducted, and the County Jail in particular may be taken as a model of good management. In the town hall are still preserved the banners carried by the Enniskilleners at the Battle of the Boyne; they are, however, sadly mutilated by time and the hands of selfish persons who have now and then clipped pieces off them to keep as memorials.

By far the most interesting of the islands in Lough Erne is Devenish, which is about two miles across the upper lake from the town of Fermanagh. It contains between seventy and eighty acres of remarkably fertile land. Here are the remains of several ancient churches and a round tower, which is considered in its present restored state to be the most perfect as well as the most beautiful in all Ireland.

The religious establishment at Devenish is said to have been founded by St Laserian, also called St Molaisse, who died in 563 AD. It was repeatedly plundered by the Danes and appears to have been re-founded in 1130 AD. The graveyard of the ancient church has long been regarded with veneration by the peasantry, and the dead are brought from far-off distances to be interred there – 'to lay their bones among their own people'. The attendant mourners embark in boats at a small promontory on the north side called

Portora, the Port of Lamentation. This lake is peculiarly liable to sudden and dangerous squalls.

The inland county of Fermanagh in the province of Ulster is bounded on the north by the counties of Tyrone and Donegal, on the east by Tyrone and Monaghan, on the south by Cavan and on the west by Donegal and Leitrim.

The county is divided into eight baronies: Clonkelly, Coole, Glenawly, Knockinny, Lurg, Magheraboy, Magherastephana and Tyrkennedy. Its principal town is Enniskillen, a town famous for centuries, and it is almost the only town of size or note that it contains.

Chapter Fourteen

LONDONDERRY

Journeying from the Giant's Causeway, the county of Londonderry is entered by way of Coleraine, the liberties of which extend to the borders of the county of Antrim. It is situated on the east bank of the river Ban, about three miles from its influx into the sea. The town appears busy and bustling and, although its commerce is comparatively limited, it still carries on a flourishing trade in the finer class of linen, in the manufacture of which it has long been pre-eminent.

The Ban is crossed by a pretty bridge, which was built in 1743 chiefly by the aid of the Irish Society. The navigation of the river is obstructed by a bar of shifting sand, and, at a distance of about two miles from the town, by a ledge of rocks – the Salmon Leap – which runs from its eastern to its western bank. A lofty, but unemployed and half-ruined mill stands upon its western border, which adds to the picturesque beauty of the scenery.

Passing through the town of Newtown-Limivady, a long broad street of poor houses, and the village of Ballykelly, a neat and peculiarly graceful village of the 'fishmongers', on the south-west borders of Lough Foyle, we soon arrive in sight of the famous city of Derry. Its character is remarkable from every point of view; covering a hill from the summit to the base, round a considerable part of which roll the waters of Lough Foyle, the houses rise in tiers one above another, with the lofty spires of the time-honoured cathedral topping all.

The walls that encompass Derry will first attract attention. They have been kept in excellent repair, and the broad walk upon them is neatly gravelled as a promenade, and the towers appear as capable of defence as they did a century and a half ago. 'By the original contract between the crown and the corporation of

London concluded in 1609, it was stipulated that the walls should be finished on the first of November in the following year, but though commenced, they were not entirely completed for several years after. They were laid out and built under the direction of Thomas Raven, of London, who had been sent over for that purpose, and the total cost of their erection 'including ports or gates,' with all the material and workmanship was £8,357.

The city gates have been kept in good repair, chiefly by grants from the Irish Society. The four original gates were called Bishop's Gate, the Ship-Quay Gate, the New Gate (now called the Butcher's Gate), and the Ferry-Port or Ferry Gate (and this is now called the Ferry Quay Gate). Two other gates, commonly called the New Gate and the Castle Gate (but not so called by any authority), were subsequently added. The Bishop's Gate and the Ship-Quay Gate are alone embellished. It was the Ferry Gate which the Prentice Boys 'shut' on 7th December 1688.

After its destruction in 1608, the city rose from its ashes, but not rapidly; in 1618-19 the houses numbered only ninety-two, and its progress continued slowly until within the present century. As recently as 1804 there was only one market – a fish market; the court house was 'unsafe from decay', and the jail was 'small and bad'. There was no dispensary, no library, no lamps, only parts of the streets were flagged and the walls were in very bad order.

The city now contains several handsome public edifices and valuable institutions; the houses within the walls and adjoining them number 2,947, and their population exceeds 10,000. It is approached from Coleraine by a singularly long and narrow wooden bridge crossing the river Foyle. The quays are good and the dock ranks among the most extensive and admirable in Ireland. The most interesting of the public structures is the Cathedral which stands upon the summit of the hill of Derry.

The maritime county of Londonderry in the province of Ulster is bounded on the south and south-west by the county of Tyrone, on the east by Antrim, on the north by the Atlantic and on the north-east by Lough Foyle, and on the west by the county of Donegal.

It is divided for the purpose of civil jurisdiction into the city and liberties of Londonderry, the town and liberties of Coleraine and the baronies of Coleraine, Tirkeeran, Kenaught and Loughinsholin. Its principal towns, besides Londonderry and Coleraine, are Newtown-Limivady, Castledawson, Dungevin, Moneymore, Drapers Town, Magherafelt, Maghera and Garvagh.

Chapter Fifteen

DONEGAL

From the immense proportion of waste land in county Donegal the reader may form some idea of the barren aspect of the county, and, at the same time, of its surpassing grandeur. Indeed, it is unequalled in Ireland for wild and rude magnificence. The most elevated of the mountains in this county is Errigal, which rises 2,463 feet above sea level. It abounds in lakes which are generally small, although some of them are very extensive. Lough Swilly and Lough Foyle also are both connected with it, the former exclusively, and its southern border is washed by the waters of Lough Erne. Its three principal rivers bear the same names, the Swilly, the Foyle and the Erne, but it abounds in water and from its mountainous character huge 'falls' are encountered in astonishing numbers.

Soon after leaving the liberties of Londonderry, proceeding northward, we entered upon the barony of Inishowen, a huge peninsula enclosed on one side by Lough Foyle, and on the other by Lough Swilly, both of which are saltwater lakes. On the southern extremity of this barony, which is distant about four miles from Derry, is the far-famed Grinnan of Aileach. The mountain upon which it stands is eight hundred and two feet high, and from its summit there is an extensive view of the two lakes with the surrounding scenery scattered over which are the ruins of several ancient castles. Within ken, although several miles distant, is the Rock of Doune, a natural fortress in the centre of a district scarcely accessible, where it is believed the ancient chieftains of Tyrconnel were inaugurated.

In the immediate vicinity of Derry there still exists a stone which appears to have been an inauguration stone of the ancient Irish kings. The stone exhibits the sculpted impressions of two feet, right and left, each of the length of ten inches.

The inauguration chair of the O'Neils of Castlereagh is still preserved. It was, for a long period, built into the wall of the Buttermarket of Belfast. The famous coronation chair in Westminster Abbey is believed to be of Irish origin, and is said to have been sent to Scotland for the coronation of Fergus, the first king of the Scots, who was 'of the blood-royal of Ireland'.

The hill of Greenan supplies a singular example of earliest architecture. It was formerly a royal residence, 'one of the most remarkable and important works of its kind ever erected by the ancient Irish'. At the base of the hill are several remarkable caves, which are considered to be associated with the ancient relics on the summit: we should remark that the cave at the base of Greenan hill is now blocked up.

The reader must be referred to the map in order to form some idea of the character of the coastal scenery of the northern districts, and the limits of our work permit us only to notice the more leading and striking features.

Along this coast too is Torry Island, which is inhabited by about five hundred persons, the greater number of whom have never visited the mainland. Some few years ago a few of its fishermen were driven on shore, and when they returned to their island homes they took with them leaves of trees as the greatest curiosities they could show to their people. Here also is a town buried beneath the sand; here, until of late years, the illicit distiller carried on his trade without the remotest dread of interruption, and the whiskey of Inishowen became proverbial for its excellence. Indeed, the coast from Moville round to Killybegs was famous for all that was rude, uncultivated and lawless.

The northern and western districts of Donegal afford rich materials for a volume. Our own journey however lies southward to Donegal Bay through a remarkably wild country, which is magnificent in the extreme, although it is infinitely less so than the rude coasts which keep out the Atlantic.

From Londonderry we verged westward to the ancient city of Raphoe, returning by the direct route to Donegal and so visiting the town of Stranorlar and the border town of Strabane. On our

LOUGH FOYLE,
LONDONDERRY

way through St Johnstown we visited a singular lake, Fort Lough, where there has always been a tradition that this lake (in common with many other lakes in Ireland) had a castle erected in the centre of the water beneath the waves. This tradition was long considered as fanciful; however, twenty years ago an attempt was made to reclaim the morass, and as the waters of the lake subsided, marks of an island became visible in the centre. By degrees regular masonry was observed ascending above the surface, and there can be now seen – even from the road – the remains of a building at the bottom of the lake, proving that the subaquatic castle was no visionary fiction, but a real existence.

About two miles from Raphoe – now a mere collection of cabins around the ruins of the Episcopal Palace – there is a high hill commanding a magnificent view of the country below. On the summit of this hill and in the centre of this view stands a Druidical temple, somewhat resembling that of Stonehenge in size and structure. The place is called Baltony, a name not uncommon in some districts of Ireland. It is supposed to be a corruption of *Baal tine*, the fire of Baal, intimating a spot where the deity – Baal – was worshipped in Ireland.

Soon after passing through Stranorlar we entered upon a district still wilder than any we had yet visited, and drove through the famous Pass of Barnes-Gap, through which the road runs to the town of Donegal; on the whole it is perhaps the most magnificent defile in Ireland. It is above four miles in length, passing between mountains of prodigious height, which soar above the comparatively narrow way and actually seem to link with the clouds that continually rest above them. When the gap had been nearly passed, we found ourselves on the brow of a hill, from which we looked down upon a rich and fertile valley, in the centre of which was Lough Eske, one of the smallest, but one of the most pleasing and beautiful of all the lakes in the county. We then drove through a luxurious vale and into the town of Donegal and examined the ruins of its ancient castle.

The castle of Donegal is not of very remote antiquity; the town is neat and clean and appears to carry on no inconsiderable trade with the interior. Our own route lay through the southern extremity of the county to Ballyshannon, but we diverged a few miles in order to examine the picturesque and venerable ruin of Kilbarron – an ancient fortalice of the O'Clearys, chiefs of the district. The nearest town is Pettigoe, a short distance from which are the remains of the old fortalice of Termon MacGrath. It commands a beautiful and extensive view of the Lower Lough Erne.

Of the town of Ballyshannon and its magnificent salmon leap we have already spoken (*Chapter Thirteen*). It is neat, clean and comfortable and has an air of business. Its situation on the northern border of Lough Erne, and within a few miles of the sea, renders it advantageous for commerce. The Erne is here crossed into Fermanagh by a bridge of fourteen arches and the adjacent scenery is exceedingly picturesque and beautiful. About four miles from Ballyshannon is the pretty village of Bundoran, near the mouth of the harbour. It is much frequented by sea-bathers, and is exceedingly healthy, with the wide ocean immediately facing it and a line of mountains enclosing it from the harsher winds.

On the other side of the town of Ballyshannon and not far out of the way from Donegal, the tourist will do well to visit a natural wonder, 'the Pulins', which is situated in the demesne of Brownhall. It is formed by the course of a mountain torrent, which runs for nearly a mile through a most singularly picturesque ravine, presenting a succession of views: a series of cascades, caves, wild cliffs, huge shattered rocks, and all amidst a profusion of the richest and most varied forms and every description of mountain plant.

The maritime county of Donegal in the province of Ulster is bounded on the east and south-east by the counties of Londonderry, Tyrone and Fermanagh. (It is separated from Londonderry by Lough Foyle.) It is bounded on the south by Donegal Bay, the northern extremity of the county of Leitrim, and on the north and west by the Atlantic Ocean.

It is divided into the baronies of Raphoe, Kilmacrenan,

Inishowen, Tyrhugh, Bannagh and Boylagh. Its principal towns are Donegal, Ballyshannon, Killybegs, Lifford, Letterkenny, St Johnstown and Stranorlar.

Chapter Sixteen

LONGFORD

We entered the county of Longford by the Royal Canal, voyaging part of the way in one of the 'Fly-boats', which are long and narrow and covered in, and with two divisions for different classes of passengers. As a mode of travelling it is exceedingly inconvenient; there is scarcely space to turn in the confined cabin, and an outside berth for more than one is impossible.

The county possesses few features of a distinctive character. It is generally flat, contains large tracts of bog and its northern boundaries are overlooked by remarkably sterile mountains. Its principal town – of the same name – is neat, clean and well-ordered, and it may be distinguished as the best-painted town in all Ireland, for the shops and houses are clean and trim, and partake very little of the negligence and indifference to appearances encountered too generally elsewhere.

The county of Longford has been rendered famous by the immortal name of Oliver Goldsmith, who was born at Pallas on 10th November 1782. This town – Pallas, Pallice or Pallasmore – which lies about two miles from the small town of Ballymahon is now a collection of mere huts. The house in which the poet was ushered into life has long been levelled with the ground and we could discover no traces of it. The village of Lissoy, generally considered the place of his birth, but certainly the place of his youth, is in the county of Westmeath, a short distance from the borders of Longford on the high road from Edgeworthstown – the home of Maria Edgeworth – to Athlone, from which it is distant about six miles. Lissoy is now, and has been for nearly a century, known as Auburn.

*

The inland county of Longford in the province of Leinster, is bounded on the south and east by that of Westmeath, on the west by that of Roscommon, from which it is separated by the Shannon and Lough Ree, and on the north by the counties of Cavan and Leitrim.

It is divided into the baronies of Abbeyshrule, Ardagh, Granard, Longford, Moydon and Rathelme. Its principal towns are Longford, Edgeworthstown, Granard and Lanesborough.

Chapter Seventeen

LEITRIM

The county of Leitrim, which possesses no features for comment, is remarkably long and narrow, its extreme length being forty-six miles, while its breadth varies from sixteen miles to two.

A very small portion of this county is maritime, and is situated between the two counties of Donegal and Sligo, in the province of Connaught. It is bounded on the north by Donegal Bay, on the west by the counties of Sligo and Roscommon, on the east by those of Cavan and Fermanagh, and on the south by that of Longford.

It is divided into the baronies of Carrigallen, Mohill, Leitrim, Dromahaire and Rossclogher. Its only town of any size is the assize town, Carrick-on-Shannon.

Chapter Eighteen

SLIGO

The town of Sligo is a seaport, but its trade is very limited, although it is the only port of much importance upon the western coast between Londonderry and Galway. Its abbey has long been famous, and its ruins are classed among the most remarkable in Ireland.

The abbey was founded in 1257 by Maurice Fitzgerald, Earl of Kildare and Lord Justice. In 1270, however, it was destroyed by fire, but was soon afterwards re-erected. In 1415 it underwent a similar fate, but it was speedily re-built during the following year, and from this era we are to date the foundation of the present structure. There are several vaults throughout the ruins, containing the remains of skulls, bones and coffins, and the abbey and yard are still used as a burying place.

The county of Sligo is rich in the picturesque; it abounds in wild mountains, surrounding fertile fields, and though not much irrigated by rivers, it is full of lakes. Its scenery and character however so nearly resemble that of the adjoining county of Mayo, a county with which we are better acquainted, and which offers far stronger temptations to the tourist, that we will pass over Sligo.

The maritime county of Sligo in the province of Connaught is bounded on the east by the county of Leitrim, on the north by the Atlantic Ocean, on the west and south by Mayo and on the south-east by the county of Roscommon.

It is divided into six baronies: Carbery, Coolavin, Corran, Leney, Tiraghrill and Tyreragh. Its principal towns are the assize town of Sligo, Ballymote and Collooney.

Chapter Nineteen

ROSCOMMON

The county of Roscommon is not particularly mountainous; the loftiest mountains are the range of Slieve Curkagh at the northern extremity and one of them, Fairymount, is described as the most elevated ground in the county. However, its rivers and loughs are abundant and extensive and it contains a considerable number of turloughs (temporary lakes which usually commence in winter and disappear in summer) which, no doubt, enterprise will ere long convert into permanently arable land. The noble and beautiful river Shannon forms the eastern boundary of Roscommon county.

Of the three principal towns of the county, Boyle is in the north, Roscommon is nearly in the centre and Athlone is in the south. Boyle is a good town, yet a very ancient one. It originally grew up round a rich and powerful abbey which was founded early in the twelfth century, the picturesque remains of which still grace the borders of the river.

In the cemetery of Kilbronan, not far from Boyle, was buried the famous Carolan, one of the last of the Irish bards, and here for several years the skull was placed in a niche of the old church and decorated with black ribbon. Carolan died in this neighbourhood in the year 1741, at a very advanced age, notwithstanding that he had been in a state of intoxication during probably seven-eighths of his entire life.

Roscommon town, although the assize-town of the county, is small and poor. This town was also indebted for its existence to one of the ecclesiastical establishments, about which the habitations gradually gathered. An abbey is said to have been founded here so early as the year 550 AD by St Coman, who gave his name to the county.

Athlone was the great gateway into Connaught for several centuries and many a bloody battle has been fought under its walls. It stands on the direct road from Dublin to Galway and protects the passage of the river Shannon at the only place where it can be forded within a distance of twenty or thirty miles. It is now used as a barrack and still exhibits proofs of prodigious strength. The bridge that conducts to it from the Leinster side is remarkably narrow and is certainly as ancient as the castle. A new bridge, however, is in the process of erection. The town of Athlone is divided into two parts. The oldest part is west of the river; the houses run up a hill and they are miserable and dirty, but indeed the more courtly part of the town is but a degree better.

The county of Roscommon was, for a considerable period, celebrated for its iron works – 'The Arigna Works', which were commenced in 1788 by three brothers of the name of O'Reilly. In previous ages the metal had been manufactured at the base of the range of Slieve-a-Neeran, which in Irish literally signifies the Iron Mountains, and the forests had consequently fallen under the axe of the woodman to be converted into charcoal.

The inland county of Roscommon is in the province of Connaught. Its boundaries on the north are the county of Leitrim, on the north-west those of Mayo and Sligo, on the south and south-west that of Galway, and on the east those of Longford, Westmeath and King's County.

It is divided into six baronies: Athlone, Ballintobber, Ballymoe, Boyle, Moycarnon and Roscommon. Its principal towns are the assize-town of Roscommon, Boyle and Tulsk. Nearly the whole of the flourishing town of Ballinaslow is in this county however, and also the major part of the ancient and famous town of Athlone, with the town being divided by the Shannon.

Chapter Twenty

MAYO

The usual route to Mayo is from Dublin, through Tuam to Castlebar, which is a distance of one hundred and thirty-six Irish miles. Soon after entering it, however, the tourist will leave to the left the old town of Cong, which lies about ten or twelve miles distant and, in order that we may meet with no interruption on our course to the far west, we shall entreat the reader to verge so much from the direct route and visit it – one of the most interesting and venerable ruins in Ireland.

To its dilapidated abbey which retains many tokens of early splendour, Roderick O'Connor, the last of the Irish kings, retired when his English enemies grew too strong for him, and here he passed the remainder of his life, living in monastic seclusion for fifteen years and here, according to tradition, he was buried. The honour of covering his remains is, however, disputed by Clonmacnois. Here at Cong the grave stands immediately under the great east window, and common stones are heaped in careless profusion above it, but it is surrounded by very perfect and beautiful sculptured buttresses, doorways and ornaments of a gorgeous character which speak of the former wealth and power of this sanctuary of kings.

It is impossible to render justice to the rich remains of this famous abbey. It is in a very perfect state, and is but a sample of the whole of the interesting structure. The windows especially are curious specimens of decorated Norman architecture, and some of the carvings seem as fresh as if they had but recently passed from the hands of the sculptor. The situation is also exceedingly beautiful and the site was happily chosen.

The village stands upon a small peninsula that pushes out into Lough Corrib. At its entrance is an ancient stone cross with an inscription in Irish, which unfortunately none of our attendants – and as it was market-day we had hundreds of them – were able to translate.

The Cross of Cong, which dates from the twelfth century, was presented to the Royal Irish Academy in 1839 by Professor Mac Cullagh, by whom it had been purchased from the Roman Catholic clergyman of Cong, who, with the funds thus supplied, was enabled to repair his chapel, which had been unroofed by a storm. Its date is supplied by the Gaelic inscriptions which are extremely clear and well cut, which covered the silver edges of the cross and which, besides giving the names of the king and a contemporary dignitary of the church, preserve that of the artist himself, who was an Irishman. A Latin inscription informs us that it contains a precious relic, a portion of the wood of the true cross, and this circumstance will account for the veneration in which it has been held for centuries, though unfortunately it was not enough to protect it from injury, for much of the ornamental work has been removed and part of the inscriptions have been torn away.

The neighbourhood of Cong is remarkably rich in natural wonders. A little to the north-west of it a narrow neck of land divides the two great lakes of Connaught, Loughs Mask and Corrib, and close to the town the water runs through a natural tunnel which lies deep under the ground for a distance of some three or four miles; thus the northern lake, Mask, joins the southern lake, Corrib, and both make their way into the Bay of Galway. Lough Mask being much higher than Lough Corrib, the stream rushes in mighty cataracts far beneath the surface of the earth – which occasionally sends up a dismal melancholy sound, keeping alive the embers of decaying superstition. Here and there the land has fallen in, exhibiting the wild rush of waters far underneath.

We went a short distance out of our way to visit one of the thus formed caves which is named the Pigeon-Hole. We were waited upon by an aged crone, as villainous a looking libel on womanhood as it has ever been our lot to encounter.

She lives in a cabin close by and watches with wolfish eyes for the coming of a *curiosity-passenger*, whom it is her business to initiate into the mysteries of the cave. We marvelled to see her with a wisp of straw in one hand and a lighted turf in the other, but their purpose was soon explained. We reached the hole, a chasm in the hill-side, the opening to which is about forty feet in circumference, and there we descended a rude and steep pathway cut into rough steps – a distance of perhaps thirty yards – to the bottom. At length we stood below with the water rushing along fiercely through a deep and narrow channel, boiling and foaming, but apparently without either ingress or egress, for the limestone rocks are enclosed about it, and the passage, both in and out, was imperceptible, except by the bubbling up at its entrance, and the smooth surface it presented when it left the cave for a still deeper cave, hidden since the creation from human eyes.

The crone, having first directed our attention to a brace of holy trout which had lived there 'since St Patrick blessed the abbey of Cong', and which we actually saw swimming merrily about in a small basin where the waters were somewhat calm, then entered deliberately upon her chief business of the day. Bending her shrivelled features over 'the coal of turf', the 'wisp of straw' was soon lighted. It was flung upon the current and carried swiftly by the rush of waters down to the farthest end of the cave, spreading a bright glow over the whole scene and exhibiting to us the parts of the cave that had previously been concealed by the darkness. Although the entire of this singular natural excavation was exhibited but for a moment, the sight was very startling, and it is worth a far longer pilgrimage to see it.

This is not the only singular object in the vicinity of Cong. On the way to Joyce's Country we saw heaps of piled-up stones on either side of the road. We left our car to examine them minutely, and learned that they were monuments to the memory of 'deceased' persons, erected by their surviving friends. The primitive tumulus is built upon death occurring – if it may be called building, since it consists of little more than placing a few large stones upon a previously unoccupied spot. Each relative of the dead adds to the heap and in time it becomes a mountain of tolerable size. The bodies are in no instance buried here, for it is not consecrated ground. We estimated that there were at least five hundred of these primitive monuments, of all shapes and sizes, along the road. In each of them we observed a small hollow, which the peasants call a window, most of which were full of pebbles and upon inquiry we learned that it is customary to fling a little stone into this 'cupboard'; the belief being that, as it gradually fills up, the soul is relieved of purgatory, and when completely full, the soul has entered paradise.

From Cong, we resume our journey northward.

We must request the reader to retrace his steps, postponing his entrance into Connamara and, regaining the great Dublin road, proceed with us to Castlebar.

The town looks thriving and prosperous; it contains some neat public buildings and a green of some extent as a promenade for the inhabitants. The suburbs are, however, exceedingly wretched as usual. The mountains surrounding Castlebar are sufficiently remote to add to their picturesque character, and in the immediate vicinity are numerous fine lakes. The neat and comfortable inn at which we abode commanded a fine prospect of both.

The district north of Castlebar is full of interest and wild beauty. About midway to Ballina, on the direct road to Sligo, the tourist passes between the lakes of Con and Cullen. A bridge was built across their juncture by the late Lord Lucan. Beneath this bridge may frequently be observed the curious appearance of the stream flowing in opposite directions during the same day, owing to the overflow of the small lake (Cullen) which has no other outlet for its superabounding waters than by sending them back again through this narrow channel.

From Castlebar we proceeded to Newport, which is called – to distinguish it from other towns of the same name – Newport-Mayo. A few years back it was little better than a collection of hovels, and a modern traveller in 1839 complains bitterly that he was domiciled in 'an ugly, mean-looking pothouse, redolent of sour beer and effete whiskey punch', the bed-chamber of which was 'small, frouze and unclean'. He adds, however, that 'Newport was intended to be a better town', and a better town it is now. The hotel is neat and comfortable, the cars are good, several pretty houses have been built along the quay and some large storehouses 'in progress' indicate increasing prosperity. At the quay a vessel of four or five hundred tons may unload. The town, and a vast district to the west of it, including nearly the whole of the island of Achill, are the property of Sir Richard O'Donnel.

To the tourist and occasional resident, Newport-Mayo has many temptations of sea, lake and land; its attractions to the sportsman and angler are abundant of every class and kind, and both may pursue their pleasure without 'let or hindrance', the sole stipulation being that they shall reside at the inn.

Here also we had the opportunity of inspecting one of the singular boats, the Corragh or Corach, the construction of which appears to have undergone little alteration for many centuries. It is of a rude form, the stem being nearly as broad as the stern. It is manufactured of wooden laths, covered with coarse tarred canvas; this canvas is manufactured by the peasantry and the cost of the whole vessel is about thirty shillings. The size is usually sufficiently large to contain four men; each man rows two oars; the oars are short, fat and broad and a hole is made in which a single trolach is introduced. The craft is, of course, very light, and rises and falls with every wave – literally dancing on the waters.

From Newport-Mayo we proceeded to the island of Achill, which lies about fourteen miles distant. It is the largest island off the coast, being sixteen miles in length by seven in breadth, and contains between 5,000 and 6,000 inhabitants. The scenery that leads to it is remarkably wild and barren; on one side are the bleak and barren mountains, and on the other is Clew Bay, for nearly half the distance until the view opens upon the broad Atlantic. In natural grandeur and rude magnificence the district is certainly unsurpassed, if indeed it can be approached, by any other in Ireland.

Nor is the neighbourhood without its interest arising from associations with the olden time; the remains of the ancient monastery of Burrishoole and the castle of Carrig-a-Hooly, one of the Castles of Grace O'Malley, are among the most striking and remarkable of the ruins in Ireland. Those of the former stand upon the east bank of the river and adjacent to the lake of Burrishoole;

CLEW BAY, FROM WESTPORT.

both afford famous sport to the angler and unrestricted permission to fish in either is, as we have intimated, readily accorded to the tourist. The venerable ruin is highly picturesque and retains many tokens of early splendour. As usual the relics of mortality are profusely scattered within and around it; it is literally a 'place of skulls' with every nook, crevice and cranny crammed with the dry bones.

The old castle was evidently built for strength. It is situated at the extremity of an arm of the sea and immediately adjoining it we were informed that there was depth enough at low water for a vessel of considerable burthen to ride in concealment and in perfect shelter from the fiercer winds. In this vicinity too are some singular caves.

About mid-way to Achill Sound is the small village of Bunown, where the tourist will certainly give his horse a rest, for probably the whole line of the Irish coast does not supply a view at once so grand and so inconceivably lovely. Yet it is all taken in at a glance. In the extreme distance, across the bay, rises a line of mountains of which the venerable and legend-haunted Croagh Patrick is the highest, with its peaked top in the clouds and mid-way is the broad bay, dotted with islands.

At length we approach the coast. The island of Achill, appearing as part of the mainland, rises in sight, the tops of its two high mountains, Croghan and Slievemore, having been visible for a long time. At Achill Sound there is a ferry-boat to the island, the passage across being a quarter of a mile at low water. The boat of course conveys the car with its passengers. At the Sound there is a plain but very comfortable inn, at which the traveller will do well to rest. It is kept by a Mr Savage, who was for several years a sub-officer of the coast guard.

The people of the island of Achill have many primitive customs. A few days before our arrival an occurrence took place which, we understood, is by no means uncommon – a race for a wife. A young man, a carpenter, named Linchigan, applied to the father of a girl named Corrigan for his daughter in marriage. A rival called Lavelle asked for her also, on the plea that he was richer and 'he wouldn't ask so much with her'. Whereupon, the factions of the swains were about to join issue and fight, when a peacemaker suggested that the boys should run for her. The race was run accordingly a distance of some miles up and down a mountain; Linchigan won and wedded the maiden.

The islanders consist almost entirely of four principal families, and we were informed that they could easily be distinguished one from the other. They have, in many respects, separate habits and customs and seldom intermarry apart from their clans:

The Lavelles are of French extraction, the descendants of French fishermen who, in former times, used to fish off the island of Boffin; they are in the most part 'light, smart and handsome men'.

The Scholefields are of English descent and 'proud of it'.

The Caulfields are dark, curly-haired men and retain tokens of Creole blood.

The Morans are of Danish descent, 'heavy and dull men', with red hair and whiskers.

The O'Malleys, Gaughans and Maughans are of the aboriginal Irish, and are 'cleverer than all the others'.

There is not a single tree upon the whole island, although there are abundant marks of its being long ago one huge and pathless forest. It is full of lakes, the shores abound in wild-fowl of every description and the mountains with grouse. The foxes are so numerous that the young lambs are never safe. Seals are seen at times in shoals among the rocks, and the ravens and eagles exist in astonishing numbers in the cliffs and recesses of the hills. A tradition exists that about a century and a half ago, an eagle bore off a child from Achill and carried it to its eyrie among the cliffs of Clare Island, which is a distance of several miles. The child was saved however, and lived to be an old man.

Our first object after entering the island was to engage the services of guides: two stout-limbed, athletic and most obliging fellows, brothers of the name of O'Malley. Under their direction we commenced the ascent of the Croghan mountain, 2,254 feet above the level of the sea. We should scarcely have been tempted to this arduous task but that the top seemed at no great distance; when we had surmounted it, however, we found ourselves at the foot of another still higher and when this difficulty was overcome, a third was before us, higher yet. In fact, we had to climb three mountains instead of one.

However, we soon obtained a view of Clew Bay, with its host of islands and Clare Island, with its tremendous precipices topping them all. Looking below we saw the village of Keem, a group of dots of stone, and further west the village of Dooagha, which had dwindled almost to a few specks, while the winding roads about the island seemed no broader than a ribbon. At length we reached the summit, and what a view! On one side was beautiful Clew Bay, and on the other a bay scarcely less beautiful – Blacksod Harbour. Behind us were the island hills and valleys and the mountain of Slievemore which, although nearly as high as Croghan, we seemed to look down upon. Before us was the broad Atlantic between us and America. It was indeed a glorious sight, but one to which no language can do justice.

From Achill we retraced our steps to Newport-Mayo, for the weather was too unsettled to permit our venturing across the bay, and from thence we proceeded through a wild and uninteresting district a distance of six miles to Westport.

Westport is a town of considerable size, containing a population of nearly five thousand. The hotel is situated on the Mall through which runs a clear stream; it is opposite the Roman Catholic church – an ugly building, the exterior of which we regretted to see defaced by 'posting bills' of sales and auctions. The inn is large and abundantly furnished, containing five sitting rooms and twenty-four bedrooms. It was built, we understood, supplied with furniture free of charge to the host, who holds it rent free, by the Marquis of Sligo, with the sole view of benefiting the town, by affording accommodation to all who are drawn thither by business or pleasure. The quay is some distance from the town; it seemed bustling and lively, notwithstanding the doleful aspect of a long line of storehouses, ostentatiously marked 'wine in bond', 'tobacco in bond', and so forth.

The seat of the Marquis of Sligo adjoins the town, through the grounds of which there is a pleasant road to the quay, a road generously left free to all comers and goers. The demesne of the

Marquis is exceedingly beautiful. The most noble peer was for some years an absentee, occupied in discharging his duties as Governor of Jamaica, but happily he is now generally at home.

The vicinity of Westport is full of attractions, and there are innumerable sources of pleasure open to the sportsman.

From Westport we proceeded to Connemara, entering this far-famed domain of Nature by way of Leenane, a small village situated at the mouth of the Killeries. The sublime, though savage scenery of Connemara may be said to commence soon after passing the pretty bridge of Errive.

The maritime county of Mayo in the province of Connaught is bounded on the east by the counties of Sligo and Roscommon, on the south by the county of Galway and on the north and west by the Atlantic Ocean.

It is divided into nine baronies: Burrishoole, Carra, Clanmorris, Costello, Erris, Gallen, Kilmain, Murrisk and Tyrawly. Its principal towns are Castlebar, the assize town, Ballina, Ballinrobe and Foxford and the seaports are Westport, Killala and Newport.

Chapter Twenty-One

CLARE

During our stay in Limerick we made a visit to Killaloe, which is situated on the Shannon, about twelve miles north of the city. It is one of the remarkable or memorable places in Ireland, for the celebrated Brien Boru, one of the most distinguished of the ancient Irish monarchs, resided in its vicinity, as did many of his ancestors as well as successors of the line. Killaloe lies on the Clare side of the river, and is approached from that of the county of Tipperary by an excellent bridge of nineteen arches, which crosses above the rapids in the only fordable part of the Shannon. Some of the arches are ancient, but three or four in the centre which are of ample span were built in 1825, and below this a ledge of rocks obstructs navigation.

The canal between Limerick and Lough Derg constructed for the avoidance of the falls terminates a little above the bridge, where the river is deeper and more tranquil, and from thence steamers ply between the town and Portumna. At either side of the bridge, occupying the extent of two small islets, are two ruinous castlets which formed the ancient defences of the pass. The town, situated on the hillside, is old, poor, small, irregular and neglected. Its population is about one thousand. It contains two cathedrals, the Protestant and the Roman Catholic; the latter, a new unfinished structure, is in a very plain pointed style. In the neighbourhood there are some excellent slate quarries, which are actively wrought, and there is also a mill for polishing and preparing marble, which is brought down the Shannon by the steamers and, when manufactured, is exported to England and elsewhere. On an island below the bridge and in front of the episcopal grounds is a stone-roofed church, which bears all the characteristics of antiquity.

The history of Killaloe is little better than a record of its various destructions and resuscitations: thus, in 1061, 1080, 1116, 1154 and 1155 it was successively burned. The only other event of its history beyond what appertains to its church is the building of a bridge here in 1054 by Turlough O'Brien, when it was called the *Clar droichet Cilledalua*, the timber bridge of Killaloe.

In front of the little bay of Skariff, which lies at the upper extremity of Lough Derg (one of the many lake-like expansions of the Shannon), is a group of three small islets, the principal of which, Iniscealtra, or Holy Island, contains twenty acres. It has been famous from early ages for its reputed sanctity, and it possesses structures belonging to the Pagan as well as the Christian periods: a round tower and seven small churches or, rather, cells or oratories. The round tower is about seventy feet high and in a good state of preservation. The principal church is called Teampol Camin, or the Chapel of St Camin, because that saint was either the founder or patron.

Holy Island continues to be a favourite burial place with the peasantry and, although its religious establishments are ruined and desecrated, the ancient sanctity of its character still endures, and pilgrims from remote distances seek its shores. On the patron day or festival day of St Camin (12th March) the crowd of its devotees is very great, but the clergy have of late years – and with much propriety – discountenanced such assemblages.

Few of the counties of Ireland contain finer monastic ruins than the county of Clare – that of 'Quin' is indeed worth a prilgrimage to see. Nor is Clare without its inland charms. The lake of Inchquin may be classed with the most beautiful lakes of the land, and it is situated about twenty miles north-west of Ennis. The principal object of the scene is the castle – a warrior pile, which though shattered and time-worn retains a stern and frowning dignity even in its decay. It stands on a small island or rather peninsula, lying in close to the northern shore, and consists of a square embattled keep, vaulted within, a curtain wall and a barbican tower. It is supposed to have been erected by Theige O'Brien, Prince of Thomond.

It is however the great ocean river, the Shannon, which gives its chief attractions to Clare County. And these attractions commence seaward with the borders of Limerick city, and terminate only with the mountain rocks that keep out the Atlantic. In the immediate vicinity of Limerick the road lies over a rich alluvial flat, which stretches from the shores of the river to the base of the highlands, which rise behind the wood of Cratloe. These flats are here called Corcass lands, a term originating in the Irish word, *corroch*, a swamp or morass, which these grounds, previously to the hand of reclamation reaching them, must unquestionably have been. They are still often overflowed by the Shannon, and along the high road which traverses them stone pillars are raised at frequent intervals as indexes of its limits on such occasions. The neighbourhood of the hamlet of Cratloe possesses two of those solitary castles so frequent in the south of Ireland, which almost seem as if they never possessed any outworks or other adjuncts. One of them is called Cratloe Castle and the other Cratloe Beg.

The voyage hence down the magnificent river Shannon to the mouth is full of interest. Sea rocks, islets and islands are abundant. We must, however, pass them by, to arrive at far-famed Scattery, which is memorable in ecclesiastical history.

The island contains about one hundred and eighty acres; twenty of which, previous to the dissolution of the monasteries, were covered with wood, although not a shrub now remains. St Sinon, or Senanus, deemed it an eligible situation in the sixth century for a monastic establishment. He was a native of Hy Conall (the present baronies of Connelloe in the county of Limerick), and studied in Ireland. He afterwards travelled to Britain, and thence to Rome. On his return to his native land he became the founder of several monasteries in Thomond (the present Clare) and in particular the one at Scattery, which was subsequently converted into a priory for regular canons, but no trace of this building is now visible. He is also said to have founded eleven churches on the same island, but the ruins of seven are all that remain. A round tower, one hundred and twenty feet high, stands a few paces to the west of 'St Sinon's Cathedral'; it measures twenty-two feet in circumference, and the doorway which faces the church is on a level with the ground, a circumstance unusual in these buildings. A long rent, from near the conic cap down to the centre, which was caused by lightning disfigures the tower and threatens its ultimate destruction.

The coast from Kilrush, on the mainland opposite the island, which is a pretty and fashionable bathing place, round to Kilkee, which faces the Atlantic, may vie for grandeur with that of any part of the kingdom. The two towns lie about eight miles distant by land, but to reach the one from the other by sea a voyage of little short of forty miles would be necessary, for the long and narrow promontory – the barony of Moyarta – stretches out between them and forms the northern boundary of the mouth of the Shannon. Some miles north of Kilkee are the famous cliffs of Moher, the highest of which is said to be 930 feet above the level of the sea. However, to supply even a faint description of the wonderful scenery in this vicinity would exceed the space to which we are limited.

The mouth of the Shannon is grand almost beyond conception. Its inhabitants point to a part of the river within the headlands, over which the tides rush with extraordinary rapidity and violence. They say that it is the site of a lost city, long buried beneath the waves, and that its towers and spires and turrets, acting as breakers against the tide water, occasion the roughness of this part of the estuary. The whole city becomes visible on every seventh year and has often been seen by the fishermen sailing over it, but the sight bodes ill-luck, for within a month the ill-fated sailor is a corpse. The time of its appearance is also rendered further disastrous by the loss of some boat or vessel, of which no vestige is thereafter found either of it or its crew.

In the summer of 1823 the city was last visible, and then a sail boat carrying a crew of fifteen men perished. The day happened to be a Sunday, and it was reported that the whole fifteen crewmen were seen about the same time at the parish chapel, mixing and

NATURAL BRIDGES, NEAR KILKEE.

conversing amongst their neighbours and relatives, although it was a few hours after that tidings of the dreadful loss reached their families.

The maritime county of Clare is in the province of Munster. It is bounded on the east and south by Lough Derg and the river Shannon, by which it is separated from the counties of Tipperary, Limerick and Kerry, on the north and north-east by the county of Galway, on the north-west by Galway Bay and on the west by the Atlantic Ocean.

It is divided into the nine baronies of Bunratty, Burren, Clonderlaw, Corcomroe, Ibickane, Inchquin, Islands, Moyarta and Tulla. Its principal towns are Ennis (the assize town), Kilrush, Killaloe, Curofin and Ennistymon.

Chapter Twenty-Two

GALWAY

Proceeding from Dublin, the county of Galway is entered on passing over the Shannon at Ballinasloe. From this pretty and prosperous town, where the grand cattle fair of Ireland is held, two great roads branch off, the north road leading to Mayo through Tuam and the west road through Aughrim and Loughrea to Galway town. Although we visited the county by the former route, we shall conduct the reader by the latter – which will enable him to examine the district in general, and Connemara in particular, to greater advantage – for to enter this region, as we did, by the Killeries, was like 'looking at a man's face behind his back'.

Proceeding thus, however, we shall miss the old town of Tuam, and no great loss, for it is a dirty and ruinous-looking place, and its Roman Catholic cathedral, which has been recently erected, is sadly out of harmony with the dull and dingy habitations upon which it looks down. Nevertheless, if it is approached from the east it has a remarkably picturesque effect as it towers above the landscape and commands an extensive prospect of the adjacent country.

The road from Ballinasloe to Galway passes through Loughrea, a remarkably neat and orderly town, and leaves on the right the ancient, but now ruinous town of Athenry, where there are several interesting remains of antiquity. Athenry was famous long before Galway became remarkable, and early records of the provincial capital distinguish it as situated near Athenry.

The comparatively unchanged character of the district soon becomes apparent and the tourist will obtain one example of this in the frequent occurrence of the 'original Connaught pig', which now exists in no other part of Ireland. He is a long, tall and usually spare animal, with a singularly sharp physiognomy, and remarkably keen eyes. His race is still preferred by the peasantry, for he will 'feed upon anything' – even the thin herbage of the common – and so the rearing costs neither trouble nor expense. For the purposes of sale, however, he is useless and, as it is often that the 'pig pays the rent' and is seldom or never brought up for 'home consumption' the Connaught pig is nearly extinct, and probably in the next few years will only be found in pictures.

On approaching Galway town the tourist perceives some other evidence that he is in a peculiar district: the dark features and coal-black hair of the people indicate their Spanish descent and they are, for the most part, so finely formed and so naturally graceful, that almost every peasant girl might serve as a model for the sculptor.

From the earliest period Galway was a famous trading port with Spain, and its merchants supplied nearly all Ireland with wine. Passing along the narrow streets the tourist is startled by greater singularities; houses with the remains of 'jalousies' and elaborately carved arched gateways mingle with modern buildings, indicating the comparatively unchanged aspect of the inhabitants and their dwellings. However, these records of old times are rapidly falling into ruin, and probably in a few years Galway will have lost its distinctive character.

If, however, the records of a peculiar people are to be found in the town, in one of the suburbs a people equally peculiar still exists, retaining today the customs and habits they have kept unchanged for centuries.

The inhabitants of the 'Claddagh' are a colony of fishermen and they, with their families, number between five and six thousand. Their market place adjoins one of the old gates of the town and is close to the remains of a fortified tower. Here they sell their fish, but it is apart from their own dominion – and their own dominion it may literally be called, for they are governed by their own king and their own laws and it is difficult, if not impossible, to make them obedient to any other.

The Claddagh is a populous district lying to the right of the harbour, consisting of streets, squares and lanes, all inhabited by fishermen. They claim the right to exercise complete and exclusive control over the bay – indeed, over all the bays of the county. They are peaceable and industrious, and their cottages are cleaner and better furnished than those of most of the Galway dwellings, but if any of the 'rights' they have enjoyed for centuries are infringed, they become so violent that nothing can withstand them.

This singular community is, as we have intimated, still governed by a king who is elected annually, and they have a number of laws of their own. At one time the king was absolute and as powerful as a veritable despot, but his power has yielded to the times, and he is now, as one of his subjects informed us, 'nothing more than the Lord Mayor of Dublin or any other city'. However, he still has much influence and literally sacrifices himself without fee or reward for 'the good of the people', and he is constantly occupied in hearing and deciding causes and quarrels, for his people never, by any chance, appeal to a higher tribunal. The king is indeed one of themselves; his rank and station being only indicated by a white sail and colours flying from the masthead of his boat when he is at sea, where he acts as admiral.

The people have many peculiar customs, but one is worthy of especial note. The wedding ring is an heir-loom in a family, and is regularly transferred by the mother to her first married daughter, and so on to their descendants. These rings are large, of solid gold and cost, not infrequently, from two to three pounds each. They are formed into the shape of two hands with a heart being clasped in each palm.

The people are, in general, comfortably clad and their houses are, for the most part, neatly furnished. We entered several of them, among others that of the ruler of the district. His majesty, however, was at sea, but we were introduced to his royal family, a group of children and grandchildren who, for ruddy health, might have been coveted by any veritable monarch of Christendom.

Among its other attractions the beautiful bay of Galway must not be forgotten, nor the magnificent lake that pours its rich tribute to the ocean through the town.

Offshore are the Aran Islands, and these are three in number;

one of them, Llanmore, is of considerable extent. During our visit to the west the weather was more than usually rough and we were unable to visit them. They were described to us as amazingly full of interesting objects, wonderfully abundant in natural scenery and containing a vast number of rude monuments of remote antiquity. The inhabitants number above three thousand. The whole of the coast round the beautiful bays – although less magnificently rugged than that which lies more to the north – abounds in picturesque objects, and the peasantry here, as well as in the less familiar districts, are rich in original character, their vicinity to the wild Atlantic, and their living remote from frequent intercourse with more civilised parts of the country having preserved much of their primitive simplicity.

Leaving Galway town, the tourist will proceed to Outerard en route to Connemara. Outerard is a small, but exceedingly neat town and close to it is the residence of the ferocious O'Flahertys, once the terror of the district, and in its immediate neighbourhood is a singular natural bridge over which the old coach road runs and under which flows one of the tributaries to Lough Corrib. The bridge is of black marble, of which there is an extensive quarry in the district.

When we were within a few miles of this pretty town, our astonishment was excited by perceiving a prodigious collection of cromleachs, of the existence of which no traveller has taken note, but which certainly demand extensive and minute investigation. These huge circles of stone were so numerous that at first we imagined them to be merely accidental occurrences in the rocky soil, but repeated examinations convinced us that they were as much artificial erections as any of the monuments of which we have encountered so many in the various parts of the country.

This great city of the Druids – for such it undoubtedly is – lies between Galway and Outerard, but much nearer the latter town upon the old road; yet the road is not so old but that searchers after antiquities must have often traversed it. It occupies the whole of an extended plain, on the height of a steep hill, and in the valley beneath the old castle of Aughanure can be seen. The space is literally covered by these stones, which are of all shapes and sizes, and it would not be difficult to count a thousand of them.

From Outerard our route lay to Clifden, which is a distance of twenty miles along a road as smooth as a bowling green and as fine a road as any in Great Britain, which leads all the way into the very heart of Connemara. This region is chiefly a waste; the cabins of the peasantry are 'few and far between' and there is but one house of entertainment on the whole route. This is a small cottage which is distinguished as 'Flyn's Hotel', and consists of two rooms with the dining hall containing three beds. It is resorted to as a 'halfway house' for refreshing horses, and is now and then used by anglers – who may be indifferent to any enjoyment except that which they find in abundance by the sides of the broad rivers and lakes. Before he reaches 'Flyn's' however, the tourist will probably turn off to the right to visit Maam, which lies about four miles distant from the main road. Maam should indeed be his resting place, for here the inland glories of Connemara are seen to great advantage.

The tourist is now, and has been for some time, in the county of lakes, where they assume all shapes and sizes which are singularly varied. Immediately at the turn from Maam is one of the most beautiful and picturesque of these lakes – the Lake of Many Islands, which is surrounded by thick underwood and is full of small islets on which the furze, broom and heather flourish luxuriantly. On the right is the western bank of Lough Corrib and occasional views are caught of the whole expanse of this great sheet of water. On the left is the noble mountain of Maam Turc, rising high above a score of lesser hills and looking down upon the loveliest, yet the loneliest of all the lakes – Lough Inah, which lies in solitary grandeur in the centre of a circle of hills, each of which is impassable except to the pedestrian or one of the little sure-footed ponies.

We have been travelling upon the road made by the justly-celebrated engineer, Mr Nimmo, and as we approach Maam, we arrive in sight of his pretty cottage which was built for his accommodation while superintending the works. It is now the 'Maam Hotel' and stands beside an elegant bridge which crosses an arm of Lough Corrib where the lake is joined by the river Bealnabrack.

At Maam the tourist must rest. He is in the midst of a host of natural wonders, within reach of all the leading beauties of the district, and he will be domiciled in one of the most comfortable inns in the kingdom. The landlord is named Rourke, and he was for some years a waiter at Gresham's Hotel, in Dublin.

There was nothing in Connemara that astonished or delighted us more than this valley through which the river winds at the base of a double line of mountains. We saw many scenes of wilder and more rugged grandeur, but none so happily mingled the sublime and beautiful. The peculiar beauty of the scene consists in the happy blending of rugged grandeur with gentle beauty, for the river moves calmly through the dell, having rushed in torrents down the sides of the mountain, and it then pursues its even course into the broad lake. Only one solitary ruin is within our ken, and that is the ivy-covered walls of Caislean na Circe, or the Hen's Castle, which is classed amongst the oldest in Ireland and which occupies a low promontory that juts out into Lough Corrib.

The road to Cong runs for a considerable way beside the lake, passing the Hen's Castle, and by degrees the lonely character of the scenery is left behind, for the view opens out upon the beautiful lough and the shore for many miles. After a while the road ascends and we reach the remarkably pretty village of Fairhill, which is not unaptly called so, and which commands an extensive and magnificent prospect of the two lakes – Corrib and Mask – for it stands upon a narrow neck of land which separates them, and under which, through a subterranean channel, the waters of the latter run to join the former, and then they voyage together into the ocean at Galway Bay.

We must now retrace our steps, return to Maam and regain the route to Clifden. Again we are in the country of the lakes, and after a few miles through barren land we reach the lake of Ballynahinch; a short way on the other side of it is the seat of the Martin family, lords of a vast portion of the soil about it. About two or three miles to the south of the demesne is the small but rising and improving town of Roundstone, which is acquiring commercial importance under the protecting care of its landlord. At Ballynahinch is the most famous of all the Connemara salmon fisheries; it is leased to a Mr Roberts, a Scottish gentleman who is very generous and liberal in his indulgences to the angler.

The town of Clifden owes its existence to the late John D'Arcy, Esq., the lord of the adjacent district, and his son and successor, Hyachinth D'Arcy, Esq., is adopting the wisest and surest means to render it an important seaport of the west. In the year 1815 Clifden contained but one house, but now there are about four hundred houses with a comfortable hotel. The town is beautifully situated with mountains surrounding it on all sides, except to the west where it is open to the Atlantic, and it stands at the head of a small bay. Here, one of the rapid rivers makes its way down from the hills and into the ocean, and presents a fine fall a little way outside the town. It is so near the congregation of dwellings indeed, that the rush of waters mingles with the voices of the inhabitants, yet, turning from the houses, it seems as lonely in its grandeur as if it were in the centre of untrodden hills.

Clifden Castle, the residence of the proprietor of the district, is within a mile and a half of the town. It is a modern castellated mansion in the midst of beautiful and magnificent scenery.

From Clifden our route lay to Leenane, round the coast. The grandeur of the scenery commences as we leave the town; the Twelve Pins – the great objects of mountain interest in Connemara – are beheld from every point of view and are varied into all conceivable forms. They are beside us to the right along the whole of the road, while every now and again to the left the prospect opens to the bold Atlantic, which can be seen between the breaks in the green hills that guard the rugged shores. As the crow would fly to Leenane the distance is perhaps six or eight miles – but what human foot has ever taken the short cut? Round the coast by the coach road – for such it now is – to Leenane is about twenty miles, but the tourist must make it thirty, for he will sacrifice the better half of his enjoyment if he does not verge to the right, to first visit the graceful shores of Renville, and the rugged passes of Salruc. Both are easily accessible, but to visit the district about Renville, which is four miles north of the main road, he will require a stout horse and a strong car, for even now the path appertains to 'old Connemara'. He will, after a fatiguing journey, reach the poor village of Tully on the northern point of a small peninsula that stands between the harbours of Ballinahill and Killery, but which lies much to the west of the latter, indeed, on the very brink of the Atlantic. It stands upon the summit of a hill, under which a lengthened slope of land, easily made arable, runs down to the sea. However, this neighbourhood exhibits many tokens of poverty.

We had to spend the night in the wretched inn of this miserable village – or rather part of a night, for we rose from our beds an hour before daybreak and pursued our journey. There was neither tea nor bread to be procured; the horse, the cow, the pigs and the hens were separated from us by a floor, through the divided boards of which they had the ample opportunity for conversing with us – which they did not fail to do.

Soon after midnight our domicile was invaded by the hostess, who required some refreshment from the cupboard for *his reverence* who had just arrived from a station, and about an hour afterwards the corn bin had to be applied to for a feed for *his reverence's* pony, for he had to make a new start. This break-in was followed by another: the boy wanted his top coat, for the rain was *powering* down; a short while afterwards the household was all in motion, and our chamber contained everything they wanted.

Here – having mentioned the rain – we should consider it necessary to advise the traveller to provide amply against the weather. A Connemara shower is like the descent of an avalanche of water and drenches everything in less than a minute. Umbrellas are perfectly useless; the hill blasts tear them into shreds before they can be raised. The wind rushes so fiercely down some of the passes that our horses found it impossible to progress faster than the rate of a mile an hour.

Continuing onwards: between Tully and Leenane a rare treat awaits the tourist, for he will walk or drive through the beautiful and magnificent pass of Kylemore. This gap in the mountains extends for about three miles and forms a deep dell through which runs a rapid river, which makes its passage into the lake near its eastern entrance.

Some two or three miles beyond this – the chief beauty of the district – the roads turn off to the north and lead beside lakes which lie at the foot of the mountains to Salruc. The pass of Salruc is said to derive its name from a certain saint – St Rock or Ruc – who is said to have resided in a cell at the foot of the mountains.

And so we pass on, by the side of, yet high above, Killery Bay. As we near Leenane we obtain another magnificent view of its whole extent. Descending from this point of view, we arrive at Leenane, and here a humble but pleasant inn greets the wayfarer, which is situated just at the head of the bay.

O'Reilly's Inn at Leenane will be found exceedingly comfortable as a resting place on the route, and here boats may be obtained to visit the beautiful scenery of Delphi on the opposite side of the bay.

In justice to Mr O'Reilly, a civil, attentive and obliging host, we cannot do better than to print from his prospectus:

The Killeries Inn – 1842 –
Anthony O'Reilly, of Leenane,
Late of the Coast-Guard Service

Begs leave most respectfully to inform travellers, tourists, and the public in general, that he has taken the house lately inhabited by Mr John Joyce, at the head of Killery Bay, and fitted it up as a hotel; determined to earn their patronage by the most strenuous exertions to please, the steadiest attention to the wants and wishes of all who honour his house with their company, and the most moderate charges.

We spent some time in the village, entering several of the houses and witnessing scenes of appalling want, that deducted largely from the enjoyment we received in visiting a place famous throughout Ireland. Perhaps it was these circumstances or perhaps because we had heard so much about it that we were disappointed in Delphi for, although it is very grand and very beautiful, it fell short of our expectations. The road to it leads through a fertile valley; on the sides of the hills there are a couple of cottages which are few and far between. In one of them a young woman lay dead, and we cannot soon forget the peculiar effect of the mournful wail that proceeded from its threshold and which was echoed by the friends of the deceased as they gathered to the wake.

HEAD OF THE KILLERIES – CONNEMARA.

The lake of Delphi is reached after a walk of about a mile. It is a lonely spot, sunk deeply in the midst of the mountains; on one of them stands a small cottage built by the Marquis of Sligo and surrounded by a plantation of trees.

We return to O'Reilly Inn, where cars may be obtained, and good cars too, well-horsed and with civil riders, to convey the tourist northward to Westport through a district of the most wonderful magnificence and beauty which is unsurpassed even in Ireland. Arriving at the little graceful bridge at Errive, we leave the county of Galway and re-enter that of Mayo.

The county of Galway is in the province of Connaught. Its boundaries on the north are the counties of Roscommon and Mayo; on the east those of Roscommon, King's County and Tipperary; on the south the county of Clare and Galway Bay, and on the west the Atlantic Ocean.

It is divided into the baronies of Aran, Athenry, Half Ballymoe, Ballynahinch, Clare, Clonmacnoon, Dunkellen, Dunmore, Kilconnel, Killian, Kiltartan, Leitrim, Longford, Loughrea, Moycullen, Ross and Tyaquin.

Besides the provincial capital, the county of Galway contains the populous towns of Tuam and Athenry, and the market-towns of Loughrea, Eyrecourt, Gort and Headford, besides the greater part of Ballinasloe, with the small but rapidly improving town of Clifden being its only seaport in addition to the port of Galway.

APPENDIX

Hall's Ireland was originally intended to be a tour of the country, but the finished product was much more. It was a personal record of the Halls' Ireland, and they reported on whatever took their interest. And their interests were wide and varied...

COTTAGES

We shall avail ourselves of the opportunity for offering some observations relative to the dwellings of the humbler, or working, classes in Ireland. There are certainly exceptions but in general, throughout the country, their condition is so wretched as to become almost revolting and to excite astonishment that human beings should continue to inhabit them, year after year, without the acquisition of a single comfort, and with scarcely a sufficiency of necessaries to render life to all appearances worth preserving.

The poor occupant of a miserable hovel loses, or rather never had, any ambition to obtain a better one, and the rich persuade themselves – easy when they find their improvements, if made, are unappreciated – that the tenant requires nothing more than the mere means of sustaining animal existence. As the father has lived, so lives the son – and so may continue to live their descendants. Undoubtedly, of late years, there has been some advance towards the civilisation of the exterior as well as the interior of the Irish cabin. They are very frequently whitewashed now – a practice which was introduced during the terrible visitation of cholera – but the progress towards a happier state of things has been grievously slow, and in the more remote districts they retain their primitive characteristics, which are absolutely degrading to human nature and shocking to humanity. This picture is not, by any means, overwrought, and the tents of the Red Indian and the huts of the Esquimaux are constructed with a greater degree of care and more attention to their rude notions of comfort than the cabin of an Irish peasant. Very frequently there is not only no window, but no chimney, with the chinks in the door alone providing the light. The thatched roof is rarely kept in repair, and it is not uncommon for the rain to drip through so that one half of its small space is continually in a 'sop'.

Many of them – indeed, most of them – consist of but one apartment, in which the whole family of grown-up young men and women eat and sleep. There is generally a truckle bed in a corner for the owner, or the 'old people', for a cabin will seldom be found in which there is neither grandfather nor grandmother, and affectionate zeal usually cares first for them; but the other members of the household commonly rest upon straw or heather which is laid on the floor, and which is covered with a blanket – if one is possessed – and the wearing apparel of the several sleepers. We have more than once entered a cabin where we have found eight or ten people of all ages recruiting body and soul for the toil of the next day. The pig – the never absent guest – a cow, if there be one, and occasionally a few fowl occupy the same chamber at night.

The furniture consists of an iron pot to boil the potatoes; a rude dresser sometimes, a couple of three-legged stools, a couple of stone seats on either side of the turf fire, a table (but not always), a 'kish' – a wickerwork basket – into which the potatoes are thrown when dressed, and the poor bed which we have mentioned, which is usually in the corner.

The dung-heap is invariably found close to every door; sometimes – indeed, frequently – right across the entrance, so that a few stepping stones are placed to pass over it. And this evil is perpetuated, in spite of all appeals on the grounds of decency and health, and seems to be almost unavoidable, for without the manure the food could not be grown. The cottager cannot trench upon the road – and in almost all instances cottages are built lining either a high-road or a by-road – and he cannot spare out of his poor modicum of earth the space thus occupied, and every inch must produce its potato. However, the stranger who 'turns up his nose' at the standing pool and still more offensive dirt heap which engenders so much disease, and is so destructive to every clean and healthy thought, may not be aware that with this sludge and refuse the cotter enriches his little potato-garden, and that to take it away without providing some spot where refuse can be gathered for the same purpose would be doing the poor fellow an irreparable injury. It will be remembered that we are speaking of the very poorest class now – but alas! we speak therefore of the great bulk of the population.

But there are cabins even more wretched than those we have described and these are to be found in the less frequented parts of the country.

A few months ago we examined one, on the island of Achill. Seven persons were housed there and we measured it: it was exactly ten feet long by seven feet broad, and five feet high. It had been built on the edge of a turf bog; within, a raised embankment of dried turf formed a bed, and besides the clothing of the more than half-naked children, a solitary ragged blanket was the only covering it contained. The family had lived here for two years; some work recently undertaken in the neighbourhood had given the man employment, and he was on the eve of building himself a better house. Close to this hovel were two others scarcely superior, and indeed nearly every cottage in the district was almost as miserable and destitute of anything approaching to comfort.

Much of this evil is no doubt attributable to the exceeding and unaccountable apathy of the peasant; for in this very locality huts were pointed out to us which were inhabited by men who were substantial enough to 'give a marriage portion of a hundred pounds with a daughter' – a common way in Ireland of estimating the possession of wealth. And – not here but in the south – we once entered a cabin, the owner of which seemed so completely a victim of poverty that we left some money on his table, which, being observed by a 'knowledgeable' companion, he then informed us that the man was richer than ourselves, for the mountain beyond his door was dotted with his sheep.

This evil – of concealing wealth – will vanish before an improved order of things; it has grown out of a long suspicion that the acquisition of money was sure to bring an increase in rent; a belief that was not ill-founded in old times. We ourselves have known instances where the purchase of a single piece of furniture, or the bare indication of thrift and decent habits was a certain notice to the landlord that it was his time to apply for arrears due; arrears being always due under the ancient system when the land was let at a nominal rent, with the real value and something above to be paid, and the remainder to be entered as a debt, and which kept the tenant in the condition of a slave, utterly and at all times in the power of his master.

Let us now picture one of the comfortable Irish cottages; for such are occasionally to be met with. A few months ago we sought shelter from a passing shower in one that will answer our purpose. It is at Erive, a small glen among the mountains that enclose the head of Killery Bay, in the county of Galway. There was no upper storey, but there was a room branching to the right and another to the left of the 'kitchen, parlour and hall' – the sleeping rooms of the family, and decently furnished. This cottage contained, indeed, nearly every article of furniture in use in such dwellings of the humbler classes. Each of them we have often seen, but very seldom have we been enabled to notice them all together.

The first object that attracted our attention was a singularly primitive chair, which is very commonly used throughout Connaught. It is roughly made of elm, with the pieces being nailed together. There is evidence that this piece of furniture has undergone little change during the last eight or ten centuries.

We next observed – and this is rarely seen anywhere now – the quern or handmill, which was a very perfect one. In appearance it took the form of two rounded stones. The upper stone was about twenty-two inches in diameter; the under stone was about an inch narrower, and convexed, so that the two surfaces might coincide, and afford an easy descent for the meal when ground. In the centre of the upper stone was a circular hole, nearly three inches in diameter, and across this stone was set a bar of wood, having a hole in its centre about half an inch deep, and the same in width, by means of which the upper stone rested *in equilibrio* upon the punthan (a strong peg or pivot in the centre of the lower stone), and by the use of little pieces of leather fitted into the hole in the bar above mentioned, the upper stone could be raised or depressed, so as to make the friction greater or lesser as the meal was meant to be coarser or finer. There was also an upright handle, which was about ten inches long, set firmly into the upper stone within about two inches of the edge, and thus was the whole machine fitted for work.

The corn was generally dried out in an iron pot over a slow fire, and kept constantly stirred to prevent it from burning, and when it arrived at a certain degree of crispness it was taken out to be ground. Two women generally worked the quern, one sitting facing the other with the quern between them, and each in her turn took hold of the handle, and turned it with a degree of velocity much greater than you would perhaps imagine. One or other of them 'fed' as it was called; that is, put the corn into the large hole which was called the eye in the upper stone. This feeding required some dexterity in avoiding a blow of the handle in its rotary motion, and at the same time to drop the corn into the eye without scattering it. The process of shelling was never performed, but the corn and husk were ground down together, so that the meal appeared at first very dark and rough, but it was sifted afterwards.

The next object that attracted our notice was the wooden drinking cup – the modern substitute for the ancient 'mether'. It is a simple rounded cup with a single handle – and such indeed are common in this country. The mether was originally square and not round, wider at the top than at the bottom, and to drink out of it was no easy task.

There was also a primitive gridiron to 'broil the red herrings'. It was made from a piece of twisted iron and a candlestick, equally rude, formed out of an iron tube inserted in a small 'slab' of oak.

The dresser we saw was well garnished with plates; there were three or four three-legged stools and 'bosses', and at either side of the chimney was a stone seat. In the chimney there were two holes, one of which was very small and which was used to hold the tobacco pipe when it was relinquished; and another, which was larger, for the 'screeching hot tumbler' of old times. A saddle hung upon a peg; and a rude and smoke-dried shelf above the chimney was garnished with plates. There was a pair of oddly-shaped tongs to place the turf on the fire, a churn, a rafter to hang the clothes upon, a salt-box, a trough for the pig (who, although domiciled in his own house, was an occasional visitor), an iron pot of course, and a crook fastened up the chimney to hang the pot upon, and there were two wheels – the wheel for wool and the wheel for flax.

This cottage then may be taken as a model of the better class, both in its interior and its exterior 'accommodations'. The roof was sound, the windows were whole and opened and shut. The stagnant pool was at a respectable distance, the pig had his separate apartment, and there was a stable for the cow and horse.

EDUCATION

Before we proceed to consider the 'National Board,' which at present holds jurisdiction over 'national education in Ireland,' it will be desirable to offer a few remarks upon the condition, as regards instruction, of the Irish people, who, all this while, were in little or no degree benefited by the national supply of means for their improvement.

The 'Irish Schoolmaster' has been pictured by nearly every writer of fiction who has dealt with the Irish character, and although he is commonly represented as odious and dangerous, this portrait is seldom overdrawn. The high estimate in which the Irish people hold learning – a fact on which we cannot lay too much stress – induced them not only to tolerate his evil habits, but tacitly to allow him a very perilous influence over their principles and conduct. Upon this topic it is needless to enlarge; there is abundant evidence by which the origin of nearly every illegal association may be traced to the cabin of the village schoolmaster.

The 'school-houses' were, for the most part, wretched hovels, in which the boys and girls mixed indiscriminately. They were usually damp and always unhealthy, and so dark that it was common practice for the pupils to learn their lessons among the adjacent hedges, and if they acquired knowledge, it was, not unfrequently, knowledge to evil rather than to good. Some of the works we found among the cabins of the humbler classes were the same *Cottage Classics of Ireland* which were in circulation some thirty years ago. These include *The History of the Seven Champions, History of Fair Rosamond and Jane Shore,* Ovid's *Art of Love, Irish Rogues and Rapparees, Francis, a notorious robber teaching the most dexterous art of Thieving, History of Celebrated Pirates, Moll Flanders, The Devil and Doctor Faustus, History of Witches and Apparitions,* etcetera. The ballads in circulation were of a still worse character. We have an extensive collection now before us; a large proportion of them are political, and filled with the very worst sentiments; others contain expressions of sympathy for men who have died on the gallows, and all are pregnant with danger.

Of late years, however, a vast improvement has taken place, and during our recent visits we found it difficult to obtain, at any of the low shops in the suburbs of large towns, copies of these books, of which they were never without an ample supply in former times. Even the *Life of James Freney, commonly called Captain Freney, from the time of his first entering upon the highway in Ireland, to the time of his surrender, being a series of five years remarkable adventures, written by himself,* is now a 'scarce book', although an edition of it has been printed in nearly every town in the south of Ireland.

These remarks have been necessary in order to exhibit, by contrast, the advantages obtained by the new order of things.

And so we proceed to treat of the existing 'Board for the Superintendence of a System of National Education in Ireland', believing it to be, all circumstances considered, the wisest and most rational project that has been devised for educating the people, and the surest to attain the great aim and object of all education – right acting from right thinking. We are very far from placing the system before the reader as in a state of perfection, or even of completeness, nor do we argue that errors which have undoubtedly been committed could not (some of them at least) have been avoided. Of late it has been the policy to conciliate the one party in Ireland without consulting with the other, and a mistake was made at the outset which it will take years to rectify.

The Board, as originally constituted, consisted of the Duke of Leinster, the Archbishop of Dublin, and Dr Sadlier – three members of the Established Church; the Roman Catholic Archbishop of Dublin and the Right Hon. A R Blake, a Roman Catholic gentleman, and the Rev J Carlile, and Robert Holmes, Esq., the one a Presbyterian, the other a Unitarian; men who, however estimable in their private lives, held opinions, political or religious, opposed to those of many whose suspicions were sure to be aroused, whose alarms were certain to be excited, and whom it was, at least equally, the duty of the Government to have conciliated. In consequence there was not a single person 'on the Board in whom the Protestants of Ireland had the least reliance' – whether they ought or ought not to have had confidence in the judgement, integrity and impartiality of the Board is another question, but the Board was, undoubtedly, so framed as to increase rather than to allay the apprehensions generally entertained by the Protestants of Ireland that 'the education scheme' was a plan for their 'discouragement'. This feeling, thus created, was certainly not diminished when they saw the school-houses spring up in the chapel-yards or immediately adjacent to the Roman Catholic chapels, and the Roman Catholic clergymen employing and paying the masons who built them, nominating the masters and supplying the books. The result was that the Protestants generally, and their clergy almost entirely, stood aloof from all contact with 'the Board,', declined to receive any portion of the state money, and permitted the Roman Catholics to possess unlimited control over the funds granted for the benefit of the whole community.

We should far exceed our limits if we were to attempt to enter upon the less important points in dispute or to detail the various arguments advanced, pro and con, in reference to this institution. We must regard the existing 'Board for superintending the education of the Irish people', as a mighty engine for their moral and social improvement, knowing that whatever defects may exist in the present system, it is immeasurably superior to the old methods of educating the lower classes of the Irish.

In lieu of the schoolmasters of former times – whose characters we have briefly sketched – a set of men, properly taught and prepared for their important task in the 'model schools' of the institution, have been substituted. They are paid by the public and are therefore responsible to the public; their habits are ascertained before they are employed and their conduct is watched during their employment by proper 'inspectors' who are duly appointed and who, in their turn, are frequently examined by the Board, and called upon to report regularly concerning all subjects concerned with their respective districts.

The school-houses, instead of being dark, close, dirty and unwholesome, are neat and commodious buildings, well-ventilated and in all respects healthful.

The books that have displaced the mischievous and deleterious publications which were formerly in universal use, are excellent in every sense of the term. Lessons in virtue are conveyed on every page with a degree of skill and judgement which is nowhere exceeded; they have been compiled with admirable tact, so as to communicate information by the simplest process, and although there is a manifest want of books that shall interest and amuse while they instruct, those that supply extracts from writers of acknowledged worth are altogether unexceptional. We procured copies of, we believe, all the books that have been issued by the Board, and we have no hesitation in stating that works better calculated for education in all the leading branches were never produced. We know of none that may so be safely recommended to schools generally, of any grade, or to families of any rank.

We have an *English Grammar*, which is exceedingly simple and comprehensive; *Books of Arithmetic* for various classes; books on the *Elements of Book-keeping*, and on the *Elements of Geometry;* a *Treatise on Mensuration;* an *Introduction to the Art of Reading, with suitable accentuation and intonation; Books of Lessons,* which commence with instructions for the very young and advance so as to suit mature students. These books consist of selections in prose and poetry from the best and most popular British authors, compiled with a view to the combination of amusement with information. The *Reading Book* is an admirable compilation we venture to say, and does not contain a single passage that could be objected to upon any ground.

There are also placards posted conspicuously in some parts of every school, and these contain, in themselves, an admirable code of wisdom.

We believe then that the system is working well – marvellously well, considering the great and manifold difficulties by which it was formerly surrounded. Many of these difficulties have been surmounted; others have been materially lessened, and those that remain may be removed by the cordial co-operation of the clergy of the Established Church. Let us hope that this will no longer be withheld.

SOCIETY

The difference between the higher classes in Ireland and those of England is, of course, very slight in all the essentials that are understood to constitute 'good society'. Indeed, of late years, the intercourse between the two countries which is so frequent and so continued, has nearly removed a distinctive character from either. The peculiarities of the old Irish gentry are all but extinct; the originals of the last century bear but a very remote resemblance to their successors; the follies and vices – the drinking, duelling and 'roistering' – which, in former times, were considered so essentially Irish, now belong exclusively to the ancestors of the present race. The habits which were once fashionable are no longer tolerated, and the boasts and glories of the past age are scorned and execrated by this one. Indeed, it was acknowledged that although the 'Irish gentleman' was often an object of suspicion, the 'gentleman from Ireland' was ever an example of courtesy, good breeding, honour and intelligence.

In higher society therefore, little of distinctive character will be perceived, except in that ease and cheerfulness of manner which make a stranger feel instantly 'at home', and the peculiar tone of the Irish voice. We do not mean that the better educated have what is understood by 'the brogue', but there is an intonation that belongs to Ireland which is never lost and which cannot be disguised.

The society of the middle class, or rather of the grade above it – the members of the learned professions, and persons on a par with them – is unquestionably agreeable and invigorating in the provinces, and equally so, but more instructive and refined, in the capital and the larger towns. It is everywhere frank and cordial, tempered by playful good humour and a keen relish for conversation, and is always distinguished by the cheerfulness that borders upon mirth and the harmony produced by a universal aptness for enjoyment.

The women of Ireland – from the highest to the lowest – represent the national character better than the other sex. Very often in the men energy degenerates into fierceness, generosity into reckless extravagance, social habits into dissipation, courage into profitless daring, confiding faith into slavish dependence, honour into captiousness and religion into bigotry, for in no country in the world is the path that divides virtue from vice so narrow.

But the Irish women have – taken in a mass – the lights without the shadows, the good without the bad or, to use a familiar expression, the 'wheat without the chaff'. Most faithful, most devoted, most pure, the best mothers, the best children, the best wives. Their information is without assumption, their cultivation without equal, their influence is never ostentatiously displayed, in no position of life do they assume an ungraceful or unbecoming independence. Their character is indeed, essentially and emphatically, feminine; the Irish woman is 'very woman' with high intellect and a sound heart.

In writing of Irish women we refer to no particular class or grade; from the most elevated to the most humble, they possess innate purity of thought, word and deed, and are certainly unsurpassed – if they can be equalled – for the qualities of heart, mind and temper, which make the best companions, the safest counsellors, the truest friends and afford the surest securities for sweet and upright discharge of duties in all the relations of life. (It will be scarcely necessary to inform the reader that these remarks proceed from but one of the authors of this work; that they give the opinions, not of an Irishwoman, but of an Englishman.)

In Ireland, as yet, the aristocracy of wealth has made little way, and to be of a 'good family' is a surer introduction to society than to be of large fortune. The prejudice in favour of 'birth' is, indeed, almost universal and pervades all ranks. Consequently, classes are to the last degree exclusive, and their divisions are distinctly marked and recognised as those determined by the etiquette of a court. Hence arises the perpetual straining after a higher station, to which many worthy families have been sacrificed; persons in business rarely persevere until they have amassed fortunes, but retire as early as possible after they have acquired competence, and the subdivisions which their properties necessarily undergo, when junior branches are to be provided for, creates a numerous class – which is almost peculiar to Ireland – of young men possessing the means of barely living without labour; disdaining the notion of 'turning to trade', unable to acquire professions and ill-suited to adorn them if obtained; content to drag on existence in a state of miserable and degrading dependence, doing nothing – literally 'too proud to work, but not too ashamed to **beg**'. This feeling operates upon the various grades of society; and the number of idlers in the busy world is fearfully large, from the 'walking gentleman' of the upper class, to the 'half-sir' in the middle, and the 'jackeen' of the class a little above the lower.

The walking gentleman is always elegantly attired, of course always unemployed and with ample leisure for the studies which originate depravity.

The half-sir is generally a younger brother with little or no income of his own, and so educated to be deprived utterly of the energy and self-dependence which create usefulness.

The jackeen is found everywhere, but most abundantly in the large towns. Happily, however, this class is not upon the increase. The jackeen might have been seen (regularly a few years ago, but now only occasionally) lounging against the college rails at early morning. He would have worn a half-intoxicated, half-insolent air that betokened a night passed in debauch; his stockings that had once been white, falling from under the drab green ill-fitting trousers over the shoes; his coat was usually of green, his waistcoat of some worn and faded finery, and the segment of collar that peeped above the stock would have been fashionable in cut but not in quality, and would be crushed and faded from its original propriety. His hat would always be a little on one side, and had a knowing 'bend' over the right eye; one of his arms would be passed, with that peculiar affectation of carelessness which evinces care, through the rails and then brought around so as to enable the hand to shift the coarse and bad cigar that nearly always rested upon his lip. There would be a torn glove upon the other hand and his dull blood-shot eyes generally winked impudently upon every girl that passed.

SERVANTS

There is one topic upon which we feel bound to offer some comments, and that is the condition of domestic servants in Ireland. Generally it is very bad, and calls loudly and earnestly for alteration and improvement.

They are insufficiently remunerated; little care is bestowed upon their wants; they are seldom properly fed and lodged; they are rarely instructed in habits of order, neatness and regularity, and an odious and evil custom largely prevails by which the domestic is often either half-starved or forced into dishonesty.

We allude to the mode of paying servants what is called 'breakfast money', that is to say, an allowance of money – usually half a crown a week – to supply themselves with bread and other necessary food. The almost inevitable consequence is that of the weekly allowance they contrive to save a considerable portion, or nearly the whole, usually with a view of devoting the quarter's wages untouched to the necessities of their more miserable families 'at home' and this custom is so general as to bear almost to be characterised as universal among Irish servants. Thus they are subjected to severe privations in the midst of plenty, if they scrupulously abstain from taking that which, by this rule, is made not to belong to them.

The Irish servant, however, will seldom consider it dishonest to take food, and thus arises an evil of even greater magnitude than subjection to privation. Throughout Ireland, indeed all classes appear to have an insurmountable object to take into account the 'aiting and drinking'. Among the upper orders the table literally groans under the weight of food, which is usually sufficient in all cases for double or treble the number of guests.

It is the servant's duty to be honest, faithful, sober, civil and industrious; to remember that he is paid not only for his labour, but for his time; and that both are his employer's property: this is his duty. His interests demand that he should be watchful to ascertain his employer's habits, small wishes and peculiarities, and to minister to them zealously and kindly, and this will perhaps win his master's regard, but, at the least, it will increase his value and he will be happier for it in the end, for a bland and yielding temper is ever wiser than one that is stern and stubborn.

But the duty is not, as some ladies and gentlemen seem to imagine, entirely on the side of the servant to the employer. In our social state all duties are more or less reciprocal, and often, when we have heard unthinking people complain of the insolence, stupidity and stubbornness with which their servants perform their duties, we have been tempted to inquire how they have performed theirs. It is not the mere duty enforced by law that is to be taken into consideration; the law compels the servant to be honest, or he will be punished; the law obliges the master to pay the servant his wages, but the duties to be exercised where the law has no power chiefly contribute to mutual comfort.

Does the employer bear in mind that he is guilty of injustice, if he expects perfection in a servant which he well knows he himself does not possess? Does the servant call himself honest, because he does not take money, though he wastes and destroys? In England servants are well paid, well fed, well housed, and the evils they suffer are minute indeed, in comparison to those endured by the

Irish servant. The maid-of-all-work in a middle-class English family has a fagging life of it, but gets through as much work as two Irish servants will, and with half the actual labour. But let it be remembered that she receives more than double the wages of a person in the same position in Ireland, and is much better fed and far better treated.

In England respectable tradespeople and the small class of farmers continually send their children into service, and consequently respectable servants may always be obtained by those who give wages, and of all false economies, paying a servant badly is the most false. In Ireland a foolish pride and, I might add, careless treatment from their employers prevent even the more respectable artisans and peasants from sending their children into service.

The greater number of Irish servants employed by the middle classes are taken from the very lowest and poorest in the country. We repeat, they are not properly fed, they are not properly lodged at night and their wages are not in proportion to their labour – and we mean even at the Irish rate of remuneration. Our hearts have often ached for these poor, ignorant but warm-hearted and affectionate creatures. We have seen the mistress of the house – perhaps an opulent tradesman's wife, such a woman as in London would give her maid-of-all-work ten or twelve pounds a year, her tea and either a pint of beer daily or beer-money, and her nursemaid eight pounds a year with the same allowances – employing a bright-faced, but half-clad girl who had to do everything as best she could for four pounds a year – wash, iron, cook, clean, scour, scrub and wait upon company; and yet her mistress descanted long and loudly on the impossibility of obtaining 'good servants'.

Now in England the middle class (the class that stamps the character of a country) prepares, as it were, the servant for a higher step. The poor Irish lass has no hope of a higher step, because she has learned nothing where she has been. She is constantly obliged to make one thing do duty in half-a-dozen ways, where there is a total want of a system, and has no idea that, unless the furnishing, cleanliness, comfort and arrangement of a kitchen are attended to, there can be nothing well-ordered throughout the house. Little or nothing is done to raise the servant in the scale of moral or intellectual being; no effort is made to improve her habits or her tastes, so that she looks upon the work of cleaning and brushing upstairs in some degree as unnecessary. She does not see the necessity of it – she does not reason as an English servant does – and why? Because there have been no pains taken to improve her knowledge of the decencies of life. We write of the habits of the middle class, and a step below them, and we say that until they treat their servants better, and pay them better, they cannot have decent servants.

A servant would consider herself well-paid, and *would* be well paid in Ireland if she received seven or eight pounds a year. Let her have her dinner at one of the clock (a servant's health and habits of order are strengthened by the system of early dining), and a third meal of plain wholesome food. Do not degrade her by supposing she would steal food like an animal. Do not treat her like a thief or you will make her one. Feed her entirely without reference to 'breakfast money'. There is something inexpressibly humiliating in bread being locked up from fellow creatures who are labouring for you.

In service, as in matrimony, there can be no 'separate maintenance' without evil arising out of it. The unselfish attachment, ready industry, willingness to labour and fidelity of the Irish servants are appreciated even where their careless, unformed and uneducated habits militate against them, and it is unquestionable that a more careful training under a better order of things would render them infinitely more valuable auxiliaries to a household either in Ireland or in England.

SECRET SOCIETIES

There can be no doubt that the secret and lawless associations in Ireland originated in the disbanded troops from the war between William and James. These were termed 'Rapparees', and they were in fact, as the name implies, formidable bands of robbers, whose depredations were by no means terminated with the cessation of hostilities.

In the course of twenty years, the Rapparees were succeeded by the Houghers – a degenerate race who were encouraged, if not organised, for a political purpose, and so long as their ebullience was allowed to freely escape into foreign services, little of the evil humour of their Irish constitution was obvious. It is stated from official documents that more than 450,000 Irishmen died in the service of France between 1691 and 1745. When, however, the vent was interrupted, when this drain of the Roman Catholic youth ceased and their services were no longer required abroad, the disaffected Irish were loosely held together at home by agents in the pay of France.

Although however such associations did, we think, unquestionably originate in political motives, they very soon lost this distinguishing characteristic – as vain and useless – and were applied to the attainment of objects more certainly and directly within their reach. A brief space will suffice to notice the several 'societies' which, under their various distinctive names, have, up to the present moment, succeeded to a considerable extent in setting the law at defiance.

The Whiteboys – whose origin we have derived from the scattered bands of Rapparees that succeeded the war of the Revolution, 'began in Tipperary', and their aggressions were 'owing to some enclosures of commons which they threw down, levelling the ditches'. In consequence of which they were first known by the name of 'levellers', but they became known as Whiteboys from their wearing their shirts over their coats for the sake of distinguishing themselves in the night.

The operations of the Whiteboys were principally limited to Munster, and they continued from the year 1760 to perhaps the year 1775. In 1785, however, they reappeared under the name of 'Right-boys' and, in imitation of their predecessors, they administered unlawful oaths, regulated the prices of land and labour, opposed the collection of taxes, and directed themselves especially to the 'reformation of tithes'. Those who resisted were subjected to horrible tortures; their favourite punishment was to bury their victim up to the head in a grave filled with thorns, and then to cut off his ears. These classes were chiefly confined to the south; within the same period however, the north had been placed in a state of insubordination by the 'Steel-boys', and the'Oak-boys'.

The 'Steel-boys' had their origin thus: an absentee nobleman of the county of Antrim, who held vast possessions, resolved upon raising a large sum of money by letting leases at small rents, but receiving large fines. A considerable portion of the tenants were unable to procure sums sufficient to obtain renewals and 'rose against the forestallers'. They said that they would pay for their farms in steel, and were called Steel-boys.

The origin of the Oak-boys is more curious: the public roads in Ireland were formerly repaired by the 'labour of the house-holders'. Each householder was compelled by law to give six days' labour in the year. They complained first that the rich were exempted from the work, and next that 'the sweat of their brows had been wasted upon private roads'. In 1764 they rose against the regulation and from the oaken branches which they wore in their hats were denominated Oak-boys. In the next year the law was altered and 'with the cause of discontent the disturbance was removed'. The evil complained of by the Steel-boys being also naturally of brief duration, both these illegal organisations were easily suppressed.

The 'Peep-of-day-boys' also originated in the north about the year 1785, and owed their title to their custom of visiting the houses of Roman Catholics at daybreak in search of arms. They were met by a counter association, 'the Defenders' – a name which explains itself. The latter, from being a defensive organisation, soon became an aggressive body, and at length were partly dissolved and partly absorbed into the body of the United Irishmen, till they were finally lost in the more important movement that gave rise to the rebellion of 1798. However, since that time their society has been revived under the name of 'Ribbonmen'.

Since the Union, however, a variety of other societies under various names have existed in several parts of Ireland, who are independent of any avowed political object. Thus we have had the Thrashers, in Connaught, which became so formidable that, according to the charge of Chief Justice Bushe in 1806, the king's judges could not move through the country upon a special commission except under a military escort, nor a criminal be executed till a general officer had marched from a distant quarter at the head of a strong force to support the civil power. We also have the Terry Alts, in Clare; the Carders (so called from the custom of flaying their victims with a wool-card); the Rockites; the Moyle Rangers; the Paddy Cars; the Shanavests and the Caravets.

The following is extracted from the report of a trial which took place in Clonmel in 1811, before a special commission. A man by the name of James Slattery was under examination.

'Which is the oldest party?'

'The Caravets were going on two years before the Shanavests stirred.'

'Why are they called Caravet?'

'A man of the name of Hanley was hanged; he was prosecuted by the Shanavests, and Paddeen Car said he wouldn't leave the place of execution till he saw a caravet about the fellow's neck; and from that time they were called Caravets.'

'For what offence was Hanley hanged?'

'For burning the house of a man who had taken land over his neighbour's head.'

'Hanley was the leader of the Caravets?'

'Before he was hanged his party was called the Moyle Rangers; the Shanavests were called Paddeen Car's party.'

'Why were they called Shanavests?'

'Because they wore old waistcoats.'

We do not hesitate our conviction that of all these societies there has not been one that has not been influenced by or designed to influence *Religion*; but that the sole object of their jurisdiction is *Land,* and that, in issuing their mandates and executing their sentences, no regard whatever is given to the consideration whether the object of them be Catholic or Protestant.

THE CONSTABULARY FORCE

We shall now avail ourselves of the opportunity to supply the information we have gathered in reference to the existing Constabulary Force of Ireland.

During our latest visit to Ireland, we had frequent opportunities of testing the advantages that had accrued to the community at large from the admirable mode in which this force is conducted. Our attention was first attracted by the exceedingly neat and clean-looking houses, fitted up as their barracks, in many instances built expressly for them, and the remarkably soldier-like air and manner of the fine-looking young men who compose the corps.

The first police station we visited was at Ballyneed, a village near Dunmanway which we were merely passing through, and of course, as our inspection was quite unlooked for, it was consequently unprepared for. The sergeant, a remarkably fine and intelligent young man, Alex Hewston, readily complied with our request to be permitted to examine his barrack.

It contained five men, strong and active fellows; the rooms were all whitewashed, the little garden was well-cultivated and free from weeds. The men slept on iron bedsteads, and the palliasses, blankets, pillows, etc., were neatly rolled up and placed at the head of each. The fire-arms and bayonets, each as polished as a mirror, were hung up over each bed, and the floors were as clean 'as a new pin'. Each man had his small box at his bed foot. All was in as perfect order as if all had been prepared in this little out-of-the-way place for the accustomed call of the inspector. The sub-inspector, we learned, visited the station once a month, and the inspector once a quarter. In this barrack the men were all bachelors; but it is usual to assign one married man with his wife to each barrack – the wife, of course, arranging the rooms, and providing the meals of the men who always mess together.

We afterwards examined many other stations and invariably found our first impressions borne out.

The first introduction of an armed police force into Ireland was in

1787: prior to that time constables were appointed by courts-leet, and by magistrates in quarter sessions. By an Act of George III, the lord-lieutenant was empowered to divide counties into districts, consisting of one or more baronies, and to appoint a chief constable to each district, with an annual salary not exceeding fifty pounds. The grand juries were empowered to appoint sixteen sub-constables 'being protestants' in each district, and to present a salary of not less than ten pounds and not more than twelve pounds for each. An allowance to constables conveying prisoners and 'armed protestants' assisting them of threepence per mile was also made. This Act was only carried into effect in thirteen counties.

In 1792 another Act was passed authorising the grand juries of the remaining counties to appoint not more than eight constables in every barony or half-barony and to present four pounds for every constable at each assizes. This sum was subsequently increased to ten pounds. The grand juries were also to raise two pounds per man once in twelve years, for arms and accoutrements, with the same allowance to 'armed protestants' as in the former Act.

The constables appointed under the above Acts, although armed, wore no uniform and in general, if not universally, followed their ordinary occupations. They were found to be so inefficient that in 1814 Sir Robert Peel, then chief secretary, introduced what is generally termed the 'Peace Preservation Act', by which the lord-lieutenant was empowered to appoint for any district comprising a county, or one or more baronies proclaimed by the privy council as in a state of disturbance, a chief magistrate, a chief constable, and fifty sub-constables whose functions were to cease on the district being declared tranquil. By this Act provision was made for the continuance of the baronial constables appointed under the Acts of 1787 and 1792.

The force employed under the 'Peace Preservation Act,' was universally known by the cognomen of 'Peelers', and for a considerable time afterwards the name was so obnoxious to the peasantry, that the service became one of great danger as well as odium; it was therefore found to be exceedingly difficult to induce men of good habits to join it.

However, as this Act was found to answer to a certain extent the object for which it had been framed, it induced the Government to introduce a more general measure; accordingly, in 1822, the 'Constabulary Act' was passed. By this Act the lord-lieutenant was empowered to appoint four general superintendents (one for each province) and one chief constable; and the magistrates were allowed to appoint sixteen sub-constables for each barony or half-barony or other division of barony. This was double the number of constables allowed by the Act of 1792. The lord-lieutenant was also authorised to appoint 'resident magistrates' and an extra number of constables at certain times. On this Act coming into operation, the chief constables and constables under the Acts of 1787 and 1792 ceased to act. But the 'Peace Preservation' force of 1814 continued in certain disturbed districts until October 1836, when the constabulary and peace preservation establishments were consolidated and placed under the control of one head (the inspector-general).

Such a measure had long been in contemplation, and different bills were from time to time brought before Parliament, but not proceeded with beyond a second reading, until Lord Normanby's government took the matter in hand, and carried the present Act. By this Act the lord-lieutenant is empowered to appoint one inspector-general, two deputy inspectors-general (to be resident in Dublin), four provincial inspectors, thirty-five sub-inspectors (now called county-inspectors) – with one for each county and riding – one chief constable (now called sub-inspector), two head constables, and sixteen constables and sub-constables for each barony, half-barony, or other division of a barony; also, one receiver and eighteen paymasters and an unlimited number of paid magistrates.

It is necessary to contrast briefly the existing establishment with the last establishments to gain the ready admission of every impartial mind that the present is a decided improvement on the former. Under the old system there were, first of all, two distinct establishments, with the one being a permanent force and the other (the Peace Preservation) co-existing with 'disturbance'. These establishments were totally independent of each other, with each acting under several heads and upon different systems. Thus the constabulary was divided (by the number of provinces in Ireland) into four distinct bodies, each under the superintendence of a provincial inspector-general. The power, however, of appointing the subordinate members of the force, that is, constables and sub-constables, and of framing rules and regulations for the control and management of the establishment of the several counties, was vested in the magistrates, who were subject, in the latter case, to the approval of the lord-lieutenant. Again, amongst the officers of each county force there was no gradation of rank, and of course no-one having any authority or superiority. Consequently, each constable acted independently within his district; a few maintained in some degree a show of discipline, but the majority preferred living quietly, or, in other words, they permitted their men to act pretty much as they pleased, and did not interfere to prevent the magistrates from employing them as they thought fit.

To meet, in some measure, this obvious defect in the Act, and the inconveniences resulting therefrom, the government of the day, as a first step towards some improvement, appointed one officer in every county (under the name of sub-inspector), who was also the paymaster, to superintend the force of his county. Several of these officers were subsequently placed in the Commission of the Peace, and continued to perform – in addition to their peculiar duties as inspectors and paymasters – those of magistrate, efficiently and satisfactorily to the public, without any increase in pay until the passing of the Act of 1836.

With respect to the Peace Preservation force, it was, in like manner, subdivided into several distinct parties, each party (not exceeding one chief constable and fifty constables and sub-constables) being under the superintendence of a chief magistrate who had the complete and sole control of it, and with which, under the special provisions of the Act, the local magistrates had no authority or right to interfere.

Thus, with the two separate establishments, each divided under several and distinct heads, all acting under different systems, and under a variety of inconsistent regulations, it could not be expected that the public service should be properly or efficiently conducted. Indeed, these manifest disadvantages were not altogether unnoticed, nor left without an effort being made to remedy and counteract them. In the majority of the counties the magistrates themselves were among the first to desire a change, and commenced a most wise and salutary reform by surrendering to the inspectors-general the right to appoint constables which, to say the least of it, had not been very judiciously exercised. In some counties a man's religion formed a principal consideration whether he should be admitted into the force or not. The number of persons too, who were generally known by the name of 'Followers', who obtained appointments were numerous, and, as a consequence, these individuals were more the servants of their patrons than of the public, in many instances acting as their stewards, gate-keepers, game-keepers or wood-rangers. On the other hand, the men nominated by the inspectors-general were selected without reference to their religious faith, and not until after a strict inquiry into their characters and general fitness for service as regard both their literate and physical qualifications. (The Act requires that every sub-constable should be able to read and write, and be an able-bodied man, and no man under the height of five feet, eight inches is taken.) As a further improvement, they were removed from among their own relations and friends, and from local influence – the bane of all discipline. It should be observed that some persons entertain the opinion that, inasmuch as local knowledge is of the first importance to a policeman, 'no man should be removed from his native county, with the localities of which he is supposed to be well acquainted'. But it will be obvious that the objects against so fixing them are numerous and strong, especially in Ireland, where the claims of relationship and 'party' are frequently paramount to all others; and it will equally be apparent that greater confidence will be placed by all the inhabitants of a district in a body known to have no predilections towards any. Indeed, those who are acquainted with the Irish character will have no difficulty in arriving at the conclusion that the arrangement, by which the natives of one part are located in another part, was exceedingly rational and judicious.

The propriety of the measure adopted by the magistracy of the majority of the counties in surrendering to the inspector-general their right of appointment, was soon manifested in the improved appearance, description and discipline of the men selected by the inspector-general, over those of the counties in which the magistrates still retained the right of appointment. There was altogether a great change for the better in the order and cleanliness of their barracks, which before this period were not paid much attention to. But a much more important result was produced by this change of system and its consequent effect on the discipline of the establishment: namely, the confidence on the part of the people in general in the members, which has continued to increase as the discipline of the force has advanced, and all religious distinctions in the selection of its members have disappeared. The consequence of this is that from having been an unpopular force, it is now quite the reverse. It is a remarkable fact that, interspersed as the Protestants and Roman Catholics are, in nearly one thousand five hundred barracks all over the kingdom, it is of extremely rare occurrence indeed that any difference has arisen on the score of religion.

Thus, in the national point of view, the constabulary force has been, and is, of the greatest advantage to Ireland, whether considered socially or morally.

The duties of the constabulary are multifarious and onerous, and are becoming every day more and more so. In fact, whatever is to be done is expected to be performed by it. Besides the ordinary and more legitimate duties as peace-preservers, the constabulary are employed in various ways, which, indirectly, creates a vast saving to the public: for instance, they had been and continue to be employed under the Poor Law Act in escorting convicts from all parts of Ireland to Dublin – a duty which was heretofore performed by the military and county jailers at a very heavy expense. They also serve notices under the various Acts of parliament; and at this moment they are engaged in taking the census of the population. They attend at all large markets, fairs, 'patrons' and public meetings within their respective districts to preserve order, as well as at all assizes, quarter and petty sessions, bankrupt courts, contested elections, etc. They also render essential service on the occasion of wrecks; in the recovery of fines and estreated recognizances – which is now a great source of income, but which was formerly consumed by the sheriff – and in the check they keep upon illicit distillation, and the suppression of unlicensed houses, which the revenue officers could never have effected without their aid. They are patrolling at all hours of the night; and the knowledge that they are invariably on the alert to detect crime has been naturally efficacious in preventing it.

FACTION FIGHTS

It seems not unnatural that some account of the ancient distinguishing characteristic – the Faction Fight – should follow our notice of the constabulary force, for we are mainly responsible to that body for their extinction. Their history belongs to old Ireland, for of late years their occurrence has been very rare, and since the establishment of temperance they have been made to appear as revolting in the eyes of the peasantry as before they would have appeared exciting.

It is unquestionable that the Faction Fight originated in a want of popular confidence in the administration of the law. However, when the peasant became satisfied that his wrongs were assured of redress, and that satisfaction for either insult or injury was to be had at all times, it was comparatively easy to induce him to abstain from 'taking the law into his own hands' and fighting out a quarrel.

Quarrels descended from father to son. There was scarcely a district in Ireland that did not recognise some hereditary dispute, and it became a sort of duty for a member of one family to insult the member of another family whenever they chanced to meet. Every relation of each family, no matter how distant, was expected to 'stand by his faction', and times and places were regularly appointed where they might meet to 'fight it out'. In the majority of cases the combatants were utterly ignorant of what they were fighting for, and even the leaders were very seldom acquainted with the original cause of the quarrel.

Generally, the magistrates were totally unable to interrupt a fight when it had begun, and usually failed to prevent it after the arrangements for it had been made; and we have more than once seen a parish priest – respected and beloved by his flock – labouring as vainly to establish peace among them as if he talked to so many sticks or stones.

Many years have passed since we witnessed one of those disgusting scenes. Unhappily, with their brutality and cruelty was frequently mixed up so much fun and humour and physical courage, that their revolting character was not immediately perceptible, although generosity was a rare ingredient in a fight, and women too frequently mingled in it. We must observe, however, that in the most ferocious encounter a woman was seldom struck – we might almost go the length of saying, never – except by accident. We recollect seeing one of the 'gentler sex' striking left and right with a terrific weapon – a huge stone in a stocking-foot – and noting several men knocked down by her blows without either of them aiming a single blow at her in return. It used to amaze us that more lives were not lost in such contests; but a man was frequently saved in consequence of the number of his adversaries, all of whom would be beating at him with their sticks, but who would generally interfere with each other so that few of the actual blows would reach him.

We call to mind one fair in particular; it took place in the vicinity of Ballydehob, about thirty miles west of Cork, and at a time when there was little dread of interruption. We shall endeavour to describe it – but briefly, however, for the subject is not pleasant, and now cannot be useful. Towards the afternoon of a spring day the rival factions began to assemble – each one armed with his stout shillelagh. The leaders parleyed somewhat before they began; they were surrounded by women and children and an old hag seemed determined that there should be no chance of peace, for she rated one of them with the term 'coward'. Actual hostilities, however, were commenced by a huge fellow running through the crowd, and stopping before each man of the opposite party, whom he greeted with the foul phrase 'liar'. His purpose was soon answered; one, less patient than the rest, struck him a blow; their sticks were crossed and in a moment hundreds had joined the melée. They fought for above an hour, and, at length, one party was beaten off the field. But, in truth we can do little good by entering into minute explanations of a scene so revolting, and we shall prefer to leave them to the reader's mind.

We might mention that the shillelagh – the chief weapon of the faction fights – derives its name from a famous wood near Arklow, in the county of Wicklow, where the best oaks and blackthorns were grown. It was generally about three feet long, although sometimes a smaller one was used which was called a 'Kippeen' or 'Cla'alpeen', or occasionally one of eight or ten feet long, called a 'Wattle'.

The peasantry were very choice in the selection of their national weapon, and especially careful in its preparation after it was cut. Sometimes it was tempered in a dung-heap, at others in slack lime, but the more usual mode was to rub it over repeatedly with butter, and place it 'up the chimney', where it would be left for a period of several months. We have in our possession one that we have pretty good evidence had been actively engaged in every fair in the neighbourhood for above twenty years, and at length came into the hands of a magistrate, from whom we received it, in consequence of its owner having been transported for manslaughter at a fight.

'The faction fights, plase your honours,' said an intelligent countryman when spoken to by us on the subject, 'the faction fights are a'most and maybe more than a'most gone off the face of the country. The boys are beginning to talk about them as things they have seen – like a show or a giant. We ask each other how we were ever drawn into them, what brought them about, and the one answer to that is – Whiskey! No gun will go off until it is primed, and sure whiskey was the priming. That made more orphans and widows than the fever or starvation. Thanks be to God, if death come upon us now, it is by the Lord's will and not our own act.'

It was encouraging to hear such a remark from one of the

people, and this was by no means a solitary instance.

The man had, he confessed, many a time when a mere child, incited by the example of the faction to whom his parents belonged, nerved his little arms to cast heavy stones into the mêlée, not caring how or where they fell. 'We usen't to mind a bit of a *shindy* in those times: if a boy was killed, why we said it was "his luck", and that it couldn't be helped. If a fellow trailed his coat over the fair green, and dared any one of us to stand a foot on it, we enjoyed the fight that was sure to follow, and we never thought how or cared how it would end. Sure. I remember my own brother – and now since he's been a Temperance man, he hasn't raised a finger in anger to any living creature – sure I mind him well, feeling the tents for heads, and when he'd get one to his liking, giving it first a good rap, and then calling on the owner to come out and fight him: sure he'd never have done that but for the whiskey. Ah,' he continued, 'that was a foolish divarshin, but there was no *heart* bitterness with it; nothing to lay heavy to the end of one's days. But the faction fights were the bitterest of all – black hatred descending from father to son against the opposite faction, as if poor Ireland hadn't enough enemies without turning to murder and destroying her own flesh and blood – like a wild beast. Now there's a poor woman,' he said, pointing to a pale patient-looking person who sat knitting at her cottage door, 'there's a poor creature! Mrs Lawler knows what factions come to and so she ought; she'll tell the lady (*Anna Maria Hall*) her story and welcome, if she has any curiosity to hear it.

'Good morrow to you, Mrs Lawler, and how's your girleen ma'am? The lady would be glad to rest while the gentleman and I get up the far hill, and you always have a welcome, like your people before you, for the stranger.'

'Kindly welcome,' said the widow. 'Mary, dust this chair, mavourneen.'

The cabin was clean and neat, and bearing no evidence of the presence of that sad poverty we had so frequently seen, though it did not dim the smile or lessen the welcome – nor was it difficult to lead the widow to the story of sorrows, which, however softened by time, were ever uppermost in her mind.

'My mother and myself were widowed by factions – plase God, my little girl won't have the same tale to tell, for the Connels and the Lawlers might put salt to each other's potatoes without fear of fighting now. It was a shocking thing to see the arm of brother raised against brother, only because as battle and murder were in the hearts of their forefathers they must continue in their own.

'I was born a Connel, and almost the first thing I learned was to hate a Lawler, from the lip out; and yet hard fortune was before me, for the very first passion my heart felt was the same love it still feels, and that was for a Lawler. It has known no change, though it has known sorrow; the first knowledge I had of the wild beatings of my own heart was when I saw that girl's father. Ah yah! it has beat with joy and terror often, but the love for my first love, and my last, was always one. And now, when it has all passed and gone, and you, Mark Lawler, are in your green quiet grave, I am prouder to have been the choice of your own fine noble spirit, than if I was this moment made the queen of all Ireland's ground.

'Oh, lady, if you could have seen him!

"Norah" said my father to me, and I winnowing at our barn door with the servant maid, "Norah, keep your eyes on the grain and not after the chaff, and don't raise them above the hedge, for there's many a Lawler will be passing the road this day on account of the fair, and I don't wish a child of mine to notice them, or to be noticed by them."

'I intended to do his bidding, and whenever I heard a horse or the voices of strangers coming down the boreen, I kept my eyes on the grain and let the chaff fly at its pleasure, until a dog broke through the hedge and attacked a little beast of my own; so as soon as that came to pass I let the sieve fall, to catch my own little dog in my arms. But there was no need for that for he was over the hedge, lighter and brighter than a sunbeam. Ah, then, I wonder, is love as quick at taking in all counties as it is here? Mark Lawler didn't speak ten words, nor I two; and yet from that moment out no-one but Mark Lawler was in my mind. I knew he was a Lawler by his eyes, and well he knew I was a Connel; but the love would have little of boy and girl love in it that would heed a faction. We, who had never met till that moment, could never go astray in the fields thereafter without meeting.

'Ah, Mary,' she continued, addressing her daughter, and yet, in her simplicity, quite forgetting the uselessness of the precept by her own confession 'ah Mary dear, if ye feel yer heart soften towards a young man, keep out of his way intirely, mavourneen; have nothing to say to him, don't drive your cow the same road he walks, nor draw water from the same well, nor go to the same chapel except if you have no other to go to. There's a deal of mischief in the chapel dear, because you think, in your innocence, that you're giving your thoughts to God, and all the time, maybe it's an idol of your own making my darling child, they would be going to – sure your mother's sorrow ought to be a warning, mavourneen!'

'Yes mother,' replied the blue-eyed girl, meekly.

'Well, my lady, my poor father thought I grew very attentive intirely to the young lambs and watchful over the flax, but at last some of the Connels whispered how it was – that Mark Lawler met his child unknownst – and he questioned me, and I told the truth, of how I had given my heart out of my bosom, and I fell at his feet and cried salt and bitter tears until they dropped upon the ground he stood on. But, seeing his heart was turning to iron, I who had ever been like a willow in his hand, roused myself and challenged him to say a word to Mark's disadvantage. I said that he was honest, sober, industrious, and my father was struck with the strength of the heart I took, and listened, until he at last made an answer – if a saint from heaven came down, and was a Lawler he would not give him a drop of water to wet his lips. He threatened me with his curse if I kept true in my love, and thought to settle the thing out of hand by marrying me to my own second cousin, but that I wouldn't hear of. God knows I did not mean to cross him, but what could I do? Mark sent to ask me to bid him farewell, or his heart would break; I thought there could be no harm in blessing him, and telling him to think of me no more. Mary, mavourneen,' she said, again addressing her daughter, 'if you really want to break off at once with a young man, take warning by me.'

'Yes mother,' was again Mary's reply.

'At that meeting we agreed to meet again; and so we did, until we got a priest to make us one. At first I was happy as a young bird, but soon my heart felt crushed, for I had to carry two faces. My father was more bitter than ever against the Lawlers; and my brother, "Dark Connel" as he was called, was more cruel than my father. At last I was forced to own that I was married. I watched the time when my brother was away, for one storm was as much as I could bear. My father cast me like a dog from the hearth I had played on when a child; in his fury he knelt to curse me, but my mother held a gospel against his lips, so I was saved his curse.

'The arms of a loving husband were open for me; and until the midsummer fair I thought my happiness was sure. I worked hard to keep Mark from it, for the factions were sure to meet there. He swore to me he would not raise a finger against my father or brother, nor let a drop of spirits pass his lips. I walked with him part of the way, and I thought all pleasure in sight left my eyes when he waved the last wave of his hat on top of the hill. As I was turning into our own field, a lark was rising above its nest, singing its glory to the heavens in its sweet voice, when a shot from the gun of one of those *squireens*, who are thick among the leaves as spider's webs, struck the bird and it fell, quivering and bleeding to the ground, close to where I knew its nest was in the corn. I opened the bending grain to see if I could find it, but it was lying quite dead, and its poor mate standing close by. The lark is a timid thing, but she never minded me, and my heart felt so sick that I went into my house crying quite bitterly.

'I could not rest; I thought that in a few hours I might be like that innocent bird, and taking my cloak about me, I walked on and on, until I came in sight of the fair green. It was a woeful sight to me – the shouts of the showmen, the scream of the sellers, the lowing of cattle and bleating of sheep were all mixed together – with the yell of the factions every now and again drowning out everything with its horrid sound. I knew my own father's voice as he shouted, "*Hurroo* for the Connels – down with the Lawlers". I saw him standing before Mark, aggravating him. My husband's hands were clenched, and he kept his arms close by his side that he might not strike. I prayed that God might keep him in that mind, and flew towards him. Just as I dropped on my knees by his side, he had raised his arm – not against my father, but against my brother who had drawn the old man back; and there they stood face to face – the two young heads of the old factions. Blows were exchanged, for Mark had been aggravated beyond all bearing; and I was trying to force myself between them, when I saw my father stretched upon the green, in the very hour and act of revenge and sin. It was by a blow from a Lawler – the old man never spoke another word – and the suddenness of his death struck a terror in them all, and the sticks fell to their sides and the great storm of oaths and voices sank into a murmur while they looked on the dying man.

'Oh, bitter, heart bitter, was my sorrow. I had shrouded my father with my arms, but he didn't feel me; the feeling had left his limbs, and the light his eyes. However hard his words had been, the knowledge that I was fatherless and my mother a widow made me forget them all.

'His death was talked of far and near; the magistrates set to putting down the factions, and the priest gave out from the altar, Sunday after Sunday, such commands that, without flying in his reverence's face, they could not keep on at the fights in public: every innocent divarshin through the country was stopped on their account, and there was outward peace.

'For as good as two years the husband, whose life was the life-beat of my worn-out heart, seldom left the cabin without my thinking he would never come back. I'd wait until he was a few yards from the door, and then steal out to watch him until he was out of sight. At ploughing, at haymaking or reaping, his whistle would come over the little hill to me while I sat at my wheel, as clear as the blackbird's, and if it stopped but for a minute my heart would sink like death, and it's to the door I'd be. If I woke in the night I could not go to sleep again without my arm across his shoulder to feel that he was safe.

'At last I persuaded him to leave the country. A new hope came to me, strong and bright, and I thought we might get away to America, and that, maybe, then he'd have a chance of living all the days that were allotted at his birth. I did not tell him that, but having got his consent, I worked night and day to get off. At last it was all settled, the day was fixed, and none of the neighbours, barring one or two of the Lawlers, knew it, and I knew my brother would not hear it from them, and my mother lived with him.

'The evening before we were to go on shipboard my husband said, "I'll go to the priest this evening, who christened, confirmed and married me, and who knows all that was in me from the time I was born; his blessing will be a guard over us, and we'll go together to his knee."

'We went, and though the parting was sad, it was sweet, and we walked home afterwards with both our hearts full. At last Mark said that but for me, he'd never have thought of leaving the old sod, but maybe it would be for the better. Now, this is a simple thing, and yet it always struck me as mighty strange intirely: we were walking through a field, and, God help me, it was a weak woman's fancy, but I never thought any harm could come to him when I was with him when all of a sudden – and startled maybe by his laugh – a lark sprung up at our feet. We both stopped to watch it, about three yards from the ditch, and while it was yet clear in sight there was a whiz, a flash, the sound of death, and my poor husband was a corpse at my feet.'

The poor woman flung her apron over her face to conceal her agitation, while she sobbed bitterly. 'The spirit of the factions,' she continued, 'was in that shot. And it was my own brother who killed him!'

ROUND TOWERS

We shall avail ourselves of this opportunity to supply information relative to the long-famed and far-famed round towers of Ireland, the peculiarities of which we have had occasion to notice frequently during the progress of our work.

Although formerly very numerous, not more than about eighty-three towers remain at present; twenty in a perfect condition, and sixty-three in a state of decay. The former vary in height from one hundred and thirty to seventy feet, and are divided into several storeys. Their general diameter is between eight and fifteen feet. The door, with but four known exceptions – Scattery, Clonmacnois, Aghaviller and Down Tower (and the latter is now no more) – is placed at a height from the ground varying from six to fifteen feet. In some instances it is arched and in others a plain oblong. Its position varies and seems to have been of no consequence. Each floor, exclusive of the basement and the attic, is lit by a single window; that at the entrance receives light by the door, and the upper storey (with the exception of the two towers in the county of Kilkenny, which have six each), is lit by four windows, which face the cardinal points. The whole structure is roofed by a conical arch of mason-work.

There are but few instances of variance between the genuinely ancient towers, and these are to be found only in Kinneagh, Ardmore, Dysart and Devenish, and we reject those of Killossy, Kevin's Kitchen and Scerkieran as spurious. Kinneagh is hexagonal at the base and rotund above; Ardmore has three external belts, Dysart one, and Devenish is sculptured below the roof. Cloyne and Kildare have received in modern renovations crenellated battlements and, at present, Cloyne, Ardmore and Clondalkin possess floors. Cloyne and Castle-Dermot are also now used as belfries.

Their origin and use have formed the subject of greatly perplexed inquiry; being claimed adversely for Pagans and Christians. Whilst upon these claims many have decided very dogmatically, it is not a little amusing to hear them avowing that an impenetrable veil still hangs over the subject, and that, like the riddle of the Sphynx, an Oedipus is wanting to expound upon it. Believing, as we do, that the formidable-looking problem is one of rather easy solution, we are not consequently of those who deem its perplexities inexplicable. In fact, we believe in their heathen antiquity, and we believe this upon grounds which we shall presently submit to the reader.

In 1830 the Royal Irish Academy proposed a prize for a satisfactory essay on the subject, and adjudicated on the claims of two writers, who delivered essays advocating opposite opinions, by giving prizes to both. Mr O'Brien, one of the victors, afterwards published his views, which were on the heathen side of the question; whilst the work of Mr Petrie, who adopted the Christian view remains still unpublished.

Before the close of the last century these structures had excited but little attention. Neither Stanihurst, Ursher, Ware, Colgan, O'Flaherty, Keating, nor the venerable Charles O'Connor had bestowed the slightest notice on them in their various works. In the seventeenth century Lynch, Walsh and Molyneux alone recognised their existence. In speaking of them, however, they fell into such absurdities as people sometimes will who have no guide but their own crude fancies, for they had no records at hand to aid them.

The first of these, Lynch, ascribed their erection to the Danes, a people who left no similar structure either in their own country or in any of their many conquests in Britain, Normandy, or Sicily. Indeed, they possessed no dominion in Ireland beyond the walled towns of Dublin, Wexford, Waterford, Cork and Limerick, after they had become Christianised.

Wright adopted Lynch's opinion, and adds that they were used as beacons.

Smith, the famous county historian, has left on record opinions of rather a conflicting character. In one of his many works he called them 'Penitentiaries', and in another, 'Belfries'. An Irish manuscript, seen by no other writer, and which was afterwards discredited by himself, led him to adopt the first view. The remaining joists of two upper floors of Ardmore Tower, which he mistook for beams to support bells, induced him to adopt the second opinion.

Doctor Campbell and Sir R Colt Hoare adhered to the Penitentiary system and assigned their era to the ninth century.

Harris, the author of a *History of the County Down*, thought they were Anchorite towers.

O'Halloran, the Irish historian, and Dr Milner adopted the same opinion, and the latter conjectured that they were built within a century or two after the conversion of the island, and that they were copied from the columns of the Eastern Anchorites (stylites). Dr Lanigan has, however, well and satisfactorily disposed of Milner's views.

The Reverend E Ledwich advocated their Danish origin, the most absurd of all the theories that have been adventured upon. For this, he stoops to misrepresenting his favourite Cambrensis (Giraldus Cambrensis – *The History and Topography of Ireland,* 1185) who, however, so far from asserting that they were of Ostmanic construction, affirms their Irish origin. Elsewhere this inconsistent antiquity endeavours to prove that Cambrensis *saw* the Irish in the act of building them.

Moores (*Origin of the Pillar Tower*) conjectured that they were repositories for church utensils, and built between the fifth and seventh centuries, by monks and pilgrims from Greece and Rome, who accompanied the first missionaries. But as neither Greece nor Rome possessed any similar structures, where, we should ask, did they find the prototype? He says their architectural style is 'Greek and Roman, strongly participating of the Gothic character, the link that combines these orders'. Gothic in the *fifth* century, and a connecting link too between Greek and Roman architecture!

Mr Petrie, as far as we can learn of his Essay, regards them as belfries, and agrees in some measure with the opinion of Moores that they were repositories for valuables belonging to the adjacent churches and monasteries.

Mr Gough thought they were Christian minarets, used before the introduction of bells to call the people to prayer.

Shea thinks that they were monuments commemorating the principal founders of Christianity in Ireland, and at the same time symbolical of the doctrine of immortality.

Mr William Willes of Cork, a gentleman who has given this subject much consideration, supposed them to have been episcopal indexes, that is, erected to point out cathedral churches. But, if so, where were the indexes of Lismore, Ferns, Emly, Cong, Clonfert, Ross, etc., or why build them on sites which were non-episcopal, as at Ram Island, Trummery, Dysery, Ardpatrick, Brigown or Kenneagh?

A learned gentleman of the South Munster Antiquarian Society who signs himself 'Quidam' suggests that these buildings might have been used for celebrating the obsequies of deceased bishops and chieftains, as the word *Torr*, a tower, and *Torav*, a waking of the dead, would indicate. But there is more of imagination than probability in this conjecture.

In this brief analysis of opinions, on the Christian side, we have seen that the leading theories are in favour of these structures having been erected either as Penitentiary and Anchorite retreats, or as Belfries. But if they were erected for the former purpose, there was no necessity for raising them to so great an elevation, and of building them of such materials, for the adjoining churches were low and small and many of them were constructed of timber. It is true that Anchoritism did greatly prevail in early Ireland, but the recluse generally selected far humbler retreats than lofty towers. We have still near many of our older churches small cells, which served them as hermitages, as at Ardfert, Scattery, and Glendalough. The cell of Declan at Ardmore – his residence in life, his grave in death – still subsists and is called Bonachan. The cell of Marianus Scotus was a similar lowly structure. Belonging to Lismore church was an Anchorite whose lands were not inconsiderable, and yet there was no round tower here. But although the towers were assuredly not erected for the reception of Anchorites, yet in after ages some few of them may have been used by these people for their penitential abodes. Such was the case with the Turaghan Ancoire (the Fire Tower of the Anchorite) on Holy Island in the Shannon.

Probability is not in favour of these towers having been erected as Belfries, for their form, as well as their separation and distance from the church, is so unlike the situation of belfries in other countries. At periods long subsequent to their foundation, as they may have been availed of by hermits, so too a bell may have been suspended; this has been the case at Cloyne for the last one hundred and fifty years, and also at Castle-Dermot.

In the Irish annals, after the introduction of belfries into Ireland at the close of the ninth century, we have frequent mention of the *Cloichteach* or Campanile. It is expressly distinguished from the *Turaghan* or *Fidneimhedh*. The Cloichteach or Clocher seems to have been generally constructed of timber, as mention occurs of some of them having been destroyed by fire. These buildings so recorded are placed in localities where no round tower appears ever to have been, as at Slane, Clonard, Emly, Telcha, etc. We have subsisting two specimens of the Cloichteach at Cashel – the earliest structures of the kind probably in Ireland. They stand at either side and form part of Cormac's Chapel, which is a structure of the ninth century. They are square and built with well-cut stones. A round tower, of very different stone and architecture, built in layers and not horizontal stands several yards north of these structures. If its purpose had been that of a belfry, there was scarcely any necessity for building the two towers just mentioned. Similar instances of a round tower near a square steeple occur at Swords and at Devenish.

It is their situation next to churches which has mainly led to the error of supposing that they were the works of ecclesiastics. But, as Mr Weld remarks, 'it might be stated that the churches were built contiguous to the towers,' and he illustrates this by the well-known disposition manifested by the early Christian missionaries to accommodate their worship to that of their Pagan proselytes – amongst the many evidences for which was the eager appropriation of heathen temples and places consecrated to their gods to Christian uses.

But to us an insuperable difficulty in the Christian theory lies in the consideration as to the source whence the supposed Christian founders derived this peculiar style of building – where they found a prototype. They are unlike any structures in use by the Christian clergy of any other country, and it will be scarcely contended that it was a spontaneous growth or invention peculiar to the Irish missionaries. Again, if these structures appertained to the Irish church, is it not more than surprising that none of the many Irish missionaries who crowded into Britain, France, Germany and Italy, where they built their churches and monasteries, ever thought of erecting round towers in any of their missionary labours? Neither Columba nor Adamman built any at Iona, nor did Aedan, Finian nor Colman, who successively governed as bishops at Lindisfarne. We find none at Glastonbury, which was an ecclesiastical colony of Irishmen. Fridolin, who founded so many churches at Poitiers, Strasburg, etc. built no towers; nor did Fingen at Metz, nor Gerard at Toul, nor Gallus at St Gall's, nor Marianus at Ratisbon.

Nor, on the other hand, at a time when the pious and the learned flocked in crowds to the Irish shores, did any of these pilgrims – and many of them were royal and noble and religious founders – import the idea into his own country and there re-erect a structure so admired in Ireland; neither Gildas, Dunstan, St Cuthbert, St David, nor Alfred thought of building one in England. We do have, it is true, a solitary round tower head as a pinnacle on St Peter's at Oxford, and a triangular-headed window at the Court of Requests at Westminster, but beyond these we have few other efforts at copying even portions of the details which are so striking and prevalent and wondered at in her Sister Isle. In France, Belgium, Germany, etc. the case is the same.

The traditional and legendary notices are equally in favour of our view of their extreme antiquity. Cambrensis relates a tradition of an ancient city which had been, in previous ages, buried beneath the waters of Lough Neagh; and states that the fishermen in serene weather were wont to point out, in passing, the round towers, 'in the waves beneath them shining'. The bardic history supports this antique tradition, by affirming that Lough Neagh burst forth suddenly in the reign of Lugad Lamh-dearg, or about the year 586 AD. Popular reports in the present day relate that these towers were universally built in one night by some holy man or other.

The vernacular name which is still used, *Cillcagh* or *Golcagh*, is a compound of two sacred words, meaning fire and the divinity. The worship of fire by the ancient Irish is a fact sufficiently vouched for by the Irish annals and the saints' lives, as well as by existing practices on the eves of May, Midsummer, etc. Its votaries were divided into two sects; one which lighted the sacred fire in the open temple, and the other which enclosed it in the Sun-Tower, or in low arched-over buildings. The tower and low square temple were equally common to the Persians with whom, as well as with most of the other early Pagan nations, fire or the sun formed a main object of adoration. In India the presiding genius of fire is still named *Agni*, a name curiously corresponding with that of the Irish tower, *Tur-aghan* or *Aidhne*, which is pronounced nearly as *Agni*. And the columnar temples belonging to the ancient worship of that element still subsist in India.

Independently of language, the similarity of structures alone would have supposed an identity of design and offer grounds for a reasonable presumption of analogous purpose. We know that the Indian towers were Mithraic, that is, consecrated to solar worship, and therefore for this, and for the other reasons mentioned, we are coerced to consider those of Ireland as similar: that they were fire temples, dedicated to the worship of the sun.

THE IRISH LANGUAGE

Irish is a language very rational and beautiful in its philosophy and far less difficult to learn than is generally imagined, for its grammar is reducible to a few simple elements which are capable of very extensive application. The alphabet originally consisted of sixteen simple elements and in this respect, as well as in the form of several of the characters, it bore the impress of its Phoenician descent, in common with the Celtiberian, the Etruscan and the Cadmean Greek. The letters have a relative position different from those of all other alphabets. Two copies of the ancient alphabet are extant: that of Forchern, who lived in the first century, and that of the Book of Lecan. Both agree in the number, power and order of the letters; but they differ in the names, with the former calling them after men and the latter after trees. This latter method evidently arose from the form of the Ogham alphabet which anteceded the alphabetic characters of which we now speak.

The Ogham Scheme resembled the stem of a tree, the letters forming the lateral branches. This species of Druidical free-masonry, as it may be termed, is often alluded to by the Cambrian or Pictish bard, Talliesin, who celebrates 'the engagement of the sprigs of the trees, and their battles with the learned'. He boasts that he could 'delineate the elementary trees and *reeds*, and speak of the *alders* at the end of the line beginning the arrangement'. Fearn, the *alder*, is placed near the beginning of the ancient Irish alphabet, being the fourth in the original arrangement. He also tells us, that when the sprigs were marked by the sages in the small *tablet* of devices, they uttered their *voice*. The ancient Irish, before the use of parchment, used beechen tablets, called *Taibhle Fileadh*, philosophic tablets, or tablets of the sages, and the alphabet was called Faodh or Daiodh, '*a voice*'. Another bard says that he 'loves the sprigs with their woven tops tied with a hundred knots, after the manner of the Celts, which the artists employed about their mystery'. From this it is evident that this custom was derived from the Guydl, or original Celtic inhabitants of Britain, who were one race with the Irish.

The Irish language is certainly the best preserved, as it is the purest of all the Celtic dialects. It contains written remains, transmitted from so remote an antiquity that the language has become almost completely unintelligible; manuscripts of so old a date that they had become ancient in the fourth and fifth centuries, and which required a gloss, and the gloss has now become nearly as obsolete as the work which it was designed to expound. To the archaeologists, to those who would inquire into the origin, the descent and the affinities of the older nations of western Europe, it is of the highest value, and its utility has long been acknowledged by some of the most eminent writers of this and of the neighbouring continental nations.

Yet, against this language, which has been so universally eulogised and so prized, the policy of the English medieval government was for centuries directed in unceasing hostility. Its use was prohibited by severe penalties, which, however, so far from proving effective, seemed but to spread that 'degeneracy' amongst the Anglo-Norman settlers, which finally gave them the character of being more Irish than the Irish – *Hibernicis Hiberniores*. Queen Elizabeth, with a good sense not participated in by her chief minister, although that minister was the great Burleigh, saw that in giving education to the people, which she intended when she founded Trinity College, her purpose would be aided through the medium of their spoken language, and suggested the appointment of an Irish professorship. But the idea found no favour with her premier.

'What!' said Burleigh, 'encourage a language more nearly allied to canine barking than to the articulation human.' And he illustrated his most calumnious assertion by pronouncing as a specimen the cacophonous alliteration – *D'ibh dubh damh obh amh*, which is pronounced *div duv dav ov av*, which means 'a black steer drank a raw egg'. The unhappy phrase lost to the university the intended professorship, and to literature such benefit as might have resulted from it.

Denounced then and shunned by the ruling class, despised as that alone of the populace, it met but little favour with the learned. The publication of the bold and beautiful figments of Macpherson – the *Poems of Ossian* – opened up a controversy which at length, though slowly, recalled attention to this too long condemned vehicle of nearly forgotten information. Little, however, has since been done in exploring or making known the treasures of history, literature, poetry, romance and philology, which our scattered manuscripts contain. But a better spirit is arousing. The great importance of the language is beginning to be understood for literary as well as religious and political purposes. The recent establishment of the Archaeological Society of Dublin, even though it is checked in its efficiency by the unwise amount of the entrance subscription, gives promise of something being done hereafter which may rescue and preserve what otherwise in a few years may be irretrievably lost.

We shall briefly notice the two most remarkable characteristics of the Irish language. The first is its expressiveness. One word is often a definition, and conveys a very complex idea; indeed, the terms in which the language abounds are so ideal, suggesting such vivid and beautiful images, that it may be termed one of the most picturesque languages in existence. As an example of this, we may mention the ancient names of places, whose etymons often not only call up delightful pictures of the localities, but also mark some important circumstances in their early history.

Another characteristic of the language is its admirable

adaptation for lyrical composition and indeed for many other species of poetry. This arises (in addition to the quality to which we have already referred) from the number of diphthongs, triphthongs and quiescent consonants with which it abounds. The bards have availed themselves of these peculiarities with such art as to render their numbers exceedingly smooth and harmonious. They have consequently brought their prosody to a perfection which is equal to that of any other language.

The Irish language, although evidently on the decline, is still the vernacular tongue of about two millions of the population. This figure is exclusive of a great number, which is probably a million, who, although they can speak Irish, yet from their rank or other circumstances now generally adopt the English tongue as their vernacular language. Its prevalence in reference to the different provinces may be expressed as follows: in Connaught it is spoken almost universally; in Munster it is spoken generally; in Leinster sparingly, and in Ulster only in the county of Donegal, and the mountainous districts. The best Irish is spoken in Connaught and Thomond, and the worst perhaps in Tipperary, although a native of that county would be highly offended at being told so. The language ceases to be spoken in the lower parts of county Tipperary, and is almost unknown in the King and Queen's Counties, part of Carlow and Wexford, Wicklow, Kildare and Dublin. The Connaught and Munster dialects differ from each other almost as much as the Hebrew and Chaldee.

The Irish language is a dialect of the Celtic and the purest dialect extant. The Celts were the aboriginal inhabitants of Europe, who possessed it before the coming of the Roman and Gothic races, by whom it was subsequently overrun. Being the earliest colonists that passed from Asia, the Celts retained a closer resemblance to the Orientals in their manners, customs and language than the other two races. Besides, they had much intercourse with the Phoenicians, and received colonies from them. This in a great measure serves to account for the difference between them and the Gothic or Teutonic nations, which consisted principally in language and religion (the religion of the Goths being gloomy in its mythology, while that of the Celts was mild and cheerful). The principal Celtic nations were the Umbrians, Sabines, Etruscans, Gauls, Celtiberians, Lusitanians and the inhabitants of the British Isles. The genuine descendants of the Celtae are now only to be found in Ireland, the Scottish highlands and isles, the Isle of Man, Wales, Brittany, Biscay and some of the Alpine valleys.

EPILOGUE

And here we close our book, grateful that we have been enabled to complete it without accident or illness, and trusting that we have succeeded in preventing our readers becoming weary of our work.

That we have left much undone and some important matters unnoticed may be readily acknowledged: our volumes, though extended beyond the original plan, afforded space too limited for the consideration of all topics and descriptions of all places that properly come under the notice of the tourist.

When our first tour was undertaken, great and important changes had been working improvements in that country. Those improvements have since wonderfully progressed, their extent and value can be estimated only by those who were familiar with the condition of Ireland twenty, or even ten years ago. During our annual visits since these volumes were commenced we have witnessed its rapid advancement, and there can be little doubt that if it continues to proceed in the same onward course, the difficulties that have for ages baulked the statesmen and thwarted the philanthropist will be encountered and overcome.

Many years will most likely pass before we again visit Ireland. The beneficial changes and vast improvements we have witnessed in progress during the last ten years will be as nothing compared to those which the next ten years must inevitably produce.

ACKNOWLEDGEMENTS

I wish to express my gratitude to the following people for their invaluable assistance:

Chris Holifield, Barbara Boote and Jim White (Sphere Books Ltd), for their unflagging enthusiasm.

Padraic O Tailliur and Tim Coughlan for their good advice. Also Paul Kelly, who got it off to a good start.

A special word of thanks to Chris Ashmore.

And to Anna.

INDEX

INDEX

TIME AFTER TIME

Molly Keane

Bestselling author of Booker Prize runner-up GOOD BEHAVIOUR

The ageing, one-eyed Jasper Swift and his three grotesque, elderly sisters, April, May and Baby June, have been waging quiet guerilla warfare against one another for years. They live together in damp, decaying Durraghglass, the country estate left to them all by darling Mummie.

Then, suddenly, their long-lost cousin returns from Vienna. Exotic Leda, whom Daddy had been so funny about all those years ago; and within days, the uneasy existence of the Swifts has been dramatically overturned, when desires, dormant for so long, flame fierce and bright as ever . . .

Poignant and hilarious, controlled yet outrageous, TIME AFTER TIME brilliantly captures the graceless setting of the sun on the eccentric Anglo-Irish aristocracy, emulating the classic comedy of Molly Keane's acclaimed novel GOOD BEHAVIOUR.

'Vivid and graceful . . . it is a joy to read.' *Spectator.*
'Sharp, deadly and irresistibly funny.' *Daily Telegraph.*
'The pleasure in grotesqueries is as gleeful as ever.' *Observer.*

FICTION 0 349 12076 5 £2.95

SILVER'S CITY

Maurice Leitch

Winner of the 1981 Whitbread Prize

It is a desolate city, a ruined landscape carved into sectors by slogan-covered walls, barbed wire barricades and khaki checkpoints. Ten years ago when Silver was put away for firing the first historic shot in the bloody sectarian war, Belfast was bitter and brutal. But violent as it was, it was still a real city, a city a man could rule. It was Silver's city.

Silver is a hero, his name a household name spelled out on gabled walls and carved forever in the unforgiving chronicles of the Loyalist movement. Sprung from behind the wire by the cold, professional new breed of gunmen, Silver is thrown into an utterly changed city ruled by assassins who kill not for the cause but for the thrill of killing. Silver turns against the tide of blood he loosed on Belfast, but it is a city ruled by mercenaries – it is no longer Silver's city.

Fiction 0 349 12179 6 £2.50

GOOD BEHAVIOUR

Molly Keane

Behind the gates of Temple Alice the aristocratic Anglo-Irish St Charles family sinks into a state of decaying grace. To Aroon St Charles, large and unlovely daughter of the house, the fierce forces of sex, money, jealousy and love seem locked out by the ritual patterns of good behaviour. But crumbling codes of conduct cannot hope to save the members of the St Charles family from their own unruly and inadmissible desires.

'An extraordinary tour de force of fictional presentation . . . a masterpiece . . . a technically remarkable work, as sharp as a blade . . . Molly Keane is a mistress of wicked comedy.' Malcolm Bradbury, *Vogue*

'Excellent . . . Molly Keane brings it off triumphantly . . . a distinguished comeback.' Piers Paul Read, *The Standard*

FICTION 0 349 12075 7 £2.95

IRELAND
a history
ROBERT KEE

the book of the major
BBC/RTE Television series

**'A careful, well-balanced, sensitive book, the fruit of long, fascinated reflection over its subject matter; it is warmly to be recommended, not only to those who know little or nothing about Irish history, but also, and especially to those who think they know a lot about it . . . an excellent book.'
Conor Cruise O'Brien, OBSERVER.**

'His achievement is to explain, lucidly and vividly, the bloodiness of the conflict . . . he is twice the man in print.' SUNDAY TIMES.

In the book of the successful, and often controversial, television series, Robert Kee examines the 'prison of Irish history', going back to its very beginnings to identify the principal groups involved in modern Ireland. He traces the emergence of each group and their links over the ages, establishing how past facts have bred present myths.

HISTORY 0 349 12081 1 £5.95